T0331781

PCI Compliance

The Payment Card Industry Data Security Standard (PCI DSS) is now in its 18th year, and it is continuing to dominate corporate security budgets and resources. If you accept, process, transmit, or store payment card data branded by Visa, MasterCard, American Express, Discover, or JCB (or their affiliates and partners), you must comply with this lengthy standard.

Personal data theft is at the top of the list of likely cybercrimes that modern-day corporations must defend against. In particular, credit or debit card data is preferred by cybercriminals as they can find ways to monetize it quickly from anywhere in the world. Is your payment processing secure and compliant? The new Fifth Edition of *PCI Compliance* has been revised to follow the new PCI DSS version 4.0, which is a complete overhaul to the standard. Also new to the Fifth Edition are: additional case studies and clear guidelines and instructions for maintaining PCI compliance globally, including coverage of technologies such as Kubernetes, cloud, near-field communication, point-to-point encryption, Mobile, Europay, MasterCard and Visa. This is the first book to address the recent updates to PCI DSS, and the only book you will need during your PCI DSS journey. The real-world scenarios and hands-on guidance will be extremely valuable, as well as the community of professionals you will join after buying this book.

Each chapter has how-to guidance to walk you through implementing concepts and real-world scenarios to help you grasp how PCI DSS will affect your daily operations. This book provides the information that you need in order to understand the current PCI Data Security Standards and the ecosystem that surrounds them, how to effectively implement security on network infrastructure in order to be compliant with the credit card industry guidelines, and help you protect sensitive and personally identifiable information. Our book puts security first as a way to enable compliance.

- Completely updated to follow the current PCI DSS, version 4.0
- Packed with tips to develop and implement an effective PCI DSS and cybersecurity strategy
- Includes coverage of new and emerging technologies such as Kubernetes, mobility, and 3D Secure 2.0
- Both authors have broad information security backgrounds, including extensive PCI DSS experience

PCI Compliance

Understand and Implement Effective PCI Data Security Standard Compliance

Fifth Edition

Dr. Branden R. Williams

James K. Adamson

CRC Press
Taylor & Francis Group
Boca Raton London New York

CRC Press is an imprint of the
Taylor & Francis Group, an **informa** business

Cover Image Credit: Shutterstock

Fifth Edition published 2023
by CRC Press
6000 Broken Sound Parkway NW, Suite 300, Boca Raton, FL 33487-2742

and by CRC Press
4 Park Square, Milton Park, Abingdon, Oxon, OX14 4RN

CRC Press is an imprint of Taylor & Francis Group, LLC

ISBN: 978-0-367-57002-6 (hbk)
ISBN: 978-0-367-57003-3 (pbk)
ISBN: 978-1-003-10030-0 (ebk)

DOI: 10.1201/9781003100300

Typeset in Times
by KnowledgeWorks Global Ltd.

Contents

Foreword

If you're reading this, it's unlikely this is your first book on Payment Card Industry (PCI). You probably play a role in the PCI ecosystem—maybe you're a security engineer, a security consultant, or a PCI Qualified Security Assessor (QSA). It's possible you're an information technology (IT) architect or administrator tasked with implementing and maintaining PCI compliance. Or perhaps you're a Chief Information Security Officer (CISO), working tirelessly to balance all the things your QSA rattles off as best practices against the confines of your business' risk appetite and IT budget. Whatever your role In the PCI ecosystem, congratulations on picking up the best book on PCI, bar none.

When I first started working heavily with PCI as a senior security engineer turned PCI QSA, the PCI Data Security Standard (DSS) was a relatively new set of rules every company that accepted credit cards had to follow. It came with a big promise to stop the rampant card breaches the world was experiencing. Everybody in the industry was talking about PCI and most hated it. As I was responsible for assessing and advising organizations on PCI compliance, I read everything I could find on the subject—white papers, documents, books, blogs, you name it. After dredging through mountains of text that did nothing but repeat the same requirements with a stunning lack of pragmatism or business understanding, an early edition of *PCI Compliance: Understand and Implement Effective PCI Data Security Standard Compliance* was a welcome relief.

Since that time, I've had the honor and responsibility of leading a number of global PCI practices. I've trained and managed hundreds of PCI consultants and QSAs, been on the front lines leading forensic investigations, recovery, and remediation efforts of some of the biggest data breaches you've heard of, and built a security assurance team responsible for protecting the shopping habits and payment information of hundreds of millions of customers. One thing remains constant: this book has become and continues to serve as the de facto training manual I throw at anyone I need to spool up on PCI and payment card security.

We all know PCI DSS amounts to doing the basics to protect cardholder data (CHD), so you might be asking yourself why was PCI so controversial in the first place. Simply put, payment card security and data breaches are an externality. In other words, before PCI, CISOs claimed they cared about security, but in reality they only cared about securing the assets that would hurt the bottom line if lost—and payment card data was not one of those assets. It took PCI compliance enforcement and post-breach fines from the card brands to create an economic incentive for merchants to invest in securing customer payment cards. In my view, enforcement of PCI compliance can be credited for virtually every advance we've seen in payment card security over the past 15 years. It's why we trust the payment card ecosystem and charge everything to our cards today.

No, PCI isn't perfect, but it's the best we've got until we develop one universal standard that covers everyone's use cases[1]. While it's super prescriptive, PCI's scope is myopic to just CHD. For immature security teams, this can lead to over-indexing on CHD protection while leaving the organization's key assets under protected. For mature security teams, on the other hand, it often drives duplicative work with security specialists working in an infinite loop of mapping PCI DSS controls against the organization's actual controls. Creating further frustration, organizations can be "PCI compliant" before a breach and then find themselves retroactively slapped with PCI noncompliance fines after. Unfortunately, there's often a big difference between thinking you're PCI compliant and actually being PCI compliant, and many QSAs are purveyors of rubber stamps for the former.

But back to why we're here—this book and how it can help you succeed in your role. This is the first text I've found on PCI that not only talks about the requirements themselves but also frames PCI in the context of business enablement. After reading this book, you will be better equipped to communicate with your business stakeholders about PCI in their language, properly and efficiently manage your PCI scope, build and maintain a realistic yet effective set of controls protecting CHD, and successfully demonstrate your organization's PCI compliance to your assessor.

As I write this, the PCI Council's presses are still smoldering from the 359-page release of PCI DSS 4.0, the first major update in over a decade. Not only does PCI 4.0 bring forth the expected myriad of updates and new requirements, it also introduces a new double-edged sword called the Customized Approach. Even for seasoned QSAs it can be pretty confusing. As such, I strongly encourage you to read this book cover-to-cover and share it with everybody in your organization who has a hand in maintaining your PCI compliance. Keep it handy as a reference for future design reviews, engineering sessions, and PCI assessments. The sooner you understand and incorporate the updated requirements into your security and compliance programs, the more prepared you and your company will be.

With this book, you are already off to a great start!

Andi Baritchi
Head of Security Assurance Engineering
at a Big Tech Company,
Prior Big 4 Consulting PCI
Practice Leader,
Prior Global PCI-QSA Practice Leader

NOTE

1. xkcd—Standards. https://xkcd.com/927/.

Acknowledgments

This project represents decades of hard work, passion, and a willingness to get my hands dirty in the depths of PCI DSS. It's my absolute delight to share it with you all. I'm proud of what we've put together in the fifth edition of this book, and it represents the largest body of overhaul work since the second edition when I first became involved in the project.

I'd like to thank James, the other half of our author team, for keeping me honest and helping to set the tone of this text. Like in previous editions, I'm certain that readers will be able to discern my voice from his, but I think this edition represents the closest voicing we've had for a collaborative text.

Yousef Hamade, my partner in crime in defending banking applications, spent hours helping us make sure the technical items were correct. Yousef improved the Microsoft-related details immensely, and the book is of much higher quality directly due to his contribution. Our interactions reminded me how much I enjoyed fighting the good fight with you at the bank. This book is so much better because of Yousef!

There are countless advisors that I reached out to during the research and development of this book. Matt Springfield (www.12feet.com) provided a sounding board for strange scenarios and did us a *huge* favor inspiring our cloud, virtualization, and containerization notes and text. There is so much available on these topics and I'm proud of the summary we put together on this.

A few bigwigs in the field of PCI that have helped in one way or another include Dr. Anton Chuvakin (who roped me into the second edition of this book 12 years ago, Andi Baritchi, Erin Jacobs, Zack Fasel, Dan Glass, Joel Weise, Derek Milroy (previous technical editor whose contribution is still present in this edition), David Mortman, and Steve Levinson. All by bouncing ideas off of each other, contributing content or ideas, digging into unique new things that we discovered leading up to the final release of PCI DSS 4.0, and trying to predict the future by reading the PCI DSS tea leaves.

There is no amount of gratitude that seems worthy enough for my family and the support they provide. My kiddos, who were babies when I started on this journey in the late 2000s and are now looking at high school and college very soon, provide inspiration as I watch them grow. Christine, for putting up with late-night writing sessions and the random "BOOM" shout from the top of the stairs. You are the reason that I get to do things like this.

Finally, it's you (*pointing at yourself?*) Yes, you. Allowing the conversation to continue off the pages here to discuss challenging topics that may start with a PCI DSS angle but quickly move into higher order business and technology discussions spark joy. I truly cherish those brain-folding moments, because as we've seen in the last few years, life is precious.

With that, I wish you all the best on your PCI DSS journey!

– Dr. Branden R. Williams

As many of our stories start, I was heading to meet Branden at a bar. This was spring of 2005 and I was living in Austin, TX, after moving back from San Francisco and pondering my next career move. Branden had been doing security consulting for Verisign and was in town for work. As we discussed the job, he wondered out loud if I would be interested in consulting. He offered a recommendation to his boss, and I jumped at the opportunity to try something new and challenging. Within a few months of being hired, I was in the Bay Area attending one of the very early training classes held by the PCI Security Standards Council and have been working in or near PCI ever since (despite a few attempts at escape). Very few opportunities have impacted my life so dramatically, and I am thankful every day that I grabbed that beer.

Thanks to all of those who helped me find my footing in consulting. Randy Kaeder, for taking a chance on a new guy. Randy Golly and Bill Uptmore, who traveled many miles with me and provided a patient experience for me to learn from. Sherri Collis, for coming into a crazy environment and just making it better than we could have. Matt Springfield, who provided guidance and brotherhood in my early career that continues to this day.

My career would not have been nearly as exciting or fulfilling without some of the great people that I have worked with over the years, especially Steve Levinson, Rob Harvey, Sandro Bucchianeri, Yvette Johnson, Erin Jacobs, Zack Fasel, and Andi Baritchi. You all have created very special environments to support and energize the people that work with you.

I have also been fortunate to have clients throughout the years that I don't just call customers, but friends. Especially early on in my consulting career, I spent a lot of time on-site and traveling with customers. To be successful in this business requires good communication and people-skills, but it makes it so much easier when you enjoy the people you are working for and truly want to help them succeed. Thanks to everyone who allowed me to assist in their PCI and security endeavors.

Moving back to the DFW Metroplex to start my consulting career had another unexpected outcome, meeting my wife, Erin. Dating through the busy travel years, chasing her to NYC, returning to Texas to start a family—she has been the constant for 15+ years and makes me a better person every day. Thanks for managing the long hours, road trips, and general craziness that accompanies life with me.

And thanks to you, the reader. I hope this book is informative, helpful, and somewhat entertaining. My career has been the most fulfilling when I have been able to educate and enlighten, and I know those goals drove the initial creation of this book. The early iterations were a great reference source for me, and I feel privileged to join the writing team and help keep the book up-to-date and useful. Enjoy!

– James K. Adamson

Authors

Dr. Branden R. Williams has more than twenty-five years of experience as a technology executive where he has served virtually every industry as an information technology and cybersecurity consultant, as well as held high-level executive roles inside banks, other financial services firms, and top cybersecurity and technology vendors. He has been working with PCI DSS, CISP, and SDP since 2004.

Branden's intuitive understanding of how information technology drives business, his use of business intelligence tools to drive revenue and innovation, and his energy and likeable personality have earned him increasing responsibility and respect in the business and academic worlds. Using his keen business insights and ability to communicate with technical and non-technical audiences, he collaborates with executives to analyze, develop, and implement enterprise-wide solutions that support key business initiatives.

Branden has global experience working on six continents as a consultant and practitioner, and holds a Masters and Doctor of Business Administration degrees. He teaches graduate-level courses at the University of Dallas as an adjunct and is a sought after speaker and author.

James K. Adamson has assisted clients in the payment security space for over 15 years as a PCI QSA and trusted advisor.

His work has included consulting with hundreds of organizations, ranging from Fortune 100s to startups, across many verticals, including retail, financial, travel, technology, medical, and service providers. He has deep expertise in assessing payment environments, reviewing security architectures and programs, and developing holistic approaches to addressing security and compliance needs.

James approaches compliance with the Payment Card Industry Data Security Standard to ensure that it helps organizations focus on protecting their customers' data, reducing risk, and improving business and security effectiveness.

1 About PCI DSS and This Book

Information in this chapter:

- Who Should Read This Book?
- How to Use the Book in Your Daily Job
- What This Book Is Not
- Organization of the Book
- Summary

The Payment Card Industry Data Security Standard (PCI DSS) celebrated its 17th year (December 15, 2004) and the PCI Security Standards Council (SSC) its 15th birthday (September 7, 2006) as of this writing. Most of you reading these words have probably heard about PCI DSS, worked on a project tied to PCI DSS compliance, or said a few words out loud about PCI DSS that would have earned at least one of us a big smack across the face from our mother. For those of you just starting with PCI DSS, we hope this book can be your guide to a successful end result—a sustainable compliance program that exceeds the baseline security standards set forth in PCI DSS 4.0.

If you are like most professionals, the idea of becoming compliant with PCI DSS (or countless other regulations) does not sound fun. Information technologists and information security professionals aren't the only ones who share this feeling. Not only have C-Level executives and other business leaders had to deal with compliance and regulation around payments at some point in the last 16 years of their career, but we have even given rise to a new C-Suite position—the Chief Compliance Officer (CCO). While the CCO is not as much a new position with articles dating back to the mid-1970s referencing the title, the challenging landscape that companies must navigate necessitated more focus on this function in the wake of Sarbanes–Oxley (SOX), PCI DSS, the Health Insurance Portability and Accountability Act (HIPAA), and others.

Compliance efforts are rarely described as fun among those working with them. Painful is probably a better description. Whether it is the pain of not knowing what to do, pain of failing the assessment, or pain of "doing compliance" without an adequate budget, there are plenty of challenges that compliance—PCI DSS compliance in particular—have in common with pain.

Thus, we face the seemingly impossible challenge to write a fun and insightful book about PCI DSS. We realize the challenge of the task ahead, and we are committed to it. We'd like to invite you, our reader, to travel with us in the hopes that when you turn the last page, you would come to realize that PCI DSS compliance can indeed be fun—or maybe you had fun learning why you want to avoid PCI DSS at all costs. The price of this book pales in comparison to the dollars companies spend complying with PCI DSS.

There are many standards and regulations out there. If your company's stock is publicly traded in the United States, you must adhere to the SOX mandates. Financial companies fall under the Gramm–Leach–Bliley Act (GLBA). Those in the energy sector build toward North American Electric Reliability Corporation (NERC), Federal Energy Regulatory Commission (FERC), or Critical Infrastructure Protection (CIP) standards. If you are in the health care industry, your network must comply with the HIPAA standards as updated in legislation focused on electronic health records. Other countries have their own "alphabet soup" of standards such as the British Science Institute (BSI), Russian GOST (Russian for "gosudarstvennyy standart" or "state standard"), worldwide International Organization for Standardization (ISO)/International Electrotechnical Commission

DOI: 10.1201/9781003100300-1

(IEC), and possibly the most intrusive regulation, the General Data Protection Regulation (GDPR) and its derivatives. PCI DSS occupies a special place among standards for two reasons: broad, worldwide applicability, and the presence of an enforcement mechanism that is seen as imminent and unavoidable, unlike other mentioned regulations (GDPR is the exception).

The overarching theme of all these standards, laws, and regulations is that organizations need to secure data and protect their networks to keep citizens' data safe. In some cases, a weak information security posture may only affect one company. However, when data on the corporate network contains personal information about patients, customers, or employees, a breach of security can have implications far beyond the victimized company. A breach dealing with hundreds of millions of customers, such as a payment card processor or Fortune 100 retailer, will have implications touching nearly every family, thus decreasing such occurrences is in the public interest. Recent breaches have brought this concept back to the forefront as malware authors have advanced their capabilities and tenacity, thus even subverting some of the very basic controls designed in many of these compliance initiatives.[1]

Visa, MasterCard, American Express, Discover, and JCB developed PCI DSS together to ensure that customer information from payment cards and the associated systems are adequately protected from loss. Breaches of customer information lead to financial loss and damaged reputations. The payment card industry wants to protect itself from financial loss or eroded consumer confidence in credit cards which could lead to expensive and invasive governmental regulation. If you ever needed a sound bite for why PCI DSS is here, it's to boost confidence in the payment system.

We will use our experience with PCI DSS, both from the PCI Qualified Security Assessor (QSA) side and the information security side, to explain the most up-to-date PCI DSS guidelines to you (version 4.0 as of this writing). Between the two of us, we've worked for merchants, acquirers, processors, security vendors, consulting firms, and even issuers. Branden also spent time on the Board of Advisors for the PCI Council and EMVCo where he shaped the futures of each standard in specific ways. The objective of this book is not only to teach you about the PCI DSS requirements but to help you understand how the PCI DSS requirements fit into an organization's information security framework and how to effectively implement information security controls so that you can be both compliant and secure. In addition, we will cover ways to do this in the easiest and most pain-free way without compromising security in the process.

This book will make constant reference to the PCI DSS. PCI DSS and its related standards are owned by the PCI SSC, sometimes known in the industry as PCI Co. Before you start reading this book, you should go to the Council's website at pcisecuritystandards.org and download the current version of PCI DSS and the Report on Compliance (ROC) Reporting Instructions. You can find the relevant documents in the Documents Library section of the website. You will find tons of additional information related to PCI DSS in this file repository, but we will focus on the standard itself. Guidance documentation is helpful, but remember that it is *not* part of the standard. That means that an assessor cannot assess against it, but it can be used to help with interpretation. Expect conflict here if you rely on it heavily.

We do not claim any ownership over PCI DSS. You will find both direct quotes and paraphrases in this text, all of which reference the set of documentation owned and managed by the PCI SSC. Please be sure to visit their site to get all the authoritative documentation, and understand that we are only referencing it here in this text while adding additional information and value to you, our reader.

As of this publication, PCI DSS is at version 4.0. This book will highlight any significant changes between the previous version 3.2.1 and this version and give you compliance tips to comply with the standard. There is also a website, pcibook.com, where you will find tools and errata in case we make a mistake or need to make an update. We're human, it happens. The website will be the primary ongoing support tool for you to reference and interact with us.

WHO SHOULD READ THIS BOOK?

Every company that accepts card payments, processes credit- or debit-card transactions, stores or transmits payment card data, or in any other way touches personal or sensitive data associated with payment card processing is affected by the PCI DSS. Nowadays, it means that virtually all businesses, no matter how big or small, need to understand how their PCI DSS scope is defined and how to implement PCI controls to reduce their compliance risk, or face penalties potentially to the point of losing their ability to cost-effectively and legally process payments.

Even with the broad audience compelled to comply with PCI DSS, this book had to be written for a specific technical level. We could have written the text in very simple terms to educate the general population about PCI DSS. We could have written an in-depth technical tome providing every bit of detail a network engineer or security administrator might need to configure and implement all controls mandated by PCI DSS. This book aims in the middle and is more of a strategic guide to help management and practitioners understand the implications of PCI DSS and what it takes to be compliant. Ultimately, our goal in writing this book was to demystify some of the challenges with PCI DSS and allow readers to understand the right questions to ask of their peers to work toward compliance.

Generally, the book is useful for every stakeholder in an organization dealing with credit cards. This would include executive management, IT and IT security management, network and server managers, developers, database managers, legal, marketing, sales, HR, front-line managers, as well as anyone interested in payment security.

We will point out areas that are relevant but out of scope for this text to give you direction on where to go next for more technical information.

Because of the wide impact that PCI DSS has on any organization, this book is like a small business with five employees—it can wear multiple hats and will appeal to multiple audiences. This book is for the IT managers and company managers who need to understand how PCI DSS applies to their organizations. This book is for the small- and medium-size businesses that don't have an IT department to delegate to. This book is also for large organizations whose PCI DSS project scope is immense. It is for all organizations that need to grasp the concepts of PCI DSS and how to implement an effective security framework that is also compliant. This book is intended as an introduction to PCI DSS, but with a deeper and more technical understanding of how to put it into action. Finally, even PCI (and anti-PCI) *literati* will benefit from our stories and case studies!

HOW TO USE THE BOOK IN YOUR DAILY JOB

You can use the book during the entire lifecycle from complete PCI unawareness to security and compliance enlightenment. Specifically, you can use it as provided in the following:

- Learn what PCI DSS is and why it is here to stay,
- Learn how to avoid PCI DSS altogether,
- Understand how it applies to you and your organization,
- Learn what to do about each of the 12 main requirements,
- Learn how to deal with PCI assessors and internal auditors,
- Learn how to plan and manage your PCI DSS project,
- Understand all the technologies referenced by PCI DSS,
- Learn how to form strategies for removing portions (or indeed all) of your company from scope, and
- Get the best experience out of what can be seen as a painful assessment and remediation process.

WHAT THIS BOOK IS NOT

While reading the book, remember that this is not the book that will unambiguously answer every PCI DSS question. There is simply no way to create a book with every use case in it with the goal of answering PCI DSS questions as the regulation applies to your own environment.

Indeed, there is a similarity in how networks and systems are deployed, but given the broad applicability of PCI DSS—from small e-commerce sites to huge worldwide retailers—there is no way to have a book "customized" for your networks, systems, and applications. It is not meant to be the final authority for all issues related to PCI DSS, and it is not the unabridged guide to all things of PCI DSS. Finally, even though the book is written using our 15-plus years of experience in virtually every part of the payment card universe, your acquiring bank[2] is the ultimate ruler of most PCI challenges you will face on your journey to compliance and your QSA[3] (or other similarly credentialed and experienced individual) should be your guide to lead you to top of PCI Compliance Mountain.

We will not discuss the myriad of other standards the Council has amassed in detail, but you will find mentions of things like the PCI Software Security Framework (SSF), Point-to-Point Encryption (P2PE) standard, and others throughout the text.

ORGANIZATION OF THE BOOK

Each chapter of the book is designed to provide you with the information you need to know in a way that you can easily understand and apply. The chapters in this book follow a common structure that, wherever possible, includes the description of the PCI DSS requirement, the value of the requirement for PCI DSS and security, common tips, and select tools useful for satisfying the requirement, as well as common mistakes and pitfalls.

In simple and direct terms, we will first explain the control or concept we are talking about in a way that illustrates its intent. Then, we explain where this concept sits in PCI DSS and why it is needed for information security (i.e., how it reduces risk). Next, we explain what you should do with this concept to be secure and compliant using examples and common practices. We add levity with detailed and entertaining case studies. When we said that we will make PCI DSS fun, we really mean it! Most chapters have a summary that provides a brief recap of the concepts discussed to reinforce what you read or to help you identify areas that you may need to re-read if you feel you don't understand them yet. Where possible, we also try to highlight common mistakes and pitfalls with these requirements or PCI concepts.

SUMMARY

This section provides a brief description of the information covered in each chapter:

- Chapter 1: About PCI DSS and This Book—You are here.
- Chapter 2: Introduction to Fraud, Identity Theft, and Regulatory Mandates—This chapter explains cybercrime and regulations and is a brief look at payment card fraud, cybercrime, identity theft, and other things around PCI DSS.
- Chapter 3: Why Is PCI Here?—This chapter gives an overview of PCI DSS and why the card industry was compelled to create it. It also includes some discussion about the benefits of PCI DSS compliance and the risks of non-compliance.
- Chapter 4: Determining and Reducing Your PCI Scope—Every successful project around PCI DSS hinges on correctly scoping the environment. Expect that you should learn exactly how to scope your environment, learn ways to reduce it, and get tips for planning your PCI DSS projects.
- Chapter 5: Building and Maintaining a Secure Network—This chapter explains fundamental steps in protecting PCI DSS and other electronic data: making your network secure in

the first place. This chapter discusses the basic components of a secure network and lays the foundation for building the rest of your PCI DSS compliance.

- Chapter 6: Strong Access Controls—This chapter covers one of the most important aspects of PCI DSS compliance: access control. The information in this chapter includes restricting access to only those individuals that need it, as well as restricting physical access to computer systems.
- Chapter 7: Protecting Cardholder Data—This chapter explains how to protect the card data stored in your systems, as well as how to protect data while it is in transit on your network.
- Chapter 8: Using Wireless Networking—This chapter covers wireless security issues and wireless security controls and safeguards managed by PCI DSS. We include concepts that can be widely applied to Wi-Fi, Bluetooth, mobile, satellite, and emerging standards like ZigBee.
- Chapter 9: Vulnerability Management—This chapter explains performing vulnerability assessments to identify weaknesses in systems and applications, and how to mitigate or remediate the vulnerabilities to protect and secure your data.
- Chapter 10: Logging Events and Monitoring the Cardholder Data Environment—This chapter discusses how to configure logging and event data to capture the information you need to be able to show and maintain PCI compliance, as well as how to perform other security monitoring tasks.
- Chapter 11: Cloud and Virtualization—This chapter is a long time in the making, and we hope will serve as a fantastic guide to the rather challenging topic of leveraging these technologies in a PCI DSS environment.
- Chapter 12: Mobile—We are increasingly becoming reliant on mobile devices in our interactions with the world from our customers to our employees. You can safely use Mobile technologies, and we will discuss how.
- Chapter 13: PCI for the Small Business—PCI DSS isn't just for big box retailers and large banks. Whether you handle millions or hundreds of cards per year, you must comply with the DSS. This chapter includes tips on how to achieve PCI Compliance in a small business, subsidiary, or satellite office setting.
- Chapter 14: PCI DSS for the Service Provider—Service Providers have extra requirements they need to comply with; we'll review those here.
- Chapter 15: Managing a PCI DSS Project to Achieve Compliance—This chapter gives an overview of the steps involved and tasks necessary to implement a successful PCI compliance project. This chapter includes a discussion of the basic elements that should be included in future projects and to proactively ensure they are PCI compliant.
- Chapter 16: Don't Fear the Assessor—This chapter makes you understand that an assessor is there to work with you to validate your compliance and help you with security. They are only your enemy if you treat them this way. This chapter explains how to use the findings from a failed assessment to build ongoing compliance and security.
- Chapter 17: The Art of Compensating Control—This chapter explains how compensating controls are often talked about and misunderstood. This chapter will help build understanding and confidence in the reader when dealing with this tricky and often ambiguous component of PCI DSS, and most importantly, give you tips on creating your own.
- Chapter 18: You're Compliant, Now What?—This chapter covers the details you need to keep in mind once you have achieved compliance. Security is not as simple as just getting it implemented. You have to monitor and maintain it. This chapter contains information about ongoing training and periodic reviews, as well as how to conduct a self-assessment to ensure continued compliance.
- Chapter 19: Emerging Technology and Alternative Payment Schemes—This chapter looks to the future of payments and how they will impact your PCI DSS strategies.

- Chapter 20: PCI DSS Myths and Misconceptions—This final chapter explains common but damaging PCI myths and misconceptions, as well as the reality behind them.
- Chapter 21: Final Thoughts—You made it to the end! We'll leave you with a few things to take away.

For those of you new to PCI DSS, we recommend going right through the chapters in order. They build upon themselves as concepts continue to get more complex and we apply what we learn. Once you are through the book, you will be able to reference specific content a little bit easier. On our Supplemental materials website (pcibook.com), you can find links to our GitHub for the book that will have actual links to the things we discuss throughout the text. This should make it easier for all of you to access material, especially as it gets updated over time. If you find a broken link, feel free to let us know!

One quick note on the use of gender in this book. The English language does not have a singular, non-binary pronoun, only plurals (they/them). We will use gendered pronouns for number agreement purposes.

In addition, both of us feel strongly that discrimination and intolerance of any type are unacceptable in this profession. We're all in this together.

And with that, let's dive into fraud, identity theft, and regulatory mandates.

NOTES

1. Those words were written almost a decade ago, and the cadence of data breach notifications is not stopping. If there were ever a reason to re-consider the data your firm uses, think about that. We will talk more about this later in the book, but you only have to secure the data you can lose.
2. Your acquirer is the entity who sends your transactions to the network for processing. We will talk about all the players in the processing system in Chapter 3.
3. The term QSA and the role of QSAs in PCI DSS assessments will be explained in Chapter 3.

2 Introduction to Fraud, Identity Theft, and Related Regulatory Mandates

Information in this chapter:

- Introduction to Fraud, Identity Theft, and Related Regulatory Mandates
- Summary

Payment card fraud, identity theft, and broader personal data misuse are problems that plague our information-dependent society and predate the Internet. Ironically, things such as automated processing of financial data that make your life easier and more convenient also make crime easier and more convenient. Moreover, the Internet allowed crime that only happened on a small scale to grow and spread globally, and the Internet's scalability turned electronic-based crimes into a global concern.

Online crimes are now automated and grew from rare to widespread. Gone are the days where criminals need to be in the same location, country, or even continent to scam you out of your hard-earned cash. Nigerian e-mail scams started decades ago and are profitable for the scammers. They send out millions of e-mails claiming to be a relative of a Nigerian dignitary with frozen assets and want you to transfer the money for them. You give them your bank account information and/or send them seed money to get things moving and end up with nothing. UK Lottery scams aren't much different with the same basic constructs to get you a cash prize (Branden literally received this scam in his e-mail while writing this chapter). Tech support, romance, and cryptocurrency scams are the new wave of electronic crimes and all are generally just variations on a theme.

An unexpected but theorized[1] pandemic forced more interactions to the digital realm in 2020, which amplified this effect dramatically. As millions of employees moved away from offices to work from home, old-school scams saw new life attacking employees who were now thrust into situations where they may start a job while never meeting anyone face to face. The year 2020 forced companies to mature quickly into combatting these scams, but we still saw a ton of breaches including EasyJet, Landry's, J-Crew, and Expedia to name a few.[2]

Criminals went high-tech and discovered that there is a significant amount of money to be made with very little risk. Hacking company databases or orchestrating a phishing attack while sitting in your pajamas and eating Nacho Fries in the living room of your house has much more appeal than physically robbing banks or convenience stores. The advancement of automated exploit kits such as Metasploit has made couch-hacking more effective for even the slightly knowledgeable. Add to that the lowered risk of a confrontation with firearms and electronic crime becomes even more attractive! Depending on the company being targeted, the sophistication of the attack, and sheer luck, sometimes the high-tech crime can also be significantly more lucrative than traditional armed robbery.

Cross-border prosecution issues significantly fuel cybercrime. When a criminal physically robs a convenience store, he will definitely be captured on a camera somewhere and there may be witnesses with phones. Law enforcement will mobilize quickly to find and catch the criminal so he may be brought to justice. Cyber-criminals have a couple of things working in their favor—the first of which is their ability to commit crimes without ever stepping into the physical location of their victim(s). Couple that with lagging cyber-security laws in most countries and the limited ability of law enforcement bodies to prosecute outside their borders and you have an idea of why cybercrime

DOI: 10.1201/9781003100300-2

is on the rise. It's used by state actors to fund government initiatives, and some locations can be havens for cyber-criminals due to outdated extradition laws. In addition, the whole ecosystem of criminal outsourcing now allows other criminals to only focus on the activities they do best, such as creating malicious software or conducting crime through botnets.

To be fair, there is cross-border prosecution of cyber-criminals, but only after the financial loss rises to a certain level where big agencies pay attention. A criminal netting $1 million in proceeds isn't enough to get the attention of law enforcement, unless it is added to a collection of crimes exceeding some baseline threshold. When talking to local agents of US Federal law enforcement bodies, generally the crime had to exceed $10–20 million before resources were used to bring that criminal to justice.

Malicious software (malware) and cyber-criminals are not the only threat. Sadly, the very companies and organizations that are entrusted with sensitive information are often to blame because they lack adequate controls to protect sensitive information. In some companies, information security is treated with apathy; in others, a lack of effective controls enables an insider to commit fraud. Consumers and businesses are faced with a wide variety of threats to their data and personal information on any given day.

Ransomware, phishing attacks, drive-by downloads, and botnets are all parts of computer attacks that are on the rise and pose a significant threat to users as they connect to the Internet. Those threats pale in comparison to the amount of personally identifiable information (PII) and sensitive data available to be compromised due to carelessness or negligence by individuals and corporations.

TOOLS

Did you know that the Privacy Rights Clearinghouse has tracked all reported breaches since the ChoicePoint breach on February 15, 2005 (as well as including additional breaches disclosed prior)? To see all these breaches with an explanation and amount of records lost, point your browser to the Privacy Rights Clearinghouse website. As of this writing, Privacy Rights Clearinghouse made their database available for download, but without anything after October 2019. They claim to be working on something bigger, but no announcement exists.

There are paid sources and other public sources (including a Wikipedia page) that you can use to learn more about specific breaches, but we'll just leave you with the notion that it is an old problem, a significant problem, and it will likely continue to be a cat and mouse type game for decades to come.

As of this writing, 68 personal information records are lost or stolen every second.[3] Every year since the ChoicePoint breach, we've seen major companies fall victim to Payment Card Industry (PCI)-related security breaches. All of these breaches continue to demonstrate both the poor state of security in these firms and the increasing sophistication of attacks who want this data and know how to profit from it.

In an "Information is King" era, when more consumers are using computers and the Internet to conduct business and make purchases, taking the proper steps to secure and protect PII and other sensitive data has never been more important. It is bad for companies, individuals, and the economy at large if consumer confidence is eroded by having personal information exposed or compromised. Credit card brands are definitely not the only entities suffering from such possible loss of confidence.

NOTE

Take a step back from the text for a minute and adjust your mindset to think of yourself as a general consumer, Internet user, or citizen—not as a security or payment professional. What data do you hold dear? Think through the following list of scenarios:

What data or information about me can be considered sensitive and should not be disclosed, be corrupted, or be made permanently or temporarily unavailable? Think of a broad range of types of information—from a rare photo to your bank account number, medical history, or information about anything you've done that you are not proud of.

Think whether this information exists in any electronic form, on your computers or anywhere else? Is that picture on your "private" Facebook page—an oxymoron if there ever was one—or present in an e-mail folder somewhere?

Next, think whether this information exists on some system connected to the Internet (possibly indexed by a helpful search engine). The answer today would be *yes* for almost all information we consider sensitive. For example:

- Credit card information—check,
- Bank account information—check,
- Personal financial records—check,
- Tax records—check,
- Legal proceedings—check,
- Sensitive personal files—check,
- Recent purchase history—check, and
- Health records—check.

What would happen if this information is seen, modified, or deleted by other people? Will it be an annoyance, a real problem, or a disaster for you? What if it's old data written on a decommissioned hard drive that fell off the back of a truck?

Finally, think about what protects that information from harm. Admittedly, in many cases, you don't know for sure. We can assure you that sometimes your assumption that the information is secure will be just that—an assumption—with no basis.

Going through this list helps you not only understand data security rationally but also feel it in your *gut*.

There are many laws and regulations designed to coax businesses into addressing their security problems that affect information technologists. Depending on what industry a company serves, they may fall under Sarbanes–Oxley (SOX), the Gramm–Leach–Bliley Act of 1999 (GLBA), the Health Insurance Portability and Accountability Act (HIPAA), Federal Information Security Management Act (FISMA), and other regulatory mandates that we mentioned at the very beginning of Chapter 1—About PCI and This Book. This hodgepodge of alphabet soup makes for a tough job understanding how to comply with all these measures, as many organizations still fail to enforce adequate security or gain consent for data usage from their customers. The Unified Compliance Framework (UCF) that can be found at unifiedcompliance.com tracks hundreds of relevant regulations, and many commercially available Governance Risk and Compliance (GRC) tools such as RSA's Archer or IBM's OpenPages can help build, manage, and reference a common control set to cover all of these compliance initiatives.

NOTE

If you feel lost and out of control, don't. Remember, all these crazy compliance initiatives are trying to minimize the risk associated with an underlying problem—poor security. Taking a step back and looking at a standard security framework, such as National Institute of Standards and Technology (NIST) Cybersecurity Framework (CSF), would do more to boost your global compliance efforts than attacking any one of these by themselves. A mature program would be able to adapt to future compliance initiatives or changes in a way that would minimize the overall impact compliance has on your organization.

Breaches often target consumer credit card information because of the revenue this type of data can generate on illicit markets. Since our last publication, Europay, MasterCard, and Visa (EMV) continues to drive the value of magnetic stripe data down, but that doesn't stop the attacks or the desire to capture other data like PII and Personal Identification Number (PIN) information. Card companies recognized the rising threat to their brands and the large payment systems they invested in, and eventually they came together to develop the Payment Card Industry Data Security Standards (PCI DSS). In essence, the credit card industry has taken steps to assure the security of credit card data and transactions in order to maintain the public trust in credit cards as a primary means of transacting business. If you want to accept cards as payment or take part in any step of the processing of the transaction, you must comply with PCI DSS. Failure to do so can result in penalties stiff enough to cause public disclosures, or worse, bankruptcy.

NOTE

Most of the above regulations focus on the issues of data protection from theft or confidentiality of sensitive data. When we think about fraud and the abuse of somebody's identity, we think about people stealing data as if it were a thing to stash in your pocket. Indeed, to assume an identity and apply for credit under that name, a thief needs that identity's most sensitive personal information. In the United States, the typical combination needed for ID theft is as follows:

- Social security number (SSN, sometimes only the last four digits),
- Your mother's maiden name,
- Your full name,
- Your current and past addresses and phone numbers, and
- Your employer's name and address.

From this pack, only the first two are not truly public (even though assignment of SSNs was geographically predictable for a long time and the secrecy of your mom's maiden name is at best debatable). The rest of the bundle can be assembled later after the most sensitive information is in the possession of the attacker thanks to social media, third-party cookie abuse, and personal data indexing services.

However, think what happens after your identity is stolen and assumed by the attacker who now lives *your* life and applies for credit cards, loans, and bank accounts using your name.

He now modifies or corrupts your data by harming your stellar credit score, reputation, standing with financial institutions, employers, and government agencies (for example, if he commits a crime and then shows fake ID—or, worse, illegally obtained *real* ID—with your name).

Thus, remember that ID theft is not only about the misuse of information, but it can also cause damage from actual changes to your personal information.

And while the attacker (excluding the most special cases which we are not prepared to discuss here...) cannot erase your life from the systems, the damage done to your future life can be significant, especially if the case of ID theft is detected late in the game.

Unlike SOX or HIPAA, the PCI DSS is not a law, though some states such as Nevada, Massachusetts, and Minnesota have enacted laws requiring that companies serving their residents comply with some or all of PCI DSS. However, in many ways, it is more effective. Non-compliance probably won't land you in jail, but on the rare and extreme side, it could mean removing your ability to accept or process payments. For some organizations, losing the ability to process credit card payments would drastically affect their ability to do business and possibly even bring about the death of the company (see the Card Systems breach in 2005). Although PCI DSS can be effective in stopping security breaches, companies still seem to struggle with its implementation.

NOTE

By the way, credit card theft and identity theft are not the same. In fact, they have little to do with each other, despite what you hear from misinformed journalists.

To explain it further, you might not care much if your credit card information is stolen due to legally mandated card liability limits (that are typically reduced even further—to $0), but you must and, in fact, will be made to care if your identity is stolen and then used by criminals to open new lines of credit.

There is nothing extraordinary or magical about the PCI DSS requirements—with the exception of the interpretation. The guidelines spelled out are all, essentially, common security practices that any organization should follow without being told. Companies with mature information security programs have few problems adding unique PCI DSS requirements to their programs, even when some had trouble proving that their controls are as good (or better) than PCI-mandated controls. Even so, some of the requirements leave room for interpretation and complying with PCI DSS can be tricky.

Here's a hint: if one particular requirement for PCI DSS seems too hard to comply with, you might be approaching it all wrong. Think less about how to get out of complying, and think more about how to incorporate and build upon the baseline of security provided by PCI DSS. Review the Customized Approach Objective to start at the beginning of what you need to do. Or even better, think about how to remove your compliance burden all together by outsourcing payments to a third party.

As with any information security regulation or guideline, you need to keep your eye on the ultimate goal. When executing a compliance program, some organizations follow the letter rather than the spirit or intent of the requirements. The end result may be that they were able to check off all the compliance boxes, declaring their network compliant but not really secure. Remember, if you follow the requirements and seek to make your network as secure as possible, you are almost guaranteed to be compliant with PCI DSS. But, if you gloss over the requirements and seek to only make your network compliant, there is a fair chance that your network could still be insecure. It could even happen while your assessors are on site!

Major retailers and larger enterprises are well aware of the PCI DSS—and have been aware of it for years. They have dedicated teams that focus on security and PCI DSS compliance. They have the resources and the budget to bring in third parties to assess and remediate issues. The scope of PCI DSS affects almost every business, from the largest retail megastores down to a self-employed single mother working from her home computer. Businesses that accept, process, transmit, or can affect the security of payment card data must comply with PCI DSS.

SUMMARY

The purpose of this book is to provide an overview of the components that make up the PCI DSS and to provide you with the information you need to know in order to get your network PCI DSS compliant and keep it that way. We've discussed how larger compliance-driven alphabet soup initiatives can really confuse the business side of operations. Security is a business issue, and a good security program puts a framework in place to address issues like compliance before they become a problem.

Each major area of security covered by the PCI DSS is discussed in some detail along with the steps you can take to implement the security measures on your network to protect your data.

Branden and James, your humble authors, are established information security professionals. We've been there and done that, and we have acquired wisdom through trial and error. We hope our experience will help you implement effective solutions that are both compliant and secure.

NOTES

1. Severe Acute Respiratory Syndrome Coronavirus as an Agent of Emerging and Reemerging Infection, by Vincent C. C. Cheng, Susanna K. P. Lau, Patrick C. Y. Woo, and Kwok Yung Yuen.
2. This data is according to identityforce.com who tracks breaches by year.
3. Sourced from DataProt.

3 Why Is PCI Here?

Information in this chapter:

- What Is PCI DSS and Who Must Comply?
- Electronic Card Payment Ecosystem
- Goal of PCI DSS
- Applicability of PCI DSS
- PCI DSS in Depth
- Quick Overview of PCI Requirements
- What's New in PCI DSS 4.0
- PCI DSS and Risk
- Benefits of Compliance
- Case Study
- Summary

Chances are you already know something about the Payment Card Industry Data Security Standard (PCI DSS), but you might not have a full and clear picture of PCI DSS—both the standard and its regulatory regime—and why they are here. This chapter covers everything from the conception of the cardholder protection programs by the individual card brands to the founding of the PCI Security Standards Council (PCI SSC) and PCI DSS development. It also explains the reasons for the arrival of the PCI DSS that are critical in understanding how to implement PCI DSS controls in your organization. Many of the questions about PCI DSS and many of the misconceptions and myths about PCI have their origins in the history of the program, so it only makes sense that we start from the beginning.

WHAT IS PCI DSS AND WHO MUST COMPLY?

First, *PCI* is not a government regulation or a law.[1] When people say "PCI," they are typically referring to PCI DSS, now at version 4.0 for this book. However, to make things easy, we will continue to use the term *PCI* to identify the payment industry standard for card data security interchangeably with PCI DSS.

Unlike many other regulations, PCI DSS has a very simple and direct answer to the question "Who must comply?" The answer is simple, but you will find that people looking to sell products and services may incorrectly name specific entities as "in" or "out." This reminds us of a quote from noted American novelist Upton Sinclair who said "It is difficult to get a man to understand something when his job depends on not understanding it."[2] PCI's answer to "who must comply?" is any organization that accepts, stores, processes, or transmits member-branded (Visa, MasterCard, American Express, Discover, and JCB) credit or debit card data.

NOTE

PCI DSS applies to you if your organization accepts, processes, stores, and/or transmits member-branded card data. Member-branded card data is any card that is part of the Visa, MasterCard, American Express, Discover, and JCB payment schemes, including their subsidiaries or international partners. Should a new member be added to this list, their cards would also be included in the scope of PCI DSS compliance. Debit cards that can be used as either

DOI: 10.1201/9781003100300-3

a debit or member-branded credit card will fall into PCI DSS scope as well. Keep a close watch on the PCI Council's website (as well as pcibook.com) for changes to this.

Keeping account data safe requires broad applicability of PCI DSS. It's pointless to protect data in a few select places. Protection is required wherever and whenever card data is physically and electronically present. You might be thinking, "why is the data present in so many places?" Visa advertises that they work with over 100 million acceptance locations worldwide. Each of those could potentially be storing months or years of payment card data in places where criminals can steal it. Keep those statistics in mind as you read through the book to provide context on both the macro and micro scales. Without jumping too far ahead into our story, we'd say that in many cases, adjusting your business processes to not touch the card data directly will save you from a lot of security, compliance, and legal challenges.

In this book, we are primarily concerned with merchants and service providers. Merchants are pretty easy to identify—they are the companies that accept credit cards in exchange for goods or services. The PCI official definition of a merchant[3] states: "a merchant is defined as any entity that accepts payment cards bearing the logos of any of the five members of PCI SSC (American Express, Discover, JCB, MasterCard, or Visa) as payment for goods and/or services" For example, a retail store that sells groceries for cash or credit cards is a merchant. An e-commerce site that sells electronic books is also a merchant.

However, when it comes to service providers, things get a bit trickier. The PCI Council provides a glossary within the PCI DSS,[4] which defines them as a: "Business entity that is not a payment brand, directly involved in the processing, storage, or transmission of cardholder data on behalf of another entity. This also includes companies that provide services that control or could impact the security of cardholder data. Examples include managed service providers that provide managed firewalls, intrusion detection systems (IDS), and other services as well as hosting providers and other entities. If an entity provides a service that involves only the provision of public network access—such as a telecommunications company providing just the communication link—the entity would not be considered a service provider for that service (although they may be considered a service provider for other services)." This definition is clunky and verbose. A better way to express service providers would be any entity that can affect the security of payment card information (excluding the same companies as the above definition does) that is not handling this data in exchange for goods or services. If you have a provider that does something that can impact the security of cardholder data, they are a service provider and should be validated as compliant with PCI DSS.

Sometimes a merchant can also be a service provider at the same time: "...a merchant that accepts payment cards as payment for goods and/or services can also be a service provider, if the services sold result in storing, processing, or transmitting cardholder data on behalf of other merchants or service providers."[5] As an example, a merchant could stand up a business model whereby a company accepts credit cards as payment for services it provides to other merchants who also accept credit cards. In this case, such an entity is both a merchant and a service provider. For example, if you provide hosted shopping cart and processing services to merchants and accept payment cards, you would be both a merchant and a service provider.

NOTE

How about a thought exercise to show how complex things can get. Let's talk about Automated Teller Machines or ATMs. If you operate a network of ATMs, are you considered a merchant or a service provider?

On one hand, the service provider definition looks like it describes the operations, but are ATMs facilitating a transaction? Are they processing, storing, or transmitting cardholder data on behalf of another entity? How would you apply requirements unique to service providers to what amounts to a self-service checkout machine?

ATM operators are merchants. Think about it this way. A customer wants to "buy" some money from a kiosk. They put in their card, punch in their PIN, select what they want, and then oftentimes pay a convenience fee of a few dollars (at least here in the United States) before their goods are delivered through a slot. Goods that could also include non-banking things like postage stamps, bill payment receipts, or lottery tickets (yes, this is actually a thing). As far as the network is concerned, it's a debit transaction over debit payment rails.

The point is that the vast majority of companies dealing with PCI DSS have a relatively straightforward business model and will have no problems understanding their classification. Only a small percentage of firms will struggle with their classification.

Now that we have some baseline definitions described, we will describe the whole payment ecosystem for the purposes of PCI DSS.

ELECTRONIC CARD PAYMENT ECOSYSTEM

Before we go into detail on PCI compliance, we'd like to describe everyone involved in the entire payment card ecosystem:

- Cardholder: a person using (holding) a credit or debit card.
- Merchant: sells goods and services and accepts cards as a form of payment.
- Service provider (sometimes a Merchant Service Provider [MSP] or an Independent Sales Organization [ISO]): provides all or some of the payment services for the merchant. In PCI DSS 4.0, we can also add Third-Party Service Providers (TPSPs) to this group. Generally, they are considered anyone that can affect the security of cardholder data.
- Payment processor: a specific type of service provider. These entities generally provide additional services through software (such as a payment gateway) or other automation (such as anti-fraud tools) to make accepting payments easier.
- Acquiring bank: connects to a card brand network for payment processing and also has a contract for payment services with a merchant or processor. You may also hear this called a Merchant Acquirer or Merchant Bank. We will generally refer to this group of entities as acquirers.
- Issuing bank: issues payment cards to consumers (who then become cardholders).
- Issuer processor: a service provider that will process issuing cards on behalf of the bank. These firms usually process for smaller banks that have not invested in their own processing systems.
- Card brand (also known as a payment brand, network, or card scheme depending on regionalization): a payment ecosystem with its own processors and acquirers, and for the purposes of PCI DSS includes the member brands (Visa, MasterCard, American Express, Discover, and JCB).

The primary focus of PCI DSS requirements is on merchants and service providers. This is understandable since this is exactly where most of the data is lost to malicious hackers. Whether TJX in 2005–2007 (45 or 90 million cards stolen, depending on the source), Heartland Payment Systems in 2008–2009 (more than 100 million reported cards stolen), Target in 2013 (more than 40 million cards), Marriott in 2018 (potentially over 100 million encrypted cards), or Capital One in 2019 (more than 106 million customers), merchants and service providers suffered from breaches that resulted in stolen cards and mounting fines (meant to offset re-issuance expenses). Prior to some of the regulations in PCI DSS becoming mainstream, issuing banks were replacing compromised cards at their own cost and incurring other administrative and fraud costs as well. PCI DSS ensures merchants and service providers understand their obligations to protect card data.

GOAL OF PCI DSS

In light of what is mentioned above, PCI DSS is here to reduce the fraud risk of payment card transactions by motivating merchants and service providers to protect card data. Whether this goal is worthy, whether there are other secondary goals, or even whether this goal is being achieved by the current version of the data security standard is irrelevant. What matters is that PCI DSS is aimed at reducing the fraud risk inherent with a payment instrument meant to represent cash in a transaction. PCI DSS seeks to accomplish that by forcing merchants and service providers to pay attention to many key aspects of data security including network security, system security, application security, security awareness, incident response, and governance. Even more importantly, it indirectly encourages merchants to drop cardholder data entirely and conduct their business in a way that eliminates costly and risky data storage and on-site processing. The focus on security practices and technologies naturally helps to reduce fraud. One of the original PCI DSS framers also described it as the following: "the original intent was to design, implement, and manage a comprehensive, cost-effective and reliable security effort"[6] rather than trying to manage a patchwork of security controls.

The "Ten Common Myths of PCI DSS" document from the PCI Council presents the six domains of PCI DSS as its goals[7]:

1. Build and maintain a secure network,
2. Protect cardholder data,
3. Maintain a vulnerability management program,
4. Implement strong access control measures,
5. Regularly monitor and test networks, and
6. Maintain an information security policy.

While the above six domains can be seen as tactical goals during a PCI DSS implementation, the strategic focus of PCI DSS is card data security, payment card risk reduction, and ultimately the reduction of fraud losses for merchants, banks, and card brands.

Overall, while motivating security improvements and reducing the risk of card fraud, PCI DSS serves an even higher goal of boosting consumer confidence in what is currently the predominant Business-to-Consumer (B2C) cashless payment system—plastic cards (or their digital representation such as Apple Pay). While we can debate whether paper, plastic, and metal money is truly on the way out, the volume of cashless transactions is increasing annually though the percentage numbers will vary depending on how you slice the research. Some countries, like Nigeria, are encouraging the use of cashless payment systems through modernized electronic banking infrastructures and disincentives to use physical cash or checks.[8] Interfering with the exchange of money directly affects our global economy. Therefore, PCI DSS defends something even bigger than "bits and bytes" in computer systems—primarily attempting to protect a major money-exchanging cog in the economic system itself.

APPLICABILITY OF PCI DSS

Though the statements about accepting, processing, storing, and transmitting payment card data will probably sound tiresome by the time you are finished reading our book, remember that PCI DSS applies to all organizations that perform the above and there are no exceptions. Chapter 20, PCI DSS Myths and Misconceptions, covers some of the common, industry-wide misbeliefs and clarifies that the above PCI applicability is indeed the reality and not the myth.

The question of validating or proving PCI compliance is a bit different from the argument of PCI DSS applicability to organizations that deal with card data. The type of validation and requirements you must follow can differ for merchants and service providers, further sliced by card brand and transaction volume.

First, there are different levels of merchants and service providers. Tables 3.1 and 3.2 show the breakdown.

TABLE 3.1
Merchant Levels

Merchant Level	Description
Level 1	Any merchant that has suffered a hack or an attack that resulted in an account data compromise (can vary based on payment brand), or any merchant deemed level 1 by any payment brand. Any merchant that processes more than 6 million Visa, MasterCard, or Discover transactions annually 2.5 million American Express Card transactions or more per year, or any merchant that has had a data incident; or any merchant that American Express otherwise deems a level. Merchants processing over 1 million JCB transactions annually, or compromised merchants (as RECOMMENDED), however, JCB doesn't have levels consistent with other brands. If you are accepting JCB, check their current tiering system and requirements (recently updated April 2018).
Level 2	Any merchant that processes between 1 and 6 million Visa or Discover transactions annually. Any merchant with greater than 1 million but less than or equal to 6 million total combined MasterCard and Maestro transactions annually. Any merchant that processes between 50,000 and 2.5 million American Express transactions annually. Merchants processing less than 1 million JCB transactions annually.
Level 3	Any merchant that processes between 20,000 and 1 million Visa or Discover card not present (e-commerce) transactions annually. Any merchant with greater than 20,000 combined MasterCard and Maestro e-commerce transactions annually but less than or equal to 1 million total combined MasterCard and Maestro e-commerce transactions annually. Any merchant that processes between 10,000 and 50,000 American Express transactions annually.
Level 4	All other Visa, MasterCard, American Express, and Discover merchants.

TABLE 3.2
Service Provider Levels

Service Provider Level	MasterCard	American Express	Visa
Level 1	All third-party providers (TPPs), all data storage entities (DSEs) that store, transmit, or process greater than 300,000 total combined MasterCard and Maestro transactions annually.	2.5 million American Express Card transactions or more per year; or any Service Provider that American Express otherwise deems a Level 1 Service Provider.	VisaNet processors or any service provider that stores, processes, or transmits over 300,000 transactions per year.
Level 2	Includes all DSEs that store, transmit, or process less than 300,000 total combined MasterCard and Maestro transactions annually.	50,000–2.5 million American Express Card transactions per year.	Any service provider that stores, processes, or transmits less than 300,000 transactions per year.
Level 3		Between 10,000 and 50,000 American Express Card transactions per year	
Level 4		Less than 10,000 American Express Card transactions per year.	

NOTE

Some levels may vary across the globe, and it is always up to an acquiring institution or payment brand to make adjustments to your level. For example, Visa Europe is a wholly owned subsidiary of Visa, Inc. as a Bank of England designated entity that has different rules—especially as it relates to compliance around their PIN Security Programme and Chip-and-PIN (EMV) transactions. For more specific information, contact your acquiring bank or card processor to provide level and validation guidance.

These levels exist for determining the type of compliance validation required as discussed in the next section. The levels are also sometimes used by the payment brands to determine which fines to impose upon the merchant for non-compliance.

A Quick Note about Appendix A3

Even with all this information, a payment brand or acquiring bank may want more validation than the standard PCI DSS requirements call for. If you are labeled as a Designated Entities Supplemental Validation (DESV) firm, you will need to have Appendix A3 completed. According to PCI DSS 4.0, the following criteria might get you tagged for this extra bit of PCI DSS love:

- Those storing, processing, and/or transmitting large volumes of account data,
- Those providing aggregation points for account data, or
- Those that have suffered significant or repeated breaches of account data.

This additional set of requirements is out of scope for this book considering the small population of companies that will need to fill them out. If you are asked to do this, you likely suffered a breach or are suspected of poorly maintaining your PCI DSS program, or maybe you have been considered too big to fail. Be sure to work with your QSA to navigate your way through this complex addition to the standard.

PCI DSS IN DEPTH

In the next section, we take a detailed look at the PCI DSS standard, its entire regulatory regime, as well as related security vendor certification programs.

NOTE

While the Customized Approach is something long overdue in the PCI DSS ecosystem, we suggest using it sparingly or not at all. Its usage could easily double, if not more, the cost of your assessments and the way you manage your program, and those costs won't go down over time. You are probably better off removing that system from scope or finding a way to make the system comply with the Defined Approach. We would expect less than 5% of firms working with PCI DSS to leverage the Customized Approach.

Compliance Deadlines

It's 2022 at the time of this writing, which means that deadlines for compliance are likely from your company changing its level or some other kind of event happening. If you are looking for a date, just assume it's in the past unless your acquirer or processor tells you something different. Dates that are in the future are more likely tied to the new requirements in PCI DSS 4.0, or indeed when you need to switch from 3.2.1 to 4.0 so firms have a period of time to adjust their operations accordingly.

Organizations can begin validating using the PCI DSS 4.0 immediately. In order to ensure groups have time to update their governance and operations to meet the new standards, the PCI DSS 3.2.1 will remain in effect and can be used for validation until March 31, 2024. The new future-dated requirements in PCI DSS 4.0 will not be part of your validation until after March 31, 2025. Completing your assessments before these dates will allow you to use the previous version of the standard if you need more time.

COMPLIANCE AND VALIDATION

As we mentioned before, depending on your company's merchant or service provider level, you will either need to go through an annual on-site PCI assessment by a Qualified Security Assessor (QSA) or Internal Security Assessor (ISA), or complete a Self-Assessment Questionnaire (SAQ) to validate compliance. In addition to this, you may have to present the results of the quarterly network perimeter scans performed by an approved scanning vendor (ASV).

If you are choosing to use the SAQ or you are performing other self-assessing under the ISA program, keep in mind that your assessment artifacts may generate more questions simply because there is no third-party validation. We recommend that you use a combination of ISA and QSA resources (where an on-site assessment is required) to perform your annual assessment to be sure you get a thorough, fair, and defensible result.

When submitting the SAQ, you will need to obtain a signature on the document by an officer of your company.[9] At the present time, there is no court precedent for officer liability as a result of false PCI DSS compliance attestation. However, industry speculation is that this person may be held accountable in a civil court, especially if he or she intentionally misrepresents information while certifying. Don't do anything unethical or illegal.

If you are planning on submitting a Report on Compliance (ROC) instead of the SAQ, you will need to download and fill out the ROC Template available on the PCI Council's website in the Document Library. This document is intended to be used by QSAs and ISAs to promote a complete and accurate report from a PCI assessment. After the SAQ has been filled out or the ROC has been completed, it must be sent along with all the necessary evidence and validation documentation to the acquiring organization or processor. It depends on who requested the compliance validation in the first place.

It is a common misconception that the degree to which you must comply with PCI DSS varies among the different levels. Both merchants and service providers must comply with the entire PCI DSS, regardless of their level and validation requirements. What varies is the way and frequency you report compliance upstream. If you determine you are a Level 4 Merchant, don't interpret the "recommended" under validation requirements to mean PCI DSS compliance is optional. Furthermore, don't download the PCI DSS Prioritized Approach from the PCI Council's Website and decide that completing milestones one through three should be fine. Visa's Web site explains it like this: "Compliance validation is required for all service providers."[10]

NOTE

Discover and JCB handle merchant PCI compliance validation differently. Contact your acquirer for more information.

The validation mechanisms, as of the time of this writing, are given in Table 3.3.

Further, the scope of PCI DSS validation differs based on the exact way the organization interfaces with card data. Specifically, quoting from the PCI Council Web site, the circumstances that affect what sections of the SAQ the merchant should complete for validation are provided in Table 3.4.

TABLE 3.3
PCI DSS Validation Requirements

Merchant or Service Provider Level	Visa	MasterCard
Level 1	QSA/ISA On-Site Assessment,[11] ASV scan, and Attestation of Compliance (AOC)	QSA/ISA On-Site Assessment and ASV scan
Level 2	SAQ, ASV scan, and AOC	QSA/ISA On-Site Assessment or assisted SAQ completion and ASV scan
Level 3	SAQ, ASV scan, and AOC	SAQ and ASV scan
Level 4	SAQ, ASV scan if requested by the acquirer	SAQ and ASV scan if requested by the acquirer

To summarize, the activities of your PCI DSS validation depend on the following:

- Merchant or service provider status,
- Transaction volume,
- Card brand, and
- The method of accepting and interacting with card data.

TABLE 3.4
SAQ Validation Types Based on Card Acceptance Methods

Card Processing	Self-Assessment Validation
Card-not-present (e-commerce or mail/telephone-order) merchants, all cardholder data functions outsourced. This would never apply to face-to-face merchants.	SAQ type A includes parts of 7 out of 12 requirements; 29 questions.
E-commerce only merchants that partially outsource their payment processing to PCI DSS validated entities and to not electronically process, store, or transmit any cardholder data.	SAQ type A-EP that covers a subset of all 12 requirements.
Imprint-only merchants with no electronic cardholder data storage, or standalone terminal merchants with no electronic cardholder data storage.	SAQ type B (for dial-only terminals) or SAQ type B-IP (for Internet Protocol [IP]-enabled terminals), which covers requirements most commonly related to those terminals.
Merchants using only web-based virtual terminals, no electronic cardholder data storage.	SAQ type C-VT, which covers sections of 10 out of 12 requirements, omitting logging (Req 10), and regular testing (Req 11).
Merchants with payment application systems connected to the Internet, no electronic cardholder data storage.	SAQ type C, which covers parts of all 12 requirements and Appendix A2.
Merchants who process payments through hardware payment terminals included in the P2PE Validated list on the Council's website.	SAQ P2PE, which includes a subset of requirements from 3, 9, and 12.
All other merchants not included in the descriptions for the SAQ types above, and all service providers defined by a payment brand as eligible to complete an SAQ.	SAQ type D (either the Merchant or Service Provider version), which includes all the 12 requirements and a full set of questions.

NOTE

Although American Express, Discover, and Visa allow Level 1 merchants to have their PCI compliance validated by the merchant's internal audit group, MasterCard does not explicitly allow this. To qualify for internal validation under MasterCard's new rules, the professional performing the assessment must be a current ISA. Check the PCI Council's website for more information on this program, including the steps required to join.

NOTE

The SAQs are generally available for download and use, and the changes include expanding some of the smaller SAQs to include new requirements and more responsibilities. There are still nine SAQs to choose from, and they generally represent the same groupings of requirements from the last version of PCI DSS. What has changed is any new requirements we will discuss in the book that will translate into new self-assessment checks in the SAQ that apply to your business.

WARNING

Don't let yourself become complacent. If you are a Level 4 merchant and are not required to do anything to validate your compliance with PCI DSS, you are still required to fully comply at all times. Even accepting one card per year gives you compliance liability and risk for PCI DSS. Many Level 4 merchants end up in big trouble when they realize they had to comply with PCI DSS irrespective of their validation requirements. In addition, due to different validation levels across major card brands, their situation in regards to PCI compliance may be much worse. Don't let a breach put you out of business from fines and fees. Ensure you are complying with PCI DSS at all times for all levels.

The specific validation requirements can change. For example, MasterCard announced in 2012 that Level 2 merchants now need to be validated via an on-site assessment from a QSA or have the person filling out the SAQ be a current ISA. We can expect validation requirements to become stricter in the future from all payment brands, especially with the advent of the Customized Approach.

WARNING

In previous versions of PCI DSS, e-commerce merchants could escape a lot of validation tasks and even compliance risk by simply loading payment pages inside inline frames (iframes). This became a hotly debated topic among QSAs and other industry leaders, so much so that SAQ A now states that Requirement 11.6.1 applies to merchants that include a TPSP's iframe payment form on their page.

If you truly want to run an e-commerce site and truly reduce your PCI DSS risk, be sure to do a redirect to your provider's hosted payment page. After payment is collected, the provider can redirect back to your page at the end.

Interestingly enough, companies can be merchants and service providers at the same time. If this is the case, the business should be described in detail in the assessment documentation and the compliance validated at the most stringent level. In other words, if a company is a Level 3 Visa merchant and a Level 1 Visa service provider, the compliance verification activities should adhere to the requirements for a Level 1 Visa service provider.

One notable PCI assessor, the late Walt Conway, related the following educational story about merchant and provider validation:

> My favorite is when the vendor replies that they are compliant as a Level 3 (or 2 or whatever) merchant. That response is completely irrelevant and inexcusably misleading. That they are compliant as a merchant is meaningless to you when you use them as a service provider. They can self-assess as a merchant—they cannot as a Level 1 service provider. That extra step is meant to protect you. If you get that kind of reply, you are likely dealing with an over-eager and/or ill-informed sales rep…ask to talk to an adult.[12]

SOMETHING NEW, THE CUSTOMIZED APPROACH

PCI DSS 4.0 introduced something new with the concept of the customized approach. You can see details of how this works in Section 8 of the front matter (page 28) and Appendices D and E (pages 333–340). Essentially, the way we have been validating compliance since December 15, 2004, is what the Council calls the "Defined Approach." Meeting requirements directly or using compensating controls according to that framework. In PCI DSS 4.0, there is a new option to validate a specific requirement and that is done with the *Customized Approach*. This new feature is part of the reason why the page count in PCI DSS 4.0 is more than double 3.2.1. While it may seem like an attractive option, managers should analyze the impact on the organization carefully.

On one hand, the benefit to the entire ecosystem is the Customized Approach Objective statements that are included with many PCI DSS requirements. If you are looking at a requirement without one of these statements, it is not eligible to be met using the Customized Approach (Requirement 3.3.1 as an example). This, with the applicability notes and guidance, provides much clearer details on what the intent of the actual requirement is. If you need to build your own set of controls that don't meet the letter of the actual requirement but will accomplish the goal stated in the Customized Approach Objective, this is now possible. Where you will typically find firms leveraging this approach is with systems or business models that are unique in ways incompatible with the requirement.

But here's the catch. Not only are the controls expected to meet or exceed the security provided by the original requirement, but QSAs are now mandated to maintain independence requirements for these controls. Much like traditional audit firms, the QSA that designs or implements the control may not be the same QSA that derives testing procedures for, assesses, or assists with the assessment of that control.

As QSAs start to wade into these waters, there will be legitimate uses of the Customized Approach to validate certain requirements. Firms will most likely continue to rely heavily on the Defined Approach for the vast majority of their compliance work and only use the Customized Approach for a subset of requirements. The Council allows for a mixed approach. Just remember, your costs will go up dramatically with every requirement using this approach, so you are better off sticking with the Defined Approach while removing a system or process that doesn't fit into that box from PCI DSS scope.

HISTORY OF PCI DSS

To better understand the PCI DSS role, motivation, and future, let's review its origins and history.

PCI DSS evolved from the efforts of payment brands battling fraud and counterfeiting. In the 1990s, the payment brands developed various standards to improve the security of sensitive information. In the case of Visa (formerly a regional association model), different regions came up with different standards because European countries and Canada were subject to different standards than the US. In June 2001, Visa launched the Cardholder Information Security Program (CISP, mostly pronounced KISP). The CISP Security Audit Procedures document version 1.0 was the great-grandfather of PCI DSS. These audit procedures went through several iterations and made it to version 2.4 in mid-2004. At this time, Visa was already collaborating with MasterCard on creating a single mechanism for merchants to go through. Their agreement was that merchants and service providers would undergo annual compliance validation according to Visa's CISP Security Audit Procedures and would follow MasterCard's rules for vulnerability scanning. Visa maintained the list of approved assessors and MasterCard maintained the list of ASVs.

This collaborative relationship had a number of problems. The lists of approved vendors was not well-maintained, and there was no clear way for security vendors to get added to the list for each particular card brand. To complicate things further, every card brand division did not endorse the program. Brands such as Discover, American Express, and JCB were running their own programs, further clouding the compliance requirements and process. The merchants and service providers in many cases had to undergo several independent assessments by different "certified" assessors just to prove compliance to each brand, which added to compliance costs and reduced the overall quality. For that and many other reasons, the five major payment brands came together and created PCI DSS 1.0, giving us the concept of PCI compliance.

Unfortunately, the issue of ownership still was not fully addressed, and just under two years later on September 7, 2006, the PCI SSC was born. Comprised of American Express, Discover Financial Services, JCB, MasterCard Worldwide, and Visa International, the PCI Council (as it came to be known) maintains the ownership of the DSS, approved vendor lists, training programs, and interpretation responsibility for the requirements.

NOTE

Since the last edition of this book, the Council continues to grow their sphere of influence. New standards include the Software-based PIN Entry on commercial off-the-shelf (SPoC), the Contactless Payments on COTS (CPoC), PCI 3-D Secure, Card Production and Provisioning Logical Security Requirements, Token Service Provider requirements, and others. There are opportunities for everyone to make a difference.

Even today, each card brand and region maintains its own security program beyond PCI DSS. These programs go beyond the data protection charter of PCI and include activities such as fraud prevention. The information on such programs can be found in Table 3.5. In certain cases, your PCI ROC may need to be submitted to a payment brand's program office separately if you have direct processing relationships with them. Keep in mind, we can't seem to keep up with the rapid changes each brand makes to their website or content. In fact, Branden got put into a kind of Internet jail with one of the brands because he was polling the site daily for changes. You should be familiar with all the brands' programs from their main websites. In addition, some payment brand requirements vary by geographical region.

TABLE 3.5
Brand Security Programs

Card Brand	Additional Program Informational
American Express	Web site: https://amex.co/3toQJX1, E-mail: EIRP@aexp.com
Discover	Web site: https://bit.ly/PCI-Disc, E-mail: DISCCompliance@discover.com
JCB	Web site: https://bit.ly/PCI-JCB
MasterCard	Web site: https://bit.ly/PCI-MC, E-mail: sdp@mastercard.com
Visa Inc.	Web site: https://vi.sa/3PK40CR, E-mail: cisp@visa.com

PCI Council

The PCI Council or, fully, PCI Security Standards Council or PCI SSC, describes itself as "a global forum that brings together payments industry stakeholders to develop and drive adoption of data security standards and resources for safe payments worldwide."[13]

The PCI Council charter provides oversight to the development of various PCI security standards (including PCI DSS, PCI Software Security Framework [SSF], and PCI PIN Transaction Security [PTS]) globally as well as maintaining the four vendor certifications programs for on-site assessments (ISA, QSA, PTS Labs, and PCI SSF Assessor), scanning companies (ASV), forensic investigators (PCI forensic investigators [PFI]), and integrator/resellers (Qualified Integrator Reseller [QIR]). The PCI Council publishes updates to the PCI DSS, which is accepted by all brands and international regions; it also updates the supporting documents such as the "PCI Quick Reference Guide" and "Prioritized Approach Tool" and a slew of supporting documents and ancillary programs ranging from interpretation guidance to output from the various Special Interest Groups (SIG).

The lists of current PCI SSF Assessors, QSA, QIR, PFI, PCI Professional (PCIP), P2PE, Qualified PIN Assessor (QPA), CPSA, PCI-Recognized Labs, and ASV companies are located in the Council's website. In addition, the Council also runs the Quality Assurance (QA) Program for QSAs, PCI SSF Assessors, and ASVs, which are aimed at boosting the overall quality and maintaining the integrity of site assessments and vulnerability scans.

The PCI Council is technically an independent industry standards body (although on the surface it looks more like a training and certification company). Since our last writing, the Council staff continues to grow, but it still remains a relatively small force of people managing the standards side of the PCI ecosystem.

The PCI ecosystem immediately felt the positive impact of the PCI Council. Merchants and service providers can now play a more active role in the compliance program and the evolution of the standard, whereas the QSA, PCI SSF Assessors, PFI, and ASV companies find it much easier to train their personnel.

TOOLS

At the time of this writing, PCI Council provides a few useful tools to help track PCI DSS compliance. These are explained in the Document Library section of the PCI Security Standards website.

- The Prioritized Approach tracking spreadsheet allows for compliance program tracking and reporting, whether internal or to the card brands or acquirers. One key note about this tool is that it is designed to be one-size-fits-all. Experience tells us that this is rarely the case, and you should customize this for your specific needs.
- The SAQ Instructions and Guidelines document is helpful for those validating PCI compliance via an SAQ. The PCI Council provides the fillable documents that can be used for tracking compliance at a small organization. All the SAQs can be obtained for free.
- AOC forms are also provided by the PCI Council. These forms accompany the SAQ during self-assessment or the ROC after the on-site assessment.

To summarize, the most important things to know about PCI Council are as follows:

- The Council maintains and updates the PCI DSS, PA Software Security Framework, and PTS, as well as all of their related supporting documents.
- The Council does *not* deal with PCI validation process and, specifically, with enforcement via fines or other means. These responsibilities are retained by the payment brands.

- The Council also certifies and maintains the lists of security vendors as QSAs, PCI SSF Assessors, ASVs, and PCIPs, as well as polices the vendors to maintain the integrity of PCI validation.

Let's look at QSAs, PCI SSF Assessors, PFIs, and ASVs in more detail as the core of the ecosystem. While there are other programs on the website, they are out of scope for this book.

QSAs

The PCI Council administers the QSA[14] program in which members are allowed to conduct on-site DSS compliance assessments. These companies have gone through the application and qualification process, having to show compliance with tough business, capability, and administrative requirements. QSAs must invest in personnel training and certification to build up a team of assessors, also called QSAs.

NOTE

QSAs are only permitted to conduct on-site DSS assessments. They are not automatically granted the right to perform perimeter vulnerability scans, unless they also certify as an Approved Scan Vendor (ASV). Many companies today can be found on multiple lists (QSAs, PCI SSFs, PFIs, and ASVs) to be able to provide complete PCI validation services to merchants and service providers.

QSAs must re-certify annually via a computer-based training module. The exact qualification process and the requirements are outlined on PCI Council Web site; however, of particular interest are the insurance requirements. QSAs are required to carry high coverage policies, much higher than typical policies for the professional service firms, which becomes important later. A lawsuit ("Merrick Bank v. Savvis," see more details in [15]) presents an example of the risk that QSAs face. In this suit, a bank is suing the assessor who validated CardSystems, a victim of a massive card data breach, as PCI compliant. Use your favorite search engine to find more lawsuits filed against prominent QSAs.

NOTE

QSAs are approved to provide services in particular markets or subsets of markets: US, Asia Pacific, CEMEA (Central Europe, Middle East, and Africa), LAC (Latin America and the Caribbean), and Canada. The qualification to service a particular market depends on the QSA's capabilities, geographic footprint, and payment of appropriate fees.

Individuals wanting to become a QSA must first and foremost work for a QSA company or for a company in the process of applying to become a QSA. Then, they must attend official training administered by the PCI Council and pass a written test. They must also undergo annual re-qualification training to maintain their status. An individual may not be a QSA, unless he or she is presently employed by a QSA company; however, a QSA can carry the certification between QSA companies when changing jobs.

TOOLS

Anybody can look up the individuals with current QSA certification by using QSA Employee Lookup on the Council's website. You can also submit feedback on individual assessors with

Verify a QSA Employee

Search by Last Name, First Initial or Certificate Number to quickly verify the certification status of a Qualified Security Assessor.

Q Jacobs, E   ✕

Search Result

Name: Erin Jacobs
Company Name: Urbane Security
Company Phone: 1-312-970-0317

CERTIFICATION	CERTIFICATE #	EXPIRATION DATE	STATUS	LEAVE FEEDBACK FOR THIS ASSESSOR
QSA	202-314	28 Oct 2022	VALID	Submit Feedback

FIGURE 3.1   QSA Query Results.

that link. If you feel compelled to share your amazing or poor experience with the council, please do.

See Figure 3.1 for an example.

We cover the tips on working with your QSA in Chapter 16, Don't Fear the Assessor. If there is one thing to remember when engaging a QSA it's to treat the QSA as a partner. Treating your QSA like an auditor will only lead to a painful process whereby both parties end up frustrated and disillusioned. This does require you to vet your QSA as not all QSAs are equal. More on this later.

ADDITIONAL PCI SSC QUALIFICATIONS

PCI SSF Assessors assess payment applications and vendors using the Secure Software Standard or the Secure Software Lifecycle (SLC) Standard as part of the PCI SSF program. The PCI SSF replaced the PA-DSS (which itself evolved from Visa's Payment Application Best Practices [PABP] program). Individuals wanting to assess applications under this standard must apply for the special designation and take additional training. You cannot be a PCI SSF Assessor without first becoming a QSA, and just like in the QSA world, your company must be signed up as a PCI SSF Company in order to perform assessments. PCI SSF and its associated standards are outside the scope of this book, but you can read about it on the PCI Security Standards website.

The P2PE (Point-to-Point Encryption) designation allows an individual to assess P2PE Solutions and Payment Applications. In order to qualify, you must work for a P2PE Assessor Company and go through the training and examination. Only those individuals who have the P2PE designation are approved to perform these assessments.

PFIs

PFIs combine all the individual payment brand programs around forensic investigations into one Council program like all the others you have read about. Like PA-QSAs, PFIs must be a QSA, and companies with the designation must also be QSAs in each region they want to do PFI work. There is no training requirement for PFIs, however, they must have experience on their resume and should include copies of certificates from their forensic-related training courses for review.

Contrary to popular belief, even though the Council manages the PFI program, they do not get copies of the forensic reports to create that closed-loop feedback channel the industry is asking for as it relates to negligence by a QSA, PA-QSA, or ASV after a breach.

PCIPs

The PCIP designation is open to anyone who passes the test and pays the fees. It was designed to be a designation that individuals can take with them, regardless of their employment status. It works like a typical certification in that manner.

QIRs

The QIR program was created to combat the rather poor job that many Point of Sale (POS) integrators or resellers do with deploying PCI DSS compliant solutions. The program has grown dramatically since our last edition and contains a large number of options by region.

ASVs

As you know, PCI DSS validation also includes network vulnerability scanning by an ASV.

To become an ASV, companies must undergo a process similar to QSA qualification. In addition to a training class for each analyst to be trained and performing ASV-related duties, ASVs must submit a scan report conducted against an outsourced test network perimeter. ASVs must certify at least two analysts before they can be approved. An organization can choose to become both a QSA and an ASV, or they could simply do one or the other.

ASVs are authorized to perform external vulnerability scans from the Internet, but PCI DSS also mandates internal vulnerability scans (performed from inside the company network), which can be performed by any qualified individual like an internal security team or consultant. Note that in PCI DSS 4.0, internal scans must be *authenticated*.

We cover all the tips on working with your ASV in Chapter 9, Vulnerability Management.

QUICK OVERVIEW OF PCI REQUIREMENTS

Now it is time to briefly run through all 12 PCI DSS requirements, which we cover in detail in the rest of this book.

PCI DSS version 4.0 is comprised of six control objectives that contain one or more requirements:

- Build and Maintain a Secure Network and Systems
  - *Requirement 1:* Install and Maintain Network Security Controls (NSCs).
  - *Requirement 2:* Apply Secure Configurations to All System Components.
- **Protect Account Data**
  - *Requirement 3:* Protect Stored Account Data.
  - *Requirement 4:* Protect Cardholder Data with Strong Cryptography During Transmission Over Open, Public Networks. Protect stored cardholder data.
- **Maintain a Vulnerability Management Program**
  - *Requirement 5:* Protect All Systems and Networks from Malicious Software.
  - *Requirement 6:* Develop and Maintain Secure Systems and Software.
- **Implement Strong Access Control Measures**
  - *Requirement 7:* Restrict Access to System Components and Cardholder Data by Business Need to Know.
  - *Requirement 8:* Identify Users and Authenticate Access to System Components.
  - *Requirement 9:* Restrict Physical Access to Cardholder Data.
- **Regularly Monitor and Test Networks**
  - *Requirement 10:* Log and Monitor All Access to System Components and Cardholder Data.
  - *Requirement 11:* Test Security of Systems and Networks Regularly.

- **Maintain an Information Security Policy**
  - *Requirement 12:* Support Information Security with Organizational Policies and Programs.

The above-mentioned 12 requirements cover a vast spectrum of information technology (IT) areas as well as venture outside of IT in Requirement 12. Some requirements are very technical in nature (e.g., Requirement 1 calls for specific settings on the NSCs such as firewalls), and some are process and policy-oriented (e.g., Requirements 7 and 12) and even go into contract law (some of the sub-requirements in Requirement 12 cover the interactions with TPSP).

The detailed coverage of controls makes things easier for both the companies that have to comply with the standards, the auditors (in the case of Sarbanes–Oxley Act of 2002 [SOX] or other laws and standards), or the assessors (in case of PCI DSS). For example, when compared to SOX, companies do not have to invent (or pay for somebody to invent) the controls for them—unless of course they are leveraging the Customized Approach. This can also create challenges as compliance initiatives become more prescriptive about their required controls, companies are forced to create a common control set and map them back to all of the individual compliance requirements.

What is interesting is that almost every time there is a discussion about PCI DSS, someone claims that PCI is too prescriptive. In reality, PCI being prescriptive is the best thing since anti-virus solutions invented automated updates (hopefully, you can detect humor here). PCI DSS prescriptive nature simply means that there is some specific guidance for people to follow and be more secure as a result (if they follow the spirit and not only the letter of PCI standards)! Sadly, in many cases, the merchants who have to comply with PCI DSS and who still think it is "too fuzzy" and "not specific enough" are the ones either fighting to comply in the first place, trying to avoid changing anything at all in spite of PCI DSS, or looking for a simple compliance and security *to do* list or a task list; and no external document that guarantees that your organization will be secure can ever be created.

In particular, when people say "PCI is too prescriptive," they actually mean to compare it to a "checklist mentality" that leads to following the letter of the mandate blindly without thinking about why it was put there in the first place. For example, deploying a shiny firewall with a basic "ALLOW ALL<->ALL" rule—an obvious exaggeration that clarifies the message here. Or, they have a firewall with a default password unchanged, or maybe slightly more secure by allowing all outbound and denying most inbound traffic. In addition, the proponents of "PCI is too prescriptive" tend to think that fuzzier guidance will lead to people actually think about the best way to do it.

Perhaps PCI DSS 4.0 perhaps made the biggest leap forward in joining these two camps with the Customized Approach guidance included in the standard. While we believe there will be lots of room for movement on whether or not a specific activity complies with the standard, we also believe that the documentation included paints arguably the clearest picture of what the Council actually intends.

So, the choices to write security-motivated regulatory guidance are as follows:

1. Mandate the tools (e.g., NSCs) and risk "checklist mentality," resulting in both insecurity and "false sense" of security.
2. Mandate the results (e.g., must be secure) and risk people saying "yes, but I don't know how" and then not acting at all, again leading to insecurity and a wide interpretation of intent.

We believe in today's reality that pill #1 works better than pill #2, but with a healthy dose of skepticism and debate. Although the organizations with less mature security programs will benefit at least a bit from #1, organizations with more mature programs might be able to operate better under #2. However, data security today has to cover the less-enlightened organizations, which makes the #1 choice (i.e., PCI DSS) the preferred one.

As a far as scope of PCI DSS within the organization is concerned, PCI compliance validation may affect more than what you consider the "cardholder environment." According to PCI DSS 4.0, the scope includes "all system components included in or connected to the cardholder data environment." Chapter 4 will help you with the scoping problem including giving you some ideas on how to reduce its impact. If you do not have basic network segmentation controls in place, the scope of PCI compliance validation will cover your entire network. Think about it: if you cannot ensure that your cardholder data is confined to a particular area, then you cannot focus on this area alone and you have to look everywhere.

NOTE

Just because a POS system is on the list of compliant payment applications, it does not mean that your particular implementation is compliant. Also, it definitely does not mean that your entire organization is PCI compliant. Only applications configured and maintained according to their Implementation Guide will be able to operate in a compliant manner. You should work with the application vendor and with your QSA to verify this.

In order for the device to be added to the PCI SSC's product and solutions list, the payment application, online shopping cart, or POS vendor has to show and document the secure method for their application deployment. However, it is ultimately the merchant's responsibility to follow the secure and compliant deployment guidance.

For merchants using an integrator or reseller, ensure they are deploying and managing your POS in a compliant manner. If they are doing things properly, they should be on the QIR list.

For the benefit of consumers who may be more familiar with a brand name rather than a parent company (e.g., TJX is the corporate parent of TJ Maxx), PCI compliance validation should always follow the merchant ID (MID). Any transaction processed under that MID, regardless of origin, should fall under that company's PCI validation process.

You may discover that you are unable to always comply with the strict letter of PCI DSS while still striving for its spirit. For example, you may need to temporarily store cardholder data unencrypted for troubleshooting purposes or to use a password of less than the mandated minimum length on a legacy system. Another example may include recording certain call-center conversations for customer service purposes. Again, card brands understand that these recordings may contain cardholder data, so accommodations must be made accordingly to protect that data.

NOTE

The Council provides additional guidance for unique situations on their website in the form of Guidance documents and a Frequently Asked Question (FAQ) library. You cannot assess against items in guidance documents or FAQs, but you can use these resources to help you understand the intent of the Council. When in doubt, always lean on your QSA to help you navigate PCI DSS requirements as they apply to your environment.

In many cases, compensating controls have to be used to achieve compliance when your company cannot exactly meet a given requirement. The important thing to remember about compensating controls is that they have to go beyond the requirements of PCI to provide the same or higher assurance of cardholder data protection. When compensating controls are used you must gather and supply additional documentation about the control. Please see Chapter 17, The Art of Compensating Control for detailed coverage of compensating controls.

How Changes to PCI DSS Happen

One of the key challenges for any security standard is to change fast enough to address the changes to the threat environment (and this changes literally every day since the criminal computer underground has to evolve to stay in business) and to change slow enough to still be considered a technical standard (and not simply advise to "do the right thing"). For prescriptive technical standards that directly call out security controls such as firewalls, network intrusion prevention, and vulnerability scanning, the challenge is even more extreme.

PCI DSS used to be criticized for being "constantly in flux" and for "not moving fast enough" at the same time, but by different people. The relatively stable nature of PCI DSS from version 3 quelled those discussions, however, PCI DSS 4.0 may just bring them back to the surface. It is a long overdue revision, and the differences in early drafts suggest that more changes will come in the next few years.

The PCI standards were historically governed by a process called the "Lifecycle Process for Changes to PCI DSS." The process broke up the life phases of the PCI DSS into three annual segments: publication of the PCI DSS, feedback on the published version, and draft revisions and final review of the next version.

The current lifecycles do not dictate strict annual windows, but still follow the same basic framework and allow time for all parties to evaluate the current version and provide feedback based on changes in technology or threat scenarios and integration of that feedback into the new version.

WHAT'S NEW IN PCI DSS 4.0

PCI DSS 4.0 represents a major overhaul from the last official version, 3.2.1. We discuss new requirements as we go through in our original topic-driven discussion here in the book, but we wanted to give a quick overview of the big themes that will change your approach. You can check the book website, pcibook.com, for more details here as we will continue to link to content designed to improve your understanding of the changes in PCI DSS 4.0.

Customized Approach

Perhaps one of the biggest signals is the notion of the Customized Approach, recently introduced into PCI DSS 4.0. This is a more audit-like approach where you can design your own controls for certain requirements. QSAs must maintain separation here (which is a diversion from previous guidance) between control design & operation and assessment. In early drafts of PCI DSS 4.0, Compensating Controls were completely removed. We believe this is a signal that you will not be able to use Compensating Controls at all in the next version of PCI DSS, instead, you will have to use the Customized Approach for any requirement you cannot meet as it is defined.

Extra Guidance

When you increase the page count from 139 to 360, you know there is going to be a ton more information available to you as a participant in the PCI DSS universe. We applaud this move as the guidance is well organized and easy to reference. There is a lot more information to become familiar with, however, we believe the majority of what you know about PCI DSS is still contained inside the requirements themselves, and you will only reference the added information in the case of an issue. Curious minds who want to learn more about the motivations of the PCI DSS framers will enjoy wading through the added detail.

NEW COUNTERMEASURES

Well, new to PCI DSS. In this version, the Council acknowledged that phishing is a serious enough threat that you must do something about it. Most firms are aware of the dangers that phishing can lead to and have some basic protections in place, so this should not be a big deal for anyone to comply with. In fact, you might already be in compliance with it today.

If you are a service provider, you will need to be able to detect and alert or prevent covert communications that are part of command-and-control structures that comprise malware. Merchants should do this too outside of PCI DSS requirements.

SKIMMERS AND WEB CONTENT

JavaScript skimmers are responsible for significant breach losses dating back to 2014, a full four years after the last version of PCI DSS, and now eight years for this version. There is a grouping of new requirements based on validating that what you are serving via a web browser to your customers is exactly what you intended. Think of it as an early warning service such that you would see malware being injected before it takes lots of customer account data. Expect slow adoption here (best practice until 2025) and you can bet the best JavaScript skimmers will build their own countermeasures to try to evade detection.

AUTHENTICATED VULNERABILITY SCANNING

Another one that most people are doing but is now required in PCI DSS. Vulnerabilities hide behind authorization gates. Compare a scan you might conduct against a system for which you have no access to versus a scan where you have administrative access. You will find many more vulnerabilities that way, and your result will be nearly devoid of false positives, thus streamlining your remediation process. So keep in mind that your vulnerability count is going to likely skyrocket if you are not doing authenticated scans today, but at the end of this process you will be an order of magnitude more secure by resolving those findings.

NOTE

An example of this in the real world. Branden was working with his team to get a more accurate understanding of outdated Java in his environment. While there were no applications running on Java 5, he found a server farm with that runtime environment installed and available to the operating system with elevated privileges. Removing that unused runtime environment raised the security of those systems dramatically—just by deleting outdated things that you would never see from a remote scan.

INVENTORY ALL THE THINGS

The amount of paper that is part of PCI DSS 4.0 doesn't stop at the weight of the standard in pages, it continues with the maintenance of new and existing inventories. If you have a piece of hardware or software, no matter how small, that is part of your CDE, you need to inventory it and keep that inventory up to date. The way the requirements are written, you can expect both your custom software to be inventoried and every single component that is used in that software as well.

The goal is to enable technology operators to discover and manage vulnerabilities in components that make their software go, like open-source libraries that enable Transport Layer Security (TLS) (OpenSSL). But this also would extend to any *glue* type software you write. Think middleware, shell scripts, Python scripts, extract/transfer/load data wrangling scripts, or anything you might write to automate a task in your CDE. It must be inventoried and that inventory must be maintained. This may represent the largest increase to Business As Usual efforts in a single PCI DSS iteration.

Scope Reviews

It's finally formalized. Older versions of PCI DSS discussed scope and required QSAs to confirm it as accurate, but there was never a specific requirement to do this. Now there is a pair of requirements (12.5.2 and 12.5.2.1) that require documentation to show that you have defined and validated your PCI DSS scope annually as a merchant, and semi-annually as a service provider.

In Place With Remediation

One of the long-standing issues around the annual compliance process was being able to have an "In Place" mark on a particular periodic requirement (that is more than annual) even if you missed one of the periods. For example, QSAs would commonly write 11.3.1 (internal vulnerability scanning) as In Place even if you were unable to produce four clean vulnerability scans by reviewing process improvement documentation that addresses the process failure. The QSA would note that he reviewed three clean scans as well as a process improvement document to address the gap that caused the firm to be one clean scan short for the year (potentially going so far as to document a compensating control requiring additional reviews or process management). In PCI DSS 4.0, QSAs will now mark the requirement "In Place with Remediation," which signals to whoever is reading your AOC or ROC that the QSA found an issue, but you were able to provide evidence that satisfies the requirement and you have addressed the process gap that caused the failure for the future.

Whether this will lead to any penalties or questions is certainly up for debate, but it is our opinion that the difference between the two is slight as previously the ROC would note the gap, but the AOC would not. For those consuming only the AOC, they would now have visibility into this lapse in control.

PCI DSS AND RISK

The relationship between PCI DSS and risk management isn't what a therapist would call healthy. PCI DSS's goal is to reduce the risk of card transactions and to build consumer confidence in the payment card networks. On the other hand, many people point out that PCI DSS presents a list of controls with no regard to an organization's own risk assessment. Let's explore the relationship of PCI and risk a bit further.

First, a common question: can one claim that complying with PCI increases the merchant's overall business risk? When people ask that question they usually imply that PCI added the risk of loss via non-compliance fines and fees to the risk of direct losses due to card theft from a merchant's environment (such as reputation damage, cost of new security measures, and monitoring). The answer is clearly a "no," since before PCI, most of the negative consequences of a card theft, even a massive one, were not falling upon the merchant's shoulders but on others such as card-issuing banks. PCI, on the other hand, represents a powerful motivation for protecting the data on the merchant side.

Still, despite that reality about PCI, many CEOs or CFOs are asking the question, "Why would I need to spend money on PCI?" And, no, the answer is not "Because there are fines" (even though there are non-compliance penalties). The answer is that the list of negative consequences due to neglecting data security and PCI DSS is much longer than fines.

Your company's contract with the acquiring bank probably has a clause in it that any fines from the card brand will be "passed through" to you. While fines are absolutely passed through, the occurrence of fines generally doesn't happen anymore unless your firm is willfully ignoring requests to present compliance attestations or you have had a breach recently. When Branden was working for a large processor, the Level 1 compliance rate was below 70% and none of them were actively being fined. Focus less on the fine aspect and more on what a breach would do to your balance sheet.

On top of that, if your organization is not compliant with PCI DSS when you are compromised, higher fines may be imposed as well. And if you find yourself in that situation, you might just end up with more data compromised, including that dreaded sensitive authentication data (SAD), which drives fines up even further. Believe it or not, this will be the least of your concerns. Possible civil and criminal liabilities could dwarf the fines from the card brands in hyper-litigious regions that cultivate class-action lawsuits. While there are research firms that place the cost of compromise at $50–$250 per stolen account (note stolen, and not one used for fraud, which will likely be a subset of the whole stolen card pool), we should not make decisions on those numbers. The research used to get to those numbers is deeply flawed and should only be used for entertainment purposes (recent versions of that research go into the limitations, they are very much worth the read). While we won't mention the firm or study in question, just understand that any firm that is aiming to estimate the cost per record of a breach and is basing that on a survey is misleading you. Smaller merchants are hit harder with penalties, especially in light of recovering from the COVID-19 pandemic, and companies in the business of protecting cardholder data don't last long after compromises.

Let's use The TJX Companies, which operates stores like TJ Maxx, Marshalls, and so on, as a case study. On January 17, 2007, TJX announced that they were compromised. Because they did not have robust monitoring capabilities such as those mandated by PCI, it took them a very long time to discover the compromise. The first breach actually occurred several years prior. TJX also announced that more than 90 million credit-card numbers were compromised. In addition to the fines, volatility in the stock price, and direct costs of dealing with the compromise, over 20 separate lawsuits were filed against TJX; some of which were converted to class-action status. This is good news for the rest of us because most of the outcomes are in the public record. It might take you some time, but with a good search engine and some time you could add up all of those losses into one big, fat scary number.

Whether you believe your company to be a target or not, the fact is that if cardholder data comes into contact with your network at some point *you are a target!* The resale value of cardholder data has plummeted dramatically in the last few years, but that doesn't mean that the size of the target on your back is smaller. You and your organization are simply someone's sheep to be fleeced, and your losses are their gains. Organized crime units profit from credit-card fraud, so your company is definitely on their list if you deal with card data. International, federal, and state law enforcement agencies are working hard to bring perpetrators to justice and shut down the infrastructure used to aid in credit-card-related crimes; however, hundreds of forum sites, Internet chat channels, and other groups on the dark web still exist where buyers can meet the sellers. Data breaches like the ones at TJX and Target are not the work of simple hackers looking for glory. Instead, well-run organizations from the Eastern European block[16] and selected Asian countries[17] sponsor such activity and earn a great living from various illegal hacking activities.

The Web site Privacy Rights Clearinghouse (https://privacyrights.org) maintained the history of the compromises and impacts in terms of lost card numbers and other records. Over 10 billion personal records (a mix of cards, identities, etc.) have been reported as compromised. This includes companies of all sizes and lines of business. Good security practices aligned with the PCI DSS can reduce the likelihood of your organization having to report that they have added to the pile of compromised records.

Finally, PCI DSS 4.0 now requires specific, targeted risk analyses in a variety of areas. Requirements 12.3.1 and 12.3.2 require an annual process to review any controls leveraging the Customized Approach, or any requirement that has some flexibility in the timing of which it must be performed. You must review all cryptographic cipher suites and protocols in use annually (Requirement 12.3.3) and also perform a detailed assessment of risks associated with hardware and software technologies in use (Requirement 12.3.4) annually. One of the best things you can do for your business is take these requirements seriously and expand it beyond the confines of cardholder data. Don't perform this to check an audit box, take it as an opportunity to get a broad look at how your business operates and the kind of risk it carries. If your firm is not currently leveraging a risk assessment framework as part of your ongoing reviews, consider looking at FAIR, ISO 31000, or the NIST RMF as your foundation.

BENEFITS OF COMPLIANCE

While the inclusion of benefits is irrelevant—after all PCI DSS compliance is *mandatory* for the organizations that deal with payment cards—it is worthwhile to highlight the fact that PCI DSS has important benefits for the merchants, acquiring banks, issuing banks, as well as for the public at large.

If we are to mention one benefit, PCI DSS has motivated security improvements in businesses (especially retail) like nothing else before it. Many of us lived through the computer virus-infested 1980s, then worm-infested and spammy 1990s, and then through heavy data loss early 2000s without doing anything on security. PCI DSS moved the needle farther toward the *secure* end for the laggards that fell victim to that reality. That's not to say breaches are not something we deal with in the 2020s, but it is something to say that PCI DSS greatly improved the baseline security for huge portions of the planet.

CASE STUDY

Much of this book focuses on case studies where a company makes a mistake or fails to do something that results in a breach. This case study is a nice change of pace where we examine someone doing something right!

THE CASE OF THE DEVELOPING SECURITY PROGRAM

Yvette's Evangelical Emporium is a small chain of 50 stores supplying religious supplies to local churches and individuals. Yvette started her business in 2013 with a single store. Throughout the 2010s, she was able to open several new stores in neighboring counties and states, eventually building a 10 retail location business. In 2015, she took advantage of low-interest rates spurred by supply-side economic policy, and using some capital from investors and a significant trust that matured, she expanded her operation to 25 stores in three years and continued to expand over the next four years to double her size.

In 2017, Yvette realized that she needed to formalize her IT division and hired Erin, a progressive and security-minded IT executive, as her chief information officer (CIO). Erin presented a plan to standardize and build out her infrastructure so that future growth could be done in a cookie-cutter fashion; thus, saving millions in deployment and maintenance costs.

By 2019, they crossed the threshold from a Level 2 Visa merchant to a Level 1 Visa merchant and knew they would quickly need to put a solid PCI compliance program in place. Erin knew from her previous experience that small companies struggled with information security and made it a point to build in basic information security fundamentals into her IT operations, but they did not meet the baseline PCI DSS requirements and needed to be reworked.

Because of her new reporting levels for PCI, Yvette hired Steve to serve as the Chief Information Security Officer, reporting directly to her. Steve's task was to build an information security program that addressed PCI immediately but would expand to be more applicable to information security such that future regulation would only require minor tweaks to the program.

Steve and Erin worked closely together to build a common set of controls to be rolled out to the entire company. Steve knew that PCI was a priority but considered everything he did in light of the ISO security framework (ISO27001). In some cases, he found that ISO far exceeded specific PCI requirements like in Business Continuity and Risk Assessments, and he found unique parts of PCI that were much more granular than ISO, like the treatment of SAD (Requirement 3.3). Steve's efforts ultimately paid off in spades as his information security program matured. Recent changes and additions to restrictions on personal data (such as the California Consumer Privacy Act) and state data breach notification laws were already addressed by the program as it matured, and Yvette's cost associated with protecting data was much less than her competitors who only chased standards with immediate non-compliance repercussions.

NOTE

The initial PCI DSS creators were well aware of ISO 17799 and other security standards. This awareness leads to the fact that if your organization has a solid security management program based on ISO IEC 27002 (a modern descendant of ISO/IEC 17799 and BS7799), your PCI effort will be relatively easier and you will gain both solid security and compliance as a result. It is also likely that compliance with other regulations will not be overly onerous. PCI is more granular, whereas ISO is broader, but they are largely in sync!

There are others to look at as well. NIST Cybersecurity Framework (CSF) is free, as are many of the FFIEC standards[18] and the Cybersecurity Assessment Tool (CAT). There's no need to pay for ISO 27001 as there are many freely available standards that will work.

Our previous technical reviewer Derek Milroy suggested using the concept of control leveling. The idea being that you define a standard or control that works for all systems, not just PCI systems, and build it into your organization's base set. This may not always work in the case of some legacy systems, but it's a good place to build fundamental security in your organization. Another example could be standards for audit lots and retention standards for all systems.

The Case of the Confusing Validation Requirements

Garrett's Gas Guzzling Garage operates 800 car repair locations across the United States. Garrett's recently opened 20 locations in Mexico City to help maintain and upgrade the fuel efficiency of old cars. Garrett is considered a Level 1 merchant in the United States but set up a different entity in Mexico City, and processes and settles locally with BBVA Bancomer. Although Garrett authorizes and settles locally in Mexico City at his small regional headquarters, he shares the data with the US-based parent for backup and analysis purposes.

His business is booming in Mexico City, and that business quickly became a Level 2 merchant. According to MasterCard's validation requirements, this would mean that Garrett must have a QSA perform an on-site assessment of compliance for both locations, or get someone internally trained under the ISA program. He was already doing this in the United States based on his Level 1 status, but now faces additional costs for doing this locally in Mexico City.

"But wait," some of you are saying, "What about Visa's rules?" Certainly glad you asked us that! According to Visa, if a smaller, wholly owned subsidiary shares infrastructure and data with a parent company considered a Level 1, then that smaller subsidiary should also be viewed as a Level 1 and perform the same level of validation.

Back to Garrett. Even though the 20 Mexico locations process through BBVA Bancomer, the data is shared with the US headquarters for backup and analysis. According to Visa's rules, the Mexican entity is considered Level 1 based on its relationship with the parent, and a Level 1 assessment must be performed.

As always, when in doubt, ask your acquirer what is expected of you. Your mileage may vary when it comes to some of these intricate rules. Some acquiring institutions may still treat certain subsidiaries as lower levels depending on the circumstances.

NOTE

There are two books that every IT and security person should read, both led by the great Gene Kim. The first is The Phoenix Project, and the second is Visible Ops Security. Do yourself a favor and buy both of these books, and don't forget to tell Gene how much you enjoyed them!

SUMMARY

PCI refers to the PCI DSS established by the payment card brands. Any company that stores, processes, or transmits cardholder data has to comply with this data protection standard. Effectively, all the target compliance dates have already passed, so if your company has not validated compliance, you are at risk of fines and other negative consequences of poor security and non-compliance. The PCI DSS is composed of 12 major requirements plus assorted appendices that cover a wide array of business areas. All companies, regardless of their respective level, have to comply with the entire standard as written. If you end up filling out a SAQ, you are responsible for validating the subset that applies to you, but don't forget about the rest of the standard, *especially* if the nature of your business changes! The actual mechanism for compliance validation varies based on the company's classification driven by the individual card brand, transaction volume, exact method of accepting cards, and other factors. The cost of dealing with data breaches continues to rise, and non-compliance exacerbates losses in case of a breach. Companies that do not take data security and compliance efforts seriously may soon find themselves out of business.

Now is the time to start the journey toward data security and compliance: get an endorsement from the company's senior management and business stakeholders, and start fulfilling your obligations and protecting the data.

NOTES

1. PCI DSS, or elements of it, are codified in actual law by a few US states at the time of this writing. Nevada explicitly called PCI DSS by reference and made it mandatory for some businesses operating in this state. Minnesota and Washington have adopted language from PCI DSS into their own information security statutes. Other state laws, such as data breach notifications or consumer privacy acts, may also include credit card account numbers in their scope.
2. Sinclair, Jr., U. B. I., Candidate for governor: and how I got licked (1935), ISBN 0-520-08198-6; repr. University of California Press; 1994. p. 109.
3. PCI Council Website, Glossary, Entry Merchant.
4. PCI Council Website, Glossary, Entry Service Provider.
5. PCI Council Website, Glossary, Entry Merchant.
6. Joel Weise, private communication, e-mail dated July 1, 2009.
7. Ten Common Myths of PCI DSS. https://bit.ly/PCI-tenmyths; 2010.
8. Central Bank of Nigeria, Cash-less Nigeria. https://bit.ly/PCI-BoN
9. This can be an electronic attestation of a full digital copy.
10. Visa's Security & Compliance web page. https://vi.sa/3PK40CR [accessed April 4, 2022].
11. For merchants, an internal security assessor may perform this instead of an external firm. We are aware of several merchants who do this in 2022.
12. https://bit.ly/PCI-Treas
13. PCI Security Standards Council website. https://www.pcisecuritystandards.org/about_us
14. In the past, there was a different name for a company (QSAC or Qualified Security Assessor Company) and an individual professional employed by such company (QSA or Qualified Security Assessor).
15. Merrick Bank versus Savvis. https://bit.ly/PCI-MBSV [accessed April 4, 2022].
16. Top 10 Organized Cybercrime Syndicates. https://bit.ly/PCI-OrgCrime [accessed April 4, 2022].
17. China state-backed hackers compromised networks of at least six U.S. state governments, research finds. https://cnb.cx/3t1odKR [accessed April 4, 2022].
18. Specifically, you should review the Appendix of the newly released Authentication and Access to Financial Institution Services and Systems summary, as well as the FFIEC IT Examination Handbook, "Information Security" booklet.

4 Determining and Reducing Your PCI Scope

Information in this chapter:

- The Basics of PCI DSS Scoping
- The "Gotchas" of PCI Scope
- Scope Reduction Tips
- Planning Your PCI Project
- Case Study
- Summary

Scoping your Payment Card Industry (PCI) environment is one of the most critical things you must get right in your quest to comply with this daunting standard. So many companies have cost themselves thousands and even millions of dollars by over- or under-scoping their environments and applying the wrong controls to the wrong systems. It also seems like the easiest way to get into a heated debate around Payment Card Industry Data Security Standard (PCI DSS) is to find something wrong with a peer's scoping process or assessment result. So many snarky comments happen in the various communities that usually start with, "You won't believe what I just read in this Report on Compliance."

One of the first Special Interest Groups (SIG) the Council put together took on the task of scoping. While the group ultimately didn't come out with a special report like other SIGs did, four different documents came out of that group's body of work, all related to scoping. The Europay, MasterCard, and Visa (EMV), Tokenization, Roadmap for Encryption, and Point-to-Point Encryption guidance documents all contain content produced by the Scoping SIG. Throughout this chapter, we will talk basics, get through some of the "gotchas," give you some tools for planning your project, talk scope reduction, and provide case studies.

THE BASICS OF PCI DSS SCOPING

Two years after we published the last edition of this book, the Council released a guidance document that is now the first one listed in PCI DSS 4.0 under the Guidance document section in Section 1. As of this publishing, the Guidance for PCI DSS Scoping and Network Segmentation document is written aligned to PCI DSS 3.2.1, but once the updated document is released we will link to it at pcibook.com. That is a great document to keep handy as a baseline.

There are other *non-canon* scoping guides out there, such as the OpenPCI Scoping Toolkit, that are available to help with determining scope (it has not been updated since 2012, however). The documentation in the front matter on scoping as well as Requirement 12.5 is the official line from the Council, and any questions coming out of this process should be addressed to your acquirer or Qualified Security Assessor (QSA).

If you look at scoping on the surface, it simply can't be as hard as people make it out to be. If your environment contains Primary Account Numbers (PANs) either in storage or flowing through it, some part of your network must comply with PCI DSS.

Simple, right? On the surface, *everything* looks simple. Especially from this high horse way up here that we're speaking from.

The majority of the discussions around scope typically end up argumentative because one person is interpreting the standard more leniently than another. Most of the discussions we have witnessed,

DOI: 10.1201/9781003100300-4

or been thrust into the middle of, start because one party didn't want to comply with the standard in part or at all. We've learned through the years that denial is a very powerful human defense mechanism. It's easy to ignore the requirements or come up with arguments to why the rules shouldn't apply to you. It's not easy to do things the right way. Reducing the scope and making business decisions about PCI DSS becomes easier when you define your scope properly from the start. It's probably better to have the scope exclusion discussion about some part of your network if you automatically include everything in scope in the beginning. Then it really comes down to a strong case on why certain components should be excluded over others from scope.

For a real-world example, multi-factor authentication (MFA) service providers Okta and Duo are often used in support of some portion of the multi-factor requirements of PCI DSS. Neither are listed on the PCI Compliant Service Provider website. Okta has since released their QSA Reviewed version of SAQ D to review, but this is a perfect example of the above. Duo and Okta traditionally didn't think they needed to be compliant, and frankly have stronger certifications around their services listed on their websites. Any company can use these services to protect their cardholder data environment (CDE) without them being on the compliant service provider list. Their status just needs to be tracked under Requirement 12.8.

Per the PCI DSS, the scope is now defined as follows:

The PCI DSS requirements apply to the CDE which is comprised of: System components, people, and processes that store, process, and transmit cardholder data (CHD) and/or sensitive authentication data, and, system components that may not store, process, or transmit CHD/SAD but have unrestricted connectivity to system components that store, process, or transmit CHD/ SAD. In addition, the PCI DSS requirements apply to system components, people, and processes that could impact the security of the CDE.[1]

The definition expands well past technology, so don't fall into a trap and stop there. You have to consider the people, processes, and technology that store, process, or transmit CHD or sensitive authentication data (SAD).

Scoping guidance like what you see above starts on page 9 of the PCI DSS, and the list of examples on that page is not meant to be exhaustive. They do provide examples of the different types of elements that should be in scope, so you should be able to find an analog for your particular item. You can expect other strange scenarios to present themselves while going through this exercise. We have gone through this process with many customers, and it's amazing how many times we've both said, "Wow... never saw that one before." Even in 2022! You will run into many scenarios like that while involved with PCI DSS, and you are better off assuming it is in scope first, and then look for ways you could possibly exclude it.

Hopefully you aren't terrified yet, but the wheels are turning. The core of your scope includes any place where cardholder information is present at any given time. The duration of time in which it is present is irrelevant, as is the complexity of an attack required to capture that information during a compromise. Don't even start with those discussions yet as it will take valuable time away from defining the size of the problem.

From there, your scope extends to systems that connect to the above systems but do not directly process, store, or transmit CHD. Things like Active Directory, Network Time Protocol (NTP), Domain Name System (DNS), and Simple Mail Transfer Protocol (SMTP) would fall into this category. These "Connected-To" systems don't necessarily drag the rest of the network in scope, but there are exceptions. In the Guidance for PCI DSS Scoping and Network Segmentation from the council, they suggest putting those shared services into a separate network zone (which would be partially or wholly in scope for the PCI DSS assessment). We will also discuss the advantages of separating the management plane from the data plane on key appliances to build resilience against vulnerabilities that have plagued F5 BigIP load balancers in the last few years.

Additionally, a good practice when you are going through defining your scope is leveraging a tool like the Socratic Method to help define the problem (check your search engine for more details). It will force you to ask the right kinds of questions in order to put all of the required elements on the table (so to speak). While this may sound extreme, defining your scope is the most critical part of this process, so find whatever tool you believe to be most effective and use it!

Smaller businesses have some advantages over larger businesses in that their processes around CHD tend to be simpler. If it is a relatively young small business, they also may be digital-first and potentially outsourced. Small businesses struggle with advanced IT concepts because they typically have neither the budget nor the staff to tackle them. Add to the fact that what used to be multi-million dollar on-premise IT installations and configurations are now available as a service—see Salesforce. com. On the other side of the fence, larger businesses typically have many of the IT processes in place to protect CHD, but they have no idea where the data is. Sure, there are areas where they can say it exists with some assurance, but for the most part they cannot exclude large portions of their environment because they have no idea if these *non-critical* areas have CHD. Perhaps, more accurately, they cannot show evidence defending the absence of CHD in areas where it should not be.

CHD is more mobile than people are willing to accept. For example, in an environment where IT people are diagnosing and fixing equipment, sensitive data routinely travels beyond its intended borders. Point-of-sale (POS) technicians debugging faulty terminals may end up with CHD on their laptops. Is it securely erased? What happens when that laptop re-joins the corporate network? Is there an automatic backup process that will further proliferate this CHD into systems in which it is not supposed to exist? What happens if that terminal starts sending these debug logs to an Elastic stack deployed in your network? It has happened, and it is ugly when it does.

Things get worse when you consider how a concierge-like service might be carried out by a small business owner. Let's say that Ryan wants to keep card information for his top customers so they only need to text an order to the shop, and it will be paid for and ready for pickup that evening. How does he store that information? Chances are, he's dropped it into the contact record for the customer. And let's say he has an iPhone, so this is now syncing to iCloud. And of course, to the other three or four machines tied into that account (iPad, Mac, etc.), one of which is also syncing information to Google, and the problem balloons out of control.

We're dragging you through this field of broken glass to help you understand that determining the scope the right way is painful and will probably require some kind of tool to rescue you. You won't be able to do this entirely on your own with sheer manpower. You need a way to proactively discover and map CHD in your environment. You may not need to go the full Data Loss Prevention (DLP) route for your environment, but you will definitely need some amalgamation of tools to help you wrangle this problem and defend your conclusions.

TOOLS

There are both free and commercially available solutions for finding certain types of data and controlling their destiny. Here are a few examples:

ccsrch from Adam Caudill. This particular tool is available, with source code, for Windows, Unix, and OS X environments and is good for singular scans. It may not scale well if you have hundreds or thousands of servers to check, but for small IT environments it is quite effective. Another alternative to this is opendlp, but it has not been updated since 2014.

GNU Grep—the original data discovery tool. Any technophile that has administered servers knows about this tool and has used it to track down wayward data in various forms. If you wanted to use this tool to triage systems and files that may contain cardholder data, you might combine it with a regular expression like this: `grep -rl "\\(\\(4\[\`
`[:digit:\]\]\\{3\\}\\)\\)\\\|\\(5\[1-5\]\[\[:digit:\]\]\\{2\\}\\)\\\|\\(6011\\)\\)\`
`[-,\[:space:\]\]\]\\?\[\[:digit:\]\]\\{4\\}\[-,\[:space:\]\]\]\\?\[\[:digit:\]\]\\`
`{4\\}\[-,\[:space:\]\]\]\\?\[\[:digit:\]\]\\{4\\}\\\|3\[4,7\]\[\[:digit:\]\]\\`
`{13\\}\\\|3\[0,6,8\]\[\[:digit:\]\]\\{12\\}"/`

The issue with this approach is the large volume of false positives you must sift through. You could pipe the output from the above to a script that could reduce the false positives by running each hit through a Luhn check, and then piping that output to a mail script to dump the contents into an e-mail box for individual follow-up (but be sure not to dump the card number in there!). But remember, any custom things you create must be inventoried (Requirement 6.3.2) and require a budget (both dollars and hours) to maintain.

Commercial solutions tend to come in two forms: system-based and network-based detection. System-based solutions will look at the systems they are installed on like endpoints or servers. Those solutions will typically be able to tell you if it is in memory somewhere or sitting on a disk unprotected. Network-based solutions will help you detect the movement of this data. Oftentimes, internal connections will be encrypted so you need to understand where you might need a proxy or decryption point to enable something like this to work.

Companies like Symantec, Digital Guardian, and SecureTrust have solutions built into their portfolio. The benefit to the commercial solutions tends to come in the form of automatic false positive reduction techniques, scalability, support, and native file format searching. When determining whether you want to roll your own solution or go with a commercial provider, be sure to include the salary cost of someone maintaining the home-grown version and run this through the "What happens if Sally wins the lottery?" scenario.

Finally, some systems now have powerful searching capabilities built into their software like Splunk or ElasticSearch. In order for them to be effective for your purposes, they must include the ability to do pattern-based searches. Because you want to search for anything that would meet the pattern of a valid credit card number, you have to be able to simplify it into something like the regular expression above. Some products will do the work for you, so you don't have to write your own query!

You will most likely end up with a combination of the above tools to accomplish your goals as none of the above are silver bullets. Each has benefits and limitations.

Once you put your tools in place, you will have to go through the process of determining what is real and what is a false positive. Branden had a customer that used a 16-digit routing number to track certain kinds of packages as they moved from location to location. Now, of course, every tracking number didn't show up as a card number to track down, only the ones that started with 36, 37, 4, 5, and 6,011, and only one in every 10 or so of those. But when one of their locations was known internally as 60110202, many packages destined for that location set off credit card data alarms. In this case, those 16-digit numbers that passed a Luhn check would not be considered CHD, but it certainly is a discussion that will be had with your assessor.

After your first tool run you may feel overwhelmed by the amount of cleanup work you have to do. Don't be. Think of it as a huge opportunity to shore up your environment and greatly reduce your liability and risk by remediating those areas. Remember, there's only one way to eat an elephant—one bite at a time.

Now, after validating all of your false positives and looking at your final pile of work to handle you will see your true scope. Yep, it really is that dire. This is the reason why you want to go through this process early so you can spend the majority of your time over the next few months by learning how the business operates and reducing the scope of your assessment by destroying data where it doesn't need to exist.

For the areas where the data absolutely must exist, you have a few options yet to help make this process easier. First, you can choose to outsource your processes to a third party, potentially transferring that liability to them. There are exceptions to that liability transfer. The cleanest solution would be to have the third party own the merchant ID (MID) and only send you wire transfers or Automated Clearing House (ACH) transfers after the transactions settle (think Square or Stripe as examples of this). You definitely don't want to resort to trying to reclaim losses from a compromise by reviewing the damages clauses of your contract with a third party if you still own the liability around the MID. Is it more expensive per transaction to have someone process payments for you? Yep, but how much of those dollars are you spending on information security related to PCI DSS? Check with your Chief Financial Officer (CFO), but we see a significant trend where companies are pushing processes like this into their operating expenses and calling it a cost of doing business (which it is). Unless you are going to invest in a payment processing mechanism to generate revenue by processing other companies' payments, outsourcing should be a serious consideration for your business.

If this is not an option—which we argue in most cases is in fact the best option—you will need to spend some time building security controls around the areas where you do have CHD. Don't try to bring your entire network into compliance with PCI DSS. You won't succeed, and it will unnecessarily cost your company thousands or millions. Instead, focus on segmentation, data centralization, and strong access controls to limit access to the raw card data.

CONNECTED-TO SYSTEMS

If you have been working with PCI Compliance in the last decade, you probably have encountered a person or third party that attempted to reduce their PCI DSS compliance and reporting requirements by claiming they were not part of the CDE, but instead were something that "Connected-To" the CDE. These Connected-To systems are going to be in scope for your PCI DSS assessment, but just because this connected-to system is included, it won't necessarily bring your entire network into scope of PCI DSS.

This has been a huge challenge for PCI DSS and depending on your interpretation, it can cause some interesting downstream effects. Scoping is one of those problems where if you ask 10 QSAs for an opinion, you will likely get 20 answers. Systems that are connected-to or security-affecting systems meet any of the following six criteria:

1. System component is on a different network (or subnet or virtual local area network [VLAN]) but can connect to or access the CDE (e.g., via internal network connectivity).
2. System component can connect to or access the CDE via another system—for example, via connection to a jump server that provides access to the CDE).
3. System component can impact the configuration or security of the CDE, or how account or secondary authentication data is handled—for example, a web redirection server or name resolution server.
4. System component provides security services to the CDE—for example, network traffic filtering, patch distribution, or authentication management.
5. System component supports PCI DSS requirements, such as time servers and audit log storage servers.
6. System component provides segmentation of the CDE from out-of-scope systems and networks—for example, firewalls configured to block traffic from untrusted networks.

In order for a system to be considered out of scope of PCI DSS according to the guidance document, it must meet all four of the following criteria:

1. System does NOT store, process, or transmit account or secondary authentication data.
2. System is NOT on the same network segment or in the same subnet or VLAN as systems that store, process, or transmit account data.
3. System cannot connect to or access any system in the CDE.
4. System cannot gain access to the CDE nor impact a security control for CDE via an in-scope system.
5. System does not meet any criteria described for connected-to or security-impacting systems, per above.

Replicating services inside the CDE may help reduce the connected-to scope, but this is where going through Requirement 12.5.2 carefully with a QSA (and possibly your acquirer) will be time well invested into your PCI DSS scoping process. We have also seen companies build a shared services enclave into their segmentation strategy. This segment has commonly shared tools like logging, NTP, Endpoint Detection & Response infrastructure, and identity services that are highly locked down so they can comply with multiple mandates. This strategy is helpful when your firm is required to manage multiple compliance and security initiatives. This is still not an easy pass, however, and introduces complexity into your infrastructure.

THE "GOTCHAS" OF PCI SCOPE

As we discussed earlier, most of the contentious discussions around PCI DSS are from people who are trying to find ways around the requirements, mostly so they don't have to make any changes to the environment for which they are responsible. We find it ironic that if people would put the same effort into complying with PCI DSS that they did into fighting it, we would see higher compliance rates and more examples of companies really doing it right. Unfortunately, both are not nearly as prevalent as they need to be regardless of what you might hear from a payment brand, acquirer, or even a merchant. If you are a techie person reading this book, you probably will walk away realizing there are a few things your company does that skirt compliance or maybe even blatantly ignore it. Remember, denial is a powerful human defense mechanism—don't let it be yours.

With that in mind, let's walk through a few examples of mistakes people have made in determining their PCI DSS scope, in both directions. There are very few examples of over-scoping a PCI DSS environment, but we'll review one now.

James was brought into a situation by the finance group of a merchant to help them determine the next steps in their PCI compliance process. The internal audit team was taking the first crack at building a case for PCI compliance and had grossly over-scoped the environment. They wanted every electronic device in the company to be included in the scope of PCI DSS and put a massive remediation budget in place, including the creation of a new department and a team of 20 heads to whip the company into shape.

The audit team's rationale for including everything in scope was not too far off the mark, but they missed some simple scope reduction techniques that were much cheaper with a smaller impact on the end systems. The company used a mainframe system to process its CHD. Once the data entered the mainframe for processing, it only left to go to the bank encrypted over a direct connection on a private, telco-provided data line. Because the mainframe was not segmented from the network, it was assumed everything should be within scope.

Data was entered into the mainframe from a specially crafted payment terminal that encrypted the traffic over the network. Once inside the mainframe, it was further encrypted and tokenized, such that the only data used by the company after settlement was token data (dummy information that is tied to a card number, but meaningless without the association to the real card number). What we suggested was to audit the access controls to that data and remove human access entirely. Then create alerts when the access control tables changed to be followed up on by the audit team. The terminals were firewalled off at the store location such that the only way to access them remotely was to use strong authentication and a Virtual Private Network (VPN) connection. With a few other controls, we were able to remove the need for the massive capital expenditure and instead helped that company boost their security and comply with the standard in a matter of months.

The "gotcha" with that example was a very loose interpretation of the scoping statement from PCI DSS. Yes, it does say *all system components included in or connected to the CDE or that could impact the security of the CDE*, but that tends to break down a bit when you ignore the capabilities of the underlying technology driving the environment. We've also learned that mainframe environments tend to throw a monkey wrench into the works because few people really understand how they work and the security implications of running one. Ultimately, there are a few ways to meet the above italicized text and still reduce the impact that PCI DSS has on your environment.

Another over-scoped example comes to us from interpreting the standard as it relates to virtualized environments. Virtualization as a technology continues to become more present in our environments, even down to our desktops and mobile devices. The PCI Council has two guidance documents on virtualization and cloud, and there was both great information and guidance as well as a terrible interpretation of some parts of the standard with editorial comments left in the document for assessors and assessees to argue over for the next couple of years. Branden helped a company educate their QSA on what virtualization can do the scope of an environment, and how tackling the "Mixed Mode" problem correctly can help IT departments meet their virtualization targets while keeping data safe and secure. The QSA argued that because the virtual host held both in and out of scope guests, all guests must comply with PCI DSS regardless of their scope determination. The QSA incorrectly made the mental leap that a virtual host could not be locked down in the same manner a physical data center could. In fact, virtualized infrastructure can be deployed in a way that makes it more secure than traditional physical deployments, but that's a topic for another book. What ultimately came out of the discussion was a scope that matched the intent of PCI DSS and focused on making the hosts and in-scope guests fully compliant with PCI DSS. The QSA was able to complete the assessment to their satisfaction, and even learned a thing or two during the assessment process that will ultimately provide their customers with a better assessment experience.

You will hear arguments on both sides of the fence here. The reality is this: we have to trust the hypervisor developers to code securely just like we trust Cisco to write their firmware securely. If a QSA asked for the source code to the firmware on your core router, he would get laughed out the door. Instead, he reviews the configuration of the device, just like a QSA should do for the hypervisor.

Now, let's discuss some under-scoped examples. One of the requirements we will discuss in this book is Requirement 2.2.3, *"Primary functions requiring different security levels are managed as follows: Only one primary function exists on a system component, OR primary functions with differing security needs that exist on the same system component are isolated from each other, OR primary functions with differing security needs on the same system component are all secured to the level required by the function with the highest security need."* Now, this can be interpreted in a number of ways as you might imagine, and this one tends to be a key area where scope can be over or underdone. In this case, a company came to Branden stating that the on-premise server that managed functions for the store location should be considered out of scope because it doesn't store any cardholder information. That particular machine performed a tremendous amount of back-of-house reporting for each store and allowed managers to check their company e-mail and do some basic web surfing, *perform local anti-virus distributions to the POS systems*, participate in the corporate Active Directory system as a tree in the forest, and contact internet systems for local DNS resolution and NTP syncing. There was no segmentation in the store, and the machine did in fact contain one day's worth of credit card data on it that was pulled from the POS controller to assist in that back-of-house reporting.

The first step was to convince the internal groups that the machine was, in fact, in scope for PCI DSS. Not only was it on the same network as the POS systems, but it contained a day of CHD on it for reporting. The company saw that they did make a mistake and the machine should be in scope. The next argument made was that it didn't violate the "one function per server" concept because its function was to support the store, and that was the only function it had. *Supporting the store* can be a broad view of a business function, but it is certainly not a single function as intended by this requirement. Once they understood the intent of the requirement, they changed a few things to keep that server functioning as intended but without the scope issues associated with leaving it connected to the same network. It was segmented off in the store, and the daily reporting information was cleaned and pushed from the POS controllers (as opposed to pulled by the in-store server) such that no PCI data was included in the dump.

Another classic under-scoping problem is calling a service provider out of scope because you have put contractual language in place between the companies to address compliance from a legal perspective. Beginning with PCI DSS version 2.0, the Council clarified the need to visit some service providers on some kind of basis to ensure they support your PCI DSS compliance. In the old days, QSAs would often see certain companies listed as service providers for certain functions and just assume they are acting in a compliant manner. Iron Mountain is a classic example of this. Rarely would you see a QSA asking to go visit the Iron Mountain facility where CHD might be stored offsite. In fact, some companies would simply call the relationship out of scope for PCI because they had earned such tremendous industry trust and they didn't want to re-open contract negotiations. This is simply not acceptable if CHD is being stored, transmitted, or otherwise processed by that service provider. They are absolutely in scope and should be evaluated just like any internal group that stores, transmits, or processes PAN data.

Now, one way to potentially remove such a service provider from scope is to send them only encrypted data with no access to any keys (meaning you can't include the keys on any media you send along). According to PCI DSS FAQ 1233, "*A third-party storage provider receives and stores encrypted CHD provided by merchants for back-up purposes. The storage provider does not have access to the encryption or decryption keys, nor do they perform any key management for their merchant customers. The provider does, however, maintain responsibility for controlling access to the encrypted data storage as part of this particular service agreement.*" There are a couple of key concepts to consider here. The delineation is means, not knowledge. So if you are using some kind of obscure crypto technique and include the means to reverse it, you can't count on the lack of the entity's knowledge to exclude them from this requirement. It also demonstrates some shared responsibility for PCI Compliance as the third party must control access to the storage.

To avoid all the gotchas associated with scoping just keep in mind that you must consider anything in scope that is included in, or connected to, the CDE. The best way to remove systems from the "connected to" clause is to deploy firewalls around the CDE's perimeter and any systems that support it, separating it from the rest of the enterprise, and eliminating data interchange over the border as much as possible. The more you can do here, the easier your assessment process will go, and the less you will have to rely on QSA interpretation to dictate your fate.

SCOPE REDUCTION TIPS

Now that you have built your scope and know how severely PCI DSS can affect your budget, you are no doubt taking a serious look at ways to reduce scope such that the impact on your organization is minimized. We have had many of these discussions over the years as companies facing PCI Compliance tend to have sloppy IT environments that focus on availability over segmentation, data privacy, and security. We love working with retailers because they tend to be some of the most innovative thinkers in running their businesses, and they don't hesitate to use every single tool in their arsenal to either solve problems or get ahead of the competition. What IT departments in retailers struggle with is the understanding of how their actions impact the company's security and compliance postures. That's where user education comes in, and why companies facing their annual assessment will typically have new problems that pop up year over year.

The first scope reduction technique has already been briefly discussed—complete outsourcing of your payment environment. Branden used to dread the confrontational discussion with Chief Information Officers (CIOs) of his clients that start something like: "What business do you have running a payment processor? You are a merchant. Your core competencies are marketing and supply chain management, not payment processing. So why on earth would you put company resources towards doing it in a half-baked way?"

These conversations aren't as contentious as they sound as they tend to be delivered with a smile, but the point is valid and it forces executives to have the hard discussion about how their business operates. PCI DSS isn't going away any time soon, and legislation around personal information is only growing. If you are considering global expansion, your regulation minefield just got scarier. Companies must focus on what is important to their bottom line, and an investment in building and maintaining a payment processing arm just isn't as good as it was in the 1980s and 1990s. Back then, we didn't have PCI DSS, and the interconnectedness of our enterprises was virtually nonexistent when you compare it to today's IT infrastructures. When CIOs work with CFOs to truly determine the amount of money spent towards maintaining these environments versus paying a point more on each transaction to outsource, they can get a better handle on what complete outsourcing means for their company. Add to that the research from in transaction cost economics, which has described how per-transaction costs are declining through automation and offshoring, and your business may benefit from an outsourcing agreement. Each enterprise is a bit different as is each processing agreement, but you can bet that more than one executive has built additional fees into their business model for the long term as opposed to continually living with compliance costs around PCI DSS.

If you are a small business, there is absolutely no reason to build your own gateway. Small businesses really get the core competency concept: "What do we do? We make the best pizzas around. So why would we invest any money on anything not related to making the best pizzas around?" Cashless payments are a way of life, and one way we conduct cashless business is via credit cards. There are many other methods that are cheaper per transaction (such as Zelle, Venmo, and CashApp), and as these new technologies incubate, every CIO and CFO should look to see if incorporating them makes a significant impact on the bottom line. Until then, outsourcing payment processing is easily one of the best decisions you can make around PCI DSS.

Now, what if you choose not to outsource? There are many options for you to reduce your scope. The first of which is to investigate tokenization. In the purest sense of the word, a token is a replacement value for another piece of data. Meaning, instead of using 4111 1111 1111 1111 for a Visa card number, you would use some other value to represent that card number and have a way to look up the original number should you need it. The token could be something alpha-numeric, numeric only, or even binary values. Based on the amount of existing data and the design of the applications using it, most tokens tend to take the form of a 16-digit numeric value.

Regardless of the makeup of the token, there should not be any mathematical relationship between the token value and the original value. The only relationship that should exist between a token and the original value is the index table of numbers you would use to associate a worthless token with a potentially valuable PAN.

NOTE

A schema for such an index might look like this:

```
CREATE TABLE Tokens {
    original_value CHAR(16) PRIMARY KEY,
    token CHAR(16)
};
```

This is a rather simplistic view, but tokens don't need to be complex to be effective. Generating tokens would happen outside of the database layer in this case, but you could build that generation process into the database layer. Making the original value the primary key will prevent two tokens from representing the same original value. Keep in mind that the original value should be encrypted. It's been a long time since either of us has done database design, so we wouldn't suggest implementing this directly. This is simply a way to illustrate a point.

Original values should not be able to be reversed or derived from token values. If they are, tokens should be treated like cipher text instead of tokens. When tokens and PANs are cryptographically related it opens the door for cryptanalysis and the potential to reverse the crypto operations.

Another concept is to look at how you process information and choose a highly centralized and protected model for doing so. One method for doing this would be to centralize all of your data into a single enclave and only provide access to the applications and data through Virtual Desktop Infrastructure like VMWare View or Citrix. Several companies have taken this approach to keep their sensitive data centralized and put a virtual air-gap between the user and the data.

In these instances, data is tightly controlled in a small environment and all interactions are done through a virtual desktop that acts like an abstraction layer. In most instances, companies will treat this as the true PCI DSS perimeter, so any user accessing the environment will typically use a token (or some other form of MFA) to meet Requirement 8.4.[2] Any traffic to and from this environment is tightly controlled via firewalls, access control choke points, other access and authorization management tools, and network monitoring including technologies like DLP. PCI DSS does not require DLP directly, however, companies use the tools to ensure their scope stays where they expect it, and to create an early warning system to alert administrators to potential problems before a breach occurs.

Reducing the scope of your PCI environment is a business decision that should be included in every journey to compliance. More often than not, simply removing the data from the environment and making it someone else's problem can go a long way to minimizing the issues most companies face when complying with PCI DSS. The main goal for minimizing the impact is to use people, process, and technology to contain the spread of CHD. The above methods are a few examples, but the general methodology you would go through is:

1. Understand how your business uses credit card information (useful for the Executive Summary section of the Report on Compliance [ROC]).
2. Understand the business and legal requirements for retention of data (Requirement 3.2).
3. Completely map the flow of CHD throughout the entire enterprise (this is much more than what is required for Requirement 1.2.4 and should include the business process flows that can map to the technology endpoints).
4. Now that you have the scope of the problem (see what we did there?), look for ways to reduce or remove CHD by changing business processes and isolating technology segments.
5. Create remediation plans for areas where you cannot remove CHD that would include budgetary requirements for maintaining the data, costs for removing the data, soft costs associated with long-term management, and a three- to five-year total cost projection.
6. Approach finance teams and business leaders to explain the available options and get buy-in from the C-level to execute a plan.
7. Execute the plan.

We have used this methodology many times to help companies reduce their compliance costs (by tens of millions of dollars) and affect change in the business to ensure a workable long-term solution.

PLANNING YOUR PCI PROJECT

If you are reading this book and working your project at the same time, you now have a really good idea of how serious the problem is, you have a solid list of projects for your company to complete during the journey, and you have executive buy-in to proceed. But what order should you go in? And how do you take a loose grouping of projects and demonstrate measured progress toward compliance? Luckily, the Council has something ready for you to use.

NOTE

The PCI Council created a tool called the Prioritized Approach for PCI DSS, which can be downloaded from the Document Library section of the PCI Security Standards website. There is both a PDF version as well as a spreadsheet version that includes graphs and completion estimates for customization to your organization. Keep in mind, that this is not a one-size-fits-all type of project. You will want to customize their milestones for your organization.

The Prioritized Approach for PCI DSS details a Council-endorsed roadmap for becoming compliant that goes through the following six key phases (pulled directly from the Prioritized Approach to Pursue PCI DSS Compliance as available at the PCI SSC website):

1. Do not store sensitive authentication data and limit cardholder data retention. This milestone targets a key area of risk for entities that have been compromised. Remember—if you do not store SAD and other CHD, the effects of a compromise will be greatly reduced. If you don't need it, don't store it.
2. Protect systems and networks and be prepared to respond to a system breach. This milestone targets controls for points of access to most compromises and the processes for responding.
3. Secure payment applications. This milestone targets controls for applications, application processes, and application servers. Weaknesses in these areas offer easy prey for compromising systems and obtaining access to CHD.
4. Monitor and control access to your systems. Controls for this milestone allow you to detect the who, what, when, and how concerning who is accessing your network and CDE.
5. Protect stored CHD. For those organizations that have analyzed their business processes and determined that they must store PANs, Milestone Five targets key protection mechanisms for that stored data.
6. Complete remaining compliance efforts, and ensure all controls are in place. The intent of Milestone Six is to complete PCI DSS requirements and finalize all remaining related policies, procedures, and processes needed to protect the CDE.

Each requirement is broken into its various sub-requirements and assigned to one of the six phases. For the large number of you reading this that validate compliance via a Self-Assessment Questionnaire (SAQ), you will need to do some editing as the tools from the Council are not broken into the various versions of the SAQ. Regardless of your level and validation requirements, you should run through the entire standard at least once to see if you are missing any of the requirements. It's better to identify and remediate issues now so that as your business grows or as the standard changes, so you are not caught with a massive remediation bill down the road. Once you complete your initial gap analysis for the requirements you must validate against, you should see how your project list lines up with the six phases. This is where the spreadsheet tool can be a huge help for your project as you can adjust the requirements to fit your projects, even if they don't exactly line up with the phases as defined by the Council. The closer you leave it to the pre-defined phases the better when talking to your acquirer or processor about your progress to compliance. They will most likely be familiar with this document, and in some geographies like Europe, you may be expected to report compliance to a certain phase to receive certain exceptions. More on this in Chapter 18, You're Compliant, Now What?

NOTE

Just a quick reminder that you cannot artificially lower your PCI Merchant Level by splitting your processing into a bunch of small, Level 4 merchants (i.e., level hiding). The card brands are quick to figure this out and will look at the grouping of MIDs that belong to your organization and aggregate them to determine your merchant level. This can also include multi-region processing. When in doubt, talk to your acquirer.

The biggest challenge you will face while remediating PCI DSS issues is during the execution of your project. You will invariably have one or two teams that cannot execute to the original remediation plan due to some unforeseen issue. This is where flexibility, knowledge, and experience really pay off in your organization. If you don't have resources on-hand to quickly assess and adjust the plans with deep knowledge and experience in PCI DSS, you should consider augmenting your staff with a contract resource. Not all contract resources are alike, and each one should be interviewed like you were going to hire them. It helps if you have been through some formal training on PCI DSS such as the Internal Security Assessor (ISA) program or even the PCI Professional (PCIP) offered through the Council. You will not only be able to handle most of the minor compliance issues yourself, but you will know what kinds of questions to ask a prospective contractor to see if they are a good fit and worth their price tag. Unfortunately, these types of issues that pop up don't have a basic formula to solve. This is where the real magic happens during your PCI journey.

For those of you who are fans of classic management tools that can help bring clarity to complex situations like PCI DSS, head over to your nearest library and grab this seminal article from 1995 as published in Sloan Management Review. Paul J. H. Shoemaker penned an article called "Scenario Planning: A Tool for Strategic Thinking" that lays out a process for helping management strategically decide the best path forward. Scenario Planning continues to be written about, so you will find new material on this today. Be prepared to have your assumptions challenged at the highest levels as your scenarios should include things like 100% outsourcing given the nature of the market.

CASE STUDY

The case studies presented in this section build upon what we have learned so far in this chapter. The first will take you through a company's quest to fully understand their data sprawl problem and the second through a company looking to reduce PCI DSS scope with business leaders that are fighting change.

THE CASE OF THE LEAKY DATA

Amelia's Automotive is just beginning their PCI project with Daniel at the helm. Daniel works for the regional retailer with 11 locations specializing in the sale and service of high-quality aftermarket automotive products. In order to compete with the larger big box retailers, Amelia created a highly customized shopping and delivery experience that values customer service and satisfaction above all else. They store extensive information on their customers in their corporate data center, as well as with several third-party providers that enable customers to watch repairs and modifications through a browser, deliver customized information to customers about their vehicles, and interactive applications that allow users to scan product codes and chat with a live expert on the integration with their vehicle.

Since Amelia's was founded on a shoe-string budget four years ago, the majority of the innovative customer interaction systems are cloud-based or delivered by third parties. Part of Amelia's secret sauce is the ability to run analytics over all of the disparate sources of information to ensure their customers receive timely updates enticing them to spend money. Daniel is a relatively new employee, now with the company for just over a year, and is in charge of starting the PCI DSS compliance process as credit card volume skyrockets. He first talks to all of the business owners of the various divisions inside of Amelia's. Daniel knows that if he doesn't have a good working knowledge of all of the service providers and data interchange points, he won't be able to properly scope the PCI environment. As he learns how the business operates, he realizes that like most small companies, the early architects at Amelia's favored utility over security and privacy, and while customer information is fairly well protected, it has no bounds by which it moves.

Daniel maps out the business processes describing how things should work inside of Amelia's systems. He then goes about validating the business process documentation by putting network sniffing technology at key choke points and working with some of the third-party providers to discover the kinds of data that Amelia uses as well as has access to. Once Daniel has that information, he updates the business process documentation to take the real-world happenings into account with the architect's vision.

Now that Daniel has a true picture of what is happening inside Amelia's, he realizes that major adjustments need to be made to the way information is processed to keep the scope manageable. As it stands today, everything is in scope because there is no real separation among the various systems and functions, and a full-scale remediation is neither affordable nor doable from a timetable perspective. He also opens discussions with his service providers to understand their compliance status as well as revisit their contracts to ensure Amelia's compliance with PCI Requirement 12.8. During this entire process, he limits the scope to two sets of systems and two third parties. He is able to set up encrypted tunnels between the providers and the systems and segment those systems from the rest of the network with firewalls. With the smaller scope defined, Daniel now looks to perform his gap analysis, plan his compliance project over the next year, and investigate tools he can use to ensure he can automatically enforce the scope definition.

THE CASE OF THE ENTRENCHED ENTERPRISE

Jason's Jump-Up, a large fitness chain targeting family health and nutrition, has grown by acquisition by merging with several regional gyms with similar cultures and customers. Jason started his business 15 years ago in Atlanta and is now a major shareholder in the larger enterprise that spans from Texas to Virginia. The board hired a new Chief Executive Officer (CEO), Chief Operating Officer (COO), and CFO to handle the larger enterprise as it plans to do an Initial Public Offering (IPO) in 24 months to raise capital for a westward expansion. For the most part, the management staff from each of the acquired companies stayed in place and each is run as a separate division with its own Profit & Loss (P&L) accountability. As the new executive management comes together, they realize that a massive overhaul in the corporate structure is necessary to sustain a larger organization, and Jason is charged with streamlining business processes across the enterprise and getting buy-in from all the divisional managers.

Jason knows how his original 18 locations operated but is unfamiliar with all the inner workings of the other various companies that merged into the fold. As he visits with each manager, he learns that not only are things very different from division to division, but the managers are quite set in their ways and have an aversion to change.

After Jason meets with everyone, he puts together several strategies for moving forward, one of which includes partnering with a third-party payment processor to manage all of the monthly membership dues and daily incidental fees that members incur by using certain amenities inside the clubs. The vast majority of the divisional managers fight the outsourcing proposal because they realize that the added fees will ultimately be charged to their divisional P&L, and they will end up with lower margins after these new fees are added to their expense lines.

In order for Jason to sell his plan, he needed to get creative. He knew that processing payments was not something he wanted the company to focus on as it took away from the core competency of health and fitness. On his initial run through the divisions, he brought a few consultants with him to analyze business processes, financials, and review the payment systems for PCI compliance. Since he had detailed information on the gaps in each environment, he was able to work with a consultant to get an approximate remediation cost and ongoing maintenance costs once the gaps were remediated. Each division's cost projections over the next five years were well into seven figures, with nearly 60% taken in the first two years. Jason went to each of the divisional managers and showed them the cost projections. He informed each of the divisions that these costs would be hitting their P&L, or they could opt for the slightly higher operating costs of outsourcing per his original plan. Jason knew that the outsourcing plan made the most financial sense for the larger company in the long term, but he put the decision to each manager to make. Overwhelmingly, the managers opted to go with the outsourced payments model, and ultimately remove some IT and operating expenses from their P&L as they spun down systems responsible for processing payments.

The key to Jason's success was not only doing all of the diligence required to paint the picture accurately but by providing complete alternatives with future cost projections while involving the managers in the decision. Each manager knew that Jason would be taking the overall analysis to the board, and that unprofitable divisions would not fall into good favor.

SUMMARY

Determining the correct scope for your PCI environment is the single most critical thing you must get right while planning anything related to PCI DSS in your company. While the officially chartered SIG didn't create the panacea for all scoping scenarios, it did produce quite a bit of content that is useful in both determining the scope and providing guidance when using more advanced technologies like EMV. The Council provided us with the Prioritized Approach for PCI DSS which can be tremendously useful in planning and executing our PCI-related projects. But no number of tools will compensate for a lack of support from the C-suite. If they don't believe that compliance is important, and reducing their exposure to compliance is equally important, you will learn what it's like to push a large rock up a very steep hill.

NOTES

1. Quoted and paraphrased for ease of formatting from Section 4 of the PCI DSS 4.0 (page 9).
2. Keep in mind that PCI DSS 4.0 Requirements 8.4.1 and 8.4.2 now mandate any access inside the CDE to have MFA, so be sure you understand the entire user experience and there is an MFA happening in the right spots.

5 Building and Maintaining a Secure Network

Information in this chapter:

- Which PCI DSS Requirements Are in This Domain?
- What Else Can You Do to Be Secure?
- Tools and Best Practices
- Common Mistakes and Pitfalls
- Case Study
- Summary

The concepts of defense-in-depth and layered security best represent the idea of building and maintaining a secure network. It would be great if organizations could rely on one type of technology or a single device to provide all of our security but that's not realistic—there can be no "silver bullets" in information security. Some professionals use the analogy that security is like an onion—it has layers. Alone, each layer might be weak and translucent, but together they're tough and solid.

A firewall is one layer, but not necessarily even the first layer and definitely not the last one. Figure 5.1 shows examples of different layers. The packet-filtering router that connects your company to the Internet may be the first layer, or there could be layers even further upstream at the Internet Service Provider (ISP)—such as for Distributed Denial of Service (DDOS) protection (which is not mandated by Payment Card Industry Data Security Standard [PCI DSS], but if your website is down due to an attack, it is pretty hard to steal the cards from it). There you might configure a small rule set to filter out basic unwanted traffic like Internet Control Message Protocol (ICMP), telnet, other outdated protocols, and anything else that you can and will live without crossing into your network space.

The next layer contains the devices that make up your internal network infrastructure. Firewalls, intrusion prevention systems (IPSs), and even switches with security functionality all contribute to this layer of security. Some organizations also choose to deploy a Web Application Firewall (WAF) that is mentioned in PCI DSS Requirement 6 as one possible choice for web application security.

Next is the host-based security that you might have installed on specific machines. Host-based intrusion detection and prevention, anti-malware software, application control, allow- and/or deny-lists, and other protective controls may include hardening of the operating system itself.

The next layer covers the application. Any hardening of the application, access controls, and file or library permissions fall into this layer. This layer also includes the encryption of the data in transit, such as with TLS or SSH.

The final layer covers protecting the data. Encrypting the data stored on the system is one of the effective ways to protect it, provided that you do need to keep that data (very likely, you don't). Don't encrypt if you can delete!

When you are designing controls for PCI and security, be sure you understand the layer at which the control you are deploying operates. You don't want to deploy a network layer control to protect the application, as there are items the application will use and process that the network layer will not. You can also reference the OSI model for another look.

DOI: 10.1201/9781003100300-5

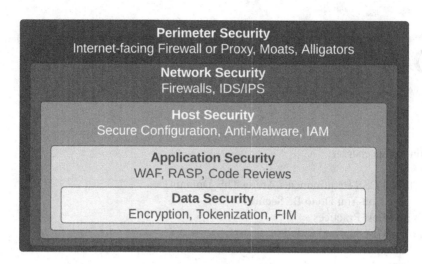

FIGURE 5.1   Layers of defense.

WHICH PCI DSS REQUIREMENTS ARE IN THIS DOMAIN?

The PCI DSS requirements begin with two sections that lay the foundation, literally, for secure networks and systems. The network access controls and configurations of the devices that are managing your network traffic ensure that only trusted traffic is allowed to reach the most secure parts of your network. Secure system configurations of all in-scope systems help to spurn the unwanted advances of attackers against your infrastructure.

This chapter assumes that the reader has a working knowledge of network security technologies and network segmentation basics as well as basic configurations of the systems and devices that are deployed. Luckily, these settings have been documented in papers and books and explored in articles all over the Internet. If you find yourself lost on a certain term, try entering it into a search engine! From time to time, we'll refer back to the PCI DSS and other PCI Security Standards Council (SSC) documents for clarification.

There are two main requirements that make up this domain:

- Install and Maintain Network Security Controls (NSCs) (Requirement 1)
- Apply Secure Configurations to All System Components (Requirement 2).

Establish NSC Configuration Standards

The first section in PCI DSS addresses how you implement and maintain your NSCs. The term NSC is new to this version of the DSS but is simply an umbrella to include any network security technologies that are used to control access or route traffic within your networks. This would include your traditional firewall or routers as well as cloud access rules, virtualization platforms, container platforms, or software-defined networking.

Requirement 1.1 has a set of two sub-requirements that will be echoed throughout each of the 12 domains in PCI DSS 4.0 as a set of common initial requirements. The first, Requirement 1.1.1, asks that all policies and operational procedures be documented. This documentation should be reviewed and updated at least annually, be actively in use, and be accessible to those who need it. Governance documents are useless if no one knows they exist. The second, Requirement 1.1.2, asks that roles and responsibilities be documented, assigned, and understood. Similar to governance, if expectations are not set for what a person or role should be doing, the likelihood it will be done diminishes quite rapidly.

These requirements may feel familiar, and that's because the requirements aren't new, just relocated. They used to be the last requirement in most of the domains, a "catch-all" requirement to list the policies and who was interviewed to confirm their knowledge. This promotion to the beginning of each section highlights the importance of governance in any organization. It also more closely resembles the flow of a typical assessment—review the policies and procedures, identify the key personnel involved, perform interviews to verify business and technical processes, and finally review the implementation of technical controls.

Requirement 1.2 guides you through the process of configuring and maintaining your NSCs. These NSCs include firewall and router configurations, network access control lists, and cloud network configurations that control how traffic moves through your network.

Requirement 1.2.1 requires a review of the configuration standards to make sure they contain, at a minimum, the security controls that are addressed throughout Requirement 1. Configuration standards should enable a team to deploy securely configured devices that are also compliant with the PCI DSS. Many configuration standards hit the PCI DSS requirements on the nose, but don't stop there—review the vendor's recommendations on secure configurations and integrate them into the documentation. The defined settings must then be reviewed against the active configurations to ensure that they were properly applied.

PCI DSS doesn't waste any time getting into change management. Requirement 1.2.2 details that "all changes to network connections and to configurations of NSCs are approved and managed in accordance with the change control process defined at Requirement 6.5.1." (Here and elsewhere in the book, quotes with no source are from the latest version of PCI DSS, 4.0 as of this writing.) Updates to the NSCs must be part of the formal change management process. Approval implies that management, or relevant delegates, must know and agree to the connection. Make sure that the other pertinent points from 6.5.1 are met as well—description, impact, testing, and rollback procedures.

It's much easier to understand what needs to be secured if you can see it on paper. Requirement 1.2.3 asks for a current network diagram: "An accurate network diagram(s) is maintained that shows all connections between the cardholder data environment (CDE) and other networks, including any wireless networks." This diagram needs to remain current at all times. Keep the network diagram up-to-date with each relevant change to ease annual review burdens.

Requirement 1.2.4 explicitly asks for a data flow diagram, not just a network topology map: "An accurate data-flow diagram(s) is maintained" that "shows all account data flows across systems and networks." The flow of data throughout the enterprise is often forgotten when putting together an accurate diagram. In fact, network diagrams in general are poor canvases for graphically depicting the flow of data due to their granularity. The data flow diagram will likely be a separate document that can show the end-to-end flow of cardholder data (CHD) through your organization. It should provide a high-level annotation of the networks, systems, and connection types.

Most diagrams are created in Visio® or a similar tool. Online drawing tools have matured, and many offer the option to import and auto-create directly from your cloud environment (as an example, James designed Figure 5.1 from this chapter with LucidChart). Other tools for data flow diagrams are sequence diagrams written with tools like PlantUML and version controlled. Just remember that you are documenting the critical intellectual property and validate that the software provides security in addition to convenience.

Although the tools are quite powerful in what they can do, most engineers think in different ways, thus creating different-looking diagrams that may represent the same underlying theme. A method for creating data flows published in an article entitled *Data Flows Made Easy* illustrates a way you can simplify this process. These flow matrices are useful to Qualified Security Assessors (QSAs) and are much easier to maintain than graphical depictions of data flows.

All ports and services allowed through the firewall must be documented—secure or not—and insecure protocols must have additional documentation about their use, business justification, and potentially a risk assessment performed against them in the environment per Requirements 1.2.5 and 1.2.6. This requirement can be easy to overlook (and easy for network teams to forget to update).

However, providing pre-approved and documented secure options for the organization to leverage can help mitigate those pains. These requirements are also a great check to automate testing or code pushes into production, helping you minimize unapproved changes to your CDE.

WARNING

The only services, ports, and protocols that are allowed are those that are required for business purposes. These must be secured and documented appropriately. A simple way to document these is to add the justification or change control ticket to the configuration in a comment field for each rule. More formal methods of documenting these items could be through an assembly of change control tickets, a firewall rule set review by a third party qualified to perform such a review (which could be an engineer or a third-party provider), or a formal corporate standards or requirements document. Remember that all documentation must be cross-checked against the current firewall ruleset, thus making documentation inline the most efficient way to handle this. Documentation is key, and if someone says, "I need that port open because I said so," a QSA will dig deeper.

Requirement 1.2.7 mandates reviews of the NSC rule sets every six months. The review should be more than a firewall engineer's rubber stamp and should include the business user who requested the rule (or functionality). Document a process that includes reviewing the changes to the rules and groups being used, business justifications are still current and in use, no insecure services or overly permissive rules were added, and no conflicts or redundancies exist between rules. Be sure to take your review process seriously and document both the review and remediation processes.

Your engineers should scrutinize every rule and ensure it needs to be there. One good way to check a rule's use is to add a command to log a message every time it is used. If you find rules that are listed in your policy but never actually used during a six-month period, chances are the rule is out of date and should be removed. If your business justifications aren't clearly defined, though, be careful of annual processes that need to happen, like pulling data for audits or financial reporting.

Finally, all configuration files for NSCs (whether they be actual configuration files or scripts or code used to push configurations) must be secured and updated so that the running configuration is the same per Requirement 1.2.8. Historically, network devices have had "stored" configurations and "running" configurations to ensure proper restoration of services on reboots. Errant changes to the stored configuration could ultimately update the running configuration and enter an insecure state. However, this requirement is just as important to cloud and software-defined networking, as any changes to the code can have massive consequences due to scaling if pushed to a dynamic cloud environment.

Denying Traffic from Untrusted Networks and Hosts

Confidentiality of CHD is at the heart of Requirement 1.3 (note that PCI DSS is less concerned about integrity and not at all concerned with the availability of CHD—that is typically your problem, not your QSA's and PCI DSS in general). We'll talk more about the Confidentiality, Integrity, and Availability (CIA) Triad in Chapter 6: Strong Access Controls. Your firewall configuration has to accomplish several things. The rule of thumb here is to deny nearly all traffic. Only the minimum traffic truly required to conduct business should be allowed through the firewall—both inbound and outbound. It is much easier—and much safer—to filter everything initially and only open the required ports and protocols on those ports leading into the CDE and towards PCI-relevant systems. This is where a good network diagram with data flows (see Requirement 1.2.4 on card data flows), coupled with an accurate list of required services, ports, and protocols (with business justification), is worth its weight in gold.

Denying all traffic from "untrusted" networks and hosts is easy to conceptualize, but not always easy to accomplish in a complex and distributed environment. Zero Trust architectures make this even more challenging. Many firewall solutions will deny all right out of the box with some degree of effectiveness. If not, there is usually a rule that can be configured to do this. It all boils down to failing safe. After processing all the traffic permitting rules in the firewall policy, all firewalls should deny everything else. For example, a common deny-all rule is called the "cleanup rule" and should be placed as the last rule in the list, whereby any traffic not matching a rule above it is automatically dropped. Another common deny-all rule is called the "stealth rule," whereby all traffic, inbound or outbound, specifically targeting the firewall device itself is dropped. Of course, before either of those rules goes into play, you must have a rule that allows an administrator to access the management function of the firewall to make changes.

With the traffic being denied for all inbound and outbound traffic, specific rules need to be applied to enable your business to function. Verify the business need against your list of ports, protocols, and services first. To add even more security, if the source of traffic can be narrowed down to specific networks or hosts, make your rule stricter and only allow those through (this approach will add to both security and your firewall management tasks). In order to pass the requirements listed under 1.3, you must lock down access to and from the CDE to only what is necessary and deny all else (Requirements 1.3.1 and 1.3.2). You must also install firewalls between any wireless networks and CHD networks (Requirement 1.3.3). But what if your cardholder network *is* wireless? See Chapter 8, Using Wireless Networking for more info.

Restricting Connections

Requirement 1.4 of PCI DSS gets pretty granular with restricting connections between publicly accessible servers and any system component in scope for PCI. Requirement 1.4.1 mandates that "NSCs are implemented between trusted and untrusted networks." What does this mean to you? The database containing CHD cannot be in a demilitarized zone (DMZ) that is publicly accessible. Stateful inspection firewalls must be used. You should never allow spoofing to occur. If traffic is not explicitly allowed in the rule set, it should be denied. Any Request for Comment (RFC) 1918 addresses are not allowed from the Internet, and Internet Protocol (IP) Masquerading should be used where appropriate with Network Address Translation (NAT) or Port Address Translation (PAT) such that those IPs cannot pass from the Internet into the DMZ and the internal IP addressing scheme is not exposed.

NOTE

The PCI DSS states in Requirement 1.4.2 that the NSCs must provide "stateful responses to communications initiated by system components in a trusted network." Most commercial and open-source firewalls have expanded beyond basic port blocking techniques and have stateful inspection capabilities. As an example, Cisco provides this capability on top of basic access lists (ACLs) in a feature called Reflexive Access Lists (or RACLs). The major cloud vendors also provide this as part of their Security Groups.

RFC 1918, originally submitted in February 1996, addressed two major challenges with the Internet and IPv4. One was the concern within the Internet community that all the globally unique address space (routable IP addresses) would be exhausted—which came true in 2011. Additionally, routing overhead could grow beyond the capabilities of the ISPs because of the sheer numbers of small blocks announced to core Internet routers. The term "private network" is a network that uses the RFC 1918 IP address space. Companies can allocate addresses from this address space for their internal systems. This alleviates the need for assigning a globally routable IPv4 address for every computer, printer, and other device that an organization uses, and this provides an easy way for these devices to remain sheltered from the Internet.

TOOLS

RFC 1918 space is often quoted and misunderstood. According to the original RFC, there are three blocks of IP addresses that are considered private and non-routable over the Internet. Those are 10.0.0.0–10.255.255.255 (10.0.0.0/8), 172.16.0.0–172.31.255.255 (172.16.0.0/12), and 192.168.0.0–192.168.255.255 (192.168.0.0/16). Any private networks in your corporation should be numbered within those allocations, or in rare cases, on non-RFC1918 space that is owned by the company and not advertised to the Internet. This can be dangerous, however, as a fat-fingered change could cause the space to be publicly routable. Avoid using IP space that is publicly routable but does not belong to you as it can be very dangerous.

Parts of Requirements 1.4.3 and 1.4.5 mandate preventing internal address space from passing through choke points to the DMZ or internal network addresses such that they can exist on both sides of an interface. Some devices call this "Anti-Spoofing" technology, mainly because an old trick to get around firewalls is to spoof internal IP addresses from external hosts. Internal addresses originating from the external side trying to come into the DMZ or internal network should raise a red flag in the logs for the device. The firewall rule set should only allow valid Internet traffic access to the DMZ, and vice versa. Also, be cautious of the potential for headers, such as "X-Forwarded-For", to pass sensitive address information where load-balancers and other reverse proxies are in use.

Requirements 1.4.1-1.4.2 add more color on restricting traffic from the Internet to only those addresses that are in the DMZ and restricting direct inbound routes from untrusted networks into the cardholder environment.

Why can't Internet traffic pass to the internal network? Because Requirement 1.4.4 requires that any system storing CHD is not directly accessible from untrusted networks. They must be on the internal network segregated from the DMZ. Cardholder databases should never be able to connect directly to the Internet. Front-end servers or services should only be accessible by the public. These servers and services access the database and return the required information on behalf of the requester just like a proxy. This prevents direct access to the database and CHD.

WARNING

There is no reason whatsoever to allow a database or other application to be directly accessed from the Internet. Along the same line, there is no reason to allow a database or other application to directly access the Internet, by passing the DMZ. This could cause cardholder information to be vulnerable to unauthorized access. It is just as risky to allow a database server to have two network interfaces: one on DMZ and one on the internal network, even if no actual routing takes place. Multi-homed servers effectively remove the security that is designed to be effective with a DMZ entirely. Can it be done? Sure. But it is another compromise point that wouldn't normally exist.

Host or Network-Based Security Controls

Finally, rounding out Requirement 1, Requirement 1.5.1 mandates the use of security controls on systems used to connect to untrusted networks to prevent threats from entering the network. The devices in question can be employee-owned (maybe a home PC with a VPN Client on it) or company-owned (such as a laptop or tablet). The scope of this requirement has increased in PCI DSS 4.0 both on applicable systems as well as the ways you can meet it. Previously, personal firewall software was the predominant way to meet the control, but the new wording allows for other types of end-point software solutions or network-based inspection. The built-in Windows Firewall can be used on Windows systems, provided that an appropriate group policy removes the capability to disable it. The controls must be actively running and cannot be disabled by the user without proper authorization.

NOTE

When you are deploying appliances either in a cloud or on premise, you will typically have multiple ways to access the appliance. In simple terms, you will have part of your appliance or server that is meant to be customer- or internet-facing, and the other part will be internal for management. You should never include management access to appliances and servers directly from the internet or on the same subnets that your customers will use to access those resources.

The more obvious reason is to make sure that you limit access to administrative interfaces, but the less obvious one is you want to ensure bugs in your administrative interfaces don't lead to a compromise of the device. F5 BIG-IP load balancers have seen recent targeted attacks toward the administrative interface that was either available from the Internet or at least available from a semi-trusted network, that allowed attackers to launch arbitrary commands or manipulate files (See CVE-2022-1388 for more details). Making sure access to these interfaces is locked down from the network can buy you the time you need to deploy a patch.

Micro-Segmentation

A full deep dive of micro-segmentation is beyond the scope of this book; however, you can absolutely use this method as part of your segmentation strategy to limit PCI DSS scope. You will sometimes hear this term used in conjunction with Zero Trust architectures. You are essentially managing security policies in a way that allow you to separate specific workloads from each other without using a NSC to do it. This is often accomplished with discretely defined subnets for each purpose and applying appropriate ACLs or even agents deployed on machines that can enforce a policy you set.

This does increase the level of skill and resources required to manage effectively, but it can be a solid strategy for introducing segmentation. If you think a micro-segmentation strategy is something your firm can use to improve its security posture and support PCI Compliance efforts, consult an expert to determine the best way forward.

Other Considerations for Requirement 1

Additional firewall considerations should be taken with regard to wireless networks and mobile or personal computers. Systems with cardholder information must be segregated from wireless networks for Requirement 1.3.3, and those firewall rules are limited only to what is necessary for business. Chapter 8, Using Wireless Networking, has more information for you on how to get your wired and wireless networks working securely. These systems may not always get critical patches in a timely manner, and security controls in place to reduce or eliminate threats from reaching those systems lessens your risk.

The Oddball Requirement 11.5

Requirement 11.5, although not grouped in with Requirements 1 or 2, is part of building and maintaining a secure network.

IDSs detect unwanted activity on networks and systems, mainly from the Internet, but increasingly on hosts (host-based intrusion detection) and Wi-Fi networks (wireless intrusion detection). This activity is usually the product of a hacker probing or executing an attack. IDS can detect malicious activity not normally prevented by firewalls including Trojan horses, worms, viruses, attacks against vulnerable services, unauthorized logins, escalation of privileges, and attacks on applications while IPS will be equipped to block it (most commercially available devices today are NIPS, not mere NIDS, but they can certainly function as a NIDS with no blocking).

In addition, the organization must "keep all intrusion-detection and prevention engines, baselines, and signatures up to date."

There are many types of intrusion detection or prevention systems that can be used to satisfy this requirement. This is an example of a requirement that companies can leverage as a component of a solid intelligence feed for their network and produce real-time threat analysis data that can be exported to various risk management software. Below, you will find many types of IDSs that could be used to demonstrate compliance with PCI DSS. For those that you are unfamiliar with, try a couple of Internet searches for updated information on these technologies.

- Network intrusion detection system (NIDS) is an independent platform that examines network traffic patterns to identify intrusions for an entire network. It needs to be placed at a choke point where all traffic traverses. A good location for this is in the DMZ.
- Host-based intrusion detection system (HIDS) analyzes system state, system calls, file-system modifications, application logs, and other system activity. Modern application allow-list tools are an evolution of a classic HIDS/Host-based intrusion prevention system (HIPS).

In most networks, an IDS is placed in one of three configurations:

- Network Test Access Port (TAP) allows passive monitoring on a network segment. TAPs are more reliable than hubs or switches and relatively inexpensive to implement. Hubs have a potential for bottlenecks and packet collisions. Switches can also cause bottlenecks depending on the amount of traffic being mirrored to the SPAN port and have a tendency to not receive error packets. Handling virtual local area network (VLAN) can be complex or impossible.
- Host-based intrusion prevention systems (HIPSs) protect workstations and servers through software that resides on the system. It catches suspect activity on the system and then either allows or disallows the event to happen, depending on the rules. Finally, it can also monitor data requests and read or write attempts and network connection attempts, potentially allowing it to be used as a compensating control for other requirements.
- Network-based intrusion prevention system (NIPS) is a network security solution, while HIPS protects hosts. It monitors all network traffic for suspect activity and either allows or disallows the traffic to pass. For a NIPS to work properly, it needs to be positioned in-line on the network segment so that all traffic traverses through the NIPS. The implementation of a NIPS is similar to a NIDS with one exception: because a NIPS has two NICS, a network TAP, switch, or hub is not required. The network only needs to be architected with the NIPS in a position where it can monitor all the network traffic inbound and outbound. Replace the "N" with a "W" and the same rules apply, but for wireless networks.
- For high availability networks, you may want to consider using external bypass units when implementing NIPS in-line.

NOTE

An IDS is a detective—not a preventive—control in nature. It only monitors and sends alerts of suspect activity. In contrast, an IPS will not only alert but can also take action to mitigate the problem. So, if the functionality of an IPS to take corrective actions is not required, why spend the money to implement an IPS? The answer to this stems from the concept of acceptable risk. An IPS solution provides the capability for corrective actions to be taken before a system administrator has the opportunity to respond, which can be desirable during an active attack against systems. Without human intervention, it is possible to cause a Type I error (or false positive) and block legitimate traffic from legitimate customers. Certain types of attack are clearly articulated and can easily be effectively blocked with an IPS. Some network IPS devices also now have "DLP Light" features that can also look for and specifically block PANs leaving the CDE automatically.

Again, PCI DSS does not dictate which solution should be used. In many cases, this may come down to cost—cost to purchase and maintain.

The QSA may "interview responsible personnel to confirm intrusion-detection and/or intrusion-prevention techniques alert personnel of suspected compromises." Thus, it is not only about buying a tool (whether NIDS or NIPS), but about having personnel that will effectively operate and run it. Big retail payment data breaches, such as the massive Target breach of 2013, revealed examples where the organization has the technology, but did not pay attention to alerts until it was way too late. Chapter 10, Logging Events and Monitoring the CDE, covers monitoring of your PCI environment and what is required.

PCI DSS 4.0 does convey in the Guidance for Requirement 10.4.1 that "Daily review of security events—for example, notifications or alerts that identify suspicious or anomalous activities—as well as logs from critical system components, and logs from systems that perform security functions, such as firewalls, IDS/IPS, file integrity monitoring (FIM) systems, etc., is necessary to identify potential issues."

Requirement 2: Defaults and Other Security Parameters

A lot of thought goes into securing a network and the systems within. You must think not only about the network devices (e.g., routers, firewalls, NIPS, WAF, etc.) but also about system defaults, configuration management, and encrypting non-console administrative access, to name a few. Requirement 2 makes sure that you "apply secure configurations to all system components." Remember that your first two requirements in this section (Requirements 2.1.1 and 2.1.2) will be to ensure all relevant security policies and procedures are documented, maintained, and known as well as documenting all roles and responsibilities for meeting the requirements.

Develop Configuration Standards

All organizations should adopt a baseline that is considered to be a minimally acceptable configuration for all systems. It is a key element of security to aid a security team's efforts in reducing the vulnerabilities on their systems from the minute they are deployed, thus reducing the overall security risk to the organization. Requirement 2.2.1 mandates that all known security weaknesses are addressed and are consistent with industry-accepted system hardening standards. If a particular vulnerability is not addressed with specific hardening techniques, workaround solutions may need to be applied to mitigate the risk. Once you have adopted a standard, the systems should be baselined to ensure all systems are built and hardened the same every time. Creating security baselines on computers and your networks is no trivial task. It takes time and effort, but the end result is priceless. A security baseline is a standard set of security settings that are established for each type of computer or network component in your organization. The baseline configuration is a "point-in-time" configuration, but it and your standards, while required to be reviewed annually for PCI compliance, should also be updated regularly as new settings are applied and new security threats emerge. Your organization's security policy should drive what security features are applied to your systems. A well-defined security policy lays the foundation for security elements that must be put in place.

TOOLS

If you are not sure where to start, the National Institute of Standards and Technology (NIST) provides checklists for almost all platforms in use today that are freely available on their website. These need to be modified and adapted for your organization. The Center for Internet Security (CIS) (cisecurity.org) is another great site for checklists, such as their CIS Benchmark tools for tons of common operating systems.

Default Passwords

Default passwords exist with almost every operating system and application. Requirement 2.2.2 states that all vendor-supplied passwords must be changed before deploying a system on the network and imposes the same mandate for wireless environments. Password policies and procedures are usually dictated by the organization. Although there are several alternatives for authentication like biometrics, smart cards, and tokens, most of us use the traditional user ID and password.

Additionally, if your organization has a procedure for adding new users and granting them access to systems, there may be some default passwords that you haven't thought about. If you can remember back to when you first received your user ID and password, you might recall that it was a preset generic password (does Password123 or Welcome1 sound familiar?). Before PCI DSS required otherwise, many system administrators used the same generic password for all new users. If your company has not changed its new user process globally to reflect the more stringent requirements for users with access to CHD, you may end up with some users that have generic passwords. For more information on this, see Chapter 6, Strong Access Controls.

Simple Network Management Protocol Defaults

Requirements 2.2 and 2.2.1 mandate all system defaults be changed before deploying a system into production. Simple Network Management Protocol (SNMP) is associated with several known vulnerabilities—specifically, versions of the protocol before Version 3—and default strings can allow someone to learn nearly everything about a device and potentially change its configuration. SNMP is a good network management tool for administrators of large infrastructures, but if it is improperly configured, it can allow hackers to do significant damage on a mass scale. Make sure SNMP defaults are changed.

NOTE

The SNMP protocol has many versions. Most modern devices now support SNMPv3 that allows for individual user authentication and encryption of the SNMP channel. Avoid prior versions of the SNMP protocol.

The most basic form of early SNMP security is the community string. There is a public community string that allows read-only access to network devices, and a private community string that allows read-write access. The default values for these community strings are "public" and "private," respectively. Remember, community strings are not unlike passwords, and any SNMP armed with those defaults can gain access to an SNMP-aware network device.

WARNING

The only thing worse than having "public" as your community string is to have a "private" community string set up with no restrictions on use. This would give anyone read access to your network devices and the ability to change its configuration. A hacker can find out a lot of information about a device through SNMP.

Delete Unnecessary Accounts

Systems and applications come with a variety of accounts built-in. Some are system accounts, and others are administrative accounts allowing vendors to support their products. All support accounts should be disabled or deleted immediately. These accounts are essentially backdoors into your system, and if not controlled closely, they can cause a compromise to easily occur. Many recent retail data breaches involve such insecure or compromised accounts.

Thus, all guest and inactive accounts should be deleted or at least disabled. The passwords should be set to something no one knows, and you should consider renaming the account if it can't be deleted. The same goes for default administrator accounts. Rename them to something inconspicuous and change the description of the account as well. It adds a layer of difficulty for an attacker looking for the account.

NOTE

Here are some common accounts to disable or set extremely long passwords. These passwords, if allowed to be used, should be stored in a secure vault (either figuratively or literally) that allows you to manage who has access to the password, how many people have access, how often you rotate and monitor when the password gets used:

- Root account on UNIX and Linux systems,
- Administrator account on Windows systems,
- SA account for Microsoft SQL Server (used to be blank by default),
- qsecofr account on AS/400, and
- "Enable" passwords on Cisco routers.

Implement Single Purpose Servers

Requirement 2.2.3 mandates that critical servers provide a single service (e.g., Domain Name System [DNS], database, e-mail, and Web) to the organization. All too often, organizations try to save money by hosting multiple services on the same host. Each service brings its own vulnerabilities and risks to the table and provides a hacker with multiple choices for attack. If too many services are provided by a single server, an exploited vulnerability on one service (i.e., DNS) can bring down or cause a denial of service to the entire server. The integrity of all the services and data is questionable at that point. As a rule of thumb, increasing the number of services provided by a single host degrades the overall security of the server and the organization.

This requirement is often debated in a number of areas, and you will have to use your best judgment many cases. For example, Windows Active Directory Domain controllers can be used to run other services such as DNS and Dynamic Host Configuration Protocol (DHCP). PCI DSS 4.0 adds clarification around this by allowing for multiple functions if "primary functions with different security levels are isolated from each other or are secured to the level required by the function with the highest security need." Because of the high level of security required for identity authentication services, you are better off moving services like DNS and DHCP to another server (though, you may be OK running them together on that server).

NOTE

If you are running a Web server that is interacting with a database, that Web server should always reside on its own host separated from the database server by a firewall. If the environment is virtualized, the Web server and database server can physically be on the same host but should be separated as individual guest systems.

The answer here is to use good sense. You don't need to have your cardholder database on a machine that also acts as your Primary Domain Controller and external e-mail server. The compliance gymnastics required to approve that would break a QSA.

Configure System Security Parameters

You might think this is a "no-brainer," but not all system administrators know exactly which services are enabled and disabled on their systems and how the system itself is secured. Requirements

2.2.4-2.2.6 describe how system administrators must handle the services that are available and running on their servers. Requirement 2.2.4 that mandates removing unnecessary scripts, drivers, features, and more. Any service, piece of software, and operating system feature that does not have business justification for running must be disabled or removed. Understand that things like Internet Explorer may not be able to be removed, but there are other controls you can put in place to mitigate the use of the software (like network or host-based firewall rules). If you absolutely must run an insecure service, protocols, or daemon, Requirement 2.2.5 states that you must document it with business justification as well as the additional security features that are implemented to reduce the risk.

WARNING

Don't forget about your network appliances and peripherals. These should also have appropriate security features applied. Yes, it even includes today's printers and copiers that are really network servers that can print or copy! The same would be said about the Internet of Things (IOT) devices like air conditioners, refrigerators, thermostats, elevators, and many other devices which typically have poor security posture and require access to insecure networks. Do not locate these devices in your CDE unless absolutely necessary.

Requirement 2.2.6 mandates the configuration of all system security parameters to prevent misuse. This particular control includes both a question-and-answer session with the system and security administrators as well as verification that common security parameter settings are included in the standard configuration. This can be accomplished by reviewing internal vulnerability scan data, as well as interacting directly with the machines. You can expect your assessor to ask things such as "What is your security knowledge?," "How would you verify secure configurations on your particular equipment?," and "What kinds of services would you disable immediately after installing a new server?"

NOTE

Remember, in most cases, default installations have numerous vulnerabilities and insecure configurations. For example, even PoS systems are often deployed by irresponsible service providers with insecure remote access tools that are strictly forbidden by PCI DSS. Today's malicious hackers know this really well and exploit such weaknesses for their nefarious gain.

A lot of these services, features, ports, protocols, and so forth were put there by the vendor, and it is well-known information that is freely available on the Internet. Even PCI SSF compliant solutions still must be configured according to the vendor-provided Implementation Guide in order to be deployed in a PCI DSS compliant manner.

Encrypt Non-Console Administrative Access

System and network administrators, by design, have access to everything. They "own" the network and are responsible for keeping it functioning. However, some of the tools they use are a little less than secure. Many of the tools are antiquated and actually pass user IDs and/or passwords in the clear (such as a legacy telnet service). To accommodate Requirement 2.2.7, encryption solutions must be used for all non-console administrative access. Most modern platforms have open-source solutions for this such as OpenSSH as a replacement for telnet. Mainframes usually require licensed software to enable encryption, so other compensating controls may be considered here.

When deploying OpenSSH, be mindful of encryption key management—freely accessible private keys do not add any security compared to easily guessable passwords.

NOTE

Compensating controls can be used for most PCI DSS controls today, so in rare cases, you may be able to run services such as telnet on your internal network. If you have a valid business case and have taken the appropriate steps to design and implement an acceptable compensating control, you may be able to use these services as long as the credentials for those services are not tied to anything else you may access. From a security perspective, allocate resources to upgrade those systems as soon as possible. Services such as telnet and even older rlogin/rsh allow users to easily capture sensitive data, remotely control hosts, and even modify data in flight. Virtually every maintained platform in use today has an encrypted non-console administrative option. For more information on compensating controls, see Chapter 17, The Art of the Compensating Control.

We suggest leaving telnet and FTP in the 1980s where they belong.

WHAT ELSE CAN YOU DO TO BE SECURE?

Secure networks are often dismissed as too hard to maintain. Why spend precious cycles chasing our tails with a locked-down configuration when we can get by fine without it?

Here is a dirty little secret that many professionals don't want you to know: security and functionality don't have to be mutually exclusive. Many messy and disorganized networks are in fact horribly insecure (hackers might know them better than their owners) and will be extremely costly to make PCI DSS compliant. On the other hand, when they are set up properly, companies can achieve both a substantial amount of flexibility and speed to market with a solid security posture.

Expanding on this requirement, we suggest going back to basics when reviewing your NSC rules. Make them start from a deny-all in both directions (yes, it means default-deny for outbound as well, very important in this day and age of pervasive malware), and then before adding any exceptions, ask yourself if this rule is really needed. Don't just stop at the PCI DSS environment; go throughout your entire enterprise with this same methodical review. Many PCI breaches start with the compromise of a system not in scope for PCI DSS; then the attacker pivots laterally into systems that are in scope on the payment network.

After you have your final set of rules, go back again and examine the network protocols and traffic that you are permitting. Can you change the software to use encrypted streams? Can you go a step further and force mutual authentication with TLS certificates (or some other means) between network hosts? If this is possible, perhaps you can further limit the types of traffic permitted through your firewall. At this point, document it and be ready to provide it to your QSA.

Finally, the best thing you can do is separate the people from the machines. No, we don't mean electrifying computer keyboards everywhere in your enterprise (but that could be a fun experiment). We mean put access controls and firewalls between your server farms and userland. Users are creative little lemurs that learn how to take the keys from an exhausted zookeeper to let all the animals out at night. Even with a massive investment into technologies to secure laptops and desktops, all it takes is one creative act to introduce unwanted software into the environment, potentially targeted at server platforms. Separating those environments will go a long way to build resilience and security into your network.

Sadly, attackers know that this level of separation is missing in many organizations. Going after a developer's personal machine can be a great starting point considering they are often located one jump away from the crown jewels of payment processing.

TOOLS AND BEST PRACTICES

Firewall and network administration are easy when you have only one or two devices like many small merchants. Larger companies have hundreds or thousands of devices distributed over dozens of locations and even countries and must use multiple tools to automate portions of the administration.

Firewalls that accept plain text configuration such as Cisco ASA/FirePOWER, Juniper Netscreen, and even Linux IPTables can easily use scripted solutions that allow one change in a file to propagate to a virtually unlimited number of sources. If all store configurations are the same, or at least can be grouped, you can input the baseline configuration into a database and then have a script that generates the appropriate configuration for each store based on variable data such as store IP addresses, special store cases/rules, and other custom configurations.

The database structure could be as simple as three tables: a store definition table that has custom elements such as IP address space, possibly other Boolean configuration switches, a baseline store configuration that all stores should conform to, and a table for supplemental rules for local customization. Basic setup scripts could easily dump a working firewall configuration for each store, and then normal distribution methods could retrieve and install them. Adding a new device to all stores or changing a global configuration could now be done with minimal effort and cost.

Most enterprise-class firewalls that use a graphical user interface to administer have the capability to administer multiple enforcement points in one central location. Many of these can be scripted as well such that you could accomplish something similar to the above but through commercially available means.

Firewalls and routers can be assessed through automated tools that review their configuration and match them up against several security standards, including PCI DSS.

COMMON MISTAKES AND PITFALLS

These requirements normally bite companies in a few specific ways. The companies requiring the most remediation under this requirement typically are companies going through PCI DSS for the first time. Small companies typically have challenges with their technology implementation (and documenting it) such that their setup does not fail-safe, or they didn't have the physical or human resources to build things to comply with PCI DSS.

Documentation continues to be one of the biggest deficiencies companies face when assessing against this domain. Your best bet is to make sure that you have documented all your firewall rules as required by PCI DSS. Simply going through that process will force several issues that will help you meet your end goal of compliance with PCI DSS. Those issues are outlined below.

EGRESS FILTERING

Firewall policies tend to forget that outbound traffic should not get a free pass. For firewalls to comply with PCI DSS (and be effective security devices), they must only permit traffic that is necessary for business—both inbound and outbound. To successfully enhance your firewall policies without interrupting your business, consider adding new rules to your firewall that permit certain types of traffic and log any hits to those rules. Rules in firewalls don't just have to block things, they can help you tag and categorize traffic that you allow through. This will allow you to quickly determine which rules will work and which ones will not. Remember, fresh installations should start from default-deny in both directions. If faced with a legacy configuration, try to find an opportunity to redo it on the same principle.

DOCUMENTATION

Without fail, documentation is one of the most tedious aspects of attaining and maintaining PCI compliance. Before your assessor comes on site, make sure that all in-scope firewall rules are documented and have all the necessary approvals. In fact, it is easier to maintain the documents than to create them every time before your QSA visits (this is one of the things that PCI Council promotes as business-as-usual).

Don't forget that all ports and services allowed in and out must have documentation associated with them. Consider performing a risk assessment on those rules and including that documentation as well.

System Defaults

Good internal vulnerability assessment (VA) tool finds most instances of default passwords or configuration on in-scope systems. Some data breaches start with a default or blank password or default to an insecure configuration. Ensure that a vulnerability management program correctly identifies these mistakes and that the management process designed to take findings through to resolution (including the all-important feedback loop) correctly reports progress on remediation activities.

CASE STUDY

For this section, we will explore three different cases to show how the requirements can be applied in both small and large companies.

The Case of the Small, Flat Store Network

Before PCI, the notion of a firewall anywhere except for the border of a network didn't exist. In fact, wasn't the old joke about security "Hey, I'm all about security! I have a firewall!"

Unfortunately for most companies, big or small, rapid growth and pressure to meet financial expectations have stifled security such that compliance initiatives like PCI become challenging. In nearly every company, network segmentation had to be addressed at some level.

Joe's Jumping Jerky Joint, a small company given to Todd by his father Joe 10 years ago, has four stores and an e-commerce website that accepts credit cards for payment. Todd was notified by one of his acquirers that he is now a Level 3 merchant and must submit an SAQ to demonstrate his compliance with the PCI DSS. As a former Level 4 merchant, his knowledge of PCI DSS was limited; thus, his stores or online site have not been validated against the controls.

The physical stores use IP-based Point of Sale (POS) terminals that he purchased off of eBay, and they share infrastructure with some nonpayment-related machines. There are two PCs that are used by the manager and assistant manager of each store to browse the Web, check e-mail, and access the order fulfillment screens from the online store. There is also one kiosk in the store that allows customers to sign up for e-mail updates. The stores also have a small cafe and tasting area where you can sample some of the jerky and have a light lunch or coffee. Todd provides free Wi-Fi to customers who come to the cafe.

Each store connects to the Internet via a high-speed service, allowing Todd to ensure certain minimum levels of bandwidth and favorable pricing when bundling other services. His service came with an upgraded router that provides the capability to create a separate protected network zone, but he has not used this functionality to date.

Todd knows that the PCs and the kiosk are not fully up-to-date with PCI standards and that the wireless network is a problem for PCI, as there is currently no segmentation between it and the wired infrastructure. In order to meet PCI DSS, some changes must be made. Todd does not want to invest thousands of dollars into added infrastructure to comply with PCI DSS. What options are out there?

Luckily for Todd, he opted for the upgraded router with his service! The separate network zone functionality on the device allows Todd to segment the POS devices onto their own network with relative ease. He needs to purchase a small managed Ethernet switch to accommodate the few POS devices per store. Finally, he needs to review the configuration of his router to ensure that the firewall settings are done appropriately according to PCI DSS. He will not be able to access the POS devices or the POS controller (if applicable) from the PCs on the network, so he may have to adjust some processes to go to those machines directly for end-of-day batch processing.

For the website, Todd must work with his hosting facility to ensure that they are providing a PCI-compliant solution. He should either ask for their completed Appendix A for his environment (to meet PCI Requirement 12.5.1 if applicable) as well as an Attestation of Compliance for any other applicable requirements. Regardless, his contract with his hosting company should comply with Requirement 12.8. See Chapter 7, Protecting Cardholder Data, for more information. If they are a compliant hosting facility or service provider, he knows he can provide documentation to satisfy his internal assessment requirements for demonstrating compliance to PCI DSS. If not, he must work with them to ensure they take the appropriate steps to become compliant. If he decided to in source his website, he would need to document all his firewall rules and make sure he had sufficient ingress and egress filtering. Oftentimes, firewalls will default to a minimal inbound ruleset without restricting outbound traffic at all.

The Case of the Large, Flat Corporate Network

Flat networks not only appear at small retailers' store locations, but also in corporate offices—often times with much higher remediation costs.

Consider the case of Christine's Car Commissary, a large retailer with 2000 stores. Christine's company has recently become a Level 1 merchant and is facing fines of $25,000 per month under the VISA Compliance Acceleration Program (CAP). She hired a QSA, and among other findings, she discovers that her internal assessors have underestimated the scope of PCI due to their flat corporate network. The store locations have large enough IT installations to make segmentation as easy (if not easier) as Joe's Jumping Jerky Joint. Instead, she is faced with massive costs associated with upgrading legacy systems not involved in card processing on her corporate network, and many of which are no longer maintained and cannot meet PCI DSS.

Christine knows that she needs to get as many systems out of scope as possible to keep her remediation costs under control. Two years ago, Christine had to upgrade several of the core switches that run her corporate infrastructure simply due to capacity limitations. She smartly purchased for growth and has both CPU cycles and bandwidth to spare. Her IT staff have several VLANs defined in the core switching infrastructure, and with the recent upgrades, they have the ability to place ACLs on some of the switching interfaces (or in some cases, directly on VLANs).

Christine must quickly deploy ACLs to isolate the cardholder environment such that her legacy computing systems are not included in the scope of the assessment. After consulting with her vendors and IT staff, she decides to take a two-prong approach. Several of her distribution switches have empty slots available. She will purchase firewall blades to boost the security and efficiency of her switching network, allowing her to accomplish several things.

1. The cardholder environment will be segmented from the rest of the core network, thus significantly reducing the scope of the PCI assessment, saving both remediation and assessment costs. She uses her new firewall blades to handle this at the network core.
2. IT and Management staff requiring access to those systems (both internally and remotely) are provided two-factor authentication tokens and have VPN software installed on their laptops. When they are in the office, they must use that two-factor token to access the environment just like if they were at home. This can effectively change the perimeter of her corporate network (as it relates to PCI), thus further reducing her scope.
3. Like Todd does in the previous example, Christine creates segmented areas inside her store locations. Christine accomplishes this differently but with the same level of effectiveness. She directs her IT staff to place RACLs in the stores to segment her POS environment from the administrative and wireless areas in the stores.
4. She also puts additional controls on the wireless network with more stringent RACLs and deploys wireless intrusion prevention systems (WIPSs) to further bolster the security around her wireless network.

5. Finally, Christine has her security staff review the overall architecture of her network and design additional enclaves to boost the security of the network and increase its overall resistance to worms, viruses, and other malware that propagates via weak network access controls.

Christine is able to focus her IT and Security staff on the above five items, saving both time and money, and successfully passes her PCI assessment by concentrating her resources on the in-scope sections of her network.

THE CASE OF THE DO OVER

Angelina's Appliances, a family business selling appliances in the Atlanta area for 20 years, has built up a significant business with seven locations covering the entire metro area. Angelina's father turned the family business over to her last year and she has been spending some time modernizing the infrastructure. The business has largely run its backend systems on a shoestring budget, investing very little in the infrastructure that connects and enables the businesses to function well. Angelina knows that certain improvements can be made, including enabling many of the internet-ready appliances in her stores to be fully functional for demos, and has spent the last few weeks with a consultant going through the infrastructure.

Her consultant, as they will, recommended a complete teardown and redo of the infrastructure that would protect both the stores and keep them interconnected with corporate. She wasn't ready to invest six figures into the infrastructure, but she knew the equipment was all relatively new and under service contracts with the manufacturer. She had the consultant build a sample ruleset that he thought she would need and log every packet that the firewalls processed. This all happened transparently to the employees and generated extremely valuable data on the back end. In the process, she learned that her payment infrastructure didn't need any internet access directly, and the few times that those machines did access the internet was to do DNS queries and access a web-based map service for planning appliance deliveries. She also learned that several of her corporate employees used remote-access services to do work from home and that some of her suppliers were connecting to her network insecurely.

Throughout the process, she learned how her networks functioned, and what she needed to do to bring herself into PCI compliance. As the consultant built her secure zones and started locking down the network, she regularly communicated with employees to talk about the changes and why they were important. The process was completed over a six-month period, well ahead of the slew of internet-ready appliances that she began selling for the holiday season.

SUMMARY

All systems must be protected from unauthorized access, whether it's from the Internet or any other source. Seemingly insignificant Internet paths such as employee e-mail, browsers, or e-commerce services such as Web servers can prove to be disastrous if not secured properly. Throughout this chapter, we have discussed Requirements 1 and 2 of PCI DSS 4.0. Understanding these two requirements is fairly easy; complying with them and actually implementing the required security features can be somewhat overwhelming. Do keep in mind that real breaches have happened—and real merchants and their customers suffered—due to the neglect of those very requirements. This is NOT compliance for compliance's sake at all!

We discussed the types of firewalls that may be effective from both an internal and external standpoint, how to update your documentation, and the best ways to manage the enormous amount of data associated with them. We also discussed administrative access to systems and components and how to handle remote or non-console administrative access.

Configuration standards must take into consideration all network devices (i.e., firewall, router, switch, NIPS) and your workstations, servers, services, and applications. Default configurations and passwords are almost always published on the Internet. For this reason alone, take precautions and change all default settings so as not to make the attacker's job easy. If an attacker makes attempts to exploit your environment and finds it difficult, chances are he'll move on to someone easier.

Next, create a baseline for your standards. Once the different types of systems and components have been hardened, establish a baseline security configuration. This takes the guesswork out of building and configuring the next similar system. It will have the same configuration as the previous one if the baseline configuration is followed. The baseline security configuration should be updated on a periodic basis to include new changes to the system and should always follow what is stated in the configuration standards and required by your organization's security policy.

Finally, take a lesson from PCI DSS: make sure that operational procedures for these and other tasks are defined, known, and in active use. Predictable and documented always beats ad hoc and firefighting!

6 Strong Access Controls

Information in this chapter:

- Which PCI DSS Requirements Are in This Domain?
- What Else Can You Do to Be Secure?
- Tools and Best Practices
- Common Mistakes and Pitfalls
- Case Study
- Summary

Access controls are fundamental to good security in almost any situation. We put locks on our cars and homes to restrict access to only authorized parties—presumably those with keys. We put passwords and leverage multi-factor authentication (MFA) and encryption on computer accounts to protect them. In this chapter, we describe some basic security principles and approaches that should be understood and implemented any time access control systems are implemented—not just for the Payment Card Industry Data Security Standard (PCI DSS). By understanding these basic principles, you will find it easier to make decisions on implementing each proposed access control. After gaining a general understanding of access controls, access controls and the PCI DSS requirements you must meet will be discussed. Then, you'll discover procedures that should be in place and how systems should be configured to enforce PCI compliance. Once you understand logical access controls, as in locking down access on your systems themselves, we'll discuss the requirements to physically secure systems and media that contain sensitive information.

NOTE

The easiest way to protect data is not to store it at all. It's a good idea to review the data you're keeping and verify that you really need to keep it. Remember, securely deleting the data is MUCH easier than safeguarding it from attackers, and this applies much more broadly than just to PCI DSS.

WHICH PCI DSS REQUIREMENTS ARE IN THIS DOMAIN?

You will find references and inferences to access controls littered throughout PCI DSS. Implementing strong access controls is important enough for PCI DSS to have a top-level heading dedicated to them, as well as three rather beefy requirements (Requirements 7–9). Requirement 7 is the shortest of the three but is probably the most important from a policy and procedure aspect. Requirement 8 focuses on identity and access management including many of the technical controls in-scope systems must enforce, and Requirement 9 concentrates on physical security. Before we go into Requirement 7, let's walk through some of the basic principles of access controls as defined by information security professionals worldwide.

PRINCIPLES OF ACCESS CONTROL

To understand the goals of access controls, it's important to understand the three pillars of security: confidentiality, integrity, and availability, sometimes commonly known as the CIA Triad. As you implement access control in your organization, you should always consider how you are meeting or violating these three pillars.

NOTE

In the last 15 years, much criticism has come upon the CIA Triad. Opponents of the triad cite that the three pillars do not fully address the basic requirements of the expanding responsibility of information assurance. One of the most notable is the "Parkerian hexad" proposed by the late information security legend Donn Parker (term coined by M. E. Kabay). Parker argued that the CIA Triad only covers half of the information security pillars. The other three proposed are Possession or Control, Authenticity, and Utility. For the sake of argument, only the basic CIA Triad pillars will be covered here, though other philosophies of information security may be relevant to your organization. CIA Triad might not be enough, but it is a very useful tool for understanding information security.

Confidentiality

The principle of confidentiality means to prevent disclosure of information to parties not authorized to receive it. For PCI DSS, we want to ensure that unauthorized users cannot access cardholder data. This data is defined as the primary account number (PAN), sensitive authentication data, and full track data, but it also includes other information about a cardholder or credit card account that is stored near the PAN. This means that an expiration date stored by itself is not considered cardholder data, but the expiration date stored next to the PAN would.

Aside from PAN data, the main focus of PCI DSS, there are many other types of information we need to block from unauthorized eyes in order to protect cardholder data. Employee passwords or encryption keys are not considered cardholder data but may be used to grant access to such data and should be kept confidential.

Integrity

The principle of integrity is an assurance that data has not been altered or destroyed in an unauthorized manner. You must put measures in place to ensure that data cannot be altered while it's being stored or while it's in transit. For example, log data that is collected for PCI DSS monitoring should be stored in a manner that an administrator would know if it had been altered from its original form. Log files are not the only data with integrity requirements. Other data include files that contain cardholder data, system files, logs, and other critical application files that would be covered under Requirements 11.5 and 11.6.

Availability

The principle of availability means that the data will be accessible to those who need it when they need it. Although the first two pillars are concerned with locking down access, this one is concerned with allowing enough access so that those who need the data can get to it. In general, PCI DSS is NOT concerned with the third triad leg—availability. The last version of the VISA CISP (version 2.4), which was retired in favor of PCI DSS 1.0, did have disaster recovery and business continuity requirements, but they were dropped. Still, availability in PCI context means that employees needing access to cardholder data and other critical information to perform their jobs are granted the necessary access as part of Requirement 7. However, if a security measure—such as data deletion—can make the card data unavailable to attackers, it is definitely a valid and effective PCI DSS control! As we pointed out elsewhere in the book, deleting the data is often a much more effective control compared to, say, encrypting it or placing stringent role-based access controls on it.

NOTE

If you are using PCI DSS as the initial foundation for your security program, keep in mind that PCI DSS does not mandate the availability of your systems and data. You should focus on the basics of PCI DSS and then progress to a more robust security program such as one based on the NIST CyberSecurity Framework (CSF).

REQUIREMENT 7: HOW MUCH ACCESS SHOULD A USER HAVE?

Let's put the principles of confidentiality, integrity, and availability (despite its somewhat tenuous connection to PCI DSS) into practice. Remember, we want to balance integrity and confidentiality (which both restrict access and ensure accuracy) with availability (which allows access and enables the business to actually function). To do this, we use the principle of least privilege. This means that we want to give an individual enough access so they can do their work but no more.

Requirement 7 mandates that all access to cardholder data be restricted by *business need-to-know*. Need-to-know is used by governments and organizations to help define what access an individual should be given. Lee is an FBI agent and has Top Secret clearance. He gained this clearance by proving he was trustworthy through extensive background checks and several years of service. Lee is at the end of his career and has been given a boring desk job. Because his caseload is fairly light, he decides to look for other Top Secret cases the FBI is investigating. Because of need-to-know, Lee is prevented from browsing through files unrelated to his cases even though he has Top Secret clearance. Unless Lee can convince his superiors that he needs access to such information, he will not be given access.

The same rules should apply in your organization. For example, Sydney's job as a purchaser is to buy inventory to sell at her company's store locations. Because her job does not dictate that she should work with customer data, she does not need access to cardholder data and should, therefore, be denied access to it.

Diving into the requirements, Requirements 7.1.1 mandates that all policies and operational procedures for Requirement 7 are documented, kept up to date, in use, and known to all affected parties. Requirement 7.1.2 mandates the documentation of roles and responsibilities for all of Requirement 7 are present and understood.

Your company must determine exactly what access each user needs. You need to make sure they can access things for their jobs, and they should be automatically locked out of everything else (Requirements 7.2.1 and 7.3.3). Companies typically do this by defining roles and assigning employees to those roles and making sure this approach is documented, approved, and has the proper risk treatment (Requirements 7.2.2, 7.2.3, and 7.3.2). The first thing you need to do is determine what access the role needs to do its job. Management must be involved in this process, and a manager should sign off on the access granted to include third-party access, and be performed every six months (Requirement 7.2.4, a new requirement). The easiest way to accomplish this is to start by assuming that no access is granted and list the areas or resources that the role must be able to access to perform its job. Once the roles are defined, the permissions should be input into the automated access control system (Requirements 7.3.1 and 7.3.2) built into the system where the data transits or is stored. For those users who are handling sensitive information, make sure that you have policies and procedures in place for restricting this access, and that the parties who do have access know that the data is sensitive and should protect it (Requirement 7.1).

Don't forget to look at how data is accessed or moved based on business applications built-in reporting tools like Tableau or PowerBI and where things may be warehoused. In Branden's last position, data warehouses and data marts broadened our scope for several compliance initiatives as data was not sanitized or removed before going into these lower tiers. Be sure you document your data flows thoroughly (Requirement 1.2.4) and you validate that those flows are accurate and always up to date.

New requirement 7.2.5 extends the controls for access management to all application and system accounts. These types of accounts include non-interactive login accounts, service accounts, Application Programming Interface (API) keys, or other accounts or permissions created by the operating system for a dedicated purpose (such as the "postgres" account in Linux that manages the PostgreSQL software). This will require additional documentation and inventory of any accounts not tied to human, interactive access. Regulated firms as well as those with mature cybersecurity and identity management programs do this today—especially when it comes to cloud-based accounts. Requirement 7.2.5.1 includes actions required for periodically reviewing this access, being sure the access is still appropriate for the function of the application, any inappropriate or incorrect access is documented and addressed, and that management acknowledges the remaining access as required and meeting the burden of 7.2.5.

Databases and Requirement 7.2.6

Databases contain lots of information valuable to a hacker, yet the security of databases is sometimes the worst in the entire enterprise. Many compromises occur because of administrator-level accounts on databases with blank passwords. Requirement 7.2.6 simplified former Requirement 8.7 as it moved into Requirement 7. Assessors must examine policies and procedures as well as interview personnel to validate the processes for Requirement 7 extend to user access to data stores that contain cardholder data. Any direct user interactions with the database must be done through programmatic methods, such as stored procedures, views, or a bespoke application that queries on the user's behalf, and that direct queries to the databases are restricted to only the responsible administrator(s). If you have power users that log into your database directly instead of going through an application, take any common actions they may perform and put them into stored procedures or functions, and then restrict their access to those elements. Better yet, code these actions into the application and force users to use that method instead.

This can be challenging depending on your infrastructure. Some versions of database servers may not be able to sufficiently distinguish users from applications, including systems that leverage NoSQL or data lakes. Consider the following example:

Matthew is a Database Administrator (DBA) and manages two main locations where enterprise data is stored. His business-critical information is stored in various locations on a mainframe. The security added to the mainframe allows batch processes to operate under non-interactive login credentials, thus preventing those credentials from being used for an interactive session with the data. Matthew's web server farm for his e-commerce site pulls its data from a PostgreSQL database. In his pg_hba.conf, he set an Internet Protocol (IP)-based restriction on the application's ID by adding in the source IPs that are valid from his application servers. He has four different installations in his enterprise, so all four of the IPs are in his pg_hba.conf, and the application IDs can only be used from those machines which are considerably locked down.

TOOLS

Here is a sample pg_hba.conf with IP-based limitations. Assume that the database is called "CommWebsite" and the ID used for access is "CommUser." Your pg_hba.conf would look like this:

```
# TYPE DATABASE USER CIDR-ADDRESS METHOD host CommWebsite CommUser
10.4.30.0/29 password
```

Keep in mind, this could be overly permissive. A /29 is six routable IP addresses, so this conceptually represents six servers (or at least six network cards) that can use this login combination. If your network does any type of Network Address Translation for private IPs (which could get confusing if you have 10-dot addresses behind more 10-dot addresses, but large networks may require this), the number of machines that have this level of access could grow much higher.

If your firm is building resilience in your infrastructure based on Site Reliability Engineering (SRE) principles, you will want to make this more restrictive by dedicating networks to a service layer or service tier. Also, this definitely does not take into account the challenges of working with Kubernetes networking. We briefly discuss that in Chapter 11, Cloud and Virtualization.

TIP

In Windows, it is the best practice to rename the built-in administrator account and set an extremely long passphrase. Activity using this account should never occur as administrators should use their own unique accounts. Events from the built-in administrator account can be monitored with a log management system.

This is relatively easy when you have centralized your identity management infrastructure leveraging technologies such as Lightweight Directory Access Protocol (LDAP) or Active Directory deployed, but it can be a challenge when you have machines that stand alone, not as part of a formal policy enforcement process.

NOTE

Today's end-user computing technologies are much more likely to force applications to run as normal or restricted users with limited access to the underlying operating system. Poorly developed software (oftentimes legacy or non-maintained) with global administrator privileges will surely lead to a root-level compromise, whereby a system is then "pwned" by an attacker. Software that needs elevated privileges must be limited to sandboxes on the servers and should never require administrators to run it under the root-level administrator account. If your vendor tells you it is a requirement, we suggest finding an alternative.

As you are looking at what access a user or application's role needs to complete its job, make a note of any information it will need read access to but not write access. For example, Abigail may need read access to cardholder information to be able to process it for settlement, but she would never need write access to change it. In this case, we would set permissions that would protect the integrity of the information. You should also determine if certain data can be retrieved via other employees when needed. For example, Abigail's manager may need access to certain financial data only once per quarter. Because Abigail works with this data every day, she could provide a quarterly report to her manager as needed.

REQUIREMENT 8: AUTHENTICATION BASICS

Requirement 8 mandates specific authentication and identification controls for individuals who have access to cardholder data as a part of their normal job. This largely sets systems up to be able to comply with Requirement 10, which we cover in Chapter 10, Logging Events and Monitoring the Cardholder Data Environment (CDE). Each user of the system must be held accountable for his or her actions on the system, and it's virtually impossible to hold an individual accountable for her actions when she shares her username and password with dozens of coworkers (which would violate Requirement 8.2.1).

Starting with Requirement 8.1, Requirement 8.1.1 mandates that all policies and operational procedures for Requirement 8 are documented, kept up to date, in use, and known to all affected parties. Requirement 8.1.2 mandates the documentation of roles and responsibilities for all of Requirement 8 are present and understood.

Requirement 8.2.1 mandates that every user is issued a unique ID before they may access systems in scope for PCI DSS. Most companies provide unique accounts for things such as network resource access and e-mail, but things fall apart when administrator-level accounts get introduced into the mix. Nearly every system comes with a common administrator or root level account for administrative purposes. Most security best practices instruct administrators to rename and disable that account before the server is placed into production. In instances where this is not possible, Requirement 8.2.2 (formerly Requirement 8.5) provides additional guidance on how to handle group, shared, or generic accounts on an exception basis. Generally, this is considered bad practice, but new computing paradigms, such as Platform as a Service (PaaS) that can be managed via a web browser, change how we have to look at generic/group accounts and control choke points (such as MFA to a browser first and logging all actions). See Chapter 11, Cloud and Virtualization for more on that topic.

In the case that you have an exception to manage an account that is shared with more than one individual, you have a few additional conditions to enforce. When using these, they should not be used as part of normal operations. Specifically, the requirement mandates that they are used only for "an exceptional circumstance." The time in which it is used must be limited to that circumstance. You of course have to document the business justification and get that approved by management. Then to ensure you have traceability, you must confirm the individual's identity using the generic account before access is granted so that every action taken under that account is attributable to an individual user.

When you are looking to build standards to harden your infrastructure, be sure to follow the CIS or NIST Hardening Guidelines as much as possible first. PCI DSS is now less prescriptive in this area for certain components (which is better and will lead to more secure implementations), so focus first on hardening that works for you, and then ensure it is documented in a way to comply with PCI DSS.

The latest update to Requirement 8 includes a major overhaul on how the requirements are listed, including updates to MFA requirements and password composition. Before your assessment begins, you should sample some of your in-scope users and make sure that they pass all of the requirements below. If, for example, you find that your authorization forms do not match the access granted, your assessor will probably find the same.

For those of you who diligently were tracking requirements on a spreadsheet, this is an example of a requirement that has been completely overhauled, and definitely for the better.

Identification, Authentication, and Requirements 8.2.4–8.2.8 and 8.3.1–8.3.9

Requirements 8.2 and 8.3 describe much of the technical and procedural aspects of handling authentication for PCI DSS. This is a general overhaul of Requirement 8 from PCI DSS 3.2.1, so while there are really no new requirements of note, there are clarifications and reorganizations that are important to discuss—including a very important change to password construction requirements. For Requirement 8.2.4, your assessor selects a sample of user IDs from your entire population, asks you to supply the documentation authorizing the access, and then validates that the access on the system is set up exactly as authorized. Be sure that you have as much automation in here as possible, as this leads to Requirement 8.2.5 for terminated users.

Another source of compromise is old or stale authentication information from users no longer employed with your company. If you terminate a user, you must immediately revoke his or her access per Requirement 8.2.5. If a user does not authenticate with his authentication factor of choice for a period of 90 days, the account must be removed or disabled per Requirement 8.2.6. Ingesting and alerting on login activity, as we cover in Chapter 10, Logging Events and Monitoring the Cardholder Data Environment, is one of the ways to track successful access from terminated employees. The account login IDs should never be associated with a successful login in access logs after their termination.

Requirement 8.2.7 mandates tight controls around accounts that vendors may use to support systems. This particular requirement when properly implemented would have prevented (or at least slowed down) the Target breach of 2013. Although vendor accounts vary in their level of authorization on systems, they should be disabled any time they are not being used and monitored while they are in use. These support accounts can come in more than one form. Sometimes the original equipment manufacturer supports it, such as IBM or Cisco, and other times you may have a third-party, such as SunGard or a division of a Big 4 to support it. Regardless, any common vendor accounts must be disabled when they are not in use. To monitor what happens during a session, you could have your vendor log into a Citrix portal to then access your machines and log the entire session. Command-based machines could make use of logging utilities built into common applications like sudo, or even using the history function of a UNIX shell and offloading the logs somewhere outside of the vendor's write access. For Unix, check out this new Secure Shell (SSH) bastion host package written in Rust (https://github.com/warp-tech/warpgate).

Locking Users Out: Requirements 8.2.8 and 8.3.4

Requirement 8.2.8 mandates that idle sessions time out after 15 minutes of inactivity. This requirement led to a myriad of interpretations, some of which actually broke a business function. For example, Matt manually runs some processes on a mainframe that takes just over an hour to complete. When he types in the command, the session essentially freezes while the task runs but becomes interactive again when the job completes. Some Qualified Security Assessors (QSAs) interpreted this to mean that after 15 minutes of starting the job, the session should time out (forcing the process to terminate abnormally). This requirement should not be applied to every possible way a session could be started but instead should be smartly applied to the environment as a whole. If all mainframe sessions must be initiated from a Windows-based workstation, then make sure the workstation meets the session timeout requirements since the mainframe session runs inside the Windows one. This may not work in every case but take the concept and find the best way to implement it in your environment. Most modern session managers can be configured in a way to allow a process to continue while locking the session.

Requirement 8.3.4 is a combination of two requirements from the last version of PCI. These controls protect accounts against brute force attacks as well as the nefarious individual from abusing an abandoned, logged-in terminal. Systems must automatically lock an account after no more than 10 failed login attempts (increased from a previous limitation of six), and those accounts must remain in a locked status for at least 30 minutes for an automated system or until an administrator resets it for a manual system after the user's identity is confirmed. To test this, an assessor should examine the system's settings to make sure it is set up properly.

NOTE

Credential stuffing is a method whereby attackers will try millions of username and password combinations against your publicly available authentication pages to try to find a match. Yousef and Branden dealt with this frequently at the bank.

For the corporate side, this is where MFA comes into play to protect accounts that have been validated but still require that second factor. You would also know that it is time to reset this password if you find multiple successful authentications with failed MFAs. This is also an attack method to cause a Denial of Service against corporate accounts through the account lockout procedure in 8.3.4.

Ultimately, you will probably need some protection against these kinds of attacks through anti-robotic defenses. There are a number of commercial and freely available (yet easily bypassed) solutions to try, but for any internet-exposed authentication for your employees or customers, find a countermeasure that works best for you.

Things Paired With Usernames

Once you have all users working off of unique, individual IDs, you must add some kind of a challenge that the user must pass in order to be authenticated to meet Requirement 8.3.1. Many security administrators look at this requirement and think, "Well DUH, guys…." The intent of this requirement is to both define acceptable methods of authentication and prod companies to think about more than just a password for their authentication needs. It is 2022, and this seems to be the biggest year for killing passwords that we can recall. Of course, the most common way companies meet Requirement 8.3.1 is by assigning a password to the unique account. The makeup of the password is described in the section "Password Design for PCI DSS," later in this chapter. Alternatively, you could choose a token (something you have), a biometric (something you do or something you are), or any combination of these for more secure authentication (this is relevant later when you need to do an MFA). Biometric authentication might include a fingerprint reader embedded into your laptop or a token could be a Fast ID Online (FIDO) compliant authenticator. Your assessor will ask you to provide documentation on the authentication methods used, as well as to perform the authentication for each method documented to ensure the design matches reality. We'll discuss some of those exact settings in the "Windows and PCI Compliance" section of this chapter.

Rendering Passwords Unreadable in Transit and Storage

Requirement 8.3.2 should be less of a problem now than it would have been in the last edition. Companies sometimes get confused about exactly what is required here and struggle with the interpretation, especially as it relates to Requirement 2.2.7 (described in Chapter 5, Building and Maintaining a Secure Network). All passwords and any additional factors of authentication for in-scope systems and users must be transmitted encrypted to the system in question to prevent someone from capturing the password with simple network sniffing technology, and all passwords or factors of authentication stored on a system must be encrypted at rest using strong cryptography. The easiest way to delineate which users and systems this requirement applies to is to ask the following question: Does this system process, store, or transmit cardholder data, meaning is it in scope for PCI? If so, then all users with administrative privileges or access to cardholder data must use some kind of encrypted channel for their authentication like SSH or Transport Layer Security (TLS).

Keep in mind, simply using SSH or TLS out of the box does not guarantee the protocols are being used securely. Older SSL or TLS versions (use only 1.2 or later) shouldn't be used and make sure you are using strong ciphers to power the connections. Only use keys issued from trusted CAs and educate users on good security practices (don't ignore certificate warnings and don't install untrusted CA certificates!) to prevent man-in-the-middle attacks.

NOTE

There is some gray area with this requirement. What if a user's authentication credential could also be used for access to systems not in scope for PCI? For example, let's say that Rob is a UNIX administrator and is responsible for both in- and out-of-scope systems. Some of the out-of-scope systems do not have SSH deployed on them (yes, in 2022 there might be a legacy system here or there that has this problem), and Rob must use telnet to administer them (as if he still lives in the 1980s and uses telnet). For ease of management, both types of systems authenticate to the same LDAP server. Would that mean that all systems must be upgraded to support SSH because credentials captured while Rob authenticates to an out-of-scope server could be used to authenticate to an in-scope server?

The best thing you can do is err on the side of common sense. Why protect a credential in one place and not another? You should deploy some kind of encryption for anything using that credential. Also, telnet and other remote access tools that expose the passwords should in fact be left in the 1980s.

Requirement 8.3.3 is another one of those "Duh, guys" moments, but you would be surprised how easily companies are compromised because they didn't check to make sure that the person on the other end of the phone asking for a password reset was the actual owner of the account! One tactic used in penetration testing is to obtain the name of an actual employee, and then call the help desk posing as that employee and request a password reset. It works more often than you imagine. Social Engineering is far beyond the scope of this book, but if you are interested in learning more you should check out Joe Gray's book called Practical Social Engineering: A Primer for the Ethical Hacker. For something more fun, check out the book or the movie titled *Catch Me If You Can* that features stories from famous con man (turned good guy) Frank Abagnale, Jr.

Requirement 8.3.3 aims to prevent enterprise account takeover by making sure that if Steve requests a password reset that the help desk person on the other side of the phone or e-mail request, or the process on the other side of the browser verifies Steve's identity before doing it. Your help desk may need access to pertinent employee data such as an employee number, last four of a national ID (Social Security Numbers [SSNs] in the United States are essentially that), address, home phone, or other types of information that are supposed to be known only to the employee but is often times now public thanks to other data breaches. A better process would be to use a document verification platform (such as PingOne Verify or ID.me) to automate and boost confidence in remote employee authentication—something that is obviously a much bigger problem today. Help desk personnel should be trained on social engineering tactics (keep in mind that PCI DSS does mandate such security awareness training) and be prepared to deal with an outsider trying to beat the system.

Password Design for PCI DSS: Requirements 8.3.5–8.3.9 and 8.3.11

When PCI DSS was really gaining steam, one big complaint from companies forced to comply was that the password controls were too stringent or could not be supported on the hardware that ran their businesses. We are unaware of any currently supported systems that do not have the capability to comply with the expanded PCI DSS password complexity requirements in PCI DSS 4.0. If you find systems that are unable to comply during your compliance efforts, check to make sure that it is still supported by the vendor and is not just horribly out of date. To simplify the sub-requirements contained within PCI DSS Requirement 8.3, see Table 6.1 that explains everything that your

TABLE 6.1
PCI DSS Password Complexity Requirements

Req. Num.	Control
8.3.5	Passwords/passphrases must be set to a unique value for first-time use *and upon reset*, and the system must force them to be changed immediately after first use
8.3.6	Passwords must contain at least one letter and one number and be at least 12 characters in length (or a minimum of eight if the system does not support 12)
8.3.7	Password must be different from the last four. When users change their passwords, they must not be able to use a password that has been used in the last four changes
8.3.8	All authentication policies and procedures are documented and communicated to users so they know how to select strong authentication mechanisms, protect their authentication factors, instructions to not reuse passwords and passphrases, and instructions to change passwords and passphrases if they suspect they may be compromised with guidance on how to report this incident
8.3.9	Expire passwords every 90 days. All users must be forced to create new passwords for their accounts at least quarterly
8.3.10	*Service Providers only* This requirement only applies when passwords or passphrases are the **only** authentication factor used (time to roll out MFA for customers!): Communicate how and when to change your customers' passwords and make sure they are changed at least every 90 days or you use a method to dynamically analyze in real time to determine when a password should be rotated
8.3.11	Authentication factors must be uniquely assigned and not shared or tied to a group. You must include physical or logical controls to ensure only the intended user can use that factor to gain access

in-scope systems must enforce for password controls. Note that this only applies if you are using passphrases or passwords as one of your authentication factors to meet Requirement 8.3.1. So if you are ready to ditch passwords as most sane security people are, here's your opportunity to go straight to FIDO and skip all these requirements.

Keep in mind that your authentication strategy is only as strong as your account recovery procedure. For example, if you have biometric-based FIDO authenticators securing your account, but the "forgot password" procedure just sends a recovery link to an e-mail address on file, then your account is really only as secure as the access to that e-mail inbox.

For these requirements, systems must enforce these controls. Having only a policy that describes the proper procedure for making passwords is not acceptable. All the above requirements can be met by modern UNIX and Windows operating systems. We'll show you how to accomplish this in the "Windows and PCI Compliance" and "POSIX (UNIX/Linux Systems) Access Control"[1] sections of this chapter.

NOTE

Forced password rotation is dumb. It creates bad behavior among users because they still have to find a way to recall these. If you are not using a password manager, you definitely should be. Users that don't might construct their password using something like a nickname for someone, with the first letter capitalized of course, and since it's forced quarterly, the two-digit month and year of when it was changed, and every password has to end with "!". People try to hack their brains to remember this stuff, but it only serves to create weaker passwords.

It's better to set a longer passphrase once (length beats complexity any day of the week) and add a second factor of authentication. If the provider sees multiple successful password authentications with a failed MFA, she knows the password has likely been compromised and should be changed.

Friends don't let friends force password rotation.

First-time passwords are often an easy way to compromise an account. For example, when Steve joined his company, he was provided with a cell phone and a laptop. His user ID was his first initial and last name, and his password was "Newuser1." The initial password was the same for every user and would technically exceed the complexity requirements of PCI DSS. The password is alphanumeric and includes a mixture of uppercase and lowercase letters. But because every user gets the same password, compromising a new account might be a trivial operation with a little bit of social engineering. Requirement 8.3.5 mandates that all new accounts have a unique password that expires immediately after its first use. We'll cover configuration methods to do these for both Windows and UNIX in the "Windows and PCI Compliance" and "POSIX (UNIX/Linux Systems) Access Control" sections of this chapter.

Requirement 8.3.8 mandates that you communicate all the authentication procedures in PCI DSS to the in-scope user base. An in-scope user is a user who has access to cardholder data as a normal part of his or her job. These users must be made aware of the authentication procedures, and your assessor will randomly sample users and ask them what they know about these procedures. Assessors may do this as a part of an interview for another area of PCI DSS, or they may specifically ask for a list of users and randomly call them for a phone interview.

Requirement 8.3.11 (and 8.2.2) mandates that all factors are uniquely assigned. This means no sharing of passwords or multi-factor tokens. This also includes a shared Public Key Infrastructure (PKI) certificate. Companies may commonly include *one* certificate for their entire user base to connect to a VPN. While this could be used to validate the device, it must not be included as one of the items for PCI Compliance.

MFA and Requirements 8.4–8.5

Requirement 8.4 mandates at least two factors of authentication for three specific access patterns. The first is any non-console access into the CDE for a person with administrative access (Requirement 8.4.1). There is a nuance here that might trip you up from the last version. In this case, the requirement mandates MFA for *any non-console access* to any system in the CDE. Where PCI used to focus solely on administrative access, they have correctly adjusted this to state that someone with authorization is accessing a lower-than-administrative account still needs to perform an MFA. Given that things like "Run As" or "sudo" are commonplace, this makes sense to ensure that lower level access has MFA included in it.

The next requirement, Requirement 8.4.2, expands and frankly supersedes 8.4.1 to the point where we would expect 8.4.1 to be deleted or incorporated into 8.4.2. Essentially, *all* access into the CDE must be paired with MFA. So if you are sitting in the same building as your data center, and you are accessing a web application that lives inside the CDE, the authentication you perform must be more than one factor. A single-factor authentication, even a strong one like a biometric, is not allowed by itself. You must use more than one factor, and the system must enforce that. This does not apply to application or system accounts performing some kind of automated functions, but you absolutely should include those in your security posture. There is no reason not to lock down those types of automated accounts as much as possible and deploy detective controls to alert you when they may not be used correctly.

Finally, Requirement 8.4.3 mandates MFA be performed for all remote network access originating from outside the entity's network that could access or affect the security of the CDE. This is for any off-site user regardless of their privileged access, as well as third parties and vendors.

This is a step up from previous versions of PCI DSS, so be sure you have clearly mapped this out with your QSA. Network or logical diagrams will help to showcase where boundaries are created and where you have deployed MFA.

Passwords by themselves are a losing battle. We link to an article from 2014 (it's shocking how accurate this article remains today) that debunks many commonly held beliefs about passwords on our GitHub. One-Time Passwords (think a code sent to an e-mail address or via SMS to your mobile) are no longer considered a second factor of authentication per NIST standards. If your authentication strategy depends on one-time passwords, consider moving to something more secure such as Mobile Push, a dedicated authentication app, or FIDO keys.

NOTE

MFA does not need to consume your entire Information Technology (IT) budget! A cost-effective solution might be leveraging free authenticators such as Google Authenticator. These types of authentication techniques (Time-based One-Time Password, or TOTP) are good, but they can be intercepted and potentially replayed (which would then be a violation of Requirement 8.5.1). The strongest authenticators you can use are FIDO2 compliant authenticators. They can be expensive to deploy at large, but they are solid. Alternatively, you can look to companies like Ping Identity to help build and execute a secure MFA strategy.

Requirement 8.5.1 adds stipulations to the strength of your MFA system. Your systems must not be susceptible to replay attacks (meaning, there has to be something dynamic to the factor, such as a rotating PIN or a One-Time PIN), they cannot be bypassed by any user including administrators (unless specifically documented on an exception basis), at least two types of factors must be used, and all factors must succeed before providing access.

A Brief Word on System Accounts and Requirement 8.6

Requirement 8.6 is new enough that it is one of those that is a best practice until March 31, 2025, but the reality is that it's something that we all either should have been doing, or we are doing in support of other PCI DSS requirements. If you are leveraging system accounts in any area, those should not be able to be used for an interactive login. In the Windows world, think about a service account. It is usually used to elevate permissions on a machine for the process it is running, but you shouldn't be able to take that username and password and log into the machine to get a desktop. In the UNIX world, it could be something like the account that your mail server runs on. In your/etc/password file, the last field that designates the shell that it will use might be something like/bin/false, or/dev/null, or/usr/sbin/nologin depending on your system. There is an exception process to use an account like this for interactive logins, but if your system requires this it is time to re-architect or replace it. This is a dangerous practice, and it will lead to a compromise. Requirement 8.6.1 reviews a number of stipulations if you choose to do this, but the best way to meet the requirement is to set any system or application account to a non-interactive login status.

Security users groan loudly when they discover credentials or keys hard coded in source code or checked into Git repositories. Requirement 8.6.2 specifically prohibits this activity and is also a best practice until March 31, 2025, but this should be tackled as soon as practical. Hard-coded passwords are easily discoverable in compiled code, and if an attacker gets access to any source code or can read scripts with this data included, it will lead to a compromise.

If you choose to use any passwords or passphrases for system or application accounts, Requirement 8.6.3 mandates that you rotate those periodically as defined in your targeted risk analysis for 12.3.1 and upon suspicion of compromise. In addition, you can vary the construction of these passwords based on the frequency of rotation.

OAuth, OIDC, SSH Keys, and SSH Certs, OH MY!

When we started working on this edition of the book, we asked the community for things they wanted to see us cover. One thing that popped up was essentially credential/secret management. While many of the items above are out of scope, there are some applications of the above technologies that can be key components of your PCI Compliance journey.

Open Authorization (OAuth) is another standard that could be leveraged in certain circumstances. Specifically, this is a method to allow access to accounts that can be controlled by the user. Visible implementations of this standard include allowing you to log into a website using your Twitter or Facebook account. These tokens can have expiration dates and can be revoked when no longer needed. If OAuth is a strategy you want to use with users, be sure to include these in your quarterly access reviews.

Open ID Connect (OIDC) is the modern iteration of Security Assertion Markup Language (SAML). Both are still in wide use, but OIDC has taken favor as the new and better kid on the block. Modern authentication enablers support both, but the idea is that you can authenticate users or processes without passwords in this open standard. A typical use case would be a link on your intranet that allows someone to access Workday without a password. But this same standard can be used to connect systems at multiple levels. Because of the abstracted process with strong cryptography, this is a valid way to authenticate processes such that you are not storing passwords.

NOTE

The advanced authentication techniques we mention can be tricky to design and deployed in insecure ways. As you begin to learn about all the different ways we can manage access, be sure to bring in an expert to help you design them securely.

SSH Keys and SSH Certificates are great for person-to-machine authentication in the UNIX world, as well as machine-to-machine access for automated processes. SSH Certificates are like SSH Keys with scope, a certificate signer (authority), and expiration. If SSH is leveraged in your organization for administration and you are not looking at an implementation of SSH Certificates, you are missing out. SSH Certificates can allow for authentication and access to a machine even when that machine has never seen your SSH key before and limit that access to a specific set of actions on the machine itself. If it trusts the certificate authority that signed your SSH Certificate, you are in! Of course, PKI is not always easy to do. But when done well in a sustainable and scalable manner, it can be a powerful way to automate your authentication and authorization.

While these technologies are not specifically mentioned in PCI DSS, they are all part of a complete authentication and authorization strategy that will allow you to comply.

Educating Users

Although PCI's password requirements are not incredibly strict, they may be stricter than what your company was using before becoming compliant. If your company is going from a very relaxed password policy to a stricter one, you will probably meet resistance from employees. Of all the changes you may have to make, this is one that affects an employee's day-to-day work. Some employees have a hard time seeing the benefits of using strict password policies—some may even grumble that this is just another way the cybersecurity department is making their lives more difficult.

Instead of forcing policy upon users and communicating it through e-mail or newsletters, meet with employees to personally explain the policy to them and answer any questions they may have. This is a great opportunity to educate them on what makes a good password and why they are important, and this could even be considered part of your security awareness training for Requirement 12.6.1 and would apply to Requirement 8.1 as well. Management should be involved in this meeting, and it makes sense to tie it to some other form of All Hands event. As we learn from our mothers (thanks Mom!), it's best to lead by example. If employees observe management interested in and adhering to the policy, they will take it more seriously. You may want to get someone from management to briefly introduce that the company will be implementing a new password policy to become more secure.

One of the things you want to cover in this meeting is the password complexity requirements that will be enforced as well as introducing the concept of MFA and reviewing the documentation required in Requirement 8.3.8. If your users have password change fatigue, now might be a good time to review all of your policies to see if you even need to rotate your passwords anymore. Passwords will still need to be changed at some point, so give them examples of passwords that both conform to and violate the policy, with details on why they do or do not comply.

NOTE

Remember that new password requirements will not be enforced until the next password change, so to be PCI compliant today, you would have to update the policy and immediately expire everyone's password. Once they log back in and reset their password to something that complies with the policy, you will have met your obligations under this requirement.

You may also want to go over some tricks to help them choose good, secure passwords that will be easy to remember. In a departure from previous editions, we want to just lay out some guidelines. Length beats complexity, and MFA beats single factor. That's all you really need to know. Picking four to five random words and stringing them together is easy to remember, but also could be upwards of 30 characters. There is no way someone who isn't a memorization champion would be able to remember a 31-character password, but you probably could remember "plenty-raw_function_pick-slowly." That is a 31-character password that goes above and beyond the base PCI DSS requirements for a password. Need a number? Add a 1 at the end. At that point it's just security theater as the complexity of a number does nothing to bolster the strength of the password (though the extra character helps strengthen the password irrespective of what it is!). A great reference is Mark

Burnett's book, *Perfect Passwords: Selection, Protection, Authentication,* (ISBN 978-1-59749-041-2, Syngress). Much of the book is dedicated to helping users select passwords that are unique and easy to remember. There's also a hilarious comic by our friends at XKCD that is worth reviewing: https://xkcd.com/936/

Users should be educated to never give out their passwords, PINs, or MFA codes under any circumstances to anyone, including the IT staff. Researchers have studied human behavior to see how quickly people would give away their passwords to strangers, and many of them chose to exchange it for a piece of chocolate. It would be interesting to perform a correlation or longitudinal study to see if this differs for kids who "passed" the delayed gratification studies done by Stanford (look up the Stanford Marshmallow Experiment). In more realistic attacks, we've seen examples of third-party support employees who make low living wages and accept a few thousand dollars in cash in exchange for their password.

If passwords are used, use this opportunity to help them understand how often password changes will be required (at least every 90 days if applicable), and that they will not be allowed to reuse old passwords (at least the last four). You should also review company policies about disclosing passwords. Passwords should never be disclosed to anybody for any reason—especially to individuals working in information technology jobs. Employees should understand the process that's in place to reset their passwords if they forget it. You should always ask users if they have any questions when rolling out a new policy.

WINDOWS AND PCI COMPLIANCE

If you work in an organization where Windows is widely deployed, you're probably using Active Directory to authenticate users. One of the great things about Active Directory is that it is easy to roll out many of the requirements for PCI to the enterprise. Using Group Policy Objects (GPOs), you can enable password-protected screen savers and set up password policies all from your domain controller. You may also have standalone Windows computers that aren't part of the domain (e.g., a Web server that's at a hosting company), so we'll show you how to configure these for PCI compliance as well.

Windows File Access Control

Windows Access Control Lists (ACLs), or Discretionary Access Control Lists (DACLs), are used to configure and enforce access control. ACLs contain a list of Access Control Entities (ACEs), and each entity defines permissions. To set ACLs for other users or groups you are not a member of in Windows, you must have proper administrative privileges. Because Windows uses discretionary access control (DAC), the owner of the file and administrators can configure ACLs for an object. When using Windows access control mechanisms, you basically have three options: you can explicitly allow permission, explicitly deny permission, or implicitly deny permission.

When you implicitly deny permission, this means that you did not explicitly allow or deny access. By default, Windows denies all access to objects that do not have rights set on them. This is a great best practice to follow for all systems and is particularly good because it helps us comply with PCI Requirement 7.3 without doing anything. Because Windows implicitly denies access (in some cases, don't try to argue that Windows leverages mandatory access control [MAC]), explicitly denying access should only be used in special cases where you are denying permission to a subset of a group. One user you would normally never deny access to is the built-in "Everyone" group because this will deny access to all users including the administrator. The correct way to do this would be to add users and groups that should have access to the file and then simply remove the Everyone group from the allowed users. Because Windows follows an implicit deny for anyone not explicitly given permission, this will likely give you the desired result. Be careful when moving files and folders around because object inheritance can cause files to gain or lose permissions in unexpected ways.

Yousef pointed out there are also other "built-in" groups that can get you in trouble such as the "Interactive" and "Authenticated Users" groups. These have broad-reaching access implications when used improperly. You should probably never use the "Everyone" group because it also includes "Guests." Instead, use the "Authenticated Users" group. These may also violate the default deny policy mandated by PCI Requirement 7.3.3.

WARNING

System administrators are busy. Sometimes they will give all users administrative rights instead of properly reducing each user's (or role's) rights to the minimum necessary to do his or her job. This is bad for many reasons, including higher support costs when "Acts of Clod" occur. With everyone acting as an administrator, Windows no longer follows the default deny policy required by PCI Requirement 7.3.3 because all users are allowed full access to all files. For the record, only administrators should have that level of access. At Branden's last company, we set a metric of administrator access enabled for less than 1% of the entire user population.

When configuring access controls in Windows, there are several tricks that can save you time in initial configuration and later maintenance. Remember the roles you created as part of the Requirement 7, "How Much Access Should a User Have?" section earlier in this chapter? Here's where we use them! Once you have the role, you must create a group with those permissions and assign all the required users to that group. With users belonging to roles or groups, you can set access permissions for the whole group instead of each user individually. This also makes maintenance much easier because you can change permissions for the entire group and remove and add users whenever needed. It's not uncommon to have users who are assigned to more than one group. For example, one user may only need access to unprocessed cardholder information, whereas another user may need access to unprocessed and processed cardholder information. In this case, both users would be members of a group with access to cardholder information, but only the second user would also be a member of a group with access to processed cardholder data.

NOTE

The process of defining roles is not a weekend or after-hours gig. Branden assisted a customer in creating a detailed set of roles for one of the top 10 financial institutions in the United States. What started as an initial set of 900 defined roles escalated to over 3,000. Even though the exercise ultimately created a much more secure company with an easily managed set of groups and permissions, the effort to complete these profiles was much larger than anticipated.

Another great time saver, but a potential minefield, is to use inheritance as much as possible. When you set permissions on a file or folder, you can also specify how subfolders will inherit those permissions. This makes it much easier to configure access control on a few folders that are near the root folder, instead of needing to configure each subfolder individually. Just remember that if you set up inheritance, by default, subfolders have the same permissions. Security templates can assist with this if you find that you have common types of folders to which you grant access often. This keeps all security settings in the same location and makes them much easier to manage.

That said, group nesting in Active Directory (AD) can absolutely lead to a compromise. In Branden's work with AD, he often found a group that was given Local Administrative rights that subsequently had another group nested underneath it, giving that group elevated rights as well. That's dangerous and can lead to users doing a bunch of bad things.

WARNING

To be able to effectively secure data natively in Windows using the operating system's controls, you should always use the New Technology File System (NTFS). FAT32 does not cut it because it does not have the capability to do access control.

Finding Inactive Accounts in Active Directory

One of the PCI requirements is to find all accounts that have been inactive for 90 days or more and remove or disable them. In Active Directory, there are several ways to find inactive accounts, although in many cases you have probably struggled to find one that works well. For some tips outside the scope of this book, check Microsoft's suite of documentation.

One peculiarity of Active Directory is that it is possible to be on the latest version of Windows and also use legacy Active Directory functionality. Yousef pointed out that the lastLogontimeStamp was not introduced until Windows 2003, so if your domain has been around for a long time and has not been updated, you may only have the lastLogon attribute (which is not replicated between domain controllers). Changing the functional level of your Active Directory domain can affect how your environment functions, so plan carefully when considering this type of upgrade.

Enforcing Password Requirements in Windows on Standalone Computers

If you have several standalone Windows systems, you can make a local security policy template and incorporate its use for all in-scope systems.

In a virtualized environment you can also make your virtual machine template(s) have these settings baked in.

To set password policies for a Windows computer that is not connected to the domain, you should use the Local Security Settings dialog box, which is set up basically the same way as a GPO, except that it will only affect the local computer.

- *Windows 10/11:* Windows key + R, then type secpol.msc in the prompt.
- *Windows Server 2019:* Search for **Local Security Policy** or use WIN+R and type secpol. msc.

Now expand Account Polices, then click on **Password Policy** (for an explanation of what these settings mean, refer to the earlier section "Enforcing a PCI Compliant Password Policy in Windows Active Directory"). Enforce password history should be changed to at least four previous passwords to meet PCI requirements. The Maximum password age should be set to at most 90 to meet PCI requirements. The password length should be at least 12 characters for PCI requirements, and passwords must meet complexity requirements and should be set to enabled. It's also a good idea to set the Minimum password age to at least 1. Otherwise, when a user is required to change their password, they could change it four times and then back to their original password. When this setting is set to 1 or more, the user must keep the same password for at least that many days before they can change it again.

You should also configure the Account Lockout Policy to comply with PCI requirements. To do this, expand the Account Lockout Policy. Double-click on **Account lockout threshold**. In the Account lockout threshold, the Properties dialog box change number of invalid login attempts to six. A dialog box will pop up and ask if it should also change the Account lockout duration and Reset account lockout counter after attributes as well. These should both be changed to 30 minutes to comply with PCI requirements, which is what the default is in this new dialog. Click **OK**.

WARNING

All these settings may be irrelevant if the users who connect to them have local administrator privileges! Do yourself a favor and remove all local administrator access from your users' accounts or look to your specific installation to ensure this cannot happen.

Enabling Password Protected Screen Savers on Standalone Windows Computers

If you have computers that are not connected to a domain, these options can be set on each computer individually, but we recommend joining Windows machines to a domain for centralized management.

- Windows 10/11 and Windows Server 2019 in a Domain: Type gpedit.msc in the Run prompt, and press Enter to open Group Policy Editor. Then navigate to User Configuration > Administrative Templates > Control Panel > Personalization. Find a policy with the name "Screen saver timeout." Double click to open it. Enable it, and then add screen timeout in seconds (15 minutes is 900 seconds).

Setting File Permissions on Standalone Windows Computers

In Windows Explorer, navigate to the file or folder you would like to modify permissions on. Right-click on the **file** or **folder** and then click on **Properties**. In the Properties dialog, click on the **Security** tab. To add a user to the list of Group or usernames, click on the **Add** button and the Select Users, Computers, or Groups dialog box will appear. You can then type in the name of a **user** or **group**. The **Advanced** button gives you more options to help you find the correct **group** or **user** to add. After you click **OK**, the user or group will appear in the previous dialog box. We suggest avoiding **"Full Control"** except to administrative groups.

POSIX (UNIX/Linux Systems) Access Control

UNIX-based systems such as Linux use POSIX-style access control lists. This means files have three permission modes: read (r), write (w), and execute (x). These modes can be assigned either using the letters just listed or they also have equivalent numbers. Read is 4, write is 2, and execute is 1. If file permissions are being set using letters, it will be a string of letters or dashes (e.g., a file with read-only permission would show r– and a file with read, write, and execute would show rwx). When using numbers, they are added to denote permissions. Read permission would simply be a 4, and read and write permission would be 6 (4 plus 2). When using POSIX-style access controls, there are three groups or users you set permissions for. The first set is for that specific user who owns the file. The second set is for the group that owns the file. The third is for all other users who do not have any ownership over the file (i.e., anyone with access to the system), similar to the Everybody group in Windows. So, a file that allows the owner to read and write, and everyone else only read access would look like this -rw-r–r– or in numeric format it would be 644.

Linux has great command-line tools for changing file permissions and file ownership. Although exploring all that these commands can do is beyond the scope of this book, we will discuss some basics here. In Linux, to list file permissions, the ls command can be used. The syntax to list the file permission and the group and user who own the file is as follows:

```
ls -lg [filename]
```

To change file permissions in Linux, you usually use the chmod command. You can run the chmod command using numbers. The following example uses POSIX permission number format to set a file to allow the user who owns it to read, write, and execute the file, and everyone else to read and execute but not write to it, similar to a standard executable file:

```
chmod 755 filename
```

Or you could use letters and specify if you are going to add them or delete them from users (u), groups (g), others (o), or all (a). For example, to allow the user who owns the file to read from it and write to it, you would do the following:

```
chmod u+rw filename
```

To take away permissions use *a hyphen or minus* in front of the permissions parameter. To deny read, write, and execute permission to the group that owns the file and to all users other than the one that owns the file, you would do the following:

```
chmod go-rwx filename
```

To change the file ownership, use the chown command. To change the user and group that owns a file, do the following:

```
chown newuser:newgroup filename
```

In POSIX-style systems, there are three additional attributes that affect how files are executed and accessed. These are the set user ID (SUID), the set group ID (SGID), and sticky. These settings work differently when they're applied to files or directories. The SUID bit can be configured to tell the file what user it should run under when the file is executed. Many times this is used to allow a non-root user to run a file as the root user. This is used if a user needs to run a file that requires root access, and you don't want to give their account root access or the root password. SGID for a file works the same way as SUID, but it specifies what group the file should execute as. The sticky has no effect on individual files. The SUID bit has no effect on directories. If the SGID bit is set on a directory, any new files created in that directory will be owned by the group specified using the SGID instead of the group of the user who created the file. This is sometimes used in directories where many users will share files. When the sticky bit is set on a directory, only the user owner of the file or root can delete or rename a file (the group owner cannot). This is sometimes used in shared directories where you don't want users other than the owner or root to delete or rename a file.

This is generally a bad idea. Many compromises have started with a process that is accessible by a normal user but executed as root. Granting elevated permissions on an executable file should not be done as a rule, but if you need to, be done with great care.

In Linux, there are also several MAC systems. Most of them are somewhat limited to protecting only a subset of files on the system (normally only critical system files). SE Linux is an example of this. SE Linux was developed by the National Security Agency (NSA) and has been incorporated since the 2.6 series Linux kernel. SE Linux uses targets to specify what files it will control and how it will control them. Other MAC systems that are currently being used in Linux include SUSE's AppArmor, Rule Set Based Access Control (RSBAC).

Linux Enforce Password Complexity Requirements

Most Linux distributions support password complexity enforcement using Pluggable Authentication Modules (PAM). This is normally set in/etc/pam.d/system-auth. To comply with PCI requirements, a password must be 12 characters long and contain alphabetic and numeric characters. pam_pwquality has parameters to help you meet these requirements. The minlen parameter is used to specify the minimum length of a password. The dcredit parameter is used to require digits, the ucredit is used to require uppercase letters, and the lcredit parameter is used to require lowercase letters. The retry parameter is used to specify how many attempts a user gets before the password program exits. pam_pwhistory can be used in conjunction with pam_pwquality to enforce password history requirements. Let's put all these together to show the entry in/etc/pam.d/system-auth:

```
password required pam_pwquality.so minlen=12 dcredit=-1 ucredit=-1
lcredit=-1 password required pam_pwhistory.so remember=4 use_authtok
```

Depending on your implementation, you may see different names for the PAM configuration files where this information is placed (e.g., in Debian, you would find this information in the/etc/pam.d/ common-password configuration file). Astute readers know that this configuration actually is more than what is required for PCI DSS, but that is due to a limitation in pam_pwquality where you have to specify upper or lower case characters but cannot just generically select alphabetic characters.

Cisco and PCI Requirements

Cisco devices have some important settings that should be used for you to become PCI compliant. All passwords should be encrypted when stored or in transit. Most operating systems do this and do not really give you an easy way to store them unencrypted even if you want to. Cisco devices are an exception, however, so it's important to check this.

Cisco Enforce Session Timeout

To force Cisco devices to automatically timeout if a session is left inactive, use the exec-timeout configuration under the appropriate line configuration. The syntax for this command is exec-timeout [minutes] [seconds]. For PCI compliance, this should be set as follows:

```
exec-timeout 15 0
```

Encrypt Cisco Passwords

The current best practice from Cisco is to always use "enable secret" and "username secret," instead of enable password. Enable password encrypts the password using a very weak encryption algorithm that has been broken for a long time. The secret command uses Message Digest 5 (MD5) to hash the password. Although MD5 has shown some weaknesses lately, this is far better than the alternative and the best Cisco is giving us right now. A better option would be to use directory-based authentication models such as LDAP or TACACS+ to prevent these usernames and passwords from being stored directly on the device. Even encrypted passwords can be vulnerable to attack when disclosed.

Setting Up SSH in a Cisco Environment

By default, Cisco routers allow Telnet access to the line vty 0 4 port for remote configuration. To disable this and set up an SSH server, you must first have an IOS version that supports IOS with the appropriate feature pack (typically the crypto pack). You need to set up either local authentication or as suggested above, tie the device to a directory. When managing any more than a few devices, pointing the authentication to a directory service makes administration much easier.

If you have already directed your device to a directory service, skip to the next configuration step. Otherwise, you need to enter this into your router after entering the "Terminal Configuration" mode by typing `config t`:

```
aaa new-model
```

The next command generates the keys required to perform SSH encryption:

```
crypto key generate rsa
```

Then finally, to disable Telnet for remote access, type the following two commands:

```
line vty 0 4
transport input ssh
```

Then, save your configuration!

Requirement 9: Physical Security

There are three basic types of physical security. The first type is obstacles such as doors, walls, and other barriers, which can help stop or at least delay intruders. The second type is detection mechanisms such as alarms, lighting, guards, and television cameras that help detect attacks. The third type is response, which includes things you would put in place to stop an attack in progress or soon after. It's important to use all these types of physical security to protect sensitive information. For example, you may put sensitive data behind a locked door and have security cameras monitoring that door, recording everybody who goes in and out. You may also have a guard on duty who can quickly respond to stop anyone who's trying to circumvent the lock. Security measures in plain sight act as a deterrent to attackers, sometimes preventing the attack in the first place. But be sure those measures actually work in case you need them (a camera that doesn't work may deter some attackers, but if you have an incident you might need a working camera).

Of course, Requirements 9.1.1 and 9.1.2 are our policy and documentation requirements. Make sure you have solid policy and procedure documents for everyone involved in physical security—and that is anyone who has any physical access to your site or anyone controlling that access. Yes, you can stop tailgaters!

Requirement 9.2.1 mandates "facility entry controls" for in-scope areas including computer rooms, data centers, and other physical areas where in-scope systems may live (i.e., the CDE). Acceptable controls include lock and key, badge access, or some other barrier that automatically locks and only unlocks for the people authorized to access these rooms (Hint: the President of your company should not have access). Requirement 9.2.1.1 mandates the use of video cameras or other access control mechanisms to monitor individual physical access to "sensitive areas within the CDE." No doubt those areas include the ones mentioned in 9.2.1, but arguably they would include a large physical storage area of paper records that contain cardholder data. These large storage areas are rare in the United States these days, but the payment systems in some countries still run on a significant amount of paper. Those areas should be protected in the same way and should have cameras monitoring access. In addition to simply placing the camera there, you must protect the video data from modification and regularly review and correlate the data, as well as store it for a minimum of three months (unless prohibited by law).

Requirements 9.2.2 and 9.2.3 aim to protect inherently vulnerable areas of your environment. Requirement 9.2.2 targets publicly accessible network jacks and mandates the access to such jacks be restricted. This one can be challenging as far as its intent. If you have conference rooms or common areas with network jacks that are outside the restricted areas of your company, you should disable them or make those public, guest networks only. This requirement would not apply to a conference room *behind* a secured area where visitors must be escorted. QSAs in the past have incorrectly read this requirement to mean that *all* conference room jacks must be disabled. This is incorrect, as only those areas that are considered publicly accessible should have their network jacks disabled (i.e., with no physical access such as a badge reader protecting them). Another area to look out for with respect to 9.2.2 is retail store locations where network jacks may be placed throughout the store in plain view (or otherwise unrestricted) that might also sit on the point of sale (POS) network (or a network where cardholder data may be processed).

It is time for a real-life example. James was working with a customer who had a chain of cafes. When sitting down at one of the tables in the cafe, a network jack was discovered slightly obscured by a plant. This jack was actually hooked up to the same network as the POS systems, and an attacker could easily hide a device that could take advantage of this major design flaw by siphoning off every transaction processed through the store.

Requirement 9.2.3, discussed in Chapter 8, Using Wireless Networking, mandates protection for wireless access points, gateways, and handheld devices.

Be sure to check any machines that are inside a sensitive area and observe that the console is locked. Requirement 9.2.4 exists because in some cases, machines would be logged in and unlocked in a data center cage for some reason. Yes, there are physical access controls required to be passed in order to get to that actual console, but that's not good enough. There should be no persistent, logged-in machines in sensitive areas.

Handling Visitors: Requirement 9.3

First, we begin with documentation! Requirement 9.3.1 talks about procedures to distinguish employees and visitors, and the testing procedures determine if the process covers granting badges, changing access, and revoking terminated or expired badges, as well as making sure you are following your own policies (9.3.1.b). Requirement 9.3.1.1 is in place to clarify that access to the systems that manage access is limited to authorized personnel. You just need some way to clearly distinguish these groups such that someone who does not know the individuals could understand what bucket they fit in.

NOTE

During your assessment, make sure you make your assessor follow the procedures you set! There is nothing that says FAIL more than when a company being assessed forgets to give the assessor a visitor badge or leaves him unescorted through a secure area.

Requirement 9.3 is a practical test for what you set up in Requirement 7. Essentially, your QSA should take a sample of individuals with physical access to sensitive areas and make sure they have authorization paperwork and that their job function requires this access. Watch out for interpretation issues here as an over-zealous QSA may decide that some of your employees don't actually need access. You should work with your QSA to ensure they are educated on the business reasons for the access. The QSA will also look through some recently terminated employees who have had access and make sure that their access is revoked.

Requirement 9.3.2 deals with visitors exclusively and is a test to make sure that the badge you give to the assessor does not open doors where sensitive information is stored. This is what the Council means by "unescorted access." You can expect your assessors to try and get their badge to open a data center door or other sensitive areas. Obviously, if you issue plain paper badges to your assessors, this will be a fairly easy requirement to pass. Your assessor will also look at the badge you give them and compare it to your badge. Requirement 9.3.2 mandates that employee badges and visitor badges visually appear different and have distinguishing marks such that an employee of your company could easily identify someone as a visitor by the badge used to identify him. Finally, Requirement 9.3.3 mandates that visitor badges are surrendered upon leaving the facility. Your assessor will probably perform the required testing procedures without you even knowing, so be sure your company is following the policies and procedures you set out!

Requirement 9.3.4 is documentation-based but not in the way you might think. When visitors are allowed to visit the facility in general, data center or other sensitive areas, they must sign in. The three items that must be captured for every access are the person's name, the firm represented, and the name of the employee authorizing the access. You must also retain this log for at least three months (unless restricted by law), so expect to add dates and times to the above three items.

Media and Physical Data Entry Points: Requirements 9.4

Up to this point, the main focus with cardholder data has been online or live data. Data is not always online or live and exists in many different places. Requirement 9.4.1 mandates physical protection of all kinds of media that contain cardholder data. The term "media" is intentionally broad here and could include computers, removable electronic media (such as USB drives), communications hardware, telecommunication lines (arguably not required if all data over the wire is encrypted), and paper (receipts, sales reports, chargeback or dispute reports, faxes, mailrooms). Although this is a procedural requirement (your assessor must review your procedures to ensure that this is addressed), your assessor may validate that you follow your procedures and ask to see areas where this type of data may be stored.

Requirements 9.4.1.1 and 9.4.1.2 deal with backup media. Backups are not required to be stored off-site, however! Several companies make use of on-site tape vaults in their primary data centers to ensure that the data remains secure. If the media goes off-site, don't send it home with one of your employees to put in her house. Be sure it is a facility that is secure and that the contracts comply with Requirement 12.8.

When media is distributed outside your company's secure facility, you must protect the media in three distinct ways. First, as a part of your compliance with Requirement 9.1, you must have a policy be put in place to strictly control the distribution of cardholder data. The fewer places you send in-scope data, the less likely you will have a breach because someone did not adequately protect the data. Requirement 9.4.2 states that all media must be classified in a manner such that it can be identified as confidential. This requirement could literally be interpreted to say that the media must have the term "CLASSIFIED" written on it, or more accurately interpreted to state that if you label media with a colored dot, the *red* ones are considered classified by your policies. Finally, Requirement 9.4.3 mandates that any media transported outside the facility is logged, done so via a secure courier or in a manner by which it can be tracked, and offsite tracking logs include details about the media location.

When media is transported off-site, you need to enter it into a log so that you know where your media inventory is at any given point. Your assessor will review several days of logs, per Requirement 9.4.3, and make sure that both the tracking information are included as well as proper management authorization. Someone capable of providing proper management authorization could be your data center manager or another person with the delegated authority (and accountability) for authorizing the transport of media.

Management must approve all transportation of media offsite (Requirement 9.4.4), including when it is sent with an individual. All electronic media with cardholder data on it must be inventoried and logged, with a manual inventory process happening at least once every 12 months (Requirements 9.4.5 and 9.4.5.1). Be sure you can show your assessor the results of your inventory. They will likely review it and spot check your work.

Requirements 9.4.6 and 9.4.7 are essentially the same with the exception of the target of the requirement—they deal with the destruction of cardholder data. In cases where you need to dispose of any media containing cardholder data, it needs to be destroyed in a manner by which the data is not recoverable. This means that if you are done with a hard drive, you must either electronically destroy the data or physically destroy the media—a simple delete does not work. When any hard copies (such as printouts) of cardholder data are no longer required for business or legal reasons, you must properly destroy it in a method that prevents its recovery. Shred bins are good options here as long as they are properly secured. The same must be done for electronic media. When electronic records are no longer needed, they must be destroyed in a manner in which they cannot be recovered. This could be bulk erasers, demagnetizers, or hardware shredders. Simply drilling a hole through it is not sufficient. Be sure you document the destruction of hardware properly with logs. Your assessor may want to review a sample of any electronically destroyed media to ensure that the data is not recoverable.

NOTE

What is periodic? Good question! PCI DSS 4.0 now includes definitions on the different time periods in Section 7 on page 25 in the front matter section. Check that when in doubt.

If you are now deploying Solid State Disks (SSDs) or use USB Flash media, you must understand that a traditional secure wipe does not work effectively to destroy data on these media. In order to protect these, be sure that you are encrypting the drive or working from an encrypted volume before deleting. This process, known as crypto-shredding, can accomplish the same effectiveness of making the data unrecoverable without access to the keys.

Protecting the Point of Interaction: Requirement 9.5

These requirements represent years of refinement dating back to PCI DSS 3.0. The Point of Interaction (POI) is the device that captures payment card data from the payment card form factor itself. It's the thing reading the swipe, dip, or tap.

Skimming was a massive issue as it relates to credit card payments (and still is an issue today), and skimmers can be found in any type of device. Some skimmers come pre-loaded into devices direct from dirty manufacturers or integrator resellers. Unattended payment terminals (think pay at the pump fuel or ATMs) are particularly susceptible because they are not watched 24×7. The bad guys are getting very creative and have some pretty incredible resources. Injection molds, lighting, and embedded electronics are all present in skimmers now such that you wouldn't necessarily be able to detect with the naked eye.

Requirement 9.5.1 states that you must protect devices that capture payment card data (payment terminals) from tampering and substitution. This includes maintaining an inventory of all POI devices (further expanded in Requirement 9.5.1.1 to include an up-to-date list with the make and model, location, and device serial number), periodically inspecting them and looking for tampering and substitution (with logs and evidence available to meet Requirement 9.5.1.2), and training personnel to be aware of suspicious behavior and how to report tampering or substitution of devices (with additional visitor verification as a part of Requirement 9.5.1.3). You will need to perform a risk assessment to determine how frequently the inspections will occur (Requirement 9.5.1.2.1). You must have logs to show your assessor all of this. In small shops, this will probably be pretty easy to do, but it will become something that you will have to work into a monthly or weekly routine. For big shops, this is an issue of scale.

Requirement 9.5.1.1 takes the concept of the big list of devices you must maintain and applies it to these very terminals. You must keep the inventory up to date and ensure that the list is accurate for added, relocated, or decommissioned devices. Your assessor should take a sample of the devices in your list and verify that they have been inspected, that they are correctly listed as operational (or decommissioned), and are in the correct location.

Requirement 9.5.1.3 is interesting in that it attempts to tackle social engineering as a risk for terminal tampering. Your front-line employees are responsible for verifying the identity of any technician dispatched and the work orders to work on payment terminals. You must train your front-line employees on how to spot suspicious behavior and give them a way to report it. If they do report it, be sure you track it and follow up with logs. Your assessor will want to review the training as well as interview front-line folks, the cashiers and POS operators, to make sure they have this training and have a method to report this behavior.

WHAT ELSE CAN YOU DO TO BE SECURE?

This chapter covers how to create PCI Compliant access controls for in-scope data. One of the most effective things you can do is reduce the amount of in-scope data stored in your systems to both make it easier to comply with these three major requirements and to improve your general security. Let's explore some areas where you might store in-scope data that could be reduced or eliminated.

Retail stores are notorious for storing data well beyond their useful lifespan for various purposes. When retailers started to embrace the concept of a computer to run their POS and process credit card transactions, it appears that the equipment first deployed was unreliable. Why else would you store 90 days of transaction logs on an in-store server? From an electronic perspective, remove all cardholder data older than two or three days from your POS controllers. POS terminals should never store this information once it has been passed to the controller (which could arguably be done on a daily batch basis). If you feel that you may need this data, collect the transaction logs or electronic journals in a central location. Bringing data from 50 stores is much easier to maintain in one place versus 50 individual places.

Next, look for paper data. If you are still printing the entire card number on the receipt that a customer signs, all of that paper must be protected in accordance with PCI. Get it centralized, then possibly imaged and destroyed. Even if you make a change to your process to mask that number when it is printed, be sure you don't have any legacy data in the stores. Branden remembers visiting a retail location that had 10 years of paper cardholder data in clearly labeled boxes next to the bathroom used by customers, even though corporate policy prohibited keeping data any longer than one year.

TOOLS

Did you know that you only need four elements to uniquely identify any transaction in your enterprise, and one of those is not the full card number? These elements are as follows:

- First six and last four (or just last four) digits of the card number,
- Date and time of purchase,
- Amount of purchase, and
- Authorization code.

Our clients who have used this method have never reported that two transactions matched these elements identically but had different complete card numbers (including the largest merchants in the world).

The PCI Security Standards Council recently updated their truncation guidance on a per-brand basis. For example, Visa cards may now be considered truncated if they have at least four digits removed, not eight. Check the PCI SSC FAQs for more details.

Do your retail stores still contain knuckle-busters, those old manual credit card contraptions that used carbon paper and made a "kerCHUNK-kerCHUNK" sound as an imprint of a customer card is made? If so, you better believe there is probably someone who has used it recently and that some data is stored on hardcopy media (i.e., paper) in that store. Just like above, be sure that once you fix the policy or remove that equipment from the store that you have removed all the legacy data.

Here's another one that you may not have thought about. If you have certain business or high-volume customers that phone or fax orders in, how do they pay for their orders? Do you keep a credit card on file so that when they come in they can just sign and leave? Work on removing that data or changing how you deal with your high-profile customers.

If you run a call center, how are calls monitored? Do the phones rely on Voice Over IP (VoIP) technologies to operate? Do you record the calls? The Council has specific Frequently Asked Questions dealing with call centers on the Council's website that will address your particular situation.

Finally, look to your corporate headquarters. Do you really need a credit card for more than a couple of minutes after the transaction was initially processed? Many companies tell you that they absolutely need it until you ask them why at least three times. Why is three the magic number? Who knows, but the truth usually sounds like "Well, we've always done it that way." Then, you ask them what they might do if the data was not available after seven days. They will usually figure out a way to either handle the dispute with a truncated number or simply realize that the cost to secure this data far exceeds the potential losses associated with not having the data. Tokenization really helps here when you work with your acquiring bank to get it set up and working. If the acquirer can deal with the token directly, there is zero reason to hold on to the original data post authorization (including for settlement and clearing).

NOTE

Propaganda is powerful. Some industry pundits think that the card brands require merchants to store data. If you have heard this, read the next sentence very carefully. Card brands do not require that you store data! In most cases, your acquirer is taking a shortcut, thus transferring risk to the merchant. In our experience, companies can easily deal with dispute resolution without the full number when they press their acquirer. Acquirers will compete for your business, so if your current acquirer is not willing to help you, consider another one. You'd be amazed how quickly something like this is resolved. Furthermore, law enforcement typically provides you with the full card number they want you to pull transactions for, so you can still assist them by asking for specific dates and times. There are some exceptions to this rule, but virtually everyone can be altered to off-load risk from the company trying to comply with PCI DSS.

TOOLS AND BEST PRACTICES

Aside from challenging the useful life of data and ensuring that you do not retain data longer than is absolutely required, here are a few other best practices you might consider.

Enforcement of a password policy in conjunction with other factors of authentication helps to protect systems from potential compromise. Here are some simple password rules, above and beyond changing default passwords that will provide stronger security. As this book is going to press, we are seeing more and more security professionals calling for the death of passwords. Since we may not see wide-scale adoption of alternative methods in the super near future, some of these tips may be useful to you:

- Accounts that have system-level privileges must have a unique password from all other accounts held by that user.
- Give administrators different accounts for administrative actions; do not tie the privileges to their primary domain accounts.
- Do not transmit passwords over the Internet without being encrypted.
- Allow users to craft long passwords in lieu of password complexity to ensure strong passwords.
- Deploy a token-based, system-wide two-factor authentication solution such that any system access to sensitive information requires a token or another factor of authentication. Even using risk-based models to define when tokens are required and what kind of token can be used can make a tremendous difference. Be sure you document the risks associated with each factor type.
- If you choose to use hardware keys like Yubikeys, be sure you have more than one. You need a backup way to access your account in case you lose or damage your primary key.
- Deploy a single sign-on solution that leverages SAML or OIDC that asserts identities so that users do not have to remember multiple passwords, thus encouraging users to select more secure passwords.
- Keep track of any tokens used for persistent access (such as OAuth tokens) and ensure they have expirations and can be revoked.
- Do not share or write passwords down insecurely (using a password vault is fine).

Many of these methods can help you bolster your overall security, but in many cases, they also make authentication easier on users. After all, if security professionals impose difficult requirements on users, they will come up with ever more creative ways to get around them!

Random Password for Users

PCI requires unique first-time passwords. There are many possible ways to do this, and a quick Google search for password generators returns many options. These may work well for you; however, if you're ultra-paranoid, then you may want to use one installed on your own computer.

Any quick search engine queries will take you to a number of password generators. These are easily scripted and most systems now will handle this for you.

COMMON MISTAKES AND PITFALLS

This section covers many pitfalls and mistakes related to this PCI domain.

POOR DOCUMENTATION

This domain of PCI DSS starts with documentation, and poor documentation will set you up for failure when you try to meet the rest of it. Companies that struggle the most with this domain have two major issues they fight. The first is a poor analysis as part of Requirement 7, thus poor (if not nonexistent) documentation to support this requirement. Because the content in Requirements 8 and 9 often rely on Requirement 7 to be completed, companies that often miss parts of Requirements 8 and 9 have set themselves up for failure by missing Requirement 7. Do your homework, and make sure Requirement 7 is handled well!

LEGACY SYSTEMS

The other big trip up is legacy systems. There aren't as many of them out there as there used to be, but with a new group of companies looking for the services of a QSA for the first time, there will be no doubt a ton of these out there. Legacy systems have many issues complying with PCI DSS, and this is one of the major ones.

Is there an avenue for a compensating control? There is almost always a possibility for a compensating control unless you are dealing with one of the few requirements that prohibit this. For these systems, you will most likely need to use network segmentation and VPNs or a jump server environment like a Citrix box or a Windows Terminal Server. Keep in mind, systems that are this old tend to be riddled with holes and struggle with just the basics of limiting network traffic to them. Most companies soon discover that this option will break their business, and they must ultimately upgrade.

CLOUD AND PaaS

PCI DSS is vague on purpose here because if they got specific, they would be releasing new versions of PCI DSS and the requirements covered in this chapter monthly. Technology evolves at a rapid pace, so be sure you are looking at all the ways that a user or process can access a particular set of infrastructure, and you have documented and secured it appropriately (most likely, according to your documentation).

PHYSICAL ACCESS MONITORING

For Requirement 9, the biggest mistakes people make are on camera coverage. Don't over-cover (i.e., put multiple cameras on every cash lane) and don't under-cover (i.e., no cameras in stores at all).

CASE STUDY

The following two case studies explore when bad things happen (or could happen) to people with good intentions. The PCI Requirements, when followed correctly, are designed to reduce the risk that companies carry by holding this data. The moral for both of these case studies is that you should store the absolute least amount possible but protect what you store like a mama bear protects her cubs.

THE CASE OF THE STOLEN DATABASE

Alice's Activity Atrium is a startup that aims to revolutionize how families shop with young children in outdoor malls. Alice pitched the concept of an activity center in a common area of her open-air mall, with a safe, indoor playground, physical security around the play area, and pagers (or notifications through their app) to reach parents if problems occur with their children. The general manager for the property granted her proposal on a trial basis, allowing her to set her business up for the back-to-school rush in an unleased storefront. Provided that things went smoothly, she would win the contract for the coveted Christmas season shopping that often occurred during November and December.

Alice bought some daycare management software for her laptop based on Microsoft Access and opened her business in late July with amazing success. Her quick rise in popularity required her to hire some additional help. Alice contracted Darlene to run the laptop during peak times so that Alice could help with keeping the kids busy and safe. The software on her laptop captured relevant information about each customer and captured a credit card for payment. Customers paid by the 10th of an hour for the service, so the card was pre-authorized for a six-hour stay, much longer than any stay she envisioned, and then finally settled for the actual amount used. The laptop was placed at her location's entrance so that customers could check in and out quickly without having to step inside the facility, and repeat customers quickly were able to drop their kids off because the information was retrieved from storage.

One evening, one of the children under Alice's care fell at an awkward angle and sprained his ankle. During the commotion of moving the child to a safe place and calling the mall's medical personnel and the child's parents, Darlene left her post to help out. A passing thief seized a rare opportunity and stole Alice's new laptop.

Some readers may stop there and say, well, it's just a stolen laptop and that's not a big deal. Except, the laptop contained customer data on it, including credit card data. Although this is definitely a small-scale breach, the concept could also occur at a well-established business (say at a daycare or jewelry store) with thousands of customers. Alice made three key mistakes when she set up her business.

First, Although Alice took every precaution to prevent a child from "escaping" from her storefront, she didn't lock down the physical assets that ran her business. A laptop out in the open of a chaotic child care facility won't last long before someone picks it up. Alice should have physically secured the laptop such that it was not openly available for a thief to steal it during a crisis.

Second, Alice's desire to make it easier for kids to be dropped off had good intentions, but fell short when she stored the cardholder data of all of her customers. Instead of storing all that data, Alice should have instructed Darlene to ask for the method of payment for every transaction. Although this request could force her customers to spend up to 1–2 minutes per transaction, she would not put her customer data at risk, and this breach's reach would be much smaller.

Finally, the software Alice used to manage her business did not protect the information it stored. Because it was written in Microsoft Access, the data is easily retrieved. The thief not only had access to each of her customers' credit card numbers but also had their home addresses and medical insurance information too! Should the thief figure this out, he has more than enough data to begin the process of stealing an identity or fraudulently charging transactions.

THE CASE OF THE LOOSE PERMISSIONS

Melissa works in the marketing department for Ben's Body Boutique, a regional fitness and health center. Ben charged Melissa with merging data from a mass mailing campaign to purchase records from the last six months. Ben wanted to determine how effective the original marketing campaign was, and if there were certain geographic areas where the response was higher, so he could concentrate future outreach programs on those areas that yielded the largest amount of business.

Melissa made a request to IT to get access to the current customer database, and through her basic database skills she learned as a business analyst in a former job, she was able to perform direct queries against the data. IT gave Melissa a different username than her normal username, and she had to use a different password from her current Windows password because the complexity requirements did not match. She had a hard time remembering the password, so she temporarily wrote it down on a sticky note and placed it inside her closed laptop.

Melissa began performing some basic queries based on the database layout provided by one of the DBAs. The data map seemed to be missing a few key elements that she needed to complete her analysis, so she tried calling the DBA. He was out sick, and nobody else was available to help her with her question. So relying on her previous experience, she ran a few commands to get a more complete layout of the schema. She noticed that most of the fields were ones she thought she would need, so to save time, she used a wildcard when listing the database columns she wanted to see, thus effectively dumping the entire contents of the table to the Excel spreadsheet she would use on her machine. Unfortunately, her wildcard selection pushed customer credit card data down to her machine without her immediate knowledge.

It was getting late in the day, and she decided to finish the analysis later that evening after she put her children to bed. Not realizing the data she had, she simply copied the customer data file and the direct mail list to a USB disk she kept in her purse, left her laptop at her desk, and headed home. After putting her kids to bed, she loaded the data on her home computer and started to perform her analysis.

Without going any farther into the story, let's stop for a minute and find the issues with this case, some of which happen every day in our companies. First, knowing Melissa's background, IT gave her a database account with unlimited select permissions on all the tables in the customer database. The IT department violated Requirement 7.2.6 by giving a user direct access into the database and not regulating her use to just the data she needed. Instead, they should have asked her for the requirements and performed the data dump themselves and further ensured that the data was not PCI related. Next, she wrote her password down because the authentication for the database was different from her main Windows account. This action should be prohibited by security and password policies. Finally, she took the data home and put it on a non-company owned or controlled PC. Although her home machine may have all of its patches and be up to date on antivirus, she may forget to delete the file and could open Ben's up for a breach further down the road if she sold the computer or fell victim to a Trojan horse or virus.

SUMMARY

Access controls are an extremely important part of protecting your data. It is important to understand your systems and the best ways to control access to your data. Once access controls are set, they must be constantly maintained to be effective. As we have talked about in this chapter, it's important to have many layers of security to be effective. Not only is it important to have strict access controls in place on computer systems, but it's also important to control physical access.

Spend time to fully define your access requirements for PCI so that you can comply with Requirement 7. Although this is the shortest of the three requirements we covered in this chapter, it may require the most amount of effort to effectively meet. Defining roles and access profiles takes time, but the work you put in will allow you to centrally manage a diverse set of permissions effectively and efficiently. Next, put those profiles into action and assign permissions to them on your systems. Put users into containers and ensure that their access complies with the diverse requirements in Requirement 8.

Then, take a step back and focus on physical security, and don't forget stores and satellite locations! Don't defeat the corporate security at your headquarters by leaving wide open electronic access to your store or satellite locations. Finally, discover how much money you can save by destroying the data quickly after settlement. Remember, you don't have to protect what you don't store!

NOTE

1 While we are not specifically calling out macOS, remember that macOS is a POSIX-based UNIX operating system.

7 Protecting Cardholder Data

Information in this chapter:

- What Is Data Protection and Why Is It Needed?
- Requirements Addressed in This Chapter
- Requirement 3: Protect Stored Account Data
- What Else Can You Do to Be Secure?
- Requirement 4 Walk-Through
- Requirement 12 Walk-Through
- How to Become Compliant and Secure
- Common Mistakes and Pitfalls
- Case Study
- Summary

Protecting account data is clearly a central goal of the Payment Card Industry Data Security Standard (PCI DSS). All of the requirements cover data protection directly or indirectly. We can even summarize PCI DSS with six words, "It's all about the account data!" There are two requirements that particularly apply to protecting card data that is stored (data at rest) or transmitted (data in motion) in your environment. This chapter covers those data security requirements, which are mostly related to avoiding the storage of data and use of encryption to protect the data you do store. We'll also cover Maintaining an Information Security Policy (Requirement 12) as a solid policy is the foundation of a successful program.

WHAT IS DATA PROTECTION AND WHY IS IT NEEDED?

Before we even start our discussion of data protection methods, we need to remind you that *the only good data is dead data.* Humor aside, dropping, deleting, not storing, and otherwise not touching cardholder data is the one weird trick to make your acquirer ignore you—or just make your PCI DSS compliance process easier. As a side benefit, total avoidance of data will de-risk your transaction processing, reduce your liability and chance of fines, and prevent breach losses.

NOTE

Many times, the easiest way to protect data is not to store it at all! It's a good idea to review the data you're keeping and verify that you really need to keep it. Most business processes dealing with cardholder data can be altered such that actual cardholder data isn't needed.

As mentioned above, PCI DSS requirements for protecting cardholder data encompass two elements:

- Protect stored account data.
- Protect cardholder data with strong cryptography during transmission over open, public networks.

The processes and activities necessary to meet these requirements and the specific sub-requirements spelled out by PCI DSS are simply the implementation of some of the fundamental components of

DOI: 10.1201/9781003100300-7

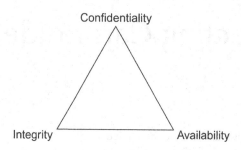

FIGURE 7.1   CIA triad.

a sound information security program—just as with other PCI DSS controls. In this particular case, the controls are about protecting *data at rest* and *data in motion*.[1]

If you have already put into place the pieces of a solid information assurance program, or you are in the process of doing so, there won't be a great deal of extra work to do. Your current processes and technology may very well serve to quickly allow you to comply with these requirements without a great deal of additional effort or cost.

THE CONFIDENTIALITY, INTEGRITY, AND AVAILABILITY TRIAD

We defined the Confidentiality, Integrity, and Availability (CIA) triad in Chapter 6, Strong Access Controls. Let's use them here to define our data protection efforts. These three tenets of information security are referred to as a triad because they are most commonly illustrated as three points of a triangle (see Figure 7.1). All three principles must be considered as you manage your data. An undue degree of emphasis on one can lead to a deficiency in one of the others.

- **Confidentiality:** Strives to ensure that information is disclosed to only those who are authorized to view it. Most PCI DSS requirements apply to this leg of the CIA triad.
- **Integrity:** Strives to ensure that information is not modified in ways that it should not be. This can refer to modifications by either people or processes. The integrity of logging data is the biggest example of how this applies to PCI DSS.
- **Availability:** Strives to ensure that data is available to the authorized parties in a reliable and timely fashion. PCI DSS does not play in this particular sandbox, with the exception of *authorized parties*. The requirement to keep the data available for your business is on you and your organization. No external guidance from the PCI Council applies, even though many general security practices, such as deploying anti-malware software as part of Requirement 5, indirectly contribute to keeping the systems humming and data available.

In addition to the CIA triad, oversight reviews in the form of audits validate that the controls you create are indeed working as designed. Specifically, the logging and monitoring requirements (covered in Chapter 10, Logging Events and Monitoring the Cardholder Data Environment) are meant to provide audit and monitoring artifacts for the infrastructure. This key tenet is about knowing who is doing what, with specific data, at any given time and being able to prove it via logging and monitoring.

Combining CIA with process-transmit-store, you arrive at the following complete structure for PCI DSS data protection (Table 7.1).

REQUIREMENTS ADDRESSED IN THIS CHAPTER

This chapter addresses the following PCI DSS requirements.

TABLE 7.1
PCI DSS Data Protection Mapped to CIA

	Transmit	Process	Store
Confidentiality	Don't transmit the data over less-secure networks, if possible. Encrypt data in transmission.	Use secure applications.	Don't store. If you have to, encrypt, mask, and truncate the data.
Integrity	Don't transmit the data over less-secure networks, and use technologies that enforce session confidentiality and integrity (i.e., encryption with signing).	Use secure applications.	Don't store data. If you have to store it, encrypt the data. Other methods do not preserve data integrity. Where appropriate use Write Once Read Many (WORM) filesystems.
Availability	PCI generally does not apply outside of the availability of all of your inventories and documentation. Your business does need card data availability to operate.	PCI generally does not apply.	PCI generally does not apply outside of the availability of all of your inventories and documentation.

- Requirement 3: Protect stored account data.
- Requirement 4: Protect cardholder data with strong cryptography during transmission over open, public networks.
- Requirement 12: Support information security with organizational policies and programs.

Other chapters, such as Chapter 5, Building and Maintaining a Secure Network, Chapter 6, Strong Access Controls, Chapter 9, Vulnerability Management and Testing, and Chapter 10, Logging Events and Monitoring the Cardholder Data Environment, cover additional requirements relevant to data protection as well:

- Requirement 7: Restrict access to system components and cardholder data by business need-to-know (see Chapter 6, Strong Access Controls).
- Requirement 10: Log and monitor all access to system components and cardholder data (see Chapter 10, Logging Events and Monitoring the Cardholder Data Environment).

REQUIREMENT 3: PROTECT STORED ACCOUNT DATA

The most effective means of ensuring that cardholder data is not exposed to unauthorized parties (confidentiality) is the proper destruction of that data.

The best means of preventing sensitive data from falling in the wrong hands is not having sensitive data at all. In fact, this is not just the best way; this is the only way that 100% guarantees it. PCI has nothing to do with data availability for your business processes (whereas the final revision of the Visa Cardholder Information Security Program [CISP] standard required business continuity and disaster recovery procedures). Instead, the general nudge present in PCI DSS is if you avoid storing and moving the data around, you can avoid a lot of trouble.

As a result, before you engage in any data protection project involving encryption, masking, sanitization, or other processes that might scrub cardholder data, consider performing a project that investigates removing the data from as many systems as possible. We are well aware of the fact that it is not possible for all organizations and every circumstance, so please read on.

By the way, we are not talking about running the commands that are as follows (both of which leave artifacts of the original data behind):

```
DEL credit_card_data.dat (Windows)
```

Or

```
/bin/rm -rf/opt/credit_card_data.data (*NIX)
```

We are talking about assessing how your organization processes payment cards and whether any parts of that business process can be simplified and improved by not storing card data, storing it in fewer places, or not storing full primary account number (PAN, which is allowed as per PCI but expands your scope). Storing some types of data is expressly prohibited by PCI DSS, and thus, no protection methods are required; such data simply must not exist in your environment.

The second-most effective means of ensuring that stored cardholder data is not exposed to unauthorized parties is using tokenization as a method to replace your stored data while keeping it in a usable format. Tokenization ensures that when data is invariably extracted from a key system for analysis, the raw card data is not included.

Finally, encryption of account data rounds out your protection mechanisms. When implemented properly, if an intruder is able to gain access to your network and your data they will not be able to use it without access to the proper encryption keys. Encryption comes in a few different forms, however, and you need to factor in any licensing or extra costs for encryption when leveraging something like a table or column level encryption inside a database or a hardware security module.

PCI standards dictate that stored cardholder data can be rendered unreadable in a number of ways, such as encrypting, masking, truncating, or tokenizing. Encryption or tokenization will protect your data from being misused by malicious individuals while maintaining some level of utility, thus reducing the risk that account data creates in your environment.

NOTE

Masking and truncating are two different methods of rendering card data unreadable. Masking is used when the data is displayed, say for example hiding the first 12 digits of an account number behind an X (XXXX XXXX XXXX 1234). The real data still exists behind it, but the viewer cannot see it. Depending on where this masking occurs (hopefully as part of a database view), you can remove large sections of your operations from scope.

Truncation is actually destroying the original data such that the masked view is what is actually stored. If data is masked, it could be unmasked to reveal the original values. Truncated data is permanently removed and you cannot reconstruct the original number from a truncated value.

Should you be unable to protect the data with strong cryptography, PCI DSS allows you to implement compensating controls to meet this requirement. See Chapter 17, The Art of Compensating Control, for more details on selecting compensating controls for encryption. Because encryption can be an effective and critical part of protecting data, we will discuss some of the details of encryption methods and the associated advantages and disadvantages.

REQUIREMENT 3 WALK-THROUGH

As with all requirements in PCI DSS, the first requirement is a policy and procedure roundup for every sub-requirement to follow. Be sure you document policies and operational procedures as well as the relevant roles and responsibilities.

PCI DSS Requirement 3.2.1 highlights the mantra about not storing data: "Keep cardholder data storage to a minimum." PCI DSS 4.0 expanded the requirement to ensure all of the documentation you build that defines your process and policy represent reality accurately. Specifically, there are two new bullets that must be addressed, "coverage for all locations of stored account data" and "coverage for any sensitive authentication data (SAD) stored prior to completion of authorization." It further specifies that an organization needs to limit storage amount and retention time to that which is required for legal, regulatory, and business requirements. If you expect to use legal or business requirements to expand your retention, you should have very detailed documentation (probably with expert help) explaining why. You would be better off deleting and destroying!

Often we would have merchants tell us they needed to store full PAN data for chargebacks, but this is not entirely true (especially today). Acquirers have other ways of handling chargebacks without mandating full-card data storage, and we are not aware of an acquirer that cannot provide an alternative method for chargeback disputes. Remember, keep cardholder data storage to a minimum. Better yet, don't store it at all.

As a real-world example, Branden was able to avoid several million dollars of remediation in an ATM servicing arm of a bank by removing the full PAN from the transaction logs in the ATM itself. The chargeback defense team thought they needed the full number until they realized that every transaction has a unique identifier provided by the network, and this could be used as part of the chargeback defense to help the network identify the transaction in question. Sometimes you have to be willing to (politely) ask the uncomfortable questions that drive policy change in positive ways. You will be a hero!

There is a common misconception about the storage of PAN data proliferated by industry pundits. If your acquirer or processor is requiring that you store the PAN data, keep in mind that is *their* requirement to fulfill, not a PCI DSS requirement for a merchant. If all else fails, choosing another acquirer is definitely within your rights. Before proceeding to the next part of Requirement 3, review all of the testing procedures for Requirement 3.2.1.a-c to ensure you are prepared for success. Your assessor should verify that nothing exceeds the retention requirements set out in your policy (testing procedure 3.2.1.b).

The next sub-requirement flat-out bans the storage of some types of data after authorization (Requirement 3.3.1): "Sensitive authentication data is not stored after authorization, even if encrypted." There is no possible way to make this any clearer in PCI DSS. *Never* store SAD after authorization. This requirement is also one of the key components of Phase 1 of the PCI DSS Prioritized Approach and is an example of a requirement that is not eligible for the Customized Approach. Requirement 3.3.3 includes new specific requirements for issuers and issuer processors, so pay attention to the wording of the requirements so you know which pieces you have to comply with.

NOTE

Both of us have worked with issuers in the past while advising on PCI DSS requirements. Here's the reality. Issuers have much bigger problems to deal with than PCI DSS. Regulations like the Gramm-Leach-Bliley Act (GLBA), General Data Protection Regulation (GDPR), and the California Consumer Privacy Act (CCPA) carry much more weight and penalties than PCI DSS would. Issuers already own the risk of fraud for their own cards, and complying with PCI DSS simply doesn't make sense.

Remember that PCI DSS is a *contractual obligation*, not a regulation in the traditional sense. Compliance with PCI DSS would need to show up in a contract that an issuer signs. Spoiler alert: it does not and likely will not anytime soon. Perhaps the only legitimate reason to include PCI DSS for an issuer would be if they run a service where they would have access to other banks' payment data, such as running an ATM Network, lockbox operations, or doing issuer processing on behalf of another bank. If you issue payment cards and are looking at PCI DSS, scoping your environment down to those areas can be a pathway to success.

Even though Requirement 3.3.3 gives guidance to say that PCI DSS is intended to include issuers, we aren't aware of a single issuer who is running PCI for anything other than their ATM network. While the payment networks use PCI DSS as a way to improve confidence in the payment system, the payment card breach problem generally is not on the issuer side of the network.

If you are an issuer processor and are looking to comply with PCI DSS, this definitely applies to you. This requirement basically follows much of the standard PCI DSS pathways in limited storage of the data to only support what is required for business, and in the future, the second bullet will require encryption of this data with strong cryptography.

There is also some EMV-friendly language around equivalent magnetic stripe data that might be found on a chip (Requirement 3.3.1.1 in the Guidance). You can also expect QSAs to ask to poke around files containing incoming transaction data, logs, history files, trace files, database schemas, and even the contents of many database tables looking for this information. If your QSA does not ask for these things, beware, you may have a QSA that is not doing a complete job.

So, what data can *never* be persistently[2] stored if you are to have any hope of PCI DSS compliance for your organization? The answer is easy:

1. Full contents of any track data or equivalent on a chip (note that modern cards come with two tracks, so there is no exception for only storing one of the tracks).
2. CAV2/CVC2/CVV2/CID code, a three- or four-digit value printed on the card.
3. Personal identification number (PIN) or the encrypted PIN block.

For example, here is a reference from PCI DSS documents (Figure 7.2).

It shows that such sensitive data must not be stored. Remember, if you are persistently storing any of the above (any track, chip-equivalents, CVV2, PIN), you are not PCI DSS compliant and cannot be validated. Above all, in the US states where PCI DSS provisions are encoded as law, it will get you in trouble with authorities as well.

		Data Elements	Storage Restrictions	Required to Render Stored Data Unreadable
Account Data	Cardholder Data	Primary Account Number (PAN)	Storage is kept to a minimum as defined in Requirement 3.2	Yes, as defined in Requirement 3.5
		Cardholder Name	Storage is kept to a minimum as defined in Requirement 3.2	No
		Service Code		
		Expiration Date		
	Sensitive Authentication Data	Full Track Data	Cannot be stored after authorization as defined in Requirement 3.3.1	Yes, data stored until authorization is complete must be protected with strong cryptography as defined in Requirement 3.3.2
		Card verification code		
		PIN/PIN Block		

FIGURE 7.2   Permitted data storage

NOTE

Track 1 contains the following data, as per ISO/IEC 7813:2006:

```
\| SS \| FC \| PAN \| FS \| CC \| Name \| FS \| Additional Data \| CC \|
LRC
The field abbreviations are as follows:
SS: start sentinel
FC: format code
PAN: primary account number
FS: field separation
Name: primary account holder name
FS: field separation
Expiration date, offset, encrypted PIN, etc.
ES: end sentinel
CC: country code (3 characters minimum)
LRC: longitudinal redundancy check
```

Track 2 contains the following data, as per ISO/IEC 7813:2006:

```
\| SS \| PAN \| FS \| ED \| SC \| Other Data \| ES \| LRC
The field abbreviations are as follows:
SS: start sentinel
PAN: primary account number
FS: field separation
ED: expiration date
SC: service code
Other data
ES: end sentinel
LRC: longitudinal redundancy check
```

This requirement results in a simple action before even looking into encryption technologies at all: find out if you have such data stored.

If there happens to be an active business process that results in such data being stored or that relies on having such data, adjust it:

- Destroy the data, and
- Make sure that no accidental/undocumented storage is taking place.

As for a real-world example, remember that the storage of prohibited data killed CardSystems back in 2005 (or at least was a contributing factor in its demise).

TOOLS

Now you know that you cannot store SAD, what does it look like? The best thing you can do is search for valid PANs first and then manually verify what data is stored around them. Card verification values that appear on either the front or the back of the physical cards can be a challenge to find programmatically. Track data is easier as it is a formally defined standard. For more information, point your browser to your favorite search engine and enter "ISO/IEC 7813" for the layout of track data. Also, a brief introduction on card track data as described in ISO/IEC 78xx family of standards is presented in the above note.

PCI DSS 4.0 moved some legacy around requirements to create Requirements 3.3.1.1, 3.3.1.2, and 3.3.1.3 which essentially require that any secondary authentication data and PIN or PIN block must be rendered unrecoverable after the authorization process.

Requirement 3.4.1 covers processes and procedures around displaying the PAN. Given that accidental disclosure of the number can lead to card fraud just as well as its theft, the DSS mandates that organizations mask the PAN when displayed. Showing the Bank Identification Number (BIN) and last four digits are noted as the maximum number of digits to be displayed. It goes without saying that this guidance cannot be mandated for the employees that need to see a full account number for their business functions, but nowadays those employees are few in number (and getting smaller by the day).

Next up we have a new requirement for PCI DSS 4.0. Requirement 3.4.2 now takes a good practice item and mandates that anyone using remote-access technologies enables technical controls that prevent copy or move functions for PANs, except for those with a documented business need. If your company already uses virtual desktops, these controls are probably in place today. Basically, version 4.0 is making sure the separation you use with something like a virtual desktop maintains its integrity and keeps data off the user's machine (and keeps it in the virtual desktop).

Now on to the fun ones. Requirement 3.5.1 mandates that the "PAN is rendered unreadable anywhere it is stored." This is another reminder to you that not storing the data will make PCI DSS easier for your organization. If it is not stored anywhere, this requirement would not require any action on behalf of your organization.

This requirement, by the way, does not expressly mandate encryption. It allows any of the following to be used:

1. One-way hashes based on strong cryptography of the entire PAN,
2. Truncation,
3. Index tokens and pads, and
4. Strong cryptography with associated key-management processes and procedures (covered in Requirements 3.6 and 3.7).

The sub-bullet under truncation in the standard itself reminds you that if you are using hashing and truncation or just different truncation formats in different parts of your data protection strategy, you have additional controls in place to prevent an attacker from exploiting the differences in the versions to reconstruct the original PAN. In addition, if you choose hashing, note the change in wording and new Requirement 3.5.1.1 that you are using encryption keys (salts) for your hashing and it is covering the entire PAN. At this point in our journey, we are comfortable stating that hashing is probably one of the least attractive measures for securing PAN of the four. The overhead required to meet the requirements and defend against attempts to reconstruct the original PAN are substantial in PCI DSS 4.0, and you would be better going off with strong cryptography instead. Truncation and tokenization remain our favorites.

Don't forget to visit the Frequently Asked Question we linked to in Chapter 6, Strong Access Controls, so you understand what specifically qualifies for truncation depending on the account number you are targeting.

All the above are equally acceptable. Some are harder to accomplish, some are harder to maintain, and some just flat won't work for your business. Remember, if it is not stored, it cannot be stolen from that area (are you sensing a theme yet?). You will gain significant ground by altering your business processes in such a way that cardholder data is not needed. We cover encryption in the next few sections in more depth.

ENCRYPTION METHODS FOR DATA AT REST

Data at rest encryption options can be broken down into three high-level categories:

- File- or folder-level encryption.
- Full disk or partition-level encryption.
- Database encryption (either table, column, or field level).

Let's examine the advantages and disadvantages of each as you consider how and where they might fit into your program for protecting cardholder data.

File- or Folder-Level Encryption

File- or folder-level encryption (or file system level) is an encryption system where specific folders, files, or volumes are encrypted by a third-party software package or a feature of the file system itself.

Advantages:

- You have more granular control over what specific information must be encrypted. Card data files that you need to encrypt can be stored in a particular folder or volume, and data that does not need to be protected can be stored elsewhere. For example, some smaller organizations that do periodic billing actually use this method to encrypt all the numbers between the billing runs, thus satisfying certain PCI DSS requirements.
- Many file-level encryption products allow you to integrate access-level restrictions. This allows you to manage who has access to what and can extend roles-based access controls making large-scale management scalable. This helps satisfy data protection and access control.
- Some file-level encryption systems offer the capability to track who attempts to access a file and when. In order to satisfy the PCI DSS logging requirements, your file-level encryption product must allow you to granularly log information about their use for Requirement 10.
- When there is a need to move the data, data can be encrypted on a file level and then moved off of the storage location. Don't forget to destroy the original data! This maintains the confidentiality of the data when it is moved to a backup medium. Remember that any missing media with cardholder data on it still constitutes a breach and must be reported.
- File-level encryption tends to consume less resource overhead, thus less impact on system performance. Modern operating systems can perform efficient file encryption on the fly.

Disadvantages:

- Performance issues can be caused for backup processes, especially with relational databases.
- Extra resources for key management are required since more keys may need to be managed, and you need to ensure that those keys are separated from the machine login.
- May require additional software not built into the operating system.
- Only offers limited protection against insiders.

Full-Disk Encryption

Full-Disk Encryption (FDE) or whole disk encryption methods encrypt every file stored on the drive (or drives), including the operating system/file system. This is usually done on a sector-by-sector basis. A filter driver that is loaded into memory at boot encrypts every file as it is written to disk and decrypts any file that is moved off of the disk. This happens transparently to the end user or the application generating the files.

Advantages

- Everything on the drive (or drives) is encrypted, including temporary files and swap space, increasing the security of all your data, not just card data. If deployed on all in-scope systems, the card data would be guaranteed encrypted unless it is in memory.

- Encryption of data is forced on end user, alleviating decisions on what or what not to encrypt.
- Encryption/decryption is transparent. When information needs to be accessed, it can be saved off the system and is automatically decrypted. If a processing application is installed on the system, the use of encrypted data is also easy.[3]
- Since all data on the drive is encrypted, even if an alternative boot medium is used against an encrypted system, the data on the drive is unreadable and therefore useless to the thief. Thus, card data is protected even when the system is turned off.

Disadvantages

- Can only be used for removable media, and if you are using it for non-removable electronic media, Requirement 3.5.1.2 essentially says it doesn't count as a control because you must add another mechanism that meets Requirement 3.5.1.
- Slight delays in writing and reading data can occur, especially with very large files and high transaction volumes.
- System password management and key management processes have to be defined and put into place. If a user loses his password that grants access to the encrypted system, he has no access to his data at all. Key management procedures defined in Requirement 3.6 are more critical for FDE. By the way, as per 3.5.1.3, decryption keys must not be tied to user accounts.
- For data centers, this technology is largely useless for security (as opposed to laptops that may be stolen or lost in the field) since most data centers have significant physical controls keeping their hardware safe.
- FDE does not necessarily protect data on a laptop if the system is compromised while in use. It primarily helps to prevent data disclosure resulting from physical theft.
- Some FDE implementations leverage Windows AD credentials. Be careful deploying such systems as it would violate Requirement 3.5.1.3.

FDE is more suited to protecting data on laptops and mobile devices, whereas file-level encryption is more useful as a method on large-volume storage devices. The much-publicized cases of database managers or analysts putting thousands of clients at risk because a laptop was stolen that had been used to download large volumes of sensitive data from a storage device only serve to demonstrate this fact.

In Figure 7.3 illustrates the difference in architecture between file-level encryption and FDE.

NOTE

Before you reach out for the encryption tools, remember and repeat the mantra: "Do I need to keep this data?" Even with "free" tools, there are management costs to operate and maintain them in your environment. Free tools are analogous to free puppies. You may not pay for the tool, but you will pay for the care and feeding. The best bet is to never carry the data in the first place.

Database (Table-, Column-, or Field-Level) Encryption

The most sensitive piece of cardholder data that is allowed to be stored is a PAN. Think of this as your crown jewel. This is the full card number that identifies both the issuer of the card and the cardholder account. PCI DSS 3.5.1 states that you must render the PAN unreadable anywhere it is stored. If PANs are stored in a relational database and not in files, the column-level encryption becomes the only rational approach for rendering the key cardholder data unreadable. Trying to do file-level encryption on database tables stored to disk is clunky—you are better finding another way.

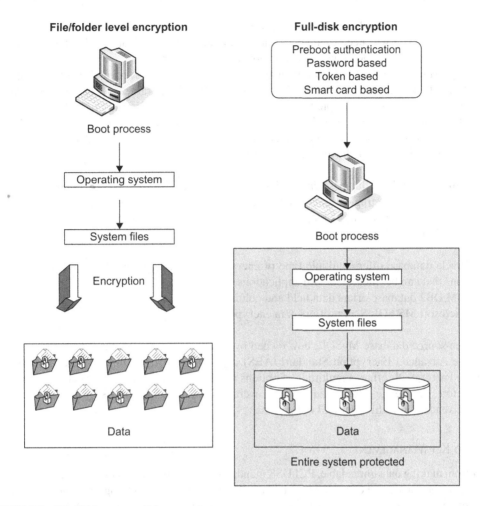

FIGURE 7.3   File/folder versus disk encryption.

Advantages

- When a table is queried for data in an *unencrypted* column, no performance impact is seen. Since no decryption activity is taking place, no delay in reading/writing and no performance hit by the system because encryption software activity is seen.
- When a query for a record with data from an encrypted field is performed, the overhead is minimal. Since the decryption activity only has to take place on the individual field or fields that are encrypted, there is much lower overhead.
- It can be used in conjunction with other controls to protect data from administrators. Separation of duties between security and database administrators (DBA) reduces the risk presented by allowing a DBA unlimited access to the data you need to secure for PCI compliance.

Disadvantages

- Database encryption requires tight integration with the database and may need to be purchased separately from a database vendor.
- It can be expensive depending on the vendor.
- It is often highly invasive to the database design. To implement column-level encryption protection after the fact, you may have to change the following (depending on implementation):
  - Data type of the field being encrypted.

- References to and queries of the encrypted field(s) will have to be modified to limit access. You will need to analyze middleware and other applications that interact with the database for documentation and potential reconfiguration.
- Key management has to be well planned; if the encryption key is hard-coded into scripts, it defeats the purpose of securing the data and violates Requirement 3.5. Keys themselves must be stored in an encrypted state and access controls placed around them.
- Merchants and service providers who perform batch processing will commonly end up storing sensitive data in flat files exported from a database. In this case, database encryption has to be combined with file or folder encryption.

As a result, column-level database encryption might be the answer for a piece of your overall plan for compliance to protecting cardholder data, but it is unlikely to be the entire plan.

At the time of writing, most major relational database vendors offer some form of database encryption. In particular:

- Oracle database offers multiple type of encrypted tables, including "transparent encryption" that can be integrated with applications.
- IBM DB2 database offers data field and column encryption.
- Microsoft MS SQL Server offers data encryption.

Free open-source database MySQL, now owned by Oracle, offers non-transparent data encryption using the Advanced Encryption Standard (AES) cryptographic algorithm, and free open-source database PostgreSQL offers a multitude of options powered by the pgcrypto() function.

As before, choose the solution that fits your overall IT strategy; you will likely not need to switch database vendors to fulfill your PCI obligations.

PCI AND KEY MANAGEMENT

Apart from making data unreadable, PCI DSS mandates certain key management practices if encryption is your chosen method of rendering data unusable. After all, the only thing that makes encryption a data protection mechanism is an encryption key. Let's continue to review PCI DSS Requirement 3.

Requirement 3.6.1 discusses the protection of encryption keys. PCI DSS details several different items for the proper management of encryption keys. They include processes, procedures, and the custodian of these keys. The management of encryption keys is probably the most resource-intensive aspect of encryption as well as the most error-prone. Critical key management practices to keep in mind are as follows:

- "Access to keys is restricted to the fewest number of custodians necessary."—Only let those who need to see the key access it; this means that not everyone who needs to see card data needs to be in possession of an encryption key.
- "Key-encrypting keys are at least as strong as the data-encrypting keys they protect."—Go read Requirement 3.6.1.2 to understand those forms, but essentially, you need to store keys encrypted on drives or use some kind of hardware security module to protect the keys. Keys must be protected from online and offline attacks. Requirement 3.5.3 now specifies that keys must be stored in the fewest possible locations.
- "Key-encrypting keys are stored separately from data-encrypting keys."—Go read Requirement 3.6.1.2 to understand the different ways this is acceptable, but essentially, you need to encrypt your data-encrypting keys where stored with a key-encrypting key that is at least as strong as the data-encrypting key. It must be stored separately. You can also use a hardware security module to protect the keys. Keys must be protected from online and offline attacks.

- "Keys are stored securely in the fewest possible locations and forms." (Requirements 3.6.1.3 and 3.6.1.4)—Your system password must not be your key to decrypt all the data in case of FDE.

Requirement 3.6.1.3 is designed to limit access to cleartext keys to the fewest number of custodians possible, and Requirement 3.6.1.4 specifies that keys must be stored in the fewest possible locations.

The next sub-requirement (3.7) addresses the process and procedure angle of encryption; namely, to fully document and implement all key-management processes and procedures to include all aspects of the key lifecycle. PCI DSS explicitly states what practices must be documented:

- Generation of strong cryptographic keys (3.7.1),
- Secure cryptographic key distribution (3.7.2),
- Secure cryptographic key storage (3.7.3),
- Periodic cryptographic key changes (3.7.4),
- Retirement or replacement of keys as deemed necessary when the integrity of the key has been weakened or keys are suspected of being compromised (3.7.5),
- Split knowledge and establishment of dual control of cryptographic keys—keep in mind, this is for manual clear-text crypto key management as automated key management systems have their own methods for doing this (3.7.6),
- Prevention of unauthorized substitution of cryptographic keys (3.7.7), and
- Requirement for cryptographic key custodians to sign a form stating that they understand and accept their key custodian responsibilities (3.7.8).

Other areas to consider:

- Ensure your private keys cannot be exported from keystores once in production.
- Use strong passphrases for private keys or HSMs.
- Don't store or transmit private keys with the passphrase that allows it to be used.
- Use a secrets manager or vault. Ones that support programmatic rotation move right to the front of the line.
- Build excellence around your internal certificate authority (CA).

Detailed coverage of cryptographic practices goes far out of the scope of this book. For more information on key management best practices, see NIST's special publication SP 800-57, Recommendations for Key Management (as well recent addendums).

WHAT ELSE CAN YOU DO TO BE SECURE?

While encryption is one of the natural ways to protect stored data, it is not the only method to protect data when stored. In some special cases, mainframe systems with mandatory access control systems such as RACF, ACF2, or TopSecret may be permitted to meet Requirement 3.5 without deploying encryption technologies. These same mandatory access control systems now exist in distributed systems such as Linux called Security-Enhanced Linux (SELinux). These circumstances are specialized, and typically require no direct user access, encrypted connections into the system, and storage limited to only a few small areas.

If you think you may fall into this category, contact a QSA and walk through the scenario to see whether they believe that it stands up to the definition of a compensating control or something that would work well under the Customized Approach. We recommend not relying on this method, however, as it has anti-future proof vibes written all over it. You are better off looking at a tokenization or encryption solution as they are readily available for mainframes and other large systems in the 2020s.

REQUIREMENT 4 WALK-THROUGH

As in the case of protecting stored data, the most reliable and efficient way to ensure that your transmitted data is not intercepted (confidentiality) or modified (integrity) is to not transmit it anywhere. At the very least, avoiding public and insecure networks will go a long way toward achieving compliance and risk reduction.

The next most reliable and efficient way to ensure that your transmitted data is not intercepted (confidentiality) or modified (integrity) is to encrypt it during transmission.

Requirement 4 spells out some specific details as it relates to these procedures for communication. Be sure you fully document your processes and procedures and roles and responsibilities are defined and understood (Requirements 4.1.1 and 4.1.2). Let's take a look at some of the specific PCI DSS sub-requirements to illuminate some of the terminology and the implications.

Requirement 4.2 mandates the use of strong cryptography and security protocols such as Transport-Layer Security (TLS), Internet Protocol Security (IPSec), or Secure Shell (SSH) to safeguard account data during transmission over open, public networks.

An open, public network is essentially any network that contains a gateway to the Internet at large. This describes the interchange in pretty much every business network. Anytime your cardholder data is transmitted over the Internet or any network you are unsure is secure, that data must be protected. Version 4.0 moved examples of these types of networks to the Guidance section of Requirement 4.2.1. Expanding on the list in the guidance, we suggest these include the Internet, any wireless network (Bluetooth, Wi-Fi, Cellular, and Satellite), Global System for Mobile Communications (GSM) or Code Division Multiple Access (CDMA), and General Packet Radio Service (GPRS) network are to be considered "open and public," while dedicated network relays are not. Others like ZigBee would fall into this category as well, so our list is not exhaustive.

The biggest change is to the newly inserted second bullet which now mandates that any company using certificates to safeguard account data must maintain a proper CA and certificate revocation list, and the certificate expiration and scope must be honored by the technology it's deployed on. You can run an internal CA, but it needs to be secured appropriately. Expired or revoked certificates must cause the technology to stop working.

Let's take a look at the specific protocols mentioned in PCI DSS and used for securing card data when transmitted over these various types of networks, and the way they are applied.

Transport Layer Security

TLS is a grouping of cryptographic protocols that are used for transferring information over networks such as the Internet. They both encrypt the data transferred between communicating endpoints as well as guarantee its integrity, such as a communication stream between a web browser and a server.

NOTE

A merchant asked Branden some time ago: if I have a TLS certificate on an e-commerce website, am I PCI DSS compliant?

After recovering from shock (after all, there are 360 pages of content that make up PCI DSS), Branden explained that TLS obviously does not guarantee PCI compliance. However, transmitting card data without TLS will certainly guarantee the absence of compliance.

All modern Web servers such as Apache, NGINX, and Microsoft IIS have long offered TLS support. Configuration of TLS on each individual server is beyond the scope of this book, but your favorite search engine offers many pointers to enabling TLS as does virtually every CA.

Don't forget, per the Council, outdated or outmoded cryptographic protocols such as all versions of SSL, SSH 1.0, and TLS prior to version 1.2 are no longer acceptable and cannot be deployed on systems that are involved in card processing and on external systems. You must at least use TLS 1.2 or later and SSH 2.0 or later. Keep up with emerging security protocols to make sure you are not caught by surprise. Various standards bodies keep recommended cipher and technology listings up to date and we suggest you reference them.

NOTE

A PCI DSS requirement clarification from the PCI Council now mandates that all approved scanning vendors (ASVs) detect the use of older cryptographic protocols and identify this as a failure to PCI validation via scanning, leading to loss of PCI compliance. We cover PCI ASV scanning in Chapter 9, Vulnerability Management and Testing. Specifically, the PCI Council stated it is imperative that an ASV identifies the use of older versions of SSL and TLS to transmit cardholder data as a failure.

To resolve these failures for PCI validation, discontinue the use of outdated SSL and TLS on all systems within the PCI scope. Having a user browse your site without that capability is not only rare, but you would be doing him a favor by directing him to a place where he can update his browser. There is an exception for older Point of Interaction (POI) terminals running outdated SSL or early TLS. Requirement A2.1.1 mandates that you confirm the devices are not susceptible to attacks that exploit those weaker protocols. Be sure to inventory these devices and prioritize them for replacement as they may not be EMV capable.

IPSEC VIRTUAL PRIVATE NETWORKS

IPsec is technically not just a protocol, but a framework or set of security protocols for data protection with cryptography. IPsec is often used for client-to-site or site-to-site virtual private networks (VPNs). A VPN can be described as a network that uses public infrastructure (like the Internet) to create a connection between a remote host or network and an organization's main or home network. This is a much less expensive proposition than using dedicated leased lines to provide this kind of privacy. VPNs set up a private tunnel using certain protocols, which causes the data to be encrypted at the sending end and decrypted at the receiving end. It can be configured in different ways, but typically involves the installation of connection software on the client, which establishes the secure tunnel to the home network and network devices on the home network end to serve as the secure gateway.

Most modern machines have various VPN technologies built into their operating system such that they do not require any additional or specialized software to be installed on the client end. When choosing a technology, you need to consider the speeds it can run at, the ease of managing the authentication aspects of the connection, and overall how this new virtual connection fits into your network diagram and security posture.

Irrespective of technology, you must maintain an inventory of the entity's trusted keys (Requirement 4.2.1.1), and any wireless networks that are involved must use industry best practices to implement strong cryptography that protects account data (Requirement 4.2.1.2).

NOTE

We mentioned some other wireless protocols that PCI DSS doesn't. GSM and CDMA refer to the communication systems that are used to support mobile phone networks. GPRS is a low-bandwidth wireless communication service that provides a connection to the Internet for data transfer for mobile phones and computers. Where this might affect a wireless network and transmission of card data would be the circumstances of using a GSM/GPRS modem card in a laptop, sled, or purpose-built device for a connection to the Internet. If the assessor observes you meeting the requirements for the implementation of a VPN and wireless protocols, it will satisfy issues related to these cards as well.

The PCI Council released the "PCI DSS 2.0 Wireless Guidelines" information supplement in August 2011 (still current as of this writing) which updates the original 2009 release to both line up with PCI DSS 2.0 as well as add new guidance for some emerging technologies to help merchants manage the security of their wireless requirements. Not too much has changed around wireless from 2.0 to 4.0, so until the council updates all of their supplemental documentation, you can use this document (found in the Document Library on the Council's website).

NOTE

One of the largest cardholder data breaches involved insufficient wireless security! In January of 2007, TJX Companies, which is the owner of several retail stores including TJ Maxx and Marshall's, reported a large data breach of customer credit and debit account numbers that occurred as early as 2003 through the beginning of 2007. TJX reported the theft of at least 94 million credit-card numbers. Attackers were able to steal the data through an insecure wireless network at a Marshall's store in Minnesota. Marshall's wireless network, which connected their credit-card processing hardware to the company's back-end systems, was not protected with Wi-Fi Protected Access (WPA) encryption, but rather was still using the unsafe and outdated WEP standard. Despite the fact that the WPA standard was introduced in 2002 and TJX had their back-end systems protected, this vulnerability gave TJX the dubious distinction of facilitating one of the largest cardholder data breaches on record.

MISCELLANEOUS CARD TRANSMISSION RULES

Finally, our Requirement 4 walk-through ends with what is simply an embodiment of common sense—Requirement 4.2.2 states that the PAN must be secured with strong cryptography when sent via end-user messaging technologies (e.g., e-mail, instant messaging, chat).

This one is a true *no-brainer* requirement with nothing else to add. Never e-mail plain card numbers—and never deal with anybody who does. By the way, this applies to attachments as well, not just to plain text e-mails.

Some merchants have asked about fax data transmission. It is obviously allowed but received faxes, especially if electronic, are subject to all the data protection rules, including physical security that governs data protection and access control. Also, if you see a fax machine in use these days, take a picture for your kids.

REQUIREMENT 12 WALK-THROUGH

Requirement 12, "Support Information Security with Organizational Policies and Programs," aims to protect card data from the non-technical side via policies and procedures. Requirement 12 is covered in several other chapters of the book. If you are looking for guidance on Service Provider Requirements 12.4, 12.5.2.1, 12.5.3, and 12.9, please see Chapter 14. For Requirements 12.5.2, 12.6.3.1, 12.6.3.2, 12.8.4, and 12.10 see Chapter 18.

Requirement 12.1.1 starts us off, mandating you establish, publish, maintain, and disseminate an overall information security policy. Details about the policy are specified in the guidance section. The main idea for compliance is that the policy exists, contains all the needed components, and is actively being used and updated on a periodic basis (Requirement 12.1.2). You will need to ensure the roles and responsibilities are clearly defined and those who are named have acknowledged and accepted their information security responsibilities (Requirement 12.1.3). Rounding out an expanded first requirement, you must formally assign a Chief Information Security Officer (or a member of the executive team with knowledge of security) for Requirement 12.1.4.

Remember, this policy should not be one massive document—it should be part of the policy framework in your governance structure. To make the document set more manageable, refrain from adding standards, guidelines, and procedures here. Stick to policy only.

While a deep dive into governance structures is out of scope for this book, let's take a moment to lay out some basic terms and what they mean. Policies are over-arching documents that define roles, limits of governance, and other ways that a company or group may act. They should not change often and should remain relatively constant. If you are changing them more than yearly, you probably have tactical or operational details buried in the policy. Next are standards, which set forth specific mandatory controls or actions for how to operationalize a procedure. These can change with the times, but should further define the sandbox in which you can play. Next are procedures, which are step-by-step instructions on completing certain tasks. Guidelines may exist, but are not required, to provide additional best practices for operations. And in some cases, you may have controls defined that give audit or other groups the ability to measure your performance against the governance program. For more information on how these governance structures work, consider looking at CoBIT.

Requirement 12.2.1 states that you must develop acceptable use policies for end-user technologies to include a list of products approved by the company for employee use, including hardware and software, acceptable uses of this technology, and explicit approval of all of this by the policy owner. This is a dramatic summarization of what made up 11 requirements in the last version of PCI DSS.

Requirement 12.3 expands the risk assessment requirements for PCI DSS 4.0. To start, every PCI DSS requirement that allows for flexibility in how frequently it is performed must have that flexible nature supported with a targeted risk assessment. For Requirement 12.3.1, you must document it fully and it must:

- Identify the assets being protected,
- Identify the threat that the requirement is protecting against,
- Identify the factors that contribute to the likelihood and/or impact of a threat being realized,
- Analyze the frequency the requirement must be performed to minimize the likelihood of the threat being realized and include justification for the result,
- Review each targeted risk analysis at least once every 12 months to determine whether the results are still valid or if an updated risk analysis is needed, and
- Perform the updated risk analyses when needed, as determined by the annual review.

Requirement 12.5.1 states that you must maintain an inventory of system components that are part of your PCI DSS scope. As we reviewed in Chapters 14 and 18, you must then confirm your scope in a formalized, documented process annually (or semi-annually for service providers). Our suggestion is to find a proper asset management tool that can be adapted to meet this requirement. Spreadsheets stored in the cloud or on SharePoint will surely cause the grandest of headaches.

Part of complying with PCI DSS means that you will build a security awareness program as an ongoing activity. Requirement 12.6.1 mandates a formal security awareness program be implemented to educate individuals working for and with your company on their role in protecting account data. It must be reviewed annually and updated as needed to reflect changes in threats or vulnerabilities the firm may face (Requirement 12.6.2). Requirement 12.6.3 states that the training is delivered upon hire and at least annually. You must use multiple methods for accomplishing this (such as small videos, formal classes, and computer-based training), but at a minimum, you must perform some kind of awareness training annually, and make your employees acknowledge that they have read and understand your security policy and procedures.

Don't forget that you must now include phishing and social engineering in your security aware-ness training (Requirement 12.6.3.1) and it must include training that covers acceptable end-user behaviors and technologies for Requirement 12.2.1 (Requirement 12.6.3.2). You must also provide specialized training for your personnel that respond to suspected and confirmed security incidents. Requirement 12.10.4.1 sets forth another targeted risk analysis that you must perform to determine the frequency of this specific type of periodic training.

PCI DSS is broad reaching in its requirements, so now we can bring in our human resource department for their very own requirement. Requirement 12.7.1 mandates employee screening, within the constraints of local laws, be performed on all employees *prior* to hiring them. The guid-ance section gives some examples of the types of checks you might do, but keep in mind this may vary from country to country depending on local laws.

One of the most critical requirements inside this section is Requirement 12.8, which covers your work with third-party service providers (TPSPs). If any cardholder data is shared with service providers, or you have service providers that could affect the security of cardholder data, you must maintain and implement policies and procedures to manage those service providers. This is one of the few requirements that is always present in your validation scope, even (especially!) if you out-source *all* operations with card data but still maintain your own Merchant ID.

One way to determine who a service provider is in the context of this requirement is to ask one question about their activities. Could Rob's IT Shop affect the security of cardholder data? If the answer is yes, add them to the list of companies covered under Requirement 12.8. Once you have your list of companies, you must maintain the list you just created (Requirement 12.8.1), ensure you have written agreements whereby the service provider acknowledges they are respon-sible for cardholder data security (Requirement 12.8.2), any *new* service provider that is brought on board must go through a diligence process before engaging them (Requirement 12.8.3), make sure you have a program to monitor your service providers' compliance to PCI DSS (Requirement 12.8.4), and finally, maintain information about which requirements are managed by each provider (Requirement 12.8.5).

NOTE

Did you notice that PCI DSS mandates that service providers must acknowledge in writing the data they will handle and that they are responsible for the security of that data? Requirement 12.8 is mostly a protection requirement for you. If you are a merchant and a breach of your data is caused by one of your service providers, you are liable. This requirement helps make both the merchant and service provider contractually aware of the security requirements. If you are a service provider that uses a service provider, things will follow the same path.

You can quickly dive into a series of dimensions you didn't realize existed. Fourth and fifth party providers can cause one of your controls to fail, putting you at risk for a breach.

The book website (www.pcibook.com) will contain sample policies and procedures, as well as links to resources that you can use to help jumpstart your Requirement 12 efforts.

HOW TO BECOME COMPLIANT AND SECURE

Now that we've looked at the particulars of the PCI requirements for protecting cardholder data and discussed some of the technologies and methods available to achieve compliance, let's take a step back and briefly discuss your approach.

Companies have been involved in handling PCI data long before PCI DSS existed. This means networks and systems designed without PCI DSS in mind all of the sudden had a different focus applied to them. If you started a company today that must comply with PCI DSS, you would most definitely design systems differently in light of PCI DSS. For example, you would probably minimize the use and transmission of card data on your network, and try to avoid storage altogether. Attempting to apply specific security standards after the fact is a different and difficult proposition.

By thinking logically through the requirement, both the letter and spirit, your business processes, and your IT environment, you can avoid a haphazard approach that can lead to problems such as inefficiency, unnecessary cost, insufficient controls, as well as unidentified risks or controls that are more restrictive than necessary.

We'd like to propose a process to satisfy these requirements. Understand that at any stage where you are doing something that increases your exposure to PCI DSS, you should provide references for discussion such that the larger team can evaluate if the assumptions that went into that initial decision are still valid. In many cases, you will find that the situation has changed in your favor, and it will allow you to accelerate your PCI DSS compliance program by reducing the scope.

STEP 1: IDENTIFY BUSINESS PROCESSES WITH CARD DATA

The first step is to simply create a list of all business processes that involve payment cards, electronic payments, card data, etc. Look at how those processes are implemented and what possible card data exposures there are. Analyze things like:

- Is account data being stored? Where? Why?
- What is my account data flow?
- Can the process be improved by reducing account data?
- Is there any prohibited data—CVV2, track, PIN, etc.—storage?

STEP 2: SHRINK THE SCOPE

After creating the list of processes that involve cards and account data—even if you outsource—focus on improving your PCI DSS program by reducing card exposure (see Chapter 4, Determining and Reducing PCI Scope, for more tips). This step needs to happen before any talk about encryption, truncation, or any other data masking begins. Also, at this stage, focus on eliminating the storage of prohibited data as this will block any chances at PCI DSS compliance.

STEP 3: IDENTIFY WHERE DATA IS STORED

Databases might house cardholder data, but where else might it be found? Flat files that are results of batch processing, log files, backup tapes, disaster recovery sites, and storage networks may all house sensitive information.

Ask the following questions:

- Where is the data located? Should it be?
- What format is it in (e.g., database, flat file)?
- What is the size of the data?

Answers to these questions will determine whether you have to make changes in your architecture to minimize the cost and work to protect the data. You will also probably need tools to validate your assumptions here. See Chapter 4, Determining and Reducing PCI Scope as well for tips.

STEP 4: DETERMINE WHAT TO DO ABOUT YOUR DATA

For each found location, consider what happens with it to bring it into compliance and reduce risk.

- Data is removed, and exposure to PCI DSS is eliminated.
- Data is truncated or hashed, thus reducing the risk of theft or loss.
- Data is encrypted using one of the discussed methods.

Only resort to encryption after you have tried other methods. Both of us have found that when you are talking to someone about removing data, they quickly push back. Change is scary. We like to kick off the conversation with something like, "The data is gone. How will you perform your daily duties?" Re-framing this as a recovery process may help access parts of your colleague's brain that remain idle when asked to brainstorm ideas on how to remove data.

NOTE

We love problem-solving! Both of us spent a significant amount of time in consulting roles, and generally being handed broken things with the "See what you can do with this" request. For a couple of classic articles with tools on problem-solving and problem re-framing, check out Dwayne Spradlin's 2012 Harvard Business Review (HBR) article "Are you solving the right problem?" and an almost identically named HBR article from 2017 by Thomas Wedell-Wedellsborg, "Are you solving the right problems?" Both of these have excellent tips for improving your problem-solving skills and can be freely obtained from hbr.org with a registered account.

STEP 5: DETERMINE WHO NEEDS ACCESS

Too often, data breaches take place simply because people and applications have access to data they do not need. You have to balance the need for access with the proper control on that access to keep doing business.

Answer these questions:

- Who currently has access to the remaining repositories of sensitive data?
- Do they need access to those repositories to do their jobs?
- What applications, such as backup applications or websites, need access?

Plan changes based on what is found.

STEP 6: DEVELOP AND DOCUMENT POLICIES

Now that you have identified what data you have, where your data is located, how it is protected, and who and what needs to access it, you can define, document, and implement information-handling policies based on what, where, who, when, and how. This is where you establish such things as policies, standards, guidelines, and procedures. These policies and procedures, as well as their implementation, are what a QSA would review to validate your PCI DSS compliance.

COMMON MISTAKES AND PITFALLS

Based on the discussions you find in the media around data protection, you might think that data encryption is everywhere. However, is this "good" encryption? Does it help you to protect the data from attackers while allowing for easy PCI compliance? A classic saying "Encryption is easy; key management is hard" illustrates one of the pitfalls that await those implementing encryption, and it is reflected in Requirement 3. While Requirement 3.5 simply states the need for encryption, the complexity of key management shows when you are reviewing Requirements 3.6 and 3.7 with their multiple sub-requirements. Let's look at some of the common mistakes that often occur when organizations try to use encryption to protect data at rest and data in transit, as well as achieve PCI compliance.

Before we start with the first mistake, how about we number this one mistake zero—thinking that PCI DSS data protection requirements are about encryption. Instead, they are about not letting the hackers get access to the data. As you've learned, *secure data deletion* is more reliable than *data encryption* as a means of denying your opponent's access to data. So, don't encrypt what you can delete, or data you don't need to store.

The first mistake is not using encryption when it is both easy and mandatory. Unencrypted protocols are outdated and largely dangerous to use these days. Every modern operating system has the capacity to do basic encryption both during transmission and storage, so start using it.

The second mistake has been mentioned by most cryptographers out there: inventing your own cryptographic algorithm. Cryptography is a science just like physics and mathematics; in fact, it is based on the latter. This is an area where amateurs have no place. Use publicly vetted algorithms and follow industry guidance on key strength and rotation, and be sure to stay up to date on which algorithms you use are no longer secure (for example, DES or SHA1).

An interesting extension of this mistake has to do with failing to correctly implement a well-designed cryptographic algorithm. Indeed, algorithm design is hard, but quality implementation isn't an easy job either. As a result, people who chose to re-invent a "known good" crypto algorithm might be doing themselves a disservice (see WEP), if a proven implementation exists (as a cryptographic library, for example).

Every reader will probably recognize the third mistake: "hard-coding" secrets, such as passwords and keys. As we know, security of a quality cryptographic algorithm does not depend on its secrecy, but on its key or password. If you inadvertently make such passwords available for attackers, the game is over. It's still a big enough problem that there are services that look for GitHub commits that contain keys. Embedding passwords in code (binaries), configuration files, Web pages, style sheets, or other "hidden" files are just providing your secret to attackers. And, no, your XORing the password with a string of characters does not count; it just replaces your credible "secured by AES" label with the purely humorous tag "protected by the power of XOR."

Hard-coded secrets led to many disasters in information security history. DVD and HD-DVD encryption breaches are just the most famous of them. The extensions of such error, where passwords are hidden in files to enable scripting or automation, have helped attackers to extend their control over the compromised networks. One cannot argue that system administrators need to automate routine tasks, but root passwords in scripts and configuration files should be as archaic as double-digit years. Don't forget that while dev environments are not typically in scope, they cultivate a sandbox mentality where secrets are often housed for ease of use in these environments. Make sure your development keys and secrets are different from your production ones, and they are not moved from development to test to production as part of your code promotion process.

As we learned in this chapter, database encryption is common and nearly all database vendors natively support it—their claim is that it is easy to just protect your database by encrypting it. Great! The task is done and the data is secured by a well-implemented encryption algorithm. The fourth mistake is not thinking rationally about where to place the key and storing it in the same place as you store the data. Branden is aware of a few organizations who sought to protect their databases by encrypting the tables with sensitive data and then storing the key in another table on the same database server.

While we're at it, think about the following as well: while you might not leave the keys in an obvious place such as a database table, do you prevent key leakage into swap files, crash dumps, logs, and other areas that might be seen by attackers? This is much more insidious, and a detailed discussion goes beyond the scope of this book.

Finally, the fifth mistake becomes relevant when you leave out procedures for data recovery. Ask yourself if your crypto implementation passes the "lottery test." If the employee who knows the keys to your encrypted data and how they are used and managed wins the lottery and disappears forever, will you be able to get your data back? PCI DSS does not mandate that you create procedures to ensure the availability of decryption keys, but it does not mean that you can avoid it.

If you implemented cryptography correctly such that there is no way to bypass the security it provides and at the same time you didn't think about data recovery, your implementation will likely not pass the lottery test. As a result, the data would be as good as gone in case of a key loss. Key revocation and data recovery is a critical piece of the security puzzle.

Data protection is a critical piece of your information security program and encryption plays a major role in it. However, try to avoid the aforementioned pitfalls and consider data encryption to be that long-sought security "silver bullet." Don't encrypt what you can destroy!

CASE STUDY

The case study below illustrates how removal of card data from the environment, as well as various security measures, helps to achieve compliance and security.

THE CASE OF THE LEAKY DATA

Kristin's Komix, a vintage cartoon and paraphernalia store, started selling online to fans back in 1997. In that ancient age of e-commerce, when the terms *new economy*, *dot-coms*, and *e-commerce* were new and cool, most website owners who wished to sell something from their sites had to find shopping cart software and install it on their sites. Often, especially for free and open-source shopping cart tools, they had to get into the code and change a few things here and there to customize and adapt the tool for their sites.

This is exactly what Kristin did: she grabbed the Bob and Garry Epic Fail of a Shopping Cart software package and dropped it on her site. After the package was installed, she checked whether the visitors of her site can click on the links and buttons, edited the code of the shopping cart to change variables, and finally configured the card processing capability.

While this scenario is unthinkable in our enlightened internet age, remember that this was 1997!

After all required configuration "magic" was done, she advertised to her customers and to a local community that she was the first to do e-commerce in the entire industry.

For a few years, Kristin was happily selling old cartoons and charging her customer's cards, totally oblivious to the threats and the emergence of PCI DSS in later years. However, as she discovered later, someone else was charging some of those cards as well. Unbeknownst to Kristin's IT team, her shopping cart was deployed in debug mode and actually logged all the cards into a big text file, located in the same directory, and anybody browsing to www.kristinskomix.com/epicfailcart/debug_card_log.txt will be able to download the ever-growing card log that contained the following:

```
date, time, name, PAN, exp, amount.
```

In other words, most of the details on the cardholders, with the exception of their address, which was not commonly needed for the transactions in the 1990s.

Unfortunately for Kristin, this file location was well-known to more than a few malicious hackers, and the cards were pilfered and used—in moderation, of course, to avoid the suspicions—for various purchases worldwide.

When Kristin came to grips that her data was being used for fraud as well as the reality of PCI, what was the first step she took?

Did she reach out for those encryption tools? Data masking? An advanced cart software?

No, she picked the right choice—she went with Stripe for all payment processing. No more cards—far less risk!

THE CASE OF THE SATELLITE LOCATION

Barbie's Booze, a specialty spirits shop in downtown Chicago was running out of room. Barbie got a fantastic deal on rent for her store and regularly had a packed location whereby she moved impressive amounts of inventory to local residents. She was beginning to need some support staff to handle all of the back office administrative requirements, and she couldn't justify removing floor space to create workstations for her staff. She decided she would open a satellite location roughly two miles away in a space purpose built for offices.

She knew she would need to connect the offices so that her electronic systems would be able to function over the distance. She found a deal on a used Checkpoint firewall set and promptly had an IT person set up a VPN for her sites to use. Unfortunately, her IT person was not well versed in this version of Checkpoint, and the VPN that was set up between the two sites did not have any encryption deployed over the link (yes, it is possible to do this). As information was being transferred from site to site, all of her daily accounting information (including credit card numbers) was exposed to a public network.

Barbie hired a QSA to do a quick review for PCI Compliance as her acquirer informed her she would soon become a Level 2 merchant. She researched and found a good QSA that really understood how her business works as well as had a background in systems and network administration. He quickly informed Barbie of the issue and gave her tips to encrypt the link between the two locations. She contacted her bank and informed them of the issue. An investigation ensued, and she dodged a bullet. Her service provider had coincidentally connected both of her lines from a single Central Office (CO), and the telco was able to walk the bank through the security controls contained inside that CO. The bank felt satisfied that no breach occurred during the 30 days where the link was used without encryption.

Barbie learned that when she was deploying technology to support her business, she needed to ensure that the people installing and configuring the technology were in fact experts, and not just generalists that could make the product work, but not work securely.

SUMMARY

PCI DSS data protection requirements are among the most challenging parts of PCI as they deal with highly technical topics like encryption algorithms, key management, and data destruction.

Here is a deceptively simple answer to your encryption worries: don't do it! If you eliminate data storage, you eliminate the need to protect data at rest, which takes care of a massive amount of complexity in Requirement 3.

Similarly, if you eliminate the movement of card data over insecure networks, Requirement 4 will become simpler. With the proper preparation and execution of your plan, you can protect the information you have been entrusted with.

NOTES

1 Sometimes *data in use* is added to this; in the context of PCI DSS, *data in use* often translated to specific requirements on the handling of account data as part of payment application security, covered by PCI SSF.

2 Temporary memory storage is implicitly allowed based on pre- versus post-authorization language, but be aware of debug-level logging of data when engineers are working on problems prior (or even in) production. In addition, the Guidance for Requirement 3.3.2 says that Issuers are the only entity that may store this data if there is a legitimate reason to do so (i.e., necessary for the performance of whatever function the issuer is doing, and not for convenience), and should refer to Requirement 3.3.3 for more information.

3 However, in this case, the unencrypted card data may be stolen while in use. Some card processor breaches were made possible by hackers using this technique. Neither data in motion nor data at rest encryption techniques could have helped for that case.

8 Using Wireless Networking

Information in this chapter:

- What Is Wireless Network Security?
- Where Is Wireless Network Security in PCI DSS?
- Why Do We Need Wireless Network Security?
- Tools and Best Practices
- Common Mistakes and Pitfalls
- Case Study
- Summary

Wireless technologies continue to advance in both speed and proliferation. In 2022, patterns have shifted such that it's rare to see small merchants running wired-only infrastructures in storefronts, and wireless technology is pretty much everywhere. Most big-box retailers already use Wi-Fi® for inventory management, curbside delivery, and customer access and have dealt with upgrading portions of their outdated technology to comply with the Payment Card Industry Data Security Standard (PCI DSS). Smaller retailers only have wireless networks in their locations, which cuts costs on store build-out and allows business owners to add additional registers in parking lots or other outdoor areas. For those who are sitting on the bleeding edge or who just love to experiment with the capabilities of radio frequency (RF) communication, point of sale (POS) networks can work over Bluetooth® or ZigBee®. We shudder to think about those kinds of networks, but it is possible and more likely to be used as those and other technologies mature. Wireless networks don't stop at Wi-Fi or Bluetooth, however.

The reliability, coverage, and speed of cellular data networks created an opportunity for a new class of card processing terminals that can process cards without Wi-Fi or hard-wired Internet connections. As we saw the effects of convergence in our mobile telephones over the last two decades, we are seeing the same effects in the payment terminal market. Not only are the terminals becoming smaller and more functional, but some companies have gone completely paperless with their field technicians. Many companies are now giving both purpose-built devices and tablet computers to their field technicians to prioritize work lists, give directions on where to go, provide traffic updates to keep their schedules efficient, keep track of spare part inventory while sending that information back to headquarters, and finally accepting a credit card for payment either via a sled or a built-in reader.

Of course, terminals don't need to be that sophisticated to be in scope! Think about the last time you went to an outdoor festival or arts and crafts fair. If you ran out of cash, you had two options. You could either run over to that ATM on the street that only seemed to need a long orange extension cord to operate or pay for your wares directly with the merchant through a credit card terminal. Depending on how hot the sun was or how many adult beverages you may have consumed, you probably didn't think too much of it. Both of those options look and feel like the ones you see indoors but with one major difference. They are not connected to any sort of wired network!

The intent of PCI DSS with respect to wireless technologies is to impose a subset of the requirements on any communication between two devices that does not occur over a wired network. If your firm leverages wireless in a way that enables the storage, processing, or transmission of account data, it is in scope. Any wireless-enabled devices connected to the CDE are also included in the scope. It's important to look for wireless technology where it shouldn't be—so even if you are here thinking *oh we don't use any wireless technologies*, you still have work to do.

DOI: 10.1201/9781003100300-8

This chapter covers some of the basics of wireless payment processing as well as the pitfalls for which you need to be aware. Although not foolproof, the basic concepts here keep your assessors and acquirers happy as well as placate the business development and security professionals at your company.

WHAT IS WIRELESS NETWORK SECURITY?

When Branden thinks about his first wireless network, he remembers that his access point (AP) was the only one within range of his laptop's Wi-Fi card. You know, the big fat credit card-sized ones that plugged into that fancy Personal Computer Memory Card International Association (PCMCIA) slot on your laptop? Or even better, that brick you carried around that plugged into the USB port?

Today we are upset if our new dishwasher isn't Wi-Fi enabled and controllable by Alexa.

Not long after his first foray into Wi-Fi, Branden noticed another wireless AP suddenly appearing as an available network to join. He protected his Wi-Fi network with a 64-bit Wired Equivalent Privacy (WEP) key (128-bit keys were not available on the hardware at the time) just to see how it worked, but he noticed that his new "target network" did not. Curious, he joined the other network.

Although the signal strength was not fantastic, he was still able to browse the Internet at a slow pace, no doubt riding the same cable modem service that was coming into his own house. He decided to probe a little bit further, and sure enough, an open file share was available on one of the machines connected to the network!

Curiosity aside, Branden's neighbor clearly believed that he was either the first person to install wireless in his area or that his signal did not extend beyond his four walls. The latter is the most common misconception carried by individuals, even though they can receive a mobile telephone, television, and radio signals inside the very same four walls that they expect will block Wi-Fi.

Now imagine that same individual several years later having a brilliant brainstorm that includes deploying Wi-Fi into his store location so he can sit out among the patrons with his laptop but still get his company business done. You can probably see where this is going. He made the fatal mistake of assuming that nobody would want to tinker with his little store's Wi-Fi network. Not long after connecting his cheap AP, he received a phone call from his acquiring bank notifying him that he may have a problem.

Wireless networks, and specifically Wi-Fi networks, are frequently the target of both nuisance and sophisticated attacks. Wi-Fi networks in particular are attractive to attackers because the cost to acquire the equipment used in the attack is minimal. Cellular network hacking is even cheap and easy due to hacked baseband radios and femtocells (those little cellular extension boxes you plug into your home network when you can't get good cellular coverage in your home). What used to cost six figures to acquire now can be had for well under $200 with some creative hacking and know-how.

In addition, smaller devices that participate in the payments system—like that little Square EMV-enabling puck that you see at some merchant shops—use other methods to connect and converse. Bluetooth, Bluetooth Low Energy, and maybe even a ZigBee network are all possible and increasingly probable.

It just goes to show that you should never trust the actual transport mechanism of your communications. Verify that it is configured securely.

Technology has come a long way and the chips our technology uses are quite capable of encrypting data before dropping it to a network connection with minimal impact to performance. Satellite networks don't have an advantage over Wi-Fi and cellular networks anymore as the equipment required to go after satellite networks is inexpensive but still requires specific training or knowledge to carry out a successful attack.[1] Satellite network hacking will continue and should have the same level of trust as Wi-Fi. These networks should never ignore things like good security and encryption, but often, the cost to acquire the equipment necessary to hack those networks is incorrectly seen as a security control (financial constraints).

To clear the air, they are not.

Early implementations of Wi-Fi only offered WEP encryption. Although the underlying algorithm was solid (RC4), the implementation of the algorithm caused encryption key information to be leaked with each packet. When used in a certain way, this information leads to the compromise of the WEP key (see the "Common Mistakes and Pitfalls" section of this chapter). With the key in hand, attackers could decode every single packet over the air, allowing him to dump information in a manner not too dissimilar from sniffing traffic via a network span port on a switch. Usernames, passwords, company secrets, and customer information were now all available until the key was changed. Because the keys could be compromised in a few minutes, key changes did not stop the attacks.

Wi-Fi attacks today are a bit more complicated, but there are devices such as the Hak5 Wi-Fi Pineapple that automate much of the attack process. Operating the device guarantees nothing, but in the right hands, modern Wi-Fi security is still very breakable. If you are concerned, remember that just like passwords, length in your Wi-Fi key will beat complexity in a strength contest. Some of the most secure passphrases we've seen are ones that are just complete sentences. Maybe something as simple as "Philly's cheese head makes every customer's heart happy!" There is nothing to say you cannot use the entire 64-character space to secure your network.

Along those lines, when connecting to networks you do not control, assume they are compromised or malicious. Your devices will give you clues when things are not right through certificate errors or simply not connecting to the Internet at all. Don't ignore these, and don't click through these errors unless you know exactly what you are doing and exactly what the risk is. For an example of some older Nation State attacks involving Wi-Fi, drop "DarkHotel attacks" into your nearest search engine to learn more.

But don't totally feel comfortable with your WPA2 or WPA3 setups either. If you so choose, you can take specific packets from a capture and upload them into a number of cloud services that will crack the password for you for a fee (use your favorite search engine to find them). The point is you should never trust the link layer encryption when packets are moving through the air.

Basic security functionality like disabling Service Set IDentifier (SSID) broadcast and Media Access Control (MAC) address filtering is more security theater than actually counting as a security control. These features are easily overcome by anyone with a basic understanding of wireless networking and the proper tools. Remember, wireless encryption only protects the payload, but it does not encapsulate the entire packet from a laptop to the AP. This means that both the SSID and MAC addresses can be seen by a casual observer regardless of the encryption technology deployed, and both of these values can be configured on any Wi-Fi card to perform a successful attack.

Worse yet, now that the casual observer has examples of legitimate hosts (and their hardware addressing) as well as the key, he could join the network and poke around looking like a legitimate device on the network. He could easily map the defenses (if any) deployed by watching for a firewall to stop his probes. For the most part, these dropped packets are not logged, or if logged are never analyzed, so he could poke around undetected for as long as he wanted. Store and internal networks in general used to be completely devoid of firewalls, but key IT investments for PCI compliance have changed that dramatically over the last decade. It's not anywhere close to the level it needs to be, but attackers are more likely to encounter a firewall today than they were 10 years ago. Many famous cardholder data compromises start like this.

WHERE IS WIRELESS NETWORK SECURITY IN PCI DSS?

For the most part, PCI DSS only sets the stage for a baseline of wireless security. PCI DSS's handling of wireless network security is a prime example of how PCI DSS compliance does not necessarily mean you are secure.

Little has changed up front in PCI DSS 4.0, but there is a small section on wireless that is helpful to review. Notice this revision still includes the acronym WLAN (Wireless LAN) in reference to wireless networks. It's pretty complete as far as giving you a definition of what is in scope for PCI DSS. When in doubt, assume it is in scope.

WARNING

Manufacturers of cellular or satellite products tell you they are safer to use because of the difficulty in intercepting the traffic, just as the ones that manufacture and sell Frequency-Hopping Spread Spectrum (FHSS) radios will. Using a more obscure spectrum like General Mobile Radio Service (GMRS), which may already be deployed in larger locations to facilitate communication among the staff, doesn't add any security to your payments either. Security by obscurity is a foolish way to protect yourself against the bad guys. Eventually, someone will (or in many cases already has) figure out a cheap way to intercept communications like this and the game will be over. The technology may lend itself to a lower risk of compromise today, but that doesn't mean it will be that way forever. Be sure you are using industry-standard stream-ciphers over these networks and consider using VPN technologies to add another layer of protection. Use Mutual TLS authentication (meaning, clients have approved certificates and are authenticated by the server before communication commences) and leverage Endpoint Detection and Response tools to protect your endpoints. And remember that any wireless technology in use must comply with these requirements!

Companies wishing to comply with PCI DSS must minimally address several requirements, even if wireless is not deployed in the target environment. Those are 1.2.3, 1.3.3, 2.3.1, 2.3.2, 4.2.1, 4.2.1.2, 9.2.3, 11.2.1, 11.2.2, 12.2.1, 12.10.1, 12.10.3, and 12.10.5. Let's explore how companies can meet those requirements.

NOTE

If you think that you have no legitimate wireless in your production environment, at a minimum you still must address the actions mandated by Requirements 11.2.1, 12.10.3, and 12.10.5. Rogue, or unauthorized, APs in your cardholder environment can be lurking without your knowledge.

REQUIREMENTS 1, 11, AND 12: DOCUMENTATION

The first step, as is with most parts of PCI, is to document! 1.2.3 was referenced in Chapter 5, Building and Maintaining a Secure Network, but it has applicability here specifically for wireless networks. Any wireless networks that are permissible in your environment should be documented in the network diagram you present to assessors. As an example, let's say that the only wireless permitted in your environment is a vendor wireless network that only has limited Internet access. Your network should already have a firewall between the unsecured wireless network and the corporate network. That action alone helps you meet most of the PCI DSS. Even though it is not connected to any card processing networks, nor does it process cards itself, placing it on the diagram helps to illustrate that you have your ducks in a row. You can also expect that your assessors will cross-reference with 11.2.1 and 11.2.2 for authorized devices.

NOTE

Good QSAs are trained to look for inconsistencies and oversights. If a QSA asks for a network diagram and you provide one that doesn't include Wi-Fi, yet the QSA is connecting to their corporate network using a Wi-Fi network from your company, they will start to ask themselves, "What else are they not telling me?"

Requirement 1.3.3 mandates that Network Security Controls (NSCs) be installed between any in-scope networks and the wireless network. This is pretty self-explanatory, but the part that can trip companies up is defining what is acceptable as an NSC. An NSC can be many different types of devices. Some are clear-cut examples such as a traditional firewall, but others—especially software-defined ones—might be trickier. You can go back to the preamble for Requirement 1 and look at Chapter 5, Building and Maintaining a Secure Network. The main point here is to put some kind of enforcement point between the wireless and wired network—preferably a logical or physical stand-alone firewall—where the wireless network exists on the untrusted side of the device.

A clarification for Requirement 1.3.3 in PCI DSS 4.0 is that if your wireless networks are part of your CDE, you still need to put NSCs to segment it "regardless of whether the wireless network is a CDE." Good practice would have NSCs between wireless and other networks, but just make sure that if you have an in-scope wireless network that is part of your CDE, you need to shore up your NSCs that protect the wired side.

Since you will be leveraging segmentation, you can expect that your QSA will want to see the report that shows how someone tested this enforcement point as well. It's part of requirement 11.4.5 in PCI DSS 4.0.

Speaking of Requirement 11, 11.2 is reorganized to include two elements that are required for compliance. 11.2.1 requires documentation to include that you mandate testing for the presence of wireless APs, all authorized and unauthorized APs are discovered and noted, that this testing occurs at least once every three months, and that any automated monitoring results in alerts that go to personnel who will respond to them. For Requirement 11.2.2, you must maintain an inventory of authorized wireless APs and that the list includes business justification for each one. Your QSA should ask to see a few of the APs around the office for verification that this is happening.

Zooming to Requirement 12, we have more documentation-related items to address. Requirement 12.2.1 is now more of a rollup of 10 requirements in the old version of PCI, including wireless technologies. Remember, this is a policy document. If you set a company policy, your internal audit group should conduct periodic reviews to ensure that the policies are being followed. Your QSA is not required to dig that deep, but if a corporate policy that has not been followed leads to a breach, you won't receive safe harbor protection under the various card brand operating rules or applicable state or federal laws. The focus for 12.2.1 targets explicit management approval, acceptable uses for any technology that falls in this scope, and a list of the hardware and software products that are approved for use.

Most companies that deploy this type of technology can address the wireless components as part of their broader policy covering Requirement 12.2.1.

Next in Requirement 12 are 12.10.1 and 12.10.3, which require that your incident response personnel are available 24/7 for both incident response and monitoring looking for any evidence of unauthorized activity, the keys and passwords used to protect wireless networks, unauthorized wireless APs, and able to manage critical IDS alerts or reports of unauthorized file changes. If you follow PCI DSS to the letter, you might be thinking that the possibility of activating this clause in your incident response plan seems fairly remote. Here's a hint: we hope it is. We'll get into that more later in the "Testing for Unauthorized Wireless: Requirement 11.2.1" section of this chapter.

Finally, Requirement 12.10.5 mandates that your incident response plan has documentation on how to handle an unauthorized wireless AP when detected.

ACTUAL SECURITY OF WIRELESS DEVICES: REQUIREMENTS 2, 4, AND 9

By now, you are probably wondering when we will get to those fancy encryption requirements! It goes without saying, but building a secure environment where you operate any sort of technology starts with good and complete documentation. Part of your wireless usage and deployment standards should include select elements from Requirements 2, 4, and 9.

Wireless encryption technologies have come a long way from their inception. Just two decades ago, the only options for wireless encryption were WEP or tunneling encryption inside your wireless connection such as a VPN or Secure Socket Layer (SSL) connection. Now, there are a multitude of options for both encryption and authentication. Be sure whatever you use in your organization is a current product that is maintained and receives security patches. Make sure it also supports the latest security features to ensure you will be able to comply with PCI DSS.

Requirements 2.3.1 and 2.3.2 list several items that QSAs must check for to validate compliance. Your wireless installation should (at a minimum):

- Have unique encryption keys (i.e., not default) that are changed anytime anyone with knowledge of the keys leaves the company or changes positions or if the key is suspected to be compromised,
- Change default Simple Network Management Protocol (SNMP) community strings,
- Change default passwords/passphrases on APs, and
- Change other security-related wireless vendor defaults.

Remember, these devices must still be receiving firmware updates to address security vulnerabilities.

This leads us quickly into Requirement 4.2.1 that mandates strong cryptography and security protocols be implemented on these networks (i.e., you cannot deploy WEP here, you must use modern, strong encryption protections). Industry best practices should be used for encryption with respect to authentication and transmission for wireless networks (Requirement 4.2.1.2).

NOTE

Some of the attacks against wireless networks start by gathering lots of traffic; either by performing injection or deauthentication (DEAUTH) attacks, or by selectively targeting certain clients to force them to connect to your AP instead of the actual one (Evil Twin). More captured traffic means more cryptanalysis and the more likely an attack against the key will be successful. On top of that, shared keys are just that—*shared*. Everything you learn about information security screams "Don't do that!"

WPA2/WPA3 provide networks with a significant boost in security by authenticating individual users through certificates or usernames and passwords. Additionally, devices that use WPA2/WPA3 benefit from mutual authentication, meaning that the device itself can authenticate the AP it uses making Evil Twin type attacks much more difficult to perform.

What constitutes an industry best practice for wireless security? For Wi-Fi installations, WPA2 or WPA3 should be deployed. New installations using Wi-Fi should absolutely use WPA2/WPA3 with some form of unique authentication, sometimes called "Enterprise" in your configuration. Don't forget to change your defaults! If you are curious what common attacks you might see depending on the type of security you deploy, seek out answers in your nearest search engine. Don't use shared keys (sometimes called WPA-Personal). They are a pain to deal with and, for large installations, virtually impossible to maintain according to PCI DSS. Often times you will see Guest Wi-Fi networks using a general password. This is acceptable as long as the guest network isn't connected to the corporate network or the CDE.

A concrete example for store locations that offer Wi-Fi access to guests is to make sure your back-of-house store network is separate from your front-of-house point of sale network, both of which would be separate from your guest Wi-Fi. Yes, that's three different networks to configure, separate, and maintain.

Given these constraints, your security is only as strong as the users that use it daily. Basic passwords may be easily cracked through cloud cracking services with only a few packets captured. Consider other methods of authentication and key derivation, and consider additive security measures to protect information going through the air.

For other wireless technologies such as satellite, cellular, or microwave, encrypt transmissions with a current stream cipher such as the Advanced Encryption Standard (AES), or Elliptical Curve

Cryptography (ECC), or an industry-accepted algorithm of equivalent or better strength. New algorithms are coming out all the time, so you have plenty to choose from. Whatever method you choose, be sure it is documented with approved configurations, and ensure you have done a proper risk assessment against the technology to understand what your periodic obligations may be. Don't rely on the cost of communication interception equipment to secure these increasingly popular forms of communication. Such reliance is both risky and could lead to a false sense of security, further putting your company at risk.

Requirement 9.2.3 mandates physical protection for wireless devices, as well networking and communications hardware and telecommunication lines. APs should be kept under lock and key, behind badged access doors, or in some cases, they should be protected with a cage. The intent of this requirement is to prevent an unauthorized user from tampering with the device. Don't rely on a high ceiling to protect the APs deployed on or above it. Ladders are readily available here in the 21st century. For that reason, don't rely on other physical hiding techniques, such as disguising your AP as a smoke detector, to secure your hardware.

Logging and Wireless Networks: Requirement 10.3.3

Wireless gets a quick mention in the logging requirements for PCI DSS. Be sure to include wireless logs from your AP in your centralized logging solution. Different vendors have different ways of communicating logging data but most can dump data via syslog. Piggybacking on the same infrastructure that collects logs from routers and switches is trivial to do.

Testing for Unauthorized Wireless: Requirement 11.2

When it comes to wireless, there is no requirement more debated than 11.2.1. Security and compliance may not be farther apart anywhere else in the standard than they are right here. On one side, merchants are equipping district managers with basic wireless tools and making sure they hit each of their stores at least once a quarter. These merchants rarely are able to be compliant with the standard all year long as invariably stores are missed and equipment fails. Managers don't understand why they have to do it, and every merchant has at least one maverick out there that would opt to buzz the tower instead of respecting the controller's wishes.

NOTE

The intent of Requirement 11.2.1 is to discover and address unauthorized wireless devices. Unauthorized devices can show up in your environment even with a "No Wireless" policy. Breaches can easily come from the wireless device you don't know is there.

On the other end of the spectrum, you have wireless defense vendors who tell their prospects that they cannot comply with PCI DSS unless they buy and deploy their wireless intrusion detection system (IDS) or intrusion prevention system (IPS) solution. Branden knows he has ruined a few salespeople's quarters by giving merchants alternatives to deploying wireless IPS. Early deployments were often costly, and retailers of any substantial size face mounting costs in deploying and operating the technology in each store. A $2,000 cash outlay for one location may be easy to swallow, but that same outlay for a hundred or a thousand locations is significant. Add to that the ongoing operational costs of maintaining the infrastructure, and things start to get out of hand.

In extremely rare cases, some merchants have sophisticated enough network equipment to positively identify every device plugged into their network with automatic quarantine capabilities when devices that should not be active are plugged in. The numbers of ways you can attack this particular requirement are numerous, and the effective security of these solutions varies greatly.

We would like all those wireless IDS and IPS vendors to cover their ears for the duration of this paragraph. Just skip the rest of this paragraph, and go to the next one. Neither James nor Branden want to see this show up in a marketing slick, seriously. For the rest of you, the wireless vendors really do have your best interests in mind when they are pushing their products as a method to meet this requirement. One vendor, in particular, has a great analogy about scanning each store once per quarter (as the requirement states). It's equivalent of turning your firewall on for a few hours on one day each quarter, then assuming nobody would want to come in and attack you until you turn it on for that one day next quarter. This analogy is fitting because it helps put things into context. It's also a great illustration of the difference between compliance and security.

With PCI DSS 4.0 and the Customized Approach, the Council has made the language here a bit more generic which offers you more options on how you wish to comply. While compliance with Requirement 11.2.1 could mean that at a minimum, you must scan each location with a wireless analyzer each quarter to identify all wireless devices, the language is such that you own the decision on the *how* portion of the detection. Should an unauthorized one show up, it should be traced down and efforts made to ensure that it is not affecting the security of the cardholder network. Alternatively, you can use a Wireless IDS or IPS to identify these devices in real-time, and in some cases, take action against them to prevent them from functioning on the network. Here is a quick breakdown of the sub-requirements:

- You must have a documented process to detect and identify wireless APs on a quarterly basis.
- Ensure the methodology used above is adequate to detect and identify all authorized and unauthorized devices.
- Alerts must be going to personnel responsible for responding to automated alerts if you choose to use those.
- You must maintain an inventory of authorized wireless devices with business justification for them all.
- Your incident response plan includes a response in the event unauthorized wireless devices are detected (overlap with 12.10.1 and 12.10.3).

If you are using a Wi-Fi POS system for your stores, do yourself a favor and deploy an AP that has IDS and IPS functionality out of the box. Then, enable it and ensure that it meets Requirement 11.2.1. If your plans include Wi-Fi POS, you should do everything you can to defend those devices. Make no mistake; if you deploy it, the attackers will come.

Quarterly Sweeps or Wireless IDS/IPS: How to Choose

As with most parts of complying with PCI DSS, there is no clear solution or silver bullet. Let's explore where one might be better than the other.

Automated solutions are slick. They provide scalability (usually) and do much of the thinking for us. If you have Wi-Fi technology in your locations, using a Wireless IDS or IPS solution is probably going to be the best way to handle security and compliance with PCI DSS. If you have a proven rapid response time in the field, a Wireless IDS may work well for you. The difference is similar to network IDS and IPS technologies we discussed in Chapter 5, Building and Maintaining a Secure Network. Wireless IDS will only tell you about the problem, and then, you must take action. In order to make IDS an effective solution, you must have some kind of 24/7 response and appropriate staffing.

Wireless IPS solutions typically come on the same hardware and carry incrementally insignificant costs over the wireless IDS solutions. If you don't have a proven response time or don't want to staff up accordingly, go with the IPS solution instead. Let it alert, but also let it take action. You will spend more time up front configuring it to not interrupt normal business activities, but overall IPS can carry a lower cost to your organization (when properly tuned and maintained).

So with all this fancy technology, why would we go the manual route? For a couple of reasons, but the number one reason typically being cost. Companies considering this option will only have limited network capabilities in their locations, such as a storefront. If all of the network connectivity comes in through a random cable from the wall into a device with four ports on it, and all four ports are in use by equipment required to run the business, regular visual inspection of this equipment (shift change is a good time to do this) may be sufficient enough to protect the enterprise and only rely on the quarterly sweep to identify any rogue devices. It's not foolproof (as any number of security pundits could no doubt come up with a list of ways to defeat this control), but based on the risk, it could definitely be both an acceptable compliance and security control. In addition, deploying technologies like 802.1X authentication or Network Access Control (NAC) can prevent a rogue AP from joining your network.

Make no mistake, quarterly, manual scanning for wireless devices might be the best example of security theater we have in PCI DSS.

Good security includes all the principles of people, process, and technology. The impact that skimmers have on credit card fraud committed against fixed devices (such as unattended fuel pumps or cash machines) will be dramatically reduced by a thorough visual inspection at a shift change and other random times during the day. This is another argument for keeping your networking simple. A shift manager or even an individual contributor taking a few minutes each day to visually inspect all equipment and network jacks can be an effective control against unauthorized wireless devices.

WHY DO WE NEED WIRELESS NETWORK SECURITY?

Corporate networks are protected by many layers of security, one of which being physical security. Think about how difficult it is to get into the data center at your company. It probably includes going through multiple layers of physical security controls such as parking access gates, fences, and security guards. Employees can easily get access to the facility, but getting access to the data center is usually limited to a select group of individuals.

Wireless networking cannot rely on physical security to completely secure it. Yes, it is possible to use directional antennas to contain the signal inside your four walls or even use specially designed mesh surfaces inside your walls to create a Faraday cage for Wi-Fi signals, but that is neither foolproof nor 100% secure. Worse, those techniques generally don't work with all wireless technologies, and it won't protect your network against a targeted attack against a user outside of the facility when they open up their laptop at the local coffee shop.

Because we lack physical security controls, we must rely almost entirely on technical controls to protect our wireless networks. Defense technologies have come a long way since the first corporate AP was deployed, but companies still need to install and configure these technologies properly in order for them to be effective.

One popular story that is part of QSA lore is a company that was in the middle of a PCI assessment and the subject of wireless technologies came up. The company's representatives were adamant that wireless technologies were expressly prohibited by policy, yet the observant QSA looked over to the head of the conference table and saw a suspicious Linksys device. When the QSA asked about that device, the company's representative just shrugged her shoulders and said, "You'll have to ask IT." Not only did IT not deploy the device, but someone had been accessing the corporate network from a neighboring parking garage for months.

PCI DSS only requires a minimum baseline for wireless security. In our opinion, companies relying on wireless technology for their business should go beyond PCI DSS and choose the appropriate defensive solution to protect their networks.

OTHER WIRELESS TECHNOLOGIES

We've spent the majority of this chapter going over Wi-Fi and cellular network communications, but there are a multitude of other common network technologies that you need to watch out for and secure. The easiest way to think about this problem is to consider how a device gets and uses its data. If you don't see a network or USB cable coming out of the device, it is using some kind of wireless technology and you need to secure it. Here is a list of some of those technologies:

- Bluetooth® is included in almost every smartphone and every new laptop that sits on a retail shelf. It was originally designed in 1994 by two individuals working for Ericsson in Sweden. As of this writing, the current specification is now up to version 5.3. Version 3 included an interesting possibility to facilitate high-speed Bluetooth networks by coupling them with 802.11 (or Wi-Fi) networks for the large transfers. Be sure to fully understand your deployment and its location in your network. Bluetooth base stations should be secured in the same manner that you would secure a Wi-Fi station.
- ZigBee® is a new wireless standard more formally known as 802.15.4. While there is a retail specification (still) in development right now, there is no plan to include payment processing as part of that specification. Ensure that if you are using this technology that you have separated this from any payment systems. The security of these implementations is largely unknown at this point in the retail space. You will see ZigBee primarily used in automation and utility management (namely electricity).
- GMRS or other packet radio as described above could be used as a local data service for companies looking to build an infrastructure outside of a phone company for a contained geographical area. This should be treated the same way Wi-Fi would be, and all communication should be encrypted independently of any link-layer encryption you might use.
- Worldwide Interoperability for Microwave Access (WiMAX) may also be a technology used in your city that could include data services for various devices that might process payments. Ensure that you have taken the appropriate steps to secure both your communications and your devices.
- Satellite communications that could be provided through your favorite satellite TV provider, Starlink, or whatever Bezos is cooking up. Modern satellite connectivity contains link-layer protection inside of it, but since the latency is much lower today than it was a decade ago, add in some additional security with a TLS or VPN tunnel.
- Backhaul Microwave or other types of long-haul wireless technologies (such as LiteBeam) bridge gaps in sparsely populated areas. You've seen these antennas on the top of tall towers when driving away from civilization on the highway. They look like bass drums and point one direction. Those are considered carrier grade, and frankly you may not even know that your internet connection is using one of those (like Multiprotocol Label Switching, MPLS), so definitely leverage additional link-layer tunneling encryption.
- Yousef pointed out that there may still be infrared transmission happening for some applications. We got a laugh out of this one when he ended the suggestion with, "Wow I'm old." #samesies.

TOOLS AND BEST PRACTICES

Wireless technologies have permeated virtually every part of our technologically advanced society from the use of cellular technology and smartphones to enter credit cards and process payments to the casual Wi-Fi device lurking at a sleepy cafe. There are numerous tools you can use to both detect networks and defend against potential hackers.

Beginning with detecting, there are both commercial and open source solutions. Commercial solutions are readily available through your favorite search engine, and most of the major AP manufacturers have similar capabilities built into their devices. The solution that fits best for you may just come down to your specific requirements and budget.

NOTE

Although wireless scanning software has come a long way over the years, especially free ones, users performing serious scanning activities should always use a combination of tools, not relying on any one single tool for all their results. As an example, some tools can be noisy with active probes while tools like Airodump-ng are stealthy and do not make themselves known.

We struggled to find good tools on the Windows side for this as most have some fees associated with them (which are well worth the price to get a professional-level tool). Acrylic Wi-Fi Home Scanner (acrylicwifi.com) is a solid entrant that covers the technologies you will see in mass deployment, and they have a free version.

On the UNIX side, two tools top our list. Kismet/KisMAC (www.kismetwireless.net and www.kismac-ng.org) uses a curses interface, so users run it from a terminal window (or natively on Mac for KisMAC), but it visually displays its information (as well as creates detailed logs with GPS data if enabled) in a format that is easy to navigate and understand. In fact, we argue that it is just as easy as using NetStumbler used to be on the Windows side when using it via the Kali Linux Live ISO. Newer implementations include more graphical options as well. The other tool to consider is aircrack-ng (www.aircrack-ng.org). It has a great traffic dumping utility but is reserved for more advanced users. This tool has excellent encryption cracking capabilities and was a staple in Branden's toolkit during wireless assessments for customers.

From the hardware side, consider getting a high-power Wi-Fi card. High-power cards with external antenna capabilities are readily available through various electronics outlets. You should also consider a good antenna. An omnidirectional antenna is probably the most useful for PCI DSS scanning, though you may have more fun with a "Pringles Can" or another yagi Wi-Fi antenna. Newer Wi-Fi networks can differ slightly in both their frequency and channel designations. Only certain channels are allowed to have a detachable antenna per the FCC requirements in the 802.11a standard. Outside the United States, check with your regulatory body for specific rules and standards. Finally, since the last writing, new Wi-Fi 6 (802.11ax) evolution proves to boost power, speed, and reach. But don't be fooled by a new technology and think you are secure because it's new.

WARNING

Keep in mind that illegally modifying equipment can land you in a heap of trouble with the various authorities that govern RF communications. Do yourself a favor and ensure that you do not break the rules!

There are plenty of tutorials for wireless scanning and penetration testing available through your favorite search engine or bookstore. If you are not a professional, your best bet is to leave this particular task to individuals who are. Whether you contract with a security consulting company or choose a wireless hardware vendor, be sure to select the most appropriate technology for your business and risk appetite. As with most things, you get what you pay for! And don't forget, use any and all of these tools at your own risk.

COMMON MISTAKES AND PITFALLS

Remember, wireless stretches the boundaries of your network past your physical walls to areas where you may not have a physical security presence. Per the requirements, one of the most basic prevention measures you can deploy is changing the default settings.

- Change the default passwords. Be sure you work with your manufacturer to find them all. Some APs come with several default accounts with varying levels of security permissions.
- Don't use shared keys. It's just not a good idea anymore and the systems to run individual keys work very well.

- Change the default SSID. The SSID differentiates one network from another. When coming up with an SSID for your AP, don't use the organization's name, address, or any identifying characteristics that would either draw attention to it or assist an attacker in singling out your company's wireless. Disabling SSID broadcasting characteristics is a good idea as well, but remember that most modern wardriving tools can still extract an SSID from packets over the air even if your AP leaves that field blank while broadcasting its beacon frames. Thus, you should not rely on "SSID Hiding" as a method of security.
- Enable enterprise strength WPA2/WPA3 for encryption. Pre-shared keys are not preferable because you have to change them frequently and have to touch every device to do so.
- Better yet, make sure any in-scope traffic is also wrapped inside a VPN tunnel over wireless connections.

NOTE

Enterprise type authentication or authentication that uses a unique username and password or certificate per device is much preferred over a pre-shared key. Most network setups can handle this type of authentication with minimal cost of hardware or software. Keep in mind, embedded systems have come under fire recently because a lack of entropy can cause the building blocks of encryption keys to be weakened. Finally, any certificates tied to AD credentials for wireless authentication do not violate Requirement 3.5.1.3.

CASE STUDY

Wireless compromises give security professionals plenty to write about when it comes to what not to do with respect to wireless. Let's walk through a couple of examples.

THE CASE OF THE UNTETHERED LAPTOP

Ashley's Archery Adventures aims to promote archery among enthusiasts and hunters alike. Ashley started her business last year and has seen steady growth as adults and kids alike take on the challenge of archery. Ashley's business is built on a small 50-acre plot of land just outside of several large suburbs. Luckily, she was close enough to those suburbs to get high-speed Internet access for her office and POS devices.

Ashley spends much of her time out in the field (literally) and has set up several small covered areas where her customers can enjoy water and packed lunches in between archery stations. Because Ashley found herself away from her desk quite often, she put a small Wi-Fi antenna on a modest 50-foot tower by the main office so that she could use her laptop. She took the appropriate precautions to secure her network and used a long pre-shared key that she changed every quarter.

One day while at the main office, she noticed some strange pop-up windows appearing on her computer and suffered intermittent network blackouts. She installed antivirus and set her automatic patch update to run weekly, so she thought that maybe it was one of her software programs automatically updating itself. If that was not the case, she thought maybe the weather caused her wireless network to go on the fritz. She made a mental note of it and went on with her day. That evening, she noticed that the problem seemed to go away and things were back to normal. Two months later, she learned that she had been compromised.

Ashley was a victim of a common attack against laptops with Wi-Fi cards called the Evil Twin. Ashley frequently visited her local coffee shop on the weekends and used their Wi-Fi connection from her laptop. When the owner of the coffee shop added free Wi-Fi for his customers, he dropped a basic wireless router with default settings on a separate broadband connection for his customers. He didn't want to mess with security settings for his customers and get involved with fixing esoteric problems with each patron's laptop. Default settings seemed to avoid those problems. He also didn't want one of his users to potentially use so much of the Wi-Fi network that his store network was at, or beyond, capacity. This solution worked well for him and his customers.

When Ashley's laptop was acting funny two weeks prior, an attacker was cycling through commonly used default SSIDs and got her laptop to associate with his attack machine. Because he provided a stronger signal than the one Ashley was using at the time, her laptop automatically associated with his machine, and he was able to launch an endpoint attack against it. Ashley's laptop had not yet downloaded and installed a patch that fixed a remote vulnerability in the operating system, allowing the attacker to exploit the vulnerability and gain control of her machine. From there, he installed a rootkit and was able to gain access to other machines on the network, including her POS devices. He was also able to grab the Wi-Fi key and casually observe and participate in the network at will.

One of the dangers of wireless networking is the devices that use it. Both of us have enjoyed watching overly confident security professionals boast about the security of their Wi-Fi networks, only to have a savvy consultant attack a laptop directly (instead of trying to break the network encryption) to gain access. Sometimes computers try to out-think their users and do things they "believe" are in the users' best interest. One of those things is to choose the strongest wireless signal to get the best possible Internet connection.

You can combat this by removing the "Auto-Join" feature for the networks that you connect to, requiring users to specifically choose each network in which they want to participate. If they have connected before and the keys are stored on the machine, they will not have to re-authenticate. It just forces the user to connect to networks with intent.

THE CASE OF THE EXPANSION PLAN

After learning her lesson, Ashley quickly cleaned up her breach and was able to refocus on her business. She kept her wireless network intact, but she added additional protection with a host-based firewall for her laptop and then removed all stored profiles except for her office Wi-Fi. Her device is the only authorized device on the network at this time, but part of her improvement plan for this year is to put small POS terminals in some of the covered areas. She plans to offer more products for sale like cold beverages and food or snack items. Each covered area would have a PC to keep track of inventory or allow employees to send quick notes via instant messages or e-mail.

Ashley has budgeted a small amount of money to purchase both the hardware for the expansion plan and to build a small back-office network to maintain these devices. She wanted to provide network services to the devices to back them up daily and put important files on a network file server for all machines to use. Being as these machines would be somewhat exposed to the elements, she knew that equipment failure was a much bigger possibility than if those devices were kept in a climate-controlled office environment.

She licenses Microsoft Azure Active Directory and sets up her new employees with usernames and passwords. Each machine must log into the domain, and her "Rent-an-IT-Guy" sets up some basic network shares and permissions for each user. After he finished setting everything up, he left a small easy-to-follow guide for Ashley should she need to make minor changes.

Now Ashley must decide how she wants these machines to connect to the wireless network. Shared keys for Wi-Fi will require additional security on top to comply, so she has an opportunity to remove shared keys altogether. What should she do?

Ashley has two choices. The first is to have her "Rent-an-IT-Guy" build an overlay VPN network on top of her existing wireless network with keys that are separate from her Wi-Fi keys. This gives Ashley the advantage of keeping her existing setup that she is familiar with.

Ashley's second choice is to upgrade her Wi-Fi infrastructure to one that will support an enterprise authentication scheme with WPA2/WPA3. From there, she can add an agent into each field computer's installation that requires users to authenticate with the network first with their existing username and password. This username and password could be part of their Active Directory credentials and may require setting up a RADIUS server on the domain controller to enable this functionality.

Before security purists jump down our throats, yes, we do realize that a single username and password that accesses all resources may add an additional risk of compromise. That said, in this instance, the risk is relatively low provided that each user receives training on how to create good passwords or passphrases, and they are protected according to the latest NIST Password guidelines. Alternatively, Ashley could deploy an inexpensive token-based solution to provide a second factor of authentication that would effectively remove this weakness.

THE CASE OF THE DOUBLE SECRET WIRELESS NETWORK

James's Junker Jubilee, a car rental facility that rents run-down automobiles for a fraction of the cost of a traditional rental company, recently went through a PCI assessment. Upon arriving at their corporate headquarters, the assessors were placed into a conference room for the duration of the assessment. When it came time to ask about wireless technologies, Sally, a risk manager, proudly stated that wireless technologies were prohibited at James's and that employees found using these technologies were reprimanded with penalties up to termination.

The lead assessor casually looked over in the corner of the conference room where the audio/visual (A/V) equipment was stored and pointed out a blue device with two antennas on it. It oddly enough had a label on it that proclaimed "Property of IT, DO NOT REMOVE." When the lead assessor examined it closer, it was an AP from a well-known supplier and was plugged into the Ethernet port in the wall. The assessor had an older model in his house, so he was sure he was looking at an AP and not something related to the A/V features of the conference room. Sally looked at the device and said, "Well, that showed up last month and we just assumed it belonged to IT and didn't touch it. The CIO has a lot of political power at James's, and most employees have learned not to cross him."

It turns out, a hacker posing as a flower delivery man gained access to the facility around Valentine's Day that year and placed the curiously labeled device in the conference room. He had been poking around the network ever since and had stolen both customer data and intellectual property. Because he had used several techniques to hide the device, the basic wireless sweeps that the company was performing did not pick up that device.

Had James's used a Wireless IDS or IPS to bolster his security instead of relying on his quarterly wireless analysis as part of Requirement 11.2.1, chances are he would have had a much better chance of catching the hacker in the act and shutting down the connection before the breach of data could occur.

The Case of the Detached POS

Karen's Kupcakes is a small bakery specializing in building delightful desserts using the cupcake as its foundation. Karen located her business in a small strip mall that is across a six-lane avenue from a large shopping mall. This year for Valentine's Day, she wants to focus on spreading the word about her business by opening a small kiosk in the parking lot outside the food court. She will sell Valentine's Day themed cupcakes with on-site customization to patrons entering and leaving the mall area. Since she will be doing the primary baking in her location, the only power she will need is for her to register to process payments for the cupcakes.

She looks at a few options like shooting 802.11a Wi-Fi across the avenue, but ultimately settles on purchasing a cellular-based payment processing terminal that will seamlessly integrate with her existing setup. She leases the equipment from a known provider, has them process the payments on her behalf, and sends over wire transfers at the end of each day. She has a security consultant take a look at the setup to ensure it complies with PCI DSS as she doesn't want her customers to be subject to a breach on her behalf. It is powered through GSM networks, so she knows that she needs to have her traffic encrypted before it hits the cellular hardware.

Overall, her kiosk was a massive success and more than paid back the investment she made in the portable payment processing hardware. Her efforts to process these payments securely paid off, and she plans to expand to multiple other kiosks in the near future.

SUMMARY

Wireless networking can be both safe and effective in extending your network's functionality for special events or as a normal course of business. From mobile users who have all-in-one devices that manage their inventory, schedules, and payments, to that cash machine at an outdoor arts festival, to a trendy bar with an outdoor patio and deck area in the spring and fall, wireless payments are here to stay.

There are several things that companies must be aware of when they venture into mobile or wireless payments. This goes without saying, but be sure you understand both the technology you are implementing and have a trusted third-party review it for compliance and security (the latter probably being much more important in the grand scheme of things). Too many companies have ventured down this road with big ideas only to deploy an insecure technology and end up with a massive compromise bill.

Finally, pay close attention to the security features of your particular infrastructure components. Use all the capacity available (that makes the most sense for your network and setup), in your keys, and use the best encryption available.

NOTE

1. Check out James Pavur's 2020 BlackHat talk entitled *Whispers Among the Stars* for more.

9 Vulnerability Management

Information in this chapter:

- Payment Card Industry Data Security Standard (PCI DSS) Requirements Covered
- Vulnerability Management in PCI
- Requirement 5 Walk-Through
- Requirement 6 Walk-Through
- Requirement 11 Walk-Through
- External Vulnerability Scanning with Approved Scanning Vendors (ASV)
- Internal Vulnerability Scanning
- Common PCI Vulnerability Management Mistakes
- Case Study
- Summary

Before we discuss Payment Card Industry (PCI) requirements related to vulnerability management in depth and find out what safeguards are prescribed there and how to address them, we need to address one underlying and confusing issue of defining some of the terms that the PCI Data Security Standard (DSS) documentation relies upon.

These are as follows:

- Vulnerability assessment,
- Penetration testing,
- Testing of controls, limitations, and restrictions, and
- Preventing vulnerabilities via secure coding practices.

Defining vulnerability assessment is a little tricky because the term has evolved over the years. We prefer to define it as a process of finding and assessing vulnerabilities on a set of systems or a network, which is a very broad definition. By the way, the term *vulnerability* is typically used to mean a software flaw or a weakness that makes the software susceptible to an attack or abuse. In the realm of information security, a vulnerability assessment is usually understood to be a vulnerability scan of the network with a scanner, implemented as installable software, a dedicated hardware appliance, or a scanning software-as-a-service (SaaS).

Sometimes using the term *network vulnerability assessment* adds more clarity to this. The terms *network vulnerability scanning* or *network vulnerability testing* are usually understood to mean the same. In addition, the separate term *application vulnerability assessment* is typically understood to mean an assessment of application-level vulnerabilities in a particular application; most frequently, a web-based application deployed publicly on the Internet or internally on the intranet.

A separate tool called an application vulnerability scanner (as opposed to the network vulnerability scanner mentioned above), is used to perform an application security assessment. By the way, concepts such as "port scan," "protocol scan," and "network service identification" belong to the domain of network vulnerability scanning, whereas concepts such as "site crawl," "Hypertext Transfer Protocol (HTTP) requests," "cross-site scripting (XSS)," and "client-side vulnerabilities" belong to the domain of Web Application Scanning (WAS). We will cover both types in this chapter as they are mandated by PCI DSS.

If you take one thing away from this chapter, remember that a vulnerability assessment and a penetration test are completely and unquestionably different. Penetration testing is usually understood to mean an attempt to break into the network by a dedicated team, which can use the network and application scanning tools mentioned above and also other nontechnical means such as dumpster diving (looking for confidential information in the trash) or social engineering (attempting to subvert authorized users to give out their access credential and other confidential information). Sometimes, penetration testers might rely on other techniques and methods such as custom-written attack tools. In fact, anybody who tries to sell you a penetration test but only plans to run a vulnerability assessment tool against your systems is misrepresenting their services.

Preventing vulnerabilities, covered in Requirement 6, addresses vulnerability management by assuring that newly created software does not contain known flaws and problems. Requirements 5, 6, and 11 also mandate various protection technologies such as antivirus, web application firewalls (WAFs), intrusion detection or prevention, and others.

The core of Requirement 11 discussed in this chapter covers all the above as well as some of the practices that help mitigate the impact of problems, such as the use of intrusion prevention tools. Such practices fall into broad domains of vulnerability management and threat management. Although there are common definitions of vulnerability management (covered below), threat management is typically defined ad hoc as "dealing with threats to information assets."

PCI DSS REQUIREMENTS COVERED

Vulnerability management controls are present in PCI DSS Requirements 5, 6, and 11.

- PCI Requirement 5: "Protect All Systems and Networks from Malicious Software" covers anti-malware measures; these are tangentially related to what is commonly seen as vulnerability management, but it helps deal with the impact of vulnerabilities.
- PCI Requirement 6: "Develop and Maintain Secure Systems and Software" covers a broad range of application security subjects, application vulnerability scanning, secure software development, and more.
- PCI Requirement 11: "Test Security of Systems and Networks Regularly" covers a broad range of security testing, including network vulnerability scanning by approved scanning vendors (ASVs), internal scanning, and other requirements. We will focus on Requirements 11.3 and 11.4 in this chapter.

VULNERABILITY MANAGEMENT IN PCI

Before we start our discussion of the role of vulnerability management for PCI compliance, we need to briefly discuss what is commonly covered under vulnerability management in the domain of information security. Vendors tend to frame vulnerability management as simple: just patch all those pesky software problems and you are done. Organizations struggle with it because the scope of platforms and applications to patch and other weaknesses to rectify is out of control in most large, diverse organizations. The problems move from intractable to downright scary when you consider the number of applications being developed in the world of modern deployments and cloud computing, including all the in-house development projects, outsourced development efforts, and partner development work. Not to mention mobile applications—many of which handle payments directly.

Vulnerability management is not the same as keeping your systems patched; it expands into software security and application security, secure development practices, configuration management, and other adjacent domains. If you are busy every first Tuesday when Microsoft releases its batch of patches, but not doing anything to eliminate a broad range of application vulnerabilities during the other 29 days in a month, you are not managing your vulnerabilities efficiently, if at all. Vulnerability management *was* a mix of technical and nontechnical processes even in the time when patching was most of what organizations needed to do to stay secure. Nowadays, it touches an even bigger part of your organization: not only network group, system group, and desktop group but also your development and development partners and cloud or mobile applications.

Clearly, vulnerability management is not only about technology and patching. Technology for discovering vulnerabilities is getting better every day. Moreover, the same technology is also used to detect configuration errors and non-vulnerability-related security issues. For instance, a fully patched system is still highly vulnerable if it has a blank administrator or root password, even though no patches are missing. The other benefit derived from vulnerability management is the detection of Shadow IT, which is sometimes deployed by business units outside of control of your IT department. Because these systems are not centrally maintained, they might not be deployed to comply with PCI DSS requirements. One of the basic tenets of adhering to the PCI Data Security Standard is to limit the scope of PCI by strictly segmenting and controlling the cardholder data environment (CDE). Proper implementation of internal and external vulnerability scanning can assist in maintaining a secure CDE.

As a result, it's useful to define vulnerability management as managing the lifecycle of processes and technologies needed to discover and then reduce (or remove) vulnerabilities in software, reducing the risks of a compromise to an acceptable threshold.

Network vulnerability scanners can detect vulnerabilities from the network side with good accuracy and from the host side with better accuracy. Host-side detection is typically accomplished via internal scans by using credentials to log into systems ("authenticated" or "trusted" scanning), so configuration files, registry entries, and file versions can be read increasing the accuracy of results. This type of scanning is generally performed from inside the network, not from the Internet.

NOTE

Vulnerability scanning tools are capable of running trusted or authenticated scanning. This is where the tools will actually log into a system, just like a regular user would, and then perform the search for vulnerabilities. Starting with PCI DSS 4.0, this is not just a suggestion but mandatory. Requirement 11.3.1.2 states that "Internal vulnerability scans are performed via authenticated scanning." This new requirement admits that attackers could gain access to privileged attacks and helps mitigate issues that could arise.

However, merchants that implement periodic vulnerability scanning at higher than a quarterly frequency have discovered that the volumes of data generated far exceed their expectations and abilities. A quick scan-then-fix approach turns into an endless wheel of pain, obviously more dramatic for PCI DSS external scanning because you have no choice in fixing vulnerabilities, which leads to validation failure (we will review the exact criteria for failure below). Historical challenges of using vulnerability scanners, including having network visibility of the critical systems, perceived or real impact on the network bandwidth, as well as system stability have almost been eliminated. Still, vulnerability management involves more processes than technology and your follow-up actions should be based on the overall risk and not simply on the volume of incoming scanner data.

STAGES OF VULNERABILITY MANAGEMENT PROCESS

Let's outline some critical stages of the vulnerability management process. Those include defining the policy, collecting the data, deciding what to remediate (i.e., fix for good) or mitigate (i.e., temporarily protect from exploitation), and then taking action.

Policy Definition

Indeed, the vulnerability management process starts from the policy definition that covers your organization's assets, such as systems and applications and their users, as well as partners, customers, and whoever touches those resources. Such documents and the accompanying detailed security procedures define the scope of the vulnerability management effort and create a "known good" state of those IT resources. Policy creation should involve business and technology teams, as well as senior management who would be responsible for overall compliance. PCI DSS requirements directly affect such policy documents and mandate its creation (see Requirement 12 that states that one needs to "maintain a policy that addresses information security"). Marking the assets that are in scope for PCI compliance is also part of this step.

Data Acquisition

The data acquisition process comes next. A network vulnerability scanner or an agent-based host scanner is a common choice; a passive vulnerability assessment tool that sniffs network traffic can also be used. Both excellent freeware and commercial solutions are available. In addition, established standards for vulnerability naming, such as Common Vulnerability and Exposures (CVE) and vulnerability scoring, such as Common Vulnerability Scoring System (CVSS) can help provide a consistent way to encode vulnerabilities, weaknesses, and organization-specific policy violations across the popular computing platforms. CVSS, specifically, is utilized for measuring vulnerability severity in PCI DSS. Moreover, an effort by the US National Institute of Standards and Technology called Security Content Automation Protocol (SCAP) has combined the above standards into a joint standard bundle to enable more automation of vulnerability management. See the NIST website for more details on SCAP.

Scanning for compliance purposes is somewhat different from scanning purely for remediation. Namely, PCI DSS requires that a Qualified Security Assessor (QSA) will validate your compliance based on the list of systems that were scanned for all PCI-relevant vulnerabilities, as well as an indication that all systems test clean. Scanning tools also provide support for Requirements 1 and 2, secure-system configurations, and many other requirements described below. This shows that while *scanning for remediation* only requires a list of vulnerable systems with their vulnerabilities, *scanning for compliance* also calls for having a list of systems found not to be vulnerable.

Prioritization

The next phase, prioritization, is a key phase in the entire process. It is highly likely that even with a well-defined specific scan policy (which is derived from PCI DSS requirements, of course) and a quality vulnerability scanner, the amount of data a scanner will generate for a large organization will be enormous. Even limiting to only the in-scope systems might lead to a firehose of data. Organizations with a flat network can have thousands of systems in scope for PCI DSS. Organizations will not fix all the problems, especially if remediation is not mandated by explicit rules. Various estimates indicate that even applying a periodic batch of Windows patches often takes longer than the period between patch releases (longer than one month). Accordingly, there is a chance that the organization will not finish the previous patching round before the next one rushes in. To intelligently prioritize vulnerabilities for remediation, you need to take into account various factors about your own IT environment as well as the outside world. Ideally, such prioritization should not only be based on PCI DSS but also on the organization's view and approach to information risk (per the note in Requirement 6.3). Also, even when working within the PCI DSS scope, it makes sense to fix vulnerabilities with higher risk to payment card data first, even if this is not mandated by PCI DSS standards.

Those include the following:

- Specific regulatory requirements: fix all medium- and high- and critical-severity vulnerabilities as indicated by the scanning vendor; fix all vulnerabilities that can lead to Structured Query Language (SQL) injection, XSS attacks, and others like these.
- Vulnerability severity for the environment: fix all other vulnerabilities on publicly exposed and then on other in-scope systems.
- Related threat information and threat relevance: fix all vulnerabilities on the frequently attacked systems.

- Public exploits available: fix vulnerabilities that have exploit code publicly available (and exploitation ongoing), and/or those used by malware.
- Business value and role information about the target system: address vulnerabilities on high-value critical servers.

To formalize this prioritization we can leverage CVSS, which takes into account various vulnerability properties such as priority, exploitability, and impact, as well as multiple, local site-specific properties. The CVSS scheme offers a way to provide a uniform way of scoring vulnerabilities on a scale from 0 to 10. PCI DSS mandates the use of CVSS by ASVs; moreover, PCI validation scanning prescribes that all vulnerabilities with the score equal to or higher than 4.0 must be fixed to pass the scan. National Vulnerability Database (NVD) provides CVSS scores for many publicly disclosed vulnerabilities. CVSS, however, can be enhanced to also account for exploit code availability and reports of active exploitation—to fix these vulnerabilities first for maximum risk reduction.

Don't forget you must show clean scans internally as well. Validation procedure 11.2.1.b states that "Rescans are performed that confirm all high-risk and critical vulnerabilities (...) have been resolved" for internal scanning.

Mitigation

The next phase of mitigation is important in many environments where immediate patching or reconfiguration is impossible, such as a critical server running unusual or custom-built applications. Despite the above, when a worm is released or a zero-day attack is seen in similar environments, protecting a system like that becomes unavoidable. In this case, you immediately need to do something to mitigate the vulnerability before you can fix it properly. This step might be performed by a host or network intrusion prevention system (IPS), but sometimes even a firewall blocking a network port will do. The important pathway forward is choosing the best mitigation strategy that keeps your business running with legitimate transaction processing. In case of a web application vulnerability, a separate dedicated device such as a WAF or Runtime Application Self-Protection (RASP) needs to be deployed in addition to the traditional network security safeguards such as firewalls, filtering routers, IPSs, and other countermeasures.

In this context, using antivirus and intrusion prevention technologies might be seen as part of vulnerability mitigation because these technologies help protect companies from vulnerability exploitation (either by malware or human attackers).

Ideally, all vulnerabilities that impact card data need to be patched or remediated as prescribed by the above prioritization procedure, taking into account the steps we took to temporarily mitigate the vulnerability above. In a large environment, it is not simply the question of "let's go patch the server." Often, a complicated workflow with multiple approval points and regression testing on different systems is required. Patching takes time, and in order to patch safely, you need to buy the operators time to test the patch to ensure it works as intended.

To make sure that vulnerability management becomes a process, an organization should monitor vulnerability management on an ongoing basis. This involves looking at the implemented technical and process controls aimed at decreasing risk. Such monitoring goes beyond vulnerability management into other security management areas. It is also important to be able to report to senior management about your risk reduction progress.

Vulnerability management is not a panacea even after all the "known" vulnerabilities are remediated. Zero-day attacks use vulnerabilities with no resolution publicly available. Protection against zero-day vulnerabilities is difficult and must be addressed by using the principle of "defense in depth" during the security infrastructure design.

Let's walk through all the requirements in PCI DSS that are related to vulnerability management, spread across Requirements 5, 6, and 11.

REQUIREMENT 5 WALK-THROUGH

While antivirus and malware solutions have little to do with finding and fixing vulnerabilities, PCI DSS includes them under the broad umbrella definition of vulnerability management. We could argue that anti-malware solutions help when a vulnerability is both present and being exploited by malware like a computer virus, worm, Trojan horse, or spyware. Thus, anti-malware tools help mitigate the consequences of exploited vulnerabilities in some scenarios.

In PCI DSS 4.0, Requirement 5 mandates keeping malware protection current. Many antivirus vendors provide daily (and some to hourly) updates of their definition files while other, more advanced Endpoint Detection and Response (EDR) tools may get updates less frequently, but in a manner consistent with the risk and performance of the tool. Needless to say, anti-malware tools need an up-to-date definition set to be fully functional. Note that this applies to your anti-malware software as well. Don't run a 5-year-old version of McAfee, even if it has new definitions.

The PCI DSS creators wisely chose to not require anti-malware protection on all systems, but instead dictate in Requirement 5.2.1 that "an anti-malware solution(s) is deployed on all system components, except for those system components identified in periodic evaluations per Requirement 5.2.3 that concludes the system components are *not at risk from malware*." While many organizations have implemented malware protection on Windows systems, other operating systems like macOS, Linux, and iOS/Android are not as widely targeted. Current malware threats have expanded to all platforms (as have malware prevention applications) and this requirement should be carefully evaluated before allowing this control to be ignored based on a risk rating. While Requirement 5.2.3 does not specify a time period, malware threats for excluded systems should be reevaluated based on a target risk-analysis, which will be formally required starting on March 31, 2025 in Requirement 5.2.3.1.

Subsection 5.2.2 states that one needs to ensure that "The deployed anti-malware solution(s): Detects all known types of malware and removes, blocks, or contains all known types of malware." They spell out not just detection, but blocking and removal of various types of malicious software knowing that such protection is highly desirable but not really achievable given the current state of malware. In fact, recent evidence suggests that a malware product's ability to protect you from all known threats is less certain everyday as viruses, Trojans, worms, spyware, ransomware, keyloggers, rootkits, malicious code, scripts, and links are spread.

Section 5.3 provides operational requirements for the malware software. Requirement 5.3.1 mandates that "The anti-malware solution(s) is kept current via automatic updates." Based on the current frequency of new threats, these definitions should be updated at least weekly, if not daily or hourly. Once definitions are up to date, Requirement 5.3.2 requires that the software "Performs periodic scans and active or real-time scans OR performs continuous behavioral analysis of systems or processes." This is a nod to new software that goes beyond definition-based detection and monitors threats based on the behavior of the user to restrict unauthorized processes from running. If you choose to use periodic scans for 5.3.2, be sure to perform your targeted risk assessment per Requirement 5.3.2.1.

Scanning should apply to internal storage as well as removable media. Requirement 5.3.3 states that scanning or behavioral analysis of removable electronic media should be performed when the media is inserted, connected, or logically mounted. (Again, another best practice until March 31, 2025). Requirements 5.3.4 and 5.3.5 aim to ensure that logs are available for each in-scope system and that users cannot disable or alter malware protection unless authorized.

NOTE

If you read between the lines on this requirement, there is an unintentional new requirement that is now part of Requirement 5.3.5. Users who are considered in scope *should not have any local administrative rights* to their machines to disable or remove these endpoint controls.

There is an exception process mentioned, but if there is a population of personnel in your firm who would fall under the scope of PCI DSS have local administrative access to their machine (Local Administrator for Windows, root/sudo access on UNIX, and Admin group for macOS), you will need to remove it unless they are legitimately an IT administrator. For any administrators that fall into that exception period, ensure you have detailed alerts for when controls are disabled and follow up on those alerts to document the reason and restoration of the control.

For larger companies, users rarely have administrative rights but your enterprise-grade anti-malware tools may have tamper protection that would apply to users provided local administration rights as well, but if your company has a large macOS or unmanaged Windows deployment, this may not be the case.

This combines three different requirements, which are sometimes overlooked by organizations that deployed antivirus products. First, they need to be current and updated as frequently as their vendor is able to push updates. Daily or hourly, not weekly or monthly, is the standard now. Second, you need to monitor the running status of your security tools. Third, as mentioned in Chapter 10, Logging Events and Monitoring the Cardholder Data Environment, logs are critical for PCI compliance. Your antivirus tools also need to generate logs, and these logs need to be reviewed in accordance with Requirement 10. Expect your Assessor to ask for logs from your anti-malware solution to substantiate this requirement, including logs from the A/V console.

Finally, Requirement 5.4.1 is brand new and requires you to implement processes and automated mechanisms to detect and protect against phishing attacks. This type of attack, especially if including spear-phishing and business e-mail compromise (BEC), is a serious threat to organizations. This control is focused on technical controls that can prevent, or at least limit, the number of e-mails with potential phishing or malware attacks. Anti-spoofing controls that can be implemented for your mail servers including Domain-based Message Authentication Reporting and Conformance (DMARC), Sender Policy Framework (SPF), and Domain Keys Identified Mail (DKIM) will count for this requirement, so ensure you have a verifiably tested installation that is documented. There are several free verification tools you can use to ensure your setup is working correctly, and your typical corporate e-mail providers may already have it set up for you. Commercial software is also available to help block or mask potential threats, such as malicious links, before the e-mail is delivered to the recipient. Don't forget to leverage your security awareness training to mature your organization's understanding of phishing.

As a side effect, a combination of the above three technologies will boost your e-mail delivery dramatically so that your employees won't have to call people they have e-mailed to ask them if their message was caught in a SPAM filter.

What to Do to Be Secure and Compliant?

1. Requirement 5 offers simple and obvious action items:
   - Deploy malware software on in-scope systems, wherever such software is available and wherever the system can suffer from malware. Free malware products can be downloaded from several vendors such as AVG or Avast.
   - Assess that systems that are not thought to be subject to malware really are not (Requirement 5.2.1)
2. Configure the obtained anti-malware software to update at least *daily*. Please forget the dated advice when weekly updates were seen as sufficient. Daily is the minimum acceptable update frequency today—but be prepared that in many cases it will be way too late as malware will already be on your systems.

3. Verify that your malware software is generating audit logs. Please refer to Chapter 10, Logging Events and Monitoring the Cardholder Data Environment, to learn how to deal with all the logs, including antivirus logs.

4. Document operational procedures related to fighting malware (QSAs are required to review such documents!)

NOTE

For example, Symantec's Norton AntiVirus and many other enterprise-grade anti-malware tools will log all detections by default; there is no need to "enable logging." To preserve, please make sure that your particular tool has the setting enabled that allows your centralized log collection system to get the logs before they are deleted.

REQUIREMENT 6 WALK-THROUGH

Another section of PCI DSS covered under the vulnerability management umbrella is Requirement 6, which covers the need to "develop and maintain secure systems and applications." This requirement touches vulnerability management from another side: making sure that those pesky flaws and holes never appear in software in the first place. At the same time, this requirement covers the need to plan and execute a patch-management program to assure that, once discovered, the flaws are corrected via software vendor patches or other means. In addition, it deals with a requirement to scan applications, especially web applications, for vulnerabilities.

We divide the mandates in Requirement 6 into three groups: those that help you prevent bugs in the in-house developed applications, those that help you patch bugs in commercial applications, and those that deal with verifying the security of web applications (Requirement 6.4).

Your vulnerability management program applies to securing any software developed in-house that could impact the security of cardholder data. Section 6.2 states that "Bespoke and custom software are developed securely (...) based on industry standards and/or best practices for secure development." The unfortunate truth, however, is that there is no single authoritative source for these security "best practices" and, at the same time, current software "industry best practices" rarely include "information security throughout the software-development life cycle." Here are some recent examples of projects that aim at standardizing security programming best practices, which are freely available for download and contain detailed technical guidance:

- BSIMM "The Building Security In Maturity Model";
- OWASP "Secure Coding Principles";
- SANS and MITRE "CWE/SANS TOP 25 Most Dangerous Programming Errors"; and
- SAFECode "Fundamental Practices for Secure Software Development".

Detailed coverage of secure programming goes far beyond the scope of this book.

Additionally, 6.2.1 requires that the applications be developed "in accordance with the PCI DSS." This is an important reason to have security involved as early in the development process as possible and be able to provide a clear list of PCI security requirements for the developers to include in their project plans. The list may change depending on how the application works. For example, how is authentication provided for the application, internally through an already PCI-scoped authorization system or using a custom list of users built into the apps (the latter in conflict with durable PCI Compliance). It may take several discussions to understand the security and PCI implications for the application in question.

The last part of 6.2.1 requires that the development incorporates "consideration of information security issues during each stage of the software development lifecycle." This bullet point ensures that security doesn't end up being an issue in final testing, long after the coding has been done. Secure coding reviews should be done similarly to saving your work in a word processor—early and often. Many Integrated Development Environments (IDEs) now have the capability to highlight common secure coding issues during editing, before the vulnerabilities are pushed into the codebase.

Requirement 6.2.2 addresses the need for developers to have the training to be able to develop their applications securely. "At least once every 12 months" software developers should go through training "relevant to their job function and development languages." There are many resources available online to provide ad hoc training for different languages that focus on common security vulnerabilities or just general coding best practices. If separate tools are used to test software in the organization, training should be provided to ensure those tools are used properly and provide accurate feedback to the developers.

Before code is promoted into production, Requirement 6.2.3 requires that code reviews are performed, look for existing and emerging vulnerabilities, and "appropriate corrections are implemented prior to release." This promotion of code for review should follow your documented progression and follow best practices such as not using public code repositories and ensuring developers have properly identified themselves prior to being allowed to commit code. Identified vulnerabilities should be reviewed to understand their risk and other controls that might be in place to protect against exploitation. These reviews can be either manual or automated depending on your environment and toolset.

If manual reviews are used, Requirement 6.2.3.1 states that they must be done by someone other than the code author, who is knowledgeable about how to review code and secure coding practices, and reviewed and approved by management prior to release. This should all be documented in change management systems or documentation that can be provided to your QSA.

Requirement 6.2.4 is reformatted from its previous incarnation as 6.5.x requirements. You no longer get 10 checkmarks for following good practices for code development, but you have more flexibility in defining the common attacks and vulnerabilities that apply to your environment. You will recognize the familiar "OWASP Top Ten" in this list. Make sure that your development or security teams have defined which types of attacks are a concern based on your environment and they are being actively reviewed or tested for during the development process. Education from the developer security training, formalized risk management practices, and the use of threat frameworks, such as MITRE ATT&CK, will help codify these definitions.

Requirement 6.3.1 continues the vulnerability management process with tasks to find and rank vulnerabilities. Note that this doesn't mean *scanning for vulnerabilities* in your environment, but looking for newly discovered vulnerabilities via vulnerability alert services. Some of these are free such as the notices from the vendors of the software in use or the Cybersecurity and Infrastructure Security Agency, or CISA (https://www.cisa.gov/uscert/), whereas others are targeted at enterprises. These services can be highly customized to only send alerts applicable to your environment and fixes for vulnerabilities that are not public. They are not free, but may surely be worth the money paid for them. Twitter can be useful here as certain streams contain excellent real-time vulnerability data.

Most, if not all, of these services provide rankings of vulnerabilities and use the CVSS, an open standard providing risk ranking based on factors such as exploitability, complexity, and impact. Following this scoring system helps meet additional requirements in 6.3.1 for using an industry best practice and identifying the high-risk and critical vulnerabilities. This should include any bespoke or custom software developed in-house.

Requirement 6.3.3 requires that any critical or high patches or updates are patched within one month. Other updates for vulnerabilities with a lower overall risk ranking should be installed as defined by your risk review. The PCI DSS gives an example of "within three months," so if your organization is going to push out patching beyond that window, there should be a documented justification in case your QSA asks.

NOTE

If you decide to use public mailing lists, you need to leverage your up-to-date inventory of bespoke software as well as any commercially available software components in your environment. You may want to set up a specific mailbox that multiple team members have access to, so new vulnerabilities are not missed when someone is out of the office. Checking these lists as part of your normal Security Operation Center (SOC) analyst duties can help ensure this activity regularly takes place. If your organization is small and does not have the resources for an in-house SOC, review those notices for awareness but consider a qualified 3rd party SOC to ensure you have full-time coverage.

Public-Facing Web Application Protection

In addition to secure coding to prevent vulnerabilities, organizations might need to take care of the existing deployed applications by looking into WAFs and WAS, sometimes also called Dynamic Application Security Testing (DAST). An interesting part of Requirement 6.4 is that PCI DSS recommends either a vulnerability scan followed by remediation ("Reviewing public-facing web applications via manual or automated application vulnerability security assessment tools") or a WAF ("Installing a WAF in front of public-facing web applications"), completely ignoring the principal of layered defense or defense-in-depth. In reality, deploying both is highly recommended for the effective protection of web applications. In fact, PCI DSS allows the WAF to be deployed in monitoring mode—with no actual protection just alerting. While this does meet the letter of the compliance requirement, this is not a recommended configuration for being secure. Also, note that Requirement 6.4.2 will require an automated tool that detects and prevents web-based attacks, but this also can be configured in a monitor and alert mode. This is a new requirement that will remove the option of doing web application scans and will supersede Requirement 6.4.1 after March 31, 2025.

Web Application Scanning (WAS)

Before progressing with the discussion of WAS, we need to remind you that XSS and SQL injection website vulnerabilities account for a significant percentage of card data loss. Others include SSL and early TLS configurations or outdated OpenSSL binaries, other injection flaws, Cross-Site Request Forgery, and JavaScript skimmers, and stolen cookies and OAuth tokens—we have quite the tall hill to climb.

You need to ensure that whichever solution you use covers current common vulnerabilities from Requirement 6.2.4 (Previously the OWASP Top 10 list). This list will change over time and you need to ensure the WAS you are using keeps up with the changes. Some WAS products will need to add or modify detections to continue to meet this requirement. If you are using a more full-featured WAS, you may need to modify the scan options from time to time as the list changes.

There are many commercial and even some free WAS solutions available. Check your nearest search engine for more, this is not an exhaustive list. Common examples of free or open-source tools are as follows:

- Nessus, free vulnerability scanner, now has some detection of Web application security issues.
- WebScarab, direct from OWASP Project is also a must for your assessment efforts. The new one, WebScrab NG, is being created as well.
- Grabber, a newer entrant into the WAS toolbelt written in Python.
- w3af is a Web Application Attack and Audit Framework, which can be used as well.
- Ratproxy is not a scanner, but a passive discovery and assessment tool.
- Another classic passive assessment tool is Paros proxy.

There are a number of commercially available tools as well that will provide support and SaaS offerings to speed your deployment.

If you are familiar with ASV network scanning (covered below in the section on Requirement 11), you need to know that Web application security scanning is often more intrusive than network-level vulnerability scanning performed by an ASV for external scan validation. For example, testing for SQL injection or XSS often requires actual attempts to perform an injection of SQL code into a database or a script into a website. Doing so may cause some databases/applications to hang or to have spurious entries appear in your Web application.

Just as with network scanning, application scanners may need to perform authentication to get access to more of your application. Many flaws that allow a regular user to become an application administrator can only be discovered with an authenticated scan. If the main page on your web application has a login form, you will need to perform an authenticated scan—one that logs in. In addition to finding flaws where a user can elevate their privileges, you also need to ensure that customers cannot intentionally, or inadvertently, manipulate the web application to see other customers' data. Authorization (AuthZ) models can be tricky when developers try to build them from scratch.

Also, depending on how your website handles authentication, you may need to log in manually first with the account you will use for scanning, grab the cookie by using a tool like Paros or WebScarab, and then load it into the scanner. Depending on time-outs, you may need to perform this activity just before the scan. In this case, do not plan on being able to schedule scans and have them run automatically. Alternatively, you might be able to store test credentials inside the scanner and run your scan against a non-production instance.

In addition, WAS requires more detailed knowledge of software vulnerabilities and attack methodologies to allow for the correct interpretation of results than network-based or traditional vulnerability scanning does. Remember to always do research in a laboratory environment, not connected to your corporate environment!

When web farms and web portals are in the mix, scoping can become somewhat cloudy. Sometimes, you may have a web portal that will send all transactions involving the transmission or processing of credit-card data to different systems. It is likely that the entire cluster will be in scope for PCI in this case.

Finally, WAS (as an option in Requirement 6.4.1) is not a substitute for the web application penetration test (mandated in Requirement 11.3). Modern web application scanners can do a lot of poking and probing, but they cannot completely perform tasks performed by a human who is attacking a web application. For example, the full discovery of cross-site request forgery (XSRF or CSRF) flaws is not possible using automated scanners today.

NOTE

Network vulnerability scanning (mandated in Requirement 11.2) and web application security testing (as an option in Requirement 6.4.1) are loosely related, but independent countermeasures. Network vulnerability scanning is mostly about looking for security issues in operating systems and off-the-shelf applications, such as Microsoft Office or Apache Web server, while web application security testing typically looks for security issues in custom and customized web applications. Simply scanning your website with a network vulnerability scanner does not satisfy Requirement 6.4.1 at all.

Some vendors offer both—but they are priced separately (and differently) and should be used based on different operational practices.

Whether network or application, the act of scanning is not sufficient by itself because it will only tell you about the issues. You need to either fix the offending lines of code or deploy a WAF to block possible exploitation of the issues.

That is what we are going to discuss next.

WARNING

While talking about network or application scanning, you rarely if ever scan to "just know what is out there." The work does not end when the scan completes—it only begins. The risk reduction from vulnerability scanning comes when you actually remediate the vulnerability or at least mitigate the possible loss. Even if scanning for PCI DSS compliance, your goal is ultimately risk reduction, which only comes when the scan results come back clean.

WEB APPLICATION FIREWALLS (WAFs)

Let's briefly address WAFs. Before the discussion of this technology, remember that a network firewall deployed in front of a website is not the same as a WAF. WAFs got their unfortunate name (the firewall bit) from the hands of marketers. They are more like an IDS/IPS specifically made for web applications.

A network firewall serves to block or allow traffic based on network protocol and port as well as source and destination (among other properties), whereas a WAF analyzes the application behavior before blocking or allowing an interaction with the web application framework.

A WAF, like a network intrusion detection system (IDS) or IPS, needs to be tuned to be effective. To tune it, review configuration guidance and understand what traffic will be monitored (TLS v1.3 introduces some challenges to typical HTTPS interception techniques). Once that's done, run reports that give total counts per violation type and tweak your rules. Often, a few messages that you determine to be acceptable traffic for your environment and applications will clean up 80% of the clutter in the alert window. This sounds like an obvious statement, but you would be amazed how many people try to tune WAF technologies in blocking mode while causing the application availability issues in your environment.

If you have a development or quality assurance (QA) environment, placing a WAF (the same type you use in production) in front of one or more of these environments (even in just read/passive mode) is a must to ensure it is functioning as designed while catching vulnerabilities before they hit production. A WAF may allow you to deploy your application to production even with a vulnerability in the code with rules to block an exploitative attempt. In addition, place a WAF in a manner that will block all the directions from where the application attacks might come from (including insider attacks). Any custom rules to mitigate vulnerabilities will need to be added to the production WAF to ensure the application does not break.

Finally, unlike the early versions, WAFs are now quite stable and can be used to protect your website from the exploitation of vulnerabilities you discover while scanning.

PAYMENT PAGES

Requirement 6.4.3 introduces a new requirement, best practice until after March 31, 2025, that applies to "all payment page scripts that are loaded and executed in the consumer's browser." These scripts must be protected to ensure that the script that runs is authorized and the same as the approved script. If applicable, consider the security risks of a script maintained by a third party or scripts that change frequently. Cookie security is also paramount here, "SECURE" and "HTTP-ONLY" are your friends here, but you also need to make sure the cookies are properly scoped to prevent data from being sent to an unintended service.

This will require an inventory of all scripts used and technical details about the script to properly ensure file integrity checking is managed properly. Many attacks over the last few years launched against e-Commerce sites, including the Magecart attacks, used this approach to substitute malicious scripts to run and forward cardholder data to the attackers, often with almost negligible differences to the customer. Both James & Branden have been shocked to see everyday large retailers we all know and love including dozens, if not over a hundred add-ins on their websites. We bet you don't know what is on your e-commerce site right now and would be shocked to see the dozens of trackers or add-ins you were not expecting.

CHANGE MANAGEMENT

Let's review some of the sub-requirements of 6.5, which are specific requirements for managing and documenting changes in your environment. Requirement 6.5.1 covers a critical area of IT governance: change control. Each record should have an easy-to-point-out section that addresses each bullet point. Change control can be considered a vulnerability management measure because unpredicted, unauthorized changes often lead to opening vulnerabilities in both custom and off-the-shelf software and systems.

The basic rule of thumb is: if you change something somewhere in your IT environment, document it. Whether it is a bound notebook (small company) or a change control system (large company) is secondary, leaving a record is primary.

To put this into context, most other IT governance frameworks, such as Control Objectives for Information (COBIT) or Information Technology Infrastructure Library (ITIL), cover change control as one of the most significant areas that directly affect system security. Indeed, having documentation and sign-off for changes and an ability to *undo* things will help achieve both security and operation goals by reducing the risk, and striving toward operational excellence.

The next requirement, 6.5.2, ensures that significant changes do not negatively change the security posture. These changes should trigger a review of applicable PCI DSS requirements and result in documentation of what requirements were considered and how the compliance was verified.

Requirement 6.5.3 considers the importance of network segmentation and access: "Pre-production environments are separated from production environments and the separation is enforced with access controls." Attackers are targeting publicly available development and testing or staging sites and have been able to take advantage of less stringent security oversight. In addition to network separation, Requirement 6.5.4 mandates that roles and functions be separated as well. The goal of this is to ensure that only changes that have been reviewed and approved are deployed to production.

A key requirement 6.5.5, which states "Live PANs are not used in pre-production environments" is of critical importance and commonly violated. Breaches happen when uninformed developers move data from the more secure production environment to a much less-protected test environment, as well as on mobile workstations, remote offices, and so on. If cardholder data *is* needed, and please interrogate your developers regarding this "need," the testing or development environment should be in the CDE and protected with all applicable PCI DSS controls.

In the opposite direction, contaminating the production environment with test code, data, and accounts is also critical (and can be just as disastrous as production data ending up on non-production systems) and is covered in Section 6.5.6, which regulates the use of "test data and test accounts." Similar to non-production networks that are not isolated, recent attackers have focused on looking for leftover administrator logins, test code, hard-coded passwords, or other unchanged default configuration.

NOTE

If you are following good data handling processes, your non-production environments will have limited exposure to PCI compliance requirements. That doesn't mean they aren't important. Where possible, implement the same security controls from production in your development and test environments. When you introduce security earlier in the development process, you reduce the risk of those environments being leveraged for attacks and compromise. While these environments are not considered production for PCI purposes, Dev environments are production for developers and UAT environments are production for Q/A—don't underestimate their importance or threat factors.

SOFTWARE SUPPLY CHAIN ATTACKS

Open source software is amazingly useful. Sharing knowledge and continual improvement allows community-sourced development at a large scale. Branden started his technology career in the mid-1990s when open source was literally powering his startup.

In recent years, the prolific use of open-source software created another problem—that of software supply chain attacks. This problem isn't only limited to open-source software as we saw with the SolarWinds event in 2020. There is so much code driving everything we build that keeping track of it all is a new problem for us to solve. These attacks have always been present, but two main areas of attack present credible threats to technology today: hijacking public repositories such as the perl.com domain or the `coa` and `rc` NPM libraries in 2021, and copycat packages that use dependency or namespace confusion for components published in large, public community repositories. A full discussion about this is beyond the scope of this book, but it's a threat we all face today.

PCI DSS only tackles a portion of this problem through the new bespoke software inventory requirements as part of Requirement 6.3.2. These inventories will be critical if there is an issue with a component you may be using. You want to know exactly where you need to target remediation and response efforts.

REQUIREMENT 11 WALK-THROUGH

The requirement name itself asks users to "Test Security of Systems and Network Regularly," which indicates that the focus of this requirement goes beyond just buffer overflows and format string vulnerabilities from the technical realm, but also includes process weaknesses vulnerabilities. An example of a process weakness is using default passwords or easily guessable passwords (such as the infamous "1234" password—or its more modern version "123456"). The above process weaknesses can be checked from the technical side, for example during the network scan by a scanner that can do authenticated policy and configuration audits, such as password strength checks.

The requirement text goes into a brief description of vulnerabilities in a somewhat illogical manner: "Vulnerabilities are being discovered continually by malicious individuals and researchers and being introduced by new software." Maybe more accurately, vulnerabilities are being introduced first by software vendors and then discovered by researchers (which are sometimes called blue teams) and attackers (red teams).

The requirement then calls for frequent testing of software for vulnerabilities: "System components, processes, and bespoke and custom software should be tested frequently to ensure security controls continue to reflect a changing environment." Notice in this section that the Council explicitly calls for testing of systems (such as operating systems software or embedded operating systems), processes (such as the password-management process examples referenced above), and custom software, but doesn't mention the commercial off-the-shelf (COTS) software applications. The reason for this is that it is included as part of the definition of "a system" because it is not only the operating system code but vendor application code that contains vulnerabilities.

Requirements 11.1.1 and 11.1.2 dictate that the policies and processes used to test networks are documented, maintained, and published as well as ensuring that roles and responsibilities are documented, assigned, and understood.

Wireless network testing (Requirement 11.2.1) states: "Authorized and unauthorized wireless access points are managed." This means scanning for both known and unknown wireless access points and cross-referencing with your inventory documentation (Requirement 11.2.2). This should be done at least once every three months, if not using an automated solution with alerting enabled. Indeed, most retail environments today make heavy use of wireless networks and POS wireless network traffic has been successfully used as an attack vector. Please refer to Chapter 7, "Using Wireless Networking," for wireless guidance.

Section 11.3 requires you to ensure that "external and internal vulnerabilities are regularly identified, prioritized, and addressed." The primary method for this is quarterly vulnerability scans that are run both internally on the CDE and externally on public-facing in-scope systems.

This requirement has an interesting twist, however. Quarterly *external* vulnerability scans required in 11.3.2 must be performed by a scan vendor qualified by the payment card industry. Thus, just using any scanner won't do. Instead, you need to select a vendor from the list of ASVs, which we mentioned in Chapter 3, Why Is PCI Here? At the same time, the requirements for scans performed after changes are more relaxed. Scans conducted after significant changes may be "performed by qualified personnel" with "organizational independence." There should be a dedicated person or team who is responsible for scanning and remediation validation, who are incentivized to provide accurate vulnerability reporting.

NOTE

Here's another place where having a valid and up-to-date inventory of systems is critical. Someone in a "Shadow IT" organization just spun up a new cloud-hosted website that's directly connected to the internet? Guess what, that's in scope! Internal server decommissioned and no longer showing up on the internal scans? QSA will notice! Be sure to review your official asset list against the vulnerability scans immediately after they run to identify any additions or omissions.

The next section covers the specifics of ASV scanning and the section after covers the internal scanning.

EXTERNAL VULNERABILITY SCANNING WITH ASV

We will look into the operational issues of using an ASV, cover some tips about picking one, and then discuss what to expect from an ASV.

WHAT IS AN ASV?

As we mentioned in Chapter 3, Why Is PCI Here?, PCI DSS validation also includes network vulnerability scanning by an ASV. To become an ASV, companies must undergo a process similar to QSA qualification. The difference is that in the case of QSAs, the individual assessors attend classroom training on an annual basis, whereas ASVs submit a scan conducted against a test network perimeter. An organization can choose to become both QSA and ASV, which allows the merchants and service providers to select a single vendor for PCI compliance validation.

ASVs are security companies that help you satisfy one of the two third-party validation requirements in PCI. ASVs go through a laboratory test process to confirm that their scanning technology is sufficient for PCI validation.

Also, it is worthwhile to mention that validation via an external ASV scan only applies to those merchants that are required to validate requirement 11. In particular, those who don't process or store any data on premises and those with dial-up (non-Internet) terminals. This is important, so it bears repeating; if you have no system to scan because you don't process or store data in-house, you don't have to scan. If this is you, you probably don't have to do too much around PCI DSS. Of course, it goes without saying that deploying a vulnerability management system to reduce your information risk is appropriate even if PCI DSS didn't exist at all.

CONSIDERATIONS WHEN PICKING AN ASV

First, your acquiring bank might have picked an ASV for you as part of their merchant security program. In this case, you might not have an option on the vendor to use. The ASV selected by your acquirer might not be the best or the cheapest.

While looking at the whole list of ASVs and then picking the one that "sounds nice" is one way to pick, it is likely not the one that will ensure trouble-free PCI validation and increased card data security as well as reduced risk of data theft. At the time of this writing, the ASV list has grown tremendously, from small consulting outlets to the IBMs and Verizons of the world, located on all the continents (save Antarctica). How do you pick?

Organizations that blindly assume that "all ASVs are the same" based on the fact that all are certified by the PCI Council to satisfy PCI DSS scan validation requirements would sometimes just pick on price. This same assumption sometimes applies to QSAs, and as many security industry insiders have pointed out (including both of us), they all are not created equal!

As a result, passing the scan validation requirement and submitting the report that indicates "Pass" will definitely confirm your PCI validation (as long as your ASV remains in good standing with the Council). Sadly, it will not do nearly enough for your cardholder data security. Even if certified, ASVs coverage of vulnerabilities varies greatly; many of them do the mandatory minimum, but more than a few cut corners and stay at that minimum (which, by the way, they are perfectly allowed to do), while others help you uncover other holes and flaws that allow malicious hackers to get to that valuable card data.

Thus, your strategy might follow these steps.

First, realize that all ASVs are not created equal; at the very least, prices for their services will be different, which should give you a hint that the value they provide will also be different.

Second, realize that all ASVs roughly fall into two groups: those that do the minimum necessary according to the above guidance documents (focus on compliance) and those that intelligently interpret the standard and help you with your data security and not just with PCI DSS compliance (focus on security). Typically, the way to tell the two groups apart is to look at the price. In addition, currently registered ASVs overwhelmingly use the scanning technologies from Qualys or Tenable to perform PCI validation.

In addition, though the pricing models for ASV services vary they roughly fall into two groups: in one model, you can scan your systems many times (unlimited scanning) while the other focuses on providing you the mandatory quarterly scan (i.e., four per year). In the latter case, if your initial scan shows the vulnerabilities and need to fix and rescan to arrive at a passing scan, you will be paying extra. Overall, it is extremely unlikely that you can get away with only scanning your network from the outside four times per year.

Third, even though an ASV does not have to be used for internal scanning, it is more logical to pick the same scanning provider for external (must be done by an ASV) and internal (must be done by somebody skilled in using vulnerability management tools). Using the same technology provider will allow you to have the same familiar report format and the same presentation of vulnerability findings. Even though external scanning does not require authenticated scanning, picking an ASV that can run authenticated scans on your internal network is useful since such scanning can be used to automate the checking for the presence of other DSS controls, such as password length, account security settings, use of encryption, and availability of anti-malware defenses.

Table 9.1 shows a sample list of PCI DSS controls that may be performed using automated scanning tools that perform authenticated or trusted scanning.

Look for how the ASV workflow matches your experience and expectation. Are there many manual tasks required to perform a vulnerability scan and create a report or is everything automated? Fully automated ASV services, where launching a scan and presenting a compliance report to your acquirer can be done from the same interface, are available. Still, if you need help with fixing the issues before you can rescan and validate your compliance, hiring an ASV that offers help with remediation is advisable. It goes without saying that picking an ASV that requires you to purchase any hardware or software is not advisable; all external scan requirements can be satisfied by scanning from the Internet.

Finally, even though this strategy focuses on picking an ASV, you and your organization have a role to play as well, namely, in fixing the vulnerabilities that the scan discovered to arrive at a compliant status—clean scan with no failures. We discuss the criteria that ASVs use for pass/fail below.

TABLE 9.1

Automatic Validation of PCI DSS Controls

Requirement	PCI DSS 4.0 Requirement	Technical Validation of PCI Requirements
1.5.1	Host-based security controls, such as personal firewall software or endpoint protection software, are installed for any computing devices that are able to connect to both untrusted networks and the CDE (for example, laptops used by employees).	Automated tools are able to check for the presence of personal firewalls deployed on servers, desktops, and laptops remotely.
2.2.1	Develop configuration standards for all system components. Assure that these standards address all known security vulnerabilities and are consistent with industry-accepted system hardening standards.	Automated tools can validate the compliance of deployed systems to configuration standards, mandated by the PCI DSS.
2.2.2	Always change vendor-supplied defaults before installing a system on the network, including but not limited to passwords, simple network management protocol (SNMP) community strings, and elimination of unnecessary accounts.	Automated tools can be used to verify that vendor defaults are not used by checking for default and system accounts on servers, desktops, and network devices.
2.2.4	Enable only necessary and secure services, protocols, daemons, etc., as required for the function of the system. Remove or disable any unnecessary functionality, such as scripts, drivers, features, subsystems, file systems, and unnecessary web servers.	Automated tools can help discover network-exposed services that are running on systems and unnecessary functionality exposed to the network, and thus significantly reduce the effort needed to bring the environment in compliance.
2.2.7	Encrypt all non-console administrative access using strong cryptography. Use technologies such as SSH, VPN, or SSL/TLS for web-based management and other non-console administrative access.	Automated tools can help validate that encrypted protocols are in use across the systems and that unencrypted communication is not enabled on servers and workstations (SSH, not Telnet; SSL, not unencrypted HTTP, etc.).
2.3.1	For wireless environments connected to the cardholder data environment or transmitting cardholder data, change wireless vendor defaults, including but not limited to default wireless encryption keys, passwords, and SNMP community strings.	Automated tools can be used to verify that default settings and default passwords are not used across wireless devices connected to the wired network.
3.5	Render PAN unreadable anywhere it is stored (including on portable digital media, backup media, and in logs).	Automated tools can confirm that encryption is in use across the PCI in-scope systems by checking system configuration settings relevant to encryption.
3.6	Protect any keys used to secure cardholder data against disclosure and misuse.	Automated tools can be used to validate security settings relevant to the protection of system encryption keys.
4.2	Use strong cryptography and security protocols to safeguard sensitive cardholder data during transmission over open, public networks.	Automated tools can be used to validate the use of strong cryptographic protocols by checking relevant system configuration settings or certificates and detect instances of insecure cipher use across the in-scope systems.
4.2.1.2	Ensure wireless networks transmitting cardholder data or connected to the cardholder data environment, use industry best practices (e.g. IEEE 802.11i) to implement strong encryption for authentication and transmission.	Automated tools can attempt to detect wireless access points from the network side and to validate the use of proper encryption across those access points.

(Continued)

TABLE 9.1 *(Continued)*
Automatic Validation of PCI DSS Controls

Requirement	PCI DSS 4.0 Requirement	Technical Validation of PCI Requirements
5.2	Deploy anti-malware software on all systems at risk for malware (particularly, personal computers and servers).	Automated tools can validate whether anti-malware software is installed on in-scope systems.
5.3.1	Ensure that all anti-malware mechanisms are current, actively running, and capable of generating audit logs.	Automated tools can be used to check for running status of anti-malware tools.
6.3.1	Establish a process to identify and assign a risk ranking to newly discovered security vulnerabilities.	Automated tools are constantly updated with new vulnerability information and can be used in tracking newly discovered vulnerabilities.
6.3.3	Ensure that all system components and software are protected from known vulnerabilities by having the latest vendor-supplied security patches installed. Install critical security patches within 1 month of release.	Automated tools can be used to detect missing OS, application patches, and security updates.
6.4.1 (6.4.2 after March 31, 2025)	For public-facing Web applications, address new threats and vulnerabilities on an ongoing basis and ensure these applications are protected against known attacks by either of the following methods: reviewing public-facing Web applications via manual or automated application vulnerability security assessment tools or methods, at least annually and after any changes.	Automated tools can be used to assess Web application security in support of PCI Requirement 6.4.
7.2.2	Limit access to system components and cardholder data to only those individuals whose job requires such access.	Automated tools can analyze database user right and permissions, looking for broad and insecure permissions.
8.2.1	Assign all users a unique ID before allowing them to access system components or cardholder data.	In partial support of this requirement, automated tools are used to look for active default, generic accounts (root, system, etc.), which indicate that account sharing takes place.
8.3.1	In addition to assigning a unique ID, use at least one of the following methods to authenticate all users: something you know (password or passphrase), something you have (token), or something you are (biometrics).	Automated tools can be used to look for user accounts with improper authentication settings, such as accounts with no passwords or with blank passwords.
8.3.2	Render all authentication factors unreadable during transmission and storage on all system components using strong cryptography.	Automated tools can be used to detect system configuration settings, permitting unencrypted and inadequately encrypted passwords across systems.
11.2	Test for the presence of wireless access points and detect all authorized and unauthorized wireless access points at least every three months.	Automated tools can attempt to detect wireless access points from the network side, thus to help the detection of rogue access points.
11.3	Perform internal and external vulnerability scans at least every three months and after any significant change in the network (such as new system component installations, changes in network topology, firewall rule modifications, and product upgrades).	Automated tools can be used to scan for vulnerabilities both from inside and from outside the network.

How ASV Scanning Works

ASVs use standard vulnerability scanning technology to detect vulnerabilities that are deemed by the PCI Council to be relevant for PCI DSS compliance. This information will help you understand what exactly you are dealing with when you retain the scanning services of an ASV. It will also help you learn how to pass or fail the PCI scan criteria and how to prepare your environment for an ASV scan.

Specifically, the ASV procedures mandate that ASV covers commonly found vulnerabilities. For more information, you can check the ASV Program Guide in the Document Library section of the PCI Council website. When you do, you will notice that PCI DSS external scanning is not everything you need to do for security. After all, PCI DSS focuses on card data loss, not on the availability of your key IT resources for your organization and not on their resistance to malicious hackers.

Each ASV will interpret the requirements a little differently. However, quality ASV identifies many different types of vulnerabilities in addition to PCI DSS.

When the scan completes, the report is generated, which can then be used to substantiate your PCI validation via vulnerability scanning.

To summarize, ASV quality scanning will detect all possible external vulnerabilities and highlight those that are reasons for PCI DSS validation failure. The same process needs to be repeated for quarterly scans—usually toward the end of the quarter but not during the last day because remediation activities need to happen before a final rescan takes place. In fact, let's talk about operationalizing the ASV scanning.

Operationalizing ASV Scanning

To recap PCI DSS Requirement 11.3 calls for quarterly scanning. In addition, every scan may lead to remediation activities, and those aren't limited to patching. Moreover, validation procedures mention that a QSA will ask for four passing reports during an assessment. If this is not provided, this requirement will generate an "In Place with Remediation" status, something new for PCI DSS 4.0. While the consequences or consistent application of an assessment finding like this is still unknown, it will note to the reader of your report on compliance that you were not maintaining good practice throughout the year.

First, it is a very good idea to scan monthly or even weekly if possible. Why would you be doing it to satisfy a quarterly scanning requirement? Well, consider the following scenario: on the last day of the quarter, you perform an external vulnerability scan and you discover a critical vulnerability. The discovered vulnerability is present on 20% of your systems, which totals to 200 systems. Now, you have exactly one day to fix the vulnerability on all systems and perform a passing vulnerability scan, which will be retained for your records. Is this realistic?

This scenario happens with companies that postpone their quarterly vulnerability scan until the very last day instead of ongoing vulnerability scanning. Considering the fact that many acquiring institutions are becoming more stringent with PCI validation requirements, you may not get an exception. Beyond the first day over the next month, the scenario will certainly incur unnecessary pain and suffering on your company and your IT staff. What is the way to avoid it? Performing scans every month or even every week. It is also a good idea to perform an external scan after you apply a patch, introduce new systems, or perform other changes to external infrastructure.

NOTE

Most companies run their external scans monthly, even though those are called "quarterly scans." That way, issues can be resolved in time to have a clean quarterly report since there are no surprises. There are known cases where organizations have been burned by waiting until the last month of a quarter to run an external scan. This can cause a serious amount of last-minute, emergency code and system configuration changes, and an overall sense of panic, which is not conducive to good security management.

After you run the scan, carefully review the results of the reports. Are those passing or failing reports? If the report indicates that you do not pass the PCI validation requirement, please note which systems and vulnerabilities do not pass the criteria. Next, distribute the report to those in your IT organization who is responsible for the systems that fail the test. Offer them some guidance on how to fix the vulnerabilities and bring those systems back to PCI compliance. These intermediate reports will absolutely not be shared with your acquiring institutions.

When you receive the indication that those vulnerabilities have been successfully fixed, rescan to obtain a clean report. Repeat this process monthly or weekly.

Finally, scan a final round before the end of the quarter and preserve the reports for the assessor. Thus, your shields will be up at all times. If you are only scanning four times a year, you're suffering from two problems. First, you are most likely not PCI compliant throughout most of the year. Second, you burden yourself with a massive emergency effort right at the end of the quarter when other people at your organization expect IT systems to operate at its peak. Don't be the one telling finance that they cannot run that quarterly report!

WHAT SHOULD YOU EXPECT FROM AN ASV?

Discussing the expectations while dealing with an ASV and working toward PCI DSS scan validation is a valuable exercise. The critical considerations are described below.

First, an ASV can scan you and present the data (report) to you. It is your job to then bring the environment in compliance. After that, the ASV can again be used to validate your compliant status and produce a clean report. Remember, ASV scanning does not make you compliant, *you do*, by making sure that no PCI-fail vulnerabilities are present in your network.

Second, you don't have to hire expensive consultants just to run an ASV scan for you every quarter. Some ASVs will automatically perform the scan with the correct settings and parameters, without you learning the ins and outs of any particular vulnerability scanner. You can sometimes even pay your scans online and get started right away.

Third, you should expect a quality ASV will discover more vulnerabilities than is required for PCI DSS compliance. You need to make your own judgment call on whether to fix them. One common case where you might want to address the issue is vulnerabilities that allow hackers to crash your systems (denial of service [DoS] vulnerabilities). Such flaws are out of scope for PCI because they cannot directly cause the theft of card data (albeit, this can depend on this cause of flaw leading to a DoS); however, by not fixing them, you are allowing the attackers to disrupt your online business operations.

Finally, some common tips on ASV scanning.

First comes the question: what system must you scan for PCI DSS compliance? The answer to this splits into two parts, for external and internal scanning.

Specifically, for external systems or those visible from the Internet, you must provide the details to your ASV as follows: "IP addresses and/or domain names of all Internet-facing systems to the ASV so the ASV can properly conduct a full scan" (page 9 of the ASV Program Guide version 3.1). The obvious answer can be "none" if your business has no connection to the Internet.

For internal systems, the answer covers all systems that are considered in-scope for PCI, which is either those involved with card processing or directly connected to them. The answer can also be "none" if you have no systems inside your perimeter, which are in-scope for PCI DSS.

Another common question is how to pass the PCI DSS scan validation? Just as above, the answer is very clear for external scans: you satisfy the above criteria. If you don't, you need to fix the vulnerabilities that are causing you to fail and the rescan. Then, you pass and get a passing report, that you can submit to your acquiring bank.

For internal scans, the pass/fail criteria are part of Requirement 11.3.1.1.

Also, people often ask whether they become "PCI compliant" if they get a passing scan for their external systems. The answer is certainly a "no." You only satisfied one of the PCI DSS requirements; namely, PCI DSS validation via an external ASV scan. This is not the end. Likely, this is the beginning.

INTERNAL VULNERABILITY SCANNING

As we mentioned in the section, "Vulnerability Management in PCI," internal vulnerability scanning must be performed every quarter and after every material system change, and no critical or high-severity vulnerability must be present in the final scan preserved for presentation to your QSA. Requirement 11.3.1 states that a merchant or service provider must perform internal vulnerability scans "at least once every three months." A QSA must then examine the report results and verify that the scan process occurred at least that often and included rescans until all high-risk and critical vulnerabilities, as defined in PCI DSS Requirement 6.2, are resolved. The remaining vulnerabilities, per Requirement 11.3.1.1 requires "those not ranked as high-risk or critical per the entity's vulnerability risk rankings defined" are addressed based on your documented risk analysis and rescanned as necessary. The scan tools will also need to be reviewed to ensure they are being kept up to date. Requirement 11.3.1.3 also mentioned internal scanning "Perform internal and external scans, and rescans as needed, after any significant change."

First, using the same template your ASV uses for external scanning is a really good idea, but you can use more reliable trusted or authenticated scanning, which will reveal key application security issues on your in-scope systems that regular, unauthenticated scanning may sometimes miss.

Remediation may take the form of hardening, patching, architecture changes, technology/tool implementations, or a combination thereof. Remediation efforts after internal scanning are prioritized based on risk and can be managed better than external ASV scans. Something to keep in mind for PCI environments is that the remediation of critical vulnerabilities on all in-scope systems is mandatory. This makes all critical and high-risk vulnerabilities found on in-scope PCI systems a top priority. Follow the same process we covered in the "operationalizing ASV scanning" section and work toward removing the high-severity vulnerabilities from the environment before presenting the clean report to the QSA.

Reports that show the finding and remediation of vulnerabilities for in-scope systems over time become artifacts that are needed to satisfy assessment requirements. You should consider that having a place to keep archives of all internal and external scan reports (summary, detailed, and remediation) for a 12-month period is a good idea. Your ASV may offer to keep them for you and also as an added service. However, it is ultimately your responsibility.

This is a continuous process. As with other PCI compliance efforts, it is important to realize that PCI compliance is an effort that takes place 24×7×365 days a year (don't take that extra day off on leap years either).

For Internal scanning, you can create different reports for technicians who will fix issues found and summary reports for management. However, overdoing it is bad as well: handing a 10,000-page report to a technician will typically not result in remediation taking place—or at least the right remediation to remain compliant. We are not even talking about a possibility of showing such a report to senior management. Working with the team responsible for remediation to ensure the reports give them actionable data, without overwhelming them, is very much worth the time spent.

Servers that are in-scope are usually scanned off-hours. Be sure your scan windows do not occur during maintenance windows or the target hosts may be off-line for maintenance. If you have workstations in-scope, scans may need to be run during business hours. For systems that must be scanned during business hours, you may need to make the scans run at a lower intensity.

WARNING

The proliferation of devices with internet connectivity (known as the Internet of Things or IoT) also introduces the need to secure the interaction of these devices with our infrastructure. Examples are office automation devices, healthcare monitoring devices, or supply chain tracking devices. These purpose-built IT solutions are being bridged to the internet to provide the ability to remotely monitor and manage. Many times the devices are built to accomplish very simple goals and not tested against good security practices or vetted for vulnerabilities prior to release.

The easiest way to avoid the vulnerabilities, of course, is to make sure that these devices are not in your cardholder data environment to begin with. Create a separate isolated network that can limit the impact if devices do have security vulnerabilities, but out of scope for PCI. If those devices cannot receive security or firmware updates, be very wary of vulnerabilities they may harbor. If you are relying on them to accept payments, you will likely need to determine a custom scanning solution that works with the device's code and ensure that you are including them in your ongoing compliance activities.

Until you have thoroughly defined processes (documentation again—many efforts in PCI DSS require both "doing" and "recording") for all scanning, remediation, and reporting functions tied to your PCI needs, you are not using a repeatable and effective process.

Finally, issues will undoubtedly occur as you begin your scanning efforts. Here, having a well-defined root cause analysis helps a lot. The sidebar covers how to handle such issues.

TOOLS

Here is a sample PCI DSS scan issue tracking process in four steps:

1. Gather inputs from the issue.
   a. Gather Host/Application information: application name, version, patch level, port usage information, etc.
      i. Was the application disrupted, a system service, or the entire operating system?
   b. What had to be done to recover from the outage? Service restart or host reboot?
2. Verify that the issue was caused by the scan. Check system logs and try to match the time of the incident to the time of the scan.
3. Place a support call with the application vendor or development team. Verify that all patches have been applied to the application for "denial of service" and "buffer overflow" problems.
4. If the issue is not resolved by the application vendor, engage support from your scanning vendor.

A special thank you to Derek Milroy for providing the sample process.

Let's also address the issues of a system change. It is your responsibility to perform a scan after these events have taken place ("Perform internal and external scans, and rescans as needed, after any significant change. Scans must be performed by qualified personnel.")

Finally, remember that internal scanning is as mandatory for in-scope systems as the ASV scanning is mandatory for external systems.

Penetration Testing

Requirement 11.4 covers penetration testing requirements. Your penetration testing methodology needs to be "defined, documented, and implemented." The logic here is again similar to vulnerability scanning: at least annually and after major changes.

Requirement 11.4.1 specifies that a penetration test must include the following:

- Industry-accepted penetration testing approaches,
- Coverage for the entire CDE perimeter and critical systems,
- Testing from both inside and outside the network,

- Testing to validate any segmentation and scope-reduction controls,
- Application-layer penetration tests to include, at a minimum, the vulnerabilities listed in Requirement 6.5,
- Network-layer penetration tests to include components that support network functions as well as operating systems,
- Review and consideration of threats and vulnerabilities experienced in the last 12 months,
- Documented approach to assessing and addressing the risk posed by exploitable vulnerabilities and security weaknesses found during penetration testing (NEW), and
- Retention of penetration testing results and remediation activities for at least 12 months.

By the way, multiple books have been written on the art and science of the penetration test. The various methods of penetration testing techniques are beyond the scope of this book. Just remember that a penetration test will always involve a skilled, human attacker, not only an automated tool.

Every penetration test begins with one concept—communication. A penetration test should be viewed by a security team as a hostile act—provided they are not asleep at the wheel. After all, the point is to break through active and passive defenses erected around an information system. Communication is important because somebody is about to break your security. During the time of the penetration test, alarm bells should ring, processes would be put into motion, and, if communication has not occurred, and appropriate permissions to perform these tests have not been obtained, law enforcement authorities may be contacted to investigate. Now wouldn't that be an embarrassment if your PCI-driven penetration test, planned for months, had not been approved by your Chief Information Officer (CIO)?

Moreover, PCI DSS dives deeper into penetration testing details. These penetration tests must include both internal penetration testing (Requirement 11.4.2) and external penetration testing (Requirement 11.4.3).

Each test should be performed in accordance with the documented methodology and at least once every 12 months or after significant changes. Per Requirement 11.4.4, each test should be repeated until clean: "Exploitable vulnerabilities and security weaknesses found during penetration testing are corrected" and "penetration testing is repeated to verify the corrections." Keep in mind, they are asking you to confirm that the vulnerability is fixed by testing that one piece again, not running the entire penetration test again for every vulnerability corrected.

In addition, they need to verify segmentation (Requirement 11.4.5) that states that "If segmentation is used to isolate the CDE from other networks, penetration tests are performed on segmentation controls."

NOTE

Documenting the methodology and scope of your penetration tests is incredibly important to ensuring that all attack vectors against the PCI CDE are being mitigated. Don't forget to make sure that technologies like VPNs, wireless access points, critical systems that could be outside of the CDE (such as perimeter firewalls, IDS/IPS, authentication servers, etc.). While PCI DSS 4.0 does not specifically require social engineering, it has certainly been a successful route to compromise for many organizations and could be included in the methodology.

COMMON PCI VULNERABILITY MANAGEMENT MISTAKES

It is worthwhile to point out a few common mistakes that organizations make while working toward satisfying the vulnerability management requirements.

We hinted at the first mistake when we described the password example. It is in focusing only on the technical assessment (which is both easier and automated) and omitting the process-based mistakes and issues. In particular, for PCI DSS, it applies to testing only the technology controls but not checking for policy controls such as security awareness, presence of plans and procedures, etc.

Thus, people often focus on the technical vulnerabilities and forget all the human vulnerabilities, such as the susceptibility of many enterprise IT users to be duped by social engineering, and other lapses of corporate controls. The way to avoid this mistake is to keep in mind that even though you use a scanning vendor, your credit-card data might still be pilfered, and addressing the softer part of security is just as critical.

Another commonly lost and forgotten item is application-level vulnerabilities, which focuses on the web applications themselves—from XSS and SQL injection flaws to cross-site request forgery to more esoteric flaws in JavaScript code and other browser-side languages.

Even when application-layer vulnerabilities are not forgotten, and patching and other remediation are happening on an aggressive schedule (patching all servers within a single day time frame is considered aggressive and potentially disruptive), there is something else to consider: vulnerabilities in the applications that were written in-house. Indeed, no vulnerability scanner vendor will have knowledge of your custom-written systems, and even if your penetration-testing consultant or an internal red team will be able to discover some of them during an annual penetration test, a lot of application code can be written in a year (and thus a lot more vulnerability introduced). The way to avoid this mistake is to train your software engineering staff to use secure programming practices to minimize the occurrence of these flaws as we discussed in a previous section on Requirement 6 (the detailed coverage of it goes well beyond the scope of this book). This can also be reinforced with tools that provide inline warnings in the IDE as well as automated verification in your release management platform. While having a good application tester on staff may not be in your budget, assessing the security of the homegrown application needs to be undertaken more frequently than once a year. It should be part of your go-live process when you promote code from non-production to production. Obviously, an initial focus on web-based and Internet-exposed applications is a must.

The last mistake we mention is misjudging the list of in-scope systems. Modern, large-scale payment processing systems are complicated and have many dependencies. Avoiding this mistake is not easy: the only way to find all the systems that might need to be scanned and protected is to have your internal staff (who know the systems best) work with an external PCI consultant or QSA (who knows the regulation best) to find out what should be in scope for your particular environment. Primarily, avoid these mistakes by documenting and being able to describe all the business processes that touch account data. This will take care of the known, authorized locations of account data and give you more ideas on reducing card data storage and processing. In addition, even though data discovery technologies are not mandated by PCI, we advise using them to discover other locations of card data, which are not authorized and are not known to be a part of the legitimate business process. The latter can be either eliminated or documented and added to PCI DSS scope: these are the only two choices, and "ignored" is not one of them.

Keeping these mistakes in mind has the chance of making your PCI compliance experience a lot less painful.

CASE STUDY

The case studies below illustrate how vulnerability management for PCI is implemented in a few real-world organizations.

PCI AT A RETAIL CHAIN

Sarah's Simple Foods did not perform any periodic network vulnerability scanning and didn't use the services of a penetration-testing firm, which put them in a clear violation of PCI DSS rules. Their IT security staff sometimes used freeware tools to scan a specific system for open ports and vulnerabilities, but all efforts were ad-hoc and not tied to any program.

Upon the approach of PCI DSS compliance deadline, their head of cybersecurity Paula began scanning using an ASV every quarter. She chose to deploy a service-based vulnerability scanning from a major vendor. Her choice of vendor was determined after a brief proof-of-concept study.

Initially, Paula had limited practical knowledge of Sarah's security posture because the scans were only ad-hoc and didn't cover the correct scope of systems. She re-baselined the scope of their scans to include all external IPs and only the in-scope internal systems.

Finding the internal systems that are in-scope was challenging because many systems have legitimate reasons to connect to the CDE. For example, their patch management system was in-scope as a Connected-To system since it pushed security patches to their transaction processing servers.

As a result, their PCI vulnerability management process took a few months following a phased approach. Paula's scope guidelines followed these steps:

1. All Internet-facing systems that can be scanned,
2. A set of internal systems that either process payments or connect to those that do, and
3. Systems that are not connected to payment processing, but are still business critical.

Even though the organization chose not to implement the intrusion detection earlier, their QSA strongly suggested that they look at some options in this area. Paula chose to upgrade Sarah's firewalls with Unified Threat Management (UTM) devices that combined the capabilities of a firewall and a network IPS. An external consultant suggested an initial intrusion prevention rule set, which the company deployed.

Overall, the project ended up with a successful, if longish, implementation of PCI Requirement 11 using a scanning service as well as UTM devices in place of their firewalls.

PCI AT AN E-COMMERCE SITE

Anna's Audiophiles recently began taking payments over her website for a custom streaming audio subscription service. Realizing that PCI compliance would be required, she assessed her current security monitoring efforts. These included the use of host IPS on their demilitarized zone (DMZ) servers as well as internal and external vulnerability scanning every three months. However, Anna realized that she needed to satisfy penetration testing requirements and file integrity check requirements.

Anna's IT staff performed extensive research on file integrity monitoring vendors, and chose one with the most advanced centralized management system (to ease the management of all the integrity-checking results). They used a small IT security outsourcing firm to perform penetration testing. These new controls required the creation of policy and procedure documentation as well as a new penetration testing methodology.

In addition, Anna's team used its previously acquired log-management solution to aggregate the host IPS and file integrity check logs and alerts and to create a distributed reporting interface for their PCI assessors. Overall, this project was a successful illustration of a security program that was following good security practices, but needed to add additional technical and non-technical controls to help it achieve PCI compliance.

SUMMARY

To conclude, PCI DSS spends a lot of effort with requirements related to software vulnerabilities. Let us summarize what areas are covered since such requirements are spread over multiple requirements, even belonging to multiple sections. Table 9.2 covers the vulnerability management activities that we covered in this chapter.

As a result, PCI allows for a fairly comprehensive, if a bit jumbled, look at the entire vulnerability landscape from coding to remediation and mitigation. Thus, you need to make sure that you look for all vulnerability-related guidance while planning your PCI-driven vulnerability management

TABLE 9.2

Vulnerability Management Activities in PCI DSS

Vulnerability-Related Activity Prescribed by PCI DSS	Requirement
Secure coding guidance in regular and web applications	6
Secure software deployment	6
Code review for vulnerabilities	6
Vulnerability scanning	11
Patching and remediation	6
Technologies that protect from vulnerability exploitation	5, 6, and 11
Site assessment and penetration testing	11

program. While focusing on vulnerability management, don't reduce your efforts to patch management only—include custom (bespoke) applications written in-house or by partners. You need to have an ongoing program to deal with discovered vulnerabilities. Wherever you can, automate the remediation of discovered vulnerabilities and focus on what you cannot. Finally, make sure that you rescan to ensure your reports come back clean.

10 Logging Events and Monitoring the Cardholder Data Environment

Information in this chapter:

- Payment Card Industry (PCI) Requirements Covered
- Why Logging and Monitoring in Payment Card Industry Data Security Standard (PCI DSS)?
- Logging and Monitoring in Depth
- PCI Relevance of Logs
- Logging in PCI Requirement 10
- Monitoring Data and Log Security Issues
- Logging and Monitoring in PCI—All Other Requirements
- PCI DSS Logging Policies and Procedures
- Tools for Logging in PCI
- Other Monitoring Tools
- Intrusion Detection and Prevention
- Integrity Monitoring
- Common Mistakes and Pitfalls
- Case Study
- Summary

When most people think about information security, they imagine blocking, deflecting, denying, or otherwise stopping a malicious hacking attack. Secure network architecture, secure server operating systems, data encryption, and other security technologies are deployed to shield your assets from that evil influence that can steal your information, commit fraud, or disrupt the operation of systems and networks.

Indeed, the visions of tall castle walls, deep moats, or more modern armor and battleships pervade most people's view of warfare as well as information security. However, there is more to warfare (and security) than armor and shields. We are talking about the other keystone of ancient as well as modern warfare: intelligence. Those archers who glance from the top of the castle walls and modern spy satellites that glance down to Earth are no less mandatory to winning (or "not losing," as we have it in the field of information security) the war than fortifications and armored divisions.

Security professionals align their security to The Five Functions from the NIST CSF:

- Identification,
- Prevention,
- Detection,
- Response, and
- Recovery.

Prevention is what covers all the blocking, deflecting, denying, or stopping attacks. Notice that it includes the actual blocking of a live attack (such as running a network intrusion prevention system)

DOI: 10.1201/9781003100300-10

as well as making sure that such an attack cannot take place (such as deploying a patch management system). However, what happens if such prevention measures actually *fail* to prevent or block an attack? Wouldn't it be nice to know that when that happens?

This is exactly where *detection* comes in. All the logging and monitoring technologies, whether relevant for the Payment Card Industry Data Security Standard (PCI DSS) or not, are things that allow you to *know*. Specifically, know that you are attacked, know that a prevention measure gave way, and know that an attacker has penetrated the network and is about to make it out with the loot. They also allow you to get better visibility into what is happening at any moment in your network.

As with any comprehensive security framework, PCI DSS requirements mandate not just prevention but detection in the form of logging, alerting, and monitoring. Your security program should expand upon PCI DSS to include Identification, Response, and Recovery.

PCI REQUIREMENTS COVERED

Contrary to popular belief, logging and monitoring are not constrained to Requirement 10, but in fact permeate all 12 of the PCI DSS requirements. Still, the key areas where logging and monitoring are mandated in PCI DSS are Requirement 10 and sections of Requirement 11.

WHY LOGGING AND MONITORING IN PCI DSS?

As mentioned above, security is not just prevention or blocking. We should review the benefits of monitoring before we go into describing what specific security monitoring measures are prescribed by PCI.

First comes situational awareness. It simply means knowing what is happening throughout the whole of your infrastructure. Examples here are "Who is doing what on that server?," "Who is accessing my network?," "What is that application doing with card data?," or "Why is that cloud resource active?" In addition, system logging helps you know not only what *is* going on but also what *was* going on—a vital component needed for investigations and incident response.

Next comes new threat discovery, which is simply knowing and analyzing what bad stuff may be happening in your environment. This illustrates one of the major use cases for collecting and reviewing logs as well as for operating intrusion detection systems (IDSs).

Third, logging helps you to get more value out of the network and security infrastructure, deployed for blocking and prevention. For example, using firewall logs for intrusion detection—often justified during assessments but not as commonly used—is an example of that.

What is even more interesting is that logging and monitoring controls (these would be considered detective controls) allow you to measure security and compliance by building metrics and trends. This means that you can use this data for a range of applications from a simple "Top users by bandwidth" report obtained from firewall logs, all the way to sophisticated tracking of Gmail cardholder data transmission and use.

Last, but not least, if the worst does happen, then you would need to have as much data as possible during your incident response process. You might not use it all, but having reliable logs, assessment trails, and network capture data from all affected systems is indispensable for a hectic post-incident environment.

Requirements 10 and 11 are easily capable of inflating PCI compliance costs to the point of consuming the small margins of card transactions. No one wants to lose money to be PCI compliant. Nowhere else in PCI compliance does the middle ground of design philosophy come into play more than in the discipline of monitoring, but this is also where minimizing the risk can hurt most.

Finally, assuming that you've designed your PCI environment to have appropriate physical and logical boundaries through the use of segregated networks and dedicated application space as we described in Chapter 4, Building and Maintaining a Secure Network, you should be able to identify the boundaries of your monitoring scope. If you haven't done this part, go back to Requirement 1 and start over!

LOGGING AND MONITORING IN DEPTH

As computer and Internet technology continues to spread and play a critical role in most of our lives, the records that they produce, such as logs and other traces, play a bigger role. From firewalls and routers to databases and enterprise applications, to wireless access points and Voice over Internet Protocol (VoIP) gateways, logs are being spewed forth at an ever-increasing pace. Both security and other IT components not only increase in numbers but also often come with more logging enabled out of the box. An example of this trend includes the Linux operating system as well as web servers, both commercial and open source, that now ship with increased levels of logging out of the box. In addition, such additional monitoring methods as full network packet capture, database audit and protection (DAP) tools, and special-purpose application monitoring are becoming common as well. And all this data begs for constant attention!

WARNING

A log management problem is to a large extent a data management problem. Thus, if you deal with logs (and deal with them you must), you'll manage plenty of data. On top of this, much of this data is often unstructured and requires normalization to get common messages into a common format and sent to a centralized place for analysis.

Still, with logs, it is much better to err on the side of keeping more—in case you need to look at it later. Storage is cheap these days. This is not the same as saying that you have to keep every log message but retaining more log data can save you in some situations.

This has led some people to proclaim that log analysis is inherently a *big data problem*. Indeed, log data does fit some of the common definitions of big data (such as based on volume, velocity, and variety), but clearly the problem of log overload predates the emergence of the field of big data and big data tools such as Hadoop. In essence, log data was big before there was big data!

This is easier written than executed. Immense volumes of monitoring data are generated minute by minute on payment card processing networks and customer-facing web resources. This results in a need to manage, store, and search all this data. Moreover, review of this data needs to happen both reactively, for instance after a suspected incident, and proactively, in search of potential risks and future problems. For example, a typical large retailer generates millions of log messages per day amounting to many terabytes or petabytes per year. An online merchant can generate millions of various log messages easily every day. One of the world's largest retailers has more than a petabyte of log data on their systems at any given time. Unlike other companies, retailers do not have the option of not managing their logs due to PCI DSS.

NOTE

Even though we often refer to retailers as a company subject to PCI DSS, PCI is not only about retailers. Remember, anyone who stores, processes, or transmits member-branded account numbers must comply with PCI DSS. This applies to e-commerce sites, hospitals, service providers, restaurants, hotels, and many other business-to-consumer companies.

To start our discussion of PCI logging and monitoring requirements, Table 10.1 shows a sample list of technologies that produce logs relevant to PCI. Though this list is not comprehensive, we bet you will find at least one system in your cardholder data environment for which logs are not being collected or monitored at all.

Despite the multitude of log sources and types, people typically start from network and firewall logs and then progress upward on the protocol stack as well as sideways toward other non-network

TABLE 10.1

Log-Producing Technologies, Monitored Using Their Logs

Type	Example Logs
Operating Systems	Linux syslog, Solaris syslog, Windows Event Log
Virtual Platforms	VMWare ESXi syslog, AWS logs, Kubernetes JSON logs
Databases	Oracle, SQL Server assessment trails
Network infrastructure	Cisco routers and switches syslog
Remote access	Virtual private network logs
Network security	Cisco ASA/FirePOWER firewalls syslog, Palo Alto syslog, Checkpoint syslog, Juniper syslog
Intrusion detection and preventions	Snort network intrusion detection system syslog and packet capture
Enterprise applications	SAP, PeopleSoft logs
Web servers	Apache logs, Internet Information Server logs
Proxy servers	BlueCoat, Squid logs
E-mail servers	Sendmail syslog, various Exchange logs
Domain Name System (DNS) servers	Bind DNS logs, MS DNS
Antivirus and antispyware	Symantec AV event logs, TrendMicro AV logs
Physical access control	IDenticard, CoreStreet
Wireless networking	Cisco Aironet AP logs

applications. For example, just about any firewall or network administrator will look at a simple summary of connections that her Cisco ASA/FirePOWER or Checkpoint firewall is logging. Many firewalls log in standard syslog format, and such logs are easy to collect and review.

For example, here is a Juniper firewall log message in syslog format:

```
NOC-FWa: NetScreen device\_id=NOC-FWa system-notification-00257(traffic):
start\_time="2020-05-01 19:17:37" duration=60 policy\_id=9 service=snmp
proto=17 src zone=noc-services dst zone=-access-ethernet action=Permit
sent=547 rcvd=432 src=10.0.12.10 dst=10.2.16.10 src\_port=1184 dst\_
port=161 src-xlated ip=10.0.12.10 port=1184
```

And, here is one from Cisco ASA/FirePOWER firewall device:

```
%ASA-6-106100: access-list outside\_access\_in denied icmp -
outside/10.88.81.77(0) -\> inside/192.10.10.246(11) hit-cnt 1 (first
hit)
```

Finally, one from a Linux IPTables firewall:

```
May 12 08:49:50 fw kernel: \[3005768.228266\] IPT-global R 25 \-- ACCEPT
IN=eth3 OUT=eth0 SRC=10.19.10.251 DST=207.232.83.70 LEN=76 TOS=0x00
PREC=0x00 TTL=63 ID=32906 DF PROTO=UDP SPT=34530 DPT=123 LEN=56
```

Reviewing network intrusion detection system (NIDS) or network IPS logs, although *interesting* in case of an incident, is often a frustrating task since NIDS can produce false alarms and dutifully log volumes of them. Still, NIDS log analysis, at least the postmortem kind for investigative purposes, often happens right after firewall logs are looked at. The NIDS logs themselves might be next, checking for signature updates, logins, and changes to the appliance.

Even though system administrators always knew to look at logs in case of problems, large-scale server operating system log analysis (both Windows and Unix/Linux variants) didn't material-ize until the late 2000s. Collecting logs from Windows servers, for example, was hindered by the lack of agentless log collection tools as well as Windows support for log centralization (included in Microsoft Server OS since Windows 2008). On the other hand, Unix server log analysis was severely undercut by a total lack of unified format for log content in syslog records.

Web server logs were long analyzed by marketing departments to check on their online campaign successes. However, because web servers don't have native log forwarding capabilities (most log files are stored on the server itself), consistent centralized web log analysis for both security and other IT purposes is still ramping up.

For example, the open-source Apache Web server has several types of logs. The most typical among them are *access_log* that contains all page requests made to the server (with their response codes) and *error_log* that contains various errors and problems. Other Apache logs relate to Secure Sockets Layer (SSL) (*ssl_engine.log*) as well as optional granular assessment logs that can be configured using tools such as ModSecurity (which produces an additional highly detailed *audit.log*).

Similarly, e-mail tracking through e-mail server logs languishes in a somewhat similar manner: people only turn to e-mail logs when something goes wrong (e-mail failures) or horribly wrong (an external party subpoenas your logs). Lack of native centralization and, to some extent, complicated log formats slowed down the e-mail log analysis initiatives.

Even more than e-mail, database logging wasn't on the radar of most IT folks for a long time. In fact, IT folks were perfectly happy with the fact that even though Relational Database Management Systems (RDBMSs) had extensive logging and data access assessment capabilities, many of them were never turned on citing performance issues. Oracle, Microsoft SQL Server, IBM DB2, and MySQL all provide excellent logging, if you know how to enable it, configure it for your specific needs, and analyze and leverage the resulting onslaught of data. In the context of PCI DSS, Database Activity Monitoring (DAM) is often performed not using logs but instead using separate software tools. Emerging big data tools such as Hadoop also process log data from various components of the framework.

What's next? Web applications and large enterprise application frameworks largely lived in a world of their own, but now people are starting to realize that their log data provides unique insight into insider attacks, insider data theft, and other trusted access abuse. Many retailers are ramping up their application log management efforts. Additionally, desktop operating system log analysis from large numbers of deployed desktops provides good early warning signals and helps support personnel diagnose and repair problems.

PCI RELEVANCE OF LOGS

Before we begin with covering additional details on logging and monitoring in PCI, one question needs to be addressed. What exactly must we log and monitor for PCI DSS compliance? The honest answer is that there is no list of what exactly you must be logging on each system. PCI, and pretty much every compliance mandate, gives you categories to start from and it is up to you to determine if the specific category falls into the "you must log this" bucket. This is still true despite the fact that PCI rules are more specific than most other recent regulations affecting information security.

The only thing that can be explained is what you *should* be logging. There is no easy "MUST-log-this" list; it is pretty much up to the individual assessor, consultant, vendor, engineer, and so forth to interpret—not simply "read," but interpret—PCI DSS guidance in your own environment. In addition, when planning what to log and monitor, it makes sense to start from compliance requirement as opposed to end with what PCI DSS suggests. After all, organizations can derive value from using it, even without regulatory or industry compliance.

So, which logs are relevant to your PCI project? In some circumstances, the answer is "all of them," but it is more likely that logs from systems that handle account information, as well as systems they connect to, will be in scope. Please refer to the data flow diagram that was described in Chapter 5, Building and Maintaining a Secure Network, to determine which systems actually PCI DSS requirements apply to all members, merchants, and service providers that store, process, or transmit cardholder data. Additionally, these requirements apply to all "system components," which are defined as "any network component, server, or application included in, or connected to, the cardholder data environment." Network components include, but are not limited to, firewalls, switches, routers, wireless access points, network appliances, and other security appliances. Servers include, but are not limited to, web, database, authentication, Domain Name System (DNS), e-mail, proxy, and Network Time Protocol (NTP). Applications include all off-the-shelf and custom-built applications, including internally facing and externally facing Web applications.

By the way, it is important to remind you that approaching logging and monitoring with the *sole* purpose of becoming PCI compliant is not only wasteful but can actually undermine the intent of PCI DSS compliance. Starting from its intent—cardholder data security—is the way to go, which we advocate.

If you've been at this for a while, you may remember an interpretation clarification that happened many years ago on the actual capture of actions, where must it happen? If the database is logging access, do I need to also log that access in the application? You will need to choose the best option for your particular system, but you only need to capture the action of accessing the data **once**. Access could be captured in the database (good for batch), application (good for interactive), or system (good for service accounts).

LOGGING IN PCI REQUIREMENT 10

Let's quickly go through Requirement 10, which directly addresses logging. We will go through it line by line and then go into details, examples, and implementation guidance.

The requirement itself is called "Log and monitor all access to system components and cardholder data" and is organized under the "Regularly monitor and test networks" heading. The theme deals with both periodic (test) and ongoing (monitor) aspects of maintaining your security, but this chapter focuses on logging and monitoring as we have addressed periodic testing in Chapter 9. More specifically, it requires a network operator to track and monitor all access to network resources and cardholder data. Thus, both network resources that handle the data and the data itself are subject to those protections. These processes and roles should all be documented, according to Requirements 10.1.1 and 10.1.2.

Further, the requirement states that logging is critical, primarily when "something does go wrong" and one needs to determine the cause of a compromise or other problem. Indeed, logs are of immense importance for incident response. However, we cannot underestimate the importance of using logs for routine user tracking and system analysis. Next, the requirement is organized in several sections on process, events that need to be logged, suggested level of details, time synchronization, assessment log security, required log review, and log retention policy.

NOTE

Question: Do I have to manually read every single log record daily to satisfy PCI Requirement 10?

Answer: No, automated log analysis and review is not only acceptable but likely the only way to get through the ever-growing stack of incoming logs. Requirement 10.4.1.1, which will be best practice until after March 31, 2025, will require automated technologies, such as security information and event management (SIEM) software for reviewing logs and creating alerts and Security Orchestration and Response (SOAR) platforms that help ingest alerts and follow pre-defined response workflows.

Section 10.2.1 requires that "audit logs are implemented to support the detection of anomalies and suspicious activity, and the forensic analysis of events," including a minimum list of system events to be logged (or, to allow "the events to be reconstructed"). Such requirements are motivated by the

TABLE 10.2

Logging Requirement and How to Address Them

Requirement Number	Requirement	Example Type of a Log Message
10.2.1.1	Individual user accesses to cardholder data	Successful logins to processing server (Unix, Windows)
10.2.1.2	Actions taken by any individual with root or administrative privileges	Sudo root actions on a processing server
10.2.1.3	Access to all audit trails	Execution of Windows event viewer
10.2.1.4	Invalid logical access attempts	Failed logins (Unix, Windows)
10.2.1.5	Use of identification and authentication mechanisms	All successful, failed, and invalid login attempts
10.2.1.6	Initialization of the audit logs	Windows audit log cleaned alert
10.2.1.7	Creation and deletion of system-level objects	Unix user added, Windows security policy updated, database created

need to assess and monitor user actions as well as other events that can affect credit-card data (such as system failures).

Following is the list of the requirements (events that must be logged) from PCI DSS:

- 10.2.1.1: Audit logs capture all individual user access to cardholder data.
- 10.2.1.2: Audit logs capture all actions taken by any individual with administrative access, including any interactive use of application or system accounts.
- 10.2.1.3: Audit logs capture all access to audit logs.
- 10.2.1.4: Audit logs capture all invalid logical access attempts.
- 10.2.1.5: Audit logs capture all changes to identification and authentication credentials including—but not limited to—creation of new accounts, elevation of privileges, and all changes, additions, or deletions to accounts with administrative access.
- 10.2.1.6: Audit logs capture all initialization of new audit logs, and all starting, stopping, or pausing of the existing audit logs.
- 10.2.1.7: Audit logs capture all creation and deletion of system-level objects.

These requirements cover data access, privileged user actions, log access and initialization, failed and invalid access attempts, authentication and authorization decisions, and system object changes. These lists have their roots in IT governance "best practices," which prescribe monitoring access, authentication, authorization change management, system availability, and suspicious activity. Other regulations, such as the Sarbanes–Oxley (SOX) Act, the Healthcare Information Portability and Accountability Act (HIPAA) (by means of related NIST guidance), and IT governance frameworks such as COBIT or ISO27001, contain or imply similar lists of events that need to be logged.

Table 10.2 is a practical example of the list on the previous page.

Moreover, PCI DSS Requirement 10 goes into an even deeper level of detail and covers specific data fields or values that need to be logged for each event. They provide a healthy minimum requirement, which is commonly exceeded by logging mechanisms in various IT platforms. In PCI DSS 4.0, these six requirements are now summarized in bullets under Requirement 10.2.2.

You must record the following for every auditable event:

- User identification,
- Type of event,
- Date and time,

- Success and failure indication,
- Origination of event, and
- Identity or name of affected data, system component, resource, or service (for example, name and protocol).

As shown, this minimum list contains all the basic attributes needed for incident analysis and for answering the questions: when, who, where, what, and where from. For example, if you are trying to discover who modified a credit-card database to copy all the transactions with all the details into a hidden file (a typical insider privilege abuse), you would need to know all of the above. Table 10.3 summarizes the above fields in this case.

NOTE

What is in the logs is as important as what is not. Most operating systems and some applications have the ability to change what events are being logged. Some, however, do it in levels or tiers that go from reporting only the most critical alerts to dumping everything event that occurs to logs. In these most verbose "debug" logs, it is very possible that data used in the event is also being recorded. This can help ensure that the software engineers can troubleshoot a problem, but it also introduces the risk of cardholder data being written to the logs and centralized logging system. Debug mode should only be used on PCI-scoped systems when actively troubleshooting a problem and other options have not worked to avoid accidental data storage. Once troubleshooting is complete, be sure to review all logs and eliminate any cardholder or sensitive data that might have been captured.

Security of the logs themselves is of paramount importance for reasons similar to the above concerns about log time synchronization. Requirement 10.3 states that one needs to ensure that "audit logs are protected from destruction and unauthorized modifications." and then clarifies various risks that need to be addressed.

MONITORING DATA AND LOG FOR SECURITY ISSUES

Although PCI is more about being compliant and protecting data than about being hacked (well, not directly), logs certainly help to answer the have I been hacked question. However, if the logs themselves are compromised by attackers, they lose nearly all value for either security or compliance

TABLE 10.3
PCI Event Details

PCI Requirement	Purpose
User identification	Which user account is associated with the event being logged? This might not necessarily mean "which person," only which username
Type of event	Was it a system configuration change? File addition? Database configuration change? Explains what exactly happened
Date and time	When did it happen? This information helps in tying the event to an actual person
Success and/or failure indication	Did he or she try to do something else that failed before his or her success in changing the configuration?
Origination of event	Where did he or she connect from? Was it local access or network access? This also helps in tying the log event to a person. Note that this can also refer to the process or application that originated the event
Identity or name of affected data, system component, resource, or service	What is the name of the database, system object, and so forth which was affected? Which server did it happen on? What protocol was used? This provides important additional information about the event

purposes. Assuring log confidentiality, integrity, and availability (CIA) is a requirement for PCI as well as a best practice for other log uses.

First, one needs to address all the CIA of logs. Section 10.3.1 of PCI DSS covers the confidentiality: "Read access to audit logs files is limited to those with a job-related need." This means that only those who need to see the logs to accomplish their jobs should be able to. What is so sensitive about logs? One of the obvious answers is that authentication-related logs will always contain usernames. Although not truly secret, username information provides 50% of the information needed for password guessing (password being the other 50%). Why give possible attackers (whether internal or external) this information? Moreover, because of users mistyping their credentials, it is not uncommon for passwords themselves to show up in logs. An engineer turning on debug logging can dump tons of extra sensitive data into log files, including data related to payment transactions such as cardholder data or sensitive authentication data (SAD). Poorly written Web applications might result in a password being logged together with the Web Uniform Resource Locator (URL) in Web server logs. Similarly, a Unix server log might contain a user password if the user accidentally presses "Enter" one extra time while logging in.

Next comes "integrity." As per Section 10.3.2 of PCI DSS, "audit log files are protected to prevent modifications by individuals." This one is blatantly obvious; because if logs can be modified by unauthorized parties (or by anybody, in fact), they stop being an objective assessment trail of system and user activities.

However, one needs to preserve the logs not only from malicious users but also from system failures and consequences of system configuration errors. This touches upon both the "availability" and "integrity" of log data. Specifically, Section 10.3.3 of PCI DSS covers that one needs for "audit log files, including those for external-facing technologies, are promptly backed up to a secure, central, internal log server(s) or other media that is difficult to modify." Indeed, centralizing logs to a server or a set of servers that can be used for log analysis is essential for both log protection and increasing log usefulness. Backing up logs to write-once read-many (WORM) media such as DVDs or tapes, for that matter, is another action you might have to perform as a result of this requirement. You should always keep in mind that logs on tape are not easily accessible and not searchable in case of an incident.

Many pieces of network infrastructure such as routers and switches are designed to log to an external server and only preserve minimum (or none) logs on the device itself. Thus, for those systems, centralizing logs is required.

To further decrease the risk of log alteration as well as to enable proof that such alteration didn't take place, Requirement 10.3.4 calls for you to confirm that "file integrity monitoring or change-detection mechanisms is used on audit logs to ensure that existing log data cannot be changed without generating alerts." At the same time, adding new log data to a log file should not generate an alert because log files tend to grow and not shrink on their own (unless logs are rotated or archived to external storage). File integrity monitoring systems use cryptographic hashing algorithms to compare files to a known good copy. The issue with logs is that log files tend to grow due to new record addition, thus undermining the utility of integrity checking. To resolve this, note that integrity monitoring can only assure the integrity of logs that are not being actively written to by the logging components. However, there are solutions that can verify the integrity of growing logs.

The next requirement is one of the most important as well as one of the most overlooked. Many PCI implementers simply forget that PCI Requirement 10 does not just call for "having logs" but for "having the logs and looking at them." Specifically, Section 10.4 states that the PCI organization must ensure "Audit logs are reviewed to identify anomalies or suspicious activity."

Thus, the requirement covers the scope of log sources that need to be "reviewed daily" and not just configured to log and have logs preserved or centralized. Given that a Fortune 1000 IT environment might produce gigabytes of logs per day, it is humanly impossible to read all of the logs. That is why guidance is added to this PCI DSS requirement that states, "Log harvesting, parsing, and alerting tools, centralized log management systems, event log analyzers, and SIEM solutions are examples of automated tools that can be used to meet this requirement." Indeed, log management tools are the only practical way to satisfy this requirement and Requirement 10.4.1.1 has been introduced to require automated tools starting after March 31, 2025.

Requirement 10.4.1 clarifies that some logs need to be reviewed daily. Specifically, "All security events, logs of all system components that store, process, or transmit CHD and/or SAD, or that could impact the security of CHD and/or SAD, logs of all critical system components and logs of all servers and system components that perform security functions" must be reviewed daily. Requirement 10.4.2 states that others can be analyzed less frequently, based on risk assessment. That risk assessment should be documented and will be required in Requirement 10.4.2.1 after March 31, 2025.

Don't forget to actually deal with those alerts. Requirement 10.4.3 requires evidence that "Exceptions and anomalies identified during the review process are addressed." Any analysis and remediation should be documented in a case tracking system to ensure the ability to show proper follow-up.

The Requirement 10.5.1 deals with another hugely important logging question—log retention. It says to, "retain audit trail history for at least 12 months, with a minimum of three months online availability." Unlike countless other requirements, this deals with the complicated log retention question directly. Thus, if you are not able to go back one year and look at the logs, you are in violation.

Requirement 10.6.1 addresses a commonly overlooked but critical requirement: a need to have accurate and consistent time for all systems so it is represented properly in all of the logs. It seems fairly straightforward that time and security event monitoring would go hand in hand as well. Time synchronization impacts your ability to perform log analysis. When analyzing your logs or ingesting into a SIEM platform, it's critical to understand the time formats and timezones used in order to perform the appropriate log correlation across platforms.

System time is generally synchronized automatically using public time servers for home or small office networks. It's whatever default values your system is using for time synchronization, or if you designed a local solution for some level of reliance, your systems are configured to obtain time synchronization from a reliable source, like official NTP servers.

Requirement 10.6.2 sets out the requirements for your time synchronization architecture: One or more designated time servers are in use.

- Only the designated central time server(s) receives time from external sources.
- Time received from external sources is based on International Atomic Time or Coordinated Universal Time (UTC).
- The designated time server(s) accept time updates only from specific industry-accepted external sources.
- Where there is more than one designated time server, the time servers peer with one another to keep accurate time.
- Internal systems receive time information only from designated central time server(s).

Using time-synchronization technology to synchronize all critical system clocks can make or break your security incident response or cause countless hours spent figuring out the actual times of events by correlating multiple sources of information together. Changing system time is a common tactic for attackers, so make sure the time synchronization settings are not easily modified and any changes will be logged (Requirement 10.6.3). In some cases, uncertainty about the log timestamps might even lead a court case to be dismissed because uncertainty about timestamps might lead to uncertainty in other claims as well. For example, "so you are saying you are not sure when exactly it happened?" might cause a skilled attorney to ask, "so maybe you are not even sure what happened?" Fortunately, this requirement is relatively straightforward to address by configuring an NTP environment and then configuring all servers to synchronize time with it. The primary NTP servers can synchronize time with *ntp://time.nist.gov* or other official time sources, also called "Stratum 1" sources. For the most part, you can use any number of official time sources, including going down to Stratum 2 or 3 type devices. The goal is to have one time for your organization that everyone can synchronize with for services. Otherwise, you will end up with outages in directory systems, some authentication systems, and performing event discovery or analytics will become a nightmare.

So, let us summarize what we have learned so far on logging in PCI:

- PCI Requirement 10 calls for logging specific events with a predefined level of details from all in-scope systems.
- PCI calls for tying the actual users to all logged actions.
- All clocks and time on the in-scope systems should be synchronized.
- The CIA of all collected logs should be protected.
- Logs should be regularly reviewed; specific logs should be reviewed at least daily or programmatically.
- All in-scope logs should be retained for at least one year.
- Organizations must have documented and actually implemented procedures and processes for log monitoring.

Now, we are ready to dig deeper to discover that logs and monitoring exist not only within Requirement 10 but in all other PCI requirements.

LOGGING AND MONITORING IN PCI—ALL OTHER REQUIREMENTS

Although many people think that logs in PCI are represented only by Requirement 10, the reality is more complicated: logs are in fact present, undercover, in all other sections. We will now reveal where they hide. Table 10.4 highlights some of the places where logging requirements are implied or mentioned. The overall theme here is that logging and log management assists with the validation and verification of many other requirements.

Now, let's dive deeper into the role of logs to further explain that logs are not only about Requirement 10. Just about every claim that is made to satisfy the requirements, such as data encryption or antivirus updates, can make effective use of log files to actually substantiate it.

For example, Requirement 1, "Install and Maintain Network Security Controls," mentions that organizations must have "a formal process for approving and testing all external network connections and changes to the firewall configuration." However, after such a process is established, you need to validate that firewall configuration changes do happen with authorization and in accordance with documented change management procedures. That is where logging becomes extremely handy, because it shows you what actually happened and not just what was supposed to happen.

Specifically, seeing a message such as this Cisco ASA/FirePOWER appliance record should indicate that someone is likely trying to modify the appliance configuration.

```
%ASA-5-502103: User priv level changed: Uname: jsmith From: privilege\_
level1 To: privilege\_level2
```

Other log-related areas within Requirement 1 include Section 1.2.5.

"All services, protocols, and ports allowed are identified, approved, and have a defined business need" where logs should be used to watch for all events triggered due to such communication.

The entire Requirement 1.3 contains guidance to firewall configuration, with specific statements about inbound and outbound connectivity. One must use firewall logs to verify this; even a review of configuration would not be sufficient, because only logs show how it really happened and not just how it was configured.

Similarly, Requirement 2 talks about password management practices as well as general security hardening, such as disabling unneeded services. Logs can show when such previously disabled services are being started, either by misinformed system administrators or by attackers.

TABLE 10.4

Logging and Monitoring Across PCI DSS Requirements

	Domain	Requirement	Logging Relevance and Recommendations
1	Build and Maintain a Secure Network and Systems	Install and Maintain Network Security Controls	Enable firewall logging, review logs for access violations, use of risky protocols, device configuration changes, accesses to critical network segments
2	Build and Maintain a Secure Network and Systems	Apply Secure Configurations to All System Components	Review logs to look for insecure services, additional services starting on servers, as well as password changes upon server deployment
3	Protect Account Data	Protect Stored Account Data	Review the logs related to key management to verify that the requirements (such as key changes) are being followed
4	Protect Account Data	Protect Cardholder Data with Strong Cryptography During Transmission Over Open, Public Networks	Look at firewall, virtual private network logs to verify that only secure network communication is used
5	Maintain a Vulnerability Management Program	Protect All Systems and Networks from Malicious Software	Verify that anti-malware software is updated by looking at antivirus logs; also look for detection and mitigation failures that might indicate that malware is present on the network
6	Maintain a Vulnerability Management Program	Develop and Maintain Secure Systems and Software	Make sure that custom applications written or customized for your environment also provide logging. Watch logs of system update and software distribution servers to make sure that patches are being deployed when needed on all relevant servers
7	Implement Strong Access Control Measures	Restrict Access to System Components and Cardholder Data by Business Need to Know	Verify that such access is indeed limited by reviewing the access logs
8	Implement Strong Access Control Measures	Identify Users and Authenticate Access to System Components	Perform log correlation to detect ID sharing in violation of this requirement; review logs indicating changes to users' privileges; verify password changes based on authentication systems logs, and so forth. Look for administrator and root accounts that can sometimes be shared (and are rarely removed from systems)
9	Implement Strong Access Control Measures	Restrict Physical Access to Cardholder Data	Collect, analyze, and review physical access control system logs
10	Regularly Monitor and Test Networks	Log and Monitor All Access to System Components and Cardholder Data	Covered above; this is the main logging and monitoring requirement
11	Regularly Monitor and Test Networks	Test Security of Systems and Networks Regularly	Monitor intrusion detection/prevention systems and file integrity checking
12	Maintain an Information Security Policy	Support Information Security with Organizational Policies and Programs	Make sure that logging and monitoring are represented in your security policy as well as operational standards, procedures, and management reports

For example, if the Apache Web server is disabled on an e-mail server system, a message such as the following should trigger an alert because the service should not be starting or restarting.

```
\[Sun May 22 04:02:09 2022\] \[notice\] Apache/1.3.19 (Unix) (Red-Hat/
Linux) mod\_ssl/2.8.1 OpenSSL/0.9.6 DAV/1.0.2 PHP/4.0.4pl1 mod\_
perl/1.24\_01 configured--- resuming normal operations
```

Further, Requirement 3, which deals with data encryption, has unambiguous links to logging. Specifically, key generation, distribution, and revocation are logged by most encryption systems, and such logs are critical for satisfying this requirement. Requirement 4, which also deals with encryption, has logging implications for similar reasons.

Requirement 5 refers to antivirus defenses. Of course, to satisfy Section 5.3, which requires that "anti-malware mechanisms and processes are active, maintained, and monitored," one needs to see such mentioned logs.

For example, Symantec Endpoint Protection might produce the following log record that occurs when the anti-malware software experiences problems and cannot continue scanning, thus putting you in violation of PCI DSS rules.

```
Product: Symantec AntiVirus---Error 1706. AntiVirus cannot continue.
```

So, even the requirement to "use and regularly update antivirus software" will likely generate requests for log data during the assessment, because the information is present in antivirus assessment logs. It is also well-known that failed antivirus updates, also reflected in logs, expose the company to malware risks because antivirus without the latest signature updates only creates a false sense of security and undermines the compliance effort.

Requirement 6 is in the same league: it calls for the organizations to "Develop and maintain secure systems and software," which is unthinkable without a strong logging function, logs useful for security analysis and incident response as well as application security monitoring.

Requirement 7, which states that one needs to "Restrict access to system components and cardholder data by business need to know," requires logs to validate who actually had access to said data. If the users who should be prevented from seeing the data appear in the log files as accessing the data usefully, remediation is needed.

Assigning a unique ID to each user accessing the system fits with other general security practices. In PCI, it is not just good practice; it is a requirement (Requirement 8, "Identify Users and Authenticate Access to System Components").

Obviously, one needs to ensure that "Addition, deletion, and modification of user IDs, authentication factors, and other identifier objects are managed." (Section 8.2.4 of PCI DSS 4.0). Most systems log such activities.

For example, the message below indicates a new user being added to an ASA/FirePOWER firewall.

```
%ASA-5-502101: New user added to local dbase: Uname: anilt Priv: 1
Encpass: 56Rt8U
```

Requirement 9 presents a different realm of security—physical access control. Even Section 9.3 that covers maintaining a visitor log (likely in the form of a physical logbook) is connected to log management if such a visitor log is electronic. There are separate data retention requirements for such logs: "A visitor log is used to maintain a physical record of visitor activity within the facility and within sensitive areas, including the visitor's name and the organization represented, the date and time of the visit, the name of the personnel authorizing physical access, and retaining the log for at least three months, unless otherwise restricted by law" (Requirement 9.3.4 of PCI DSS 4.0).

Requirement 10 is all about logging. It's why you are here in this chapter.

Requirement 11 addresses the need to scan the in-scope systems for vulnerabilities. However, it also calls for the use of IDS or IPS in Section 11.4: "Intrusion-detection and/or intrusion prevention techniques are used to detect and/or prevent intrusions into the network" including to confirm that "personnel are alerted to suspected compromises." Intrusion detection is only useful if monitored!

Requirement 12 covers the issues on a higher level—security policy as well as security standards and daily operational procedures (e.g., a procedure for daily log review mandates by Requirement 10 should be reflected here). However, it also has logging implications because logging should be a part of every security policy. In addition, incident response requirements are also tied to logging: "An incident response plan exists and is ready to be activated in the event of a suspected or confirmed security incident" is unthinkable to satisfy without effective collection and timely review of log data. Don't forget to track changes and review approval for all of your documentation.

Thus, event logging and security monitoring in the PCI DSS program go much beyond Requirement 10.

PCI DSS LOGGING POLICIES AND PROCEDURES

At this stage, we went through all of the PCI guidelines and uncovered where logging and monitoring are referenced. We now have a mammoth task ahead—how to address all those requirements?

In light of the above discussion, a PCI-derived logging policy must at least contain the following:

- Adequate logging, that covers both logged event types and details,
- Log aggregation and retention (one year),
- Log protection, and
- Log review.

Let's start focusing in depth on log review as the most complex of the requirements. PCI testing and validation procedures for log review mandate that a QSA should "examine documentation and interview personnel to verify that security policies and operational procedures identified in Requirement 10." QSA must also "interview personnel with responsibility for performing activities in Requirement 10 to verify that roles and responsibilities are assigned as defined and are understood."

Thus the organization should at least address the following:

1. Log review practices, procedures, and tasks, and
2. Exception investigation and analysis.

These procedures can be implemented using automated log management tools as well as manually when tools are not available.

The overall connection between the three types of PCI mandates is as follows (see Figure 10.1).

In other words, "Periodic Log Review Practices" are performed every day (or less frequently, if daily review is impossible) and any discovered exceptions are escalated to "Exception Investigation and Analysis."

The basic principle of PCI DSS periodic log review (further referred to as "daily log review" even if it might not be performed daily for all the applications) is to accomplish the following:

- Assure that cardholder data has not been compromised by the attackers,
- Detect possible risks to cardholder data, as early as possible, and
- Satisfy the explicit PCI DSS requirement for log review.

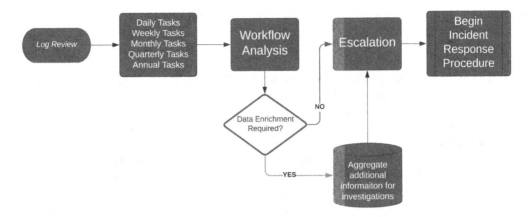

FIGURE 10.1   PCI log flow review with mandates.

Even given the fact that PCI DSS is the motivation for daily log review, other goals are accomplished by performing daily log review:

- Assure that systems that process cardholder data are operating securely and efficiently, and
- Reconcile all possible anomalies observed in logs with other systems activities (such as application code changes or patch deployments).

In light of the above goals, the daily log review is built around the concept of "baselining" or learning and documenting normal set of messages appearing in logs. Baselining is then followed by the process of finding "exceptions" from the normal routine and investigating them to assure that no breach of cardholder data has occurred or is imminent.

The process can be visualized as follows (see Figure 10.2).

Before PCI daily log review is put into practice, you must become familiar with normal activities logged on each of your applications.

Explicit event types might not always be available for some log types. For example, some Java application logs and some Unix logs don't have explicit log or event types recorded in logs. You have to create an implicit event type. The procedure for this case is as follows:

1. Review the log message,
2. Identify which part of the log message identifies what it is about,
3. Determine whether this part of the message is unique, and
4. Create an event ID from this part of the message.

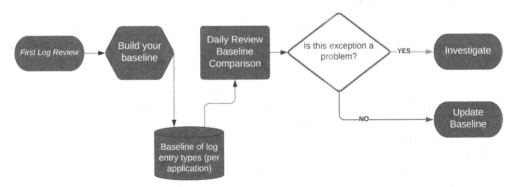

FIGURE 10.2   Documenting log reviews.

Even though log management tools perform the process automatically, it makes sense to go through an example of doing it manually in case a manual log review procedure is utilized.

For example:

1. Review the log message **The log message is:** *[Mon May 23 22:55:37 2022] [notice] Digest: generating secret for digest authentication.*
2. Identify which part of the log message identifies what it is about **It is very likely that the key part of the message is "generating secret for digest authentication" or even "generating secret."**
3. Determine whether this part of the message is unique **A review of other messages in the log indicates that no other messages contain the same phase and thus this phrase can be used to classify a message as a particular type.**
4. Create an event ID from this part of the message **We can create a message ID or message type as "generating_secret." Now, we can update our baseline that this type of message was observed today.**

BUILDING AN INITIAL BASELINE MANUALLY

To build a baseline without using a log management tool has to be done when logs are not compatible with an available tool, or the available tool has a poor understanding of log data. To do it, perform the following:

1. Make sure that relevant logs from a PCI application are saved in one location,
2. Select a time period for an initial baseline: "90 days" or "all time" if logs have been collected for less than 90 days; check the timestamp on the earliest logs to determine that,
3. Review log entries starting from the oldest to the newest, attempting to identify their types,
4. Manually create a summary of all observed types; if realistic, collect the counts of time each message was seen (not likely in case of high log data volume), and
5. Assuming that no breaches of card data have been discovered in that time period, we can accept the above report as a baseline for "routine operation."
6. An additional step should be performed while creating a baseline: even though we assume that no compromise of card data has taken place, there is a chance that some of the log messages recorded over the 90-day period triggered some kind of action or remediation. Such messages are referred to as "known bad" and should be marked as such.

The logs could be very large text and .csv files. During your analysis, tools like `notepad++` and `csved` can help. They also have good search features and counting functions within them.

GUIDANCE FOR IDENTIFYING "KNOWN BAD" MESSAGES

The following are some rough guidelines for marking some messages as "known bad" during the process of creating the baseline. If generated, these messages will be looked at first during the daily review process.

1. Login and other "access granted" log messages occurring at unusual hour,
2. Credential and access modifications log messages occurring outside of a change window,
3. Multiple invalid login attempts and account lockouts
4. Any log messages produced by the expired user accounts,
5. Reboot/restart messages outside of the maintenance window (if defined),
6. Backup/export of data outside of backup windows (if defined),
7. Log data deletion,
8. Logging termination on system or application,
9. Any change to logging configuration on the system or application,

10. Any log message that has triggered any action in the past: system configuration, investigation, add/deletes,
11. Modification of key configuration files or other files logged by your tamper prevention tools,
12. Creation or modification of systems drivers, scheduled tasks/cron jobs, and startup processes/services (common methods of rootkits), and
13. Other logs are clearly associated with security policy violations.

As we can see, this list is also very useful for creating "what to monitor in near-real-time?" policy and not just for logging. Over time, this list should be expanded based on the knowledge of local application logs and past investigations.

After we built the initial baselines, we can start the daily log review.

Main Workflow: Daily Log Review

This is the very central piece of the log review—comparing the logs produced over the last day (in case of a daily review) with an accumulated baseline.

Daily workflow follows this model (see Figure 10.3). This diagram summarizes the actions of the log analyst who performs the daily log review.

EXCEPTION INVESTIGATION AND ANALYSIS

A message not fitting the profile of a normal is flagged "an exception." It is important to note that an exception is not the same as a security incident, but it might be an early indication that one is taking place.

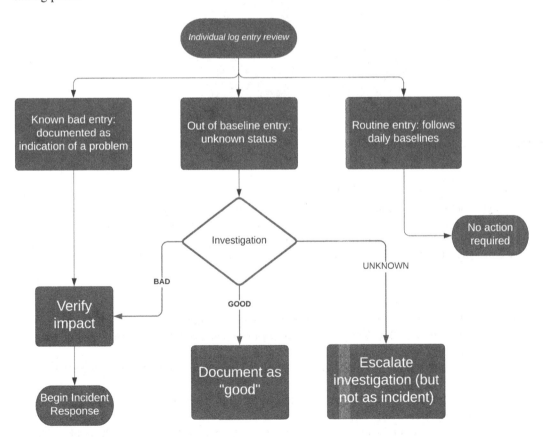

FIGURE 10.3 Daily log workflow.

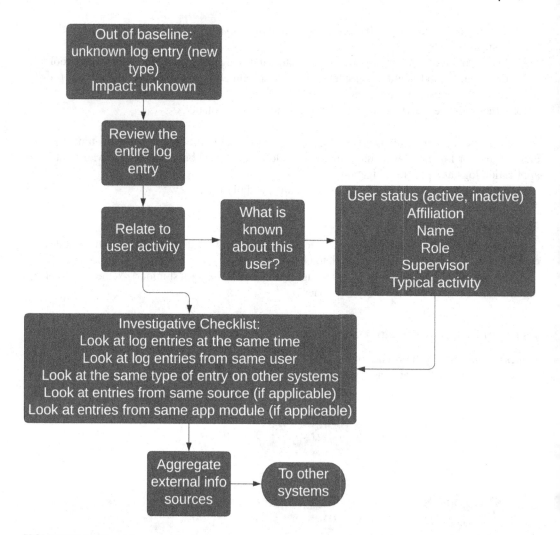

FIGURE 10.4 Exception entry log review.

At this stage we have an individual log message that is outside of routine/normal operation. How do we figure out whether it is significant, determine its impact on security and PCI compliance status?

The following high-level investigative process ("Initial Investigation") is used on each "exception" entry (more details are added further in the document) (see Figure 10.4).

Specifically, the above process makes use of a log investigative checklist, which is explained below in more details.

1. **Look at log entries at the same time**: this technique involves looking at an increasing range of time periods around the log message that is being investigated. Most log management products can allow you to review logs or to search for all logs within a specific time frame. For example:
    1. First, look at other log messages triggered one minute before and one minute after the "suspicious" log
    2. Second, look at other log messages triggered 10 minutes before and 10 minutes after the "suspicious" log
    3. Third, look at other log messages triggered one hour before and one hour after the "suspicious" log

2. **Look at other entries from same user:** this technique includes looking for other log entries produced by the activities of the same user. It often happens that a particular logged event of a user activity can only be interpreted in the context of other activities of the same user. Most log management products can allow you to "drill down into" or search for a specific user within a specific time frame.

3. **Look at the same type of entry on other systems:** this method covers looking for other log messages of the same type, but on different systems in order to determine its impact. Learning when the same message was produced on other systems may hold clues to understanding the impact of this log message.

4. **Look at entries from same source (if applicable):** this method involves reviewing all other log messages from the network source address (where relevant).

5. **Look at entries from same app module (if applicable):** this method involves reviewing all other log messages from the same application module or components. While other messages in the same time frame (see item 1. above) may be significant, reviewing all recent logs from the same components typically helps to reveal what is going on.

Validation of Log Review

Final and critical part of compliance-motivated log review is making sure that there is sufficient evidence of the process, its real-world implementation and diligence in following the process. The good news here is that the same data can be used for management reporting about the logging and log review processes.

Let's determine what documentation should be produced as proof of log review.

First, a common misconception is that just having logs actually provides that log review documentation. That is not really true: "having logs" and "having logs reviewed" are completely different and sometime years of maturing the security and compliance program separates one and the other.

Just to remind you, we have several major pieces that we need to prove for PCI DSS compliance validation. Unlike other sections, here we will cover proof of logging and not just proof of log review since the latter is so dependent on the former:

- Presence and adequacy of logging,
- Presence of log review processes and its implementation, and
- Exception handling process and its implementation.

If you are using a SIEM or SOAR platform to assist in the review, look to see if it has tools to help you track your log analysis processes. These reports or alert acknowledgment, triage, and remediation can be a good source of information for your QSA to review.

PCI Compliance Evidence Package

Overall, it is useful to create a "PCI Compliance Evidence Package" to show it to the QSA that will establish our three keys of PCI DSS logging requirements:

- Presence and adequacy of logging,
- Presence of log review processes and its implementation, and
- Exception handling process and its implementation.

While it is possible to prepare the evidence package before the assessment, it is much easier to maintain it on an ongoing basis and build scripts or other automated processes to refresh evidentiary data used during your assessment. For example, keep printed or electronic copies of the following:

1. Logging policy that covers all of the PCI DSS in-scope systems,
2. Logging and log review procedures (this document),

3. List of log sources—all systems and their components (applications) from the in-scope environment,
4. Sampling of configuration files that indicate that logging is configured according to the policy (e.g./etc/syslog.conf for Unix, screenshots of audit policy for Windows, etc.),
5. Sampling of logs from in-scope systems that indicate that logs are being generated according to the policy and satisfy PCI DSS logging requirements,
6. Exported or printed report from a log management tool that shows that log reviews are taking place, and
7. Up-to-date logbook defined above.

This will allow you to establish a compliant status and prove ongoing compliance.

Finally, let's summarize all the operational tasks the organization should be executing in connection with the log review.

PERIODIC OPERATIONAL TASK SUMMARY

The following contains a summary of operational tasks related to logging and log review. Some of the tasks are described in detail in the document above; others are auxiliary tasks needed for the successful implementation of PCI DSS log review program.

DAILY TASKS

Table 10.5 contains daily tasks, responsible role that performs them as well as what record or evidence is created of their execution:

Now we are ready to discuss the tools you might use for logging while meeting PCI DSS compliance.

TOOLS FOR LOGGING IN PCI

First, if we are talking about a single server and a single piece of network gear such as a router there might be no need for automation and tools. One can easily configure logging and then look at the logs (measuring a few pages of text a day or more), as well as save a copy of said logs to make sure that one can go back a year and review the old logs if needed. However, this approach fails

---

TABLE 10.5
PCI DSS Daily Tasks

Task	Responsible Role	Evidence
Review all the types of logs produced over the last day as described in the daily log review procedures	Security administrator, security analyst, (if authorized) application administrator	Record of reports being run on a log management tool
(As needed) investigate the anomalous log entries as described in the investigative procedures	Security administrator, security analyst, (if authorized) application administrator	Recorded logbook entries for investigated events
(As needed) take actions as needed to mitigate, remediate or reconcile the results of the investigations	Security administrator, security analyst, (if authorized) application administrator, other parties	Recorded logbook entries for investigated events and taken actions
Verify that logging is taking place across all in-scope applications	Application administrator	Create a spreadsheet to record such activities for future assessment
(As needed) enabled logging if disabled or stopped	Application administrator	Create a spreadsheet to record such activities for future assessment

miserably when the number of systems grows from 1 to, say, 10. In reality, a large e-commerce site or a whole chain of stores might easily have thousands of in-scope systems, starting from mainframes with customer databases down to servers to complex network architectures (including classic LANs, WANs, wireless networks, and remote access systems with hundreds of remote users) to point of sale (POS) systems and all the way down to wireless card scanners. A handheld wireless card scanner is "a credit-card processing system" and thus is in scope for PCI compliance.

Once it has been accepted that manual review of logs is not feasible or effective, the next attempt to satisfy the requirements usually comes in the form of scripts written by system administrators, to filter, review, and centralize the logs as well as makeshift remote logging collectors (usually limited to those log sources that support syslog, which is easy to forward to another system).

For example, you might configure all in-scope Unix servers to log a single "log server" and then write a Perl script that will scan the logs for specific strings (such as "fail," "attack," "denied," "modify," and so forth) and then send an e-mail to the administrator upon finding one of those strings. Another script might be used to summarize the log records into a simple "report" that highlights, for example, "Top Users" or "Top IP Addresses." A few creative tools were written to implement various advanced methods of log analysis, such as rule-based or stateful correlation.

When you can physically touch each server or device, it's easy to conceptually understand that you need to enable logging and log forwarding. Don't forget about your cloud and container infrastructure. Major cloud providers offer robust logging methods for their services, as well as log analysis and alerting mechanisms. Cloud infrastructure offerings are now so mature that many third-party vendors provide cloud-based solutions of their SIEM platforms. Cloud compute and container environments are also challenging due to the ephemeral (temporary) quality of elastic compute environments. Logs need to be forwarded immediately to avoid data loss when the instances themselves disappear.

The reality in these days is you probably already have a centralized logging system that you can tie into that will perform this type of analysis automatically.

If not, that basic analysis can work well in a smaller environment and does not require any initial investment. Other advantages include:

- You are likely to get exactly what you want because you design and build the tool for your environment.
- You can develop tools that have capabilities not offered by any commercial tool vendor.
- The choice of platform, development tools, analysis methods, and everything else is yours alone.
- You can later customize the solution to suit your future needs.
- There is no up-front cost for buying software and even hardware (if you are reusing some old unused servers, which is frequently the case for such log analysis projects), however, you may run into cost allocations around storage.
- Many system administrators think that "it is a fun thing to do."

What makes it even easier is the availability of open source and freeware tools to address some of the pieces of log management for PCI. For example, Table 10.6 summarizes a few popular tools that have been used in PCI log management projects.

On the other hand, many organizations turn to commercial vendors when looking for solutions to PCI logging and monitoring challenges. On the logging side, commercial log management solutions can aggregate all data from the in-scope entities, whether applications, servers, or network gear. Such solutions enable satisfying the log data collection, monitoring, analysis, data protection, and data retention.

NOTE

Why do we keep saying "retention" where some people would have used to term "storage?" Retention usually implies making sure that data is stored but on a schedule and lifecycle.

TABLE 10.6

Logging Tools Useful for PCI DSS

Origin	Tool	License	Purpose	Satisfied PCI Requirement
Quest	syslog-ng	Open source	General purpose syslog replacement and secure log transfer	Multiple sections of Requirement 10 and others; enabling infrastructure
Project LASSO	Project LASSO	Open source	Remote Windows event collection	Windows logging centralization; enables analysis of Windows logs covered by Requirement 10
Various	Stunnel, OpenSSH, FreeS/WAN	Open source	Secure data (including log) transfer	Log protection sections in Requirement 10
Various	MySQL, PostgreSQL	Open source	Data (including log) storage	Log retention section of Requirement 10
Various	Swatch, logwatch, logsentry	Open source	Small scripts for log filtering, alerting, and simple monitoring automation	Automated log review in Requirement 10
Risto Vaarandi	SEC	Open source	Log correlation and rule-based analysis	Automated log review in Requirement 10 on a more advanced level
OSSEC team	OSSEC	Open source	Log analysis	Automated log review in Requirement 10 on a more advanced level
Security Onion Solutions	SecurityOnion	Open Source	IDS, NSM, and Log Management	Requirements 10 and 11
AlienVault, by AT&T	OSSIM	Open source	Log analysis and correlation across logs and other information sources	Automated security monitoring across various systems

Vendors also help with system configuration guidance to enable optimum logging (sometimes for a fee as professional services). Advantages of such an approach are obvious: on day one, you get a supported solution as well as a degree of certainty that the vendor will maintain and improve the technology as well as have a roadmap for addressing other log-related organization needs beyond PCI compliance.

Fortunately, there are simple things you can do to avoid the pitfalls of unmet requirements when acquiring a log management solution.

- Review PCI logging guidance (as well as the standard itself) to clarify the standard's requirements.
- Consider how a log management solution would work in your environment.
- Define the need by talking to all the stakeholders in your PCI project and have the above information in mind.

Look through various commercial log management and SIEM tools such as TIBCO LogLogic (tibco.com), MicroFocus/CyberRes ArcSight (microfocus.com), Splunk (splunk.com), Elastic (elastic.co), Sumo Logic (sumologic.com), NetWitness or others to see what is out there. Here are some useful ideas on how to best talk to those vendors:

- How does your tool collect and aggregate 100% of all log data from all in-scope log sources on the network?
- How are your logs transported and stored securely to satisfy the CIA of log data?

- Describe the packaged reports that suit the needs of your PCI projects stakeholders such as IT, assessors, maybe even Finance, or Human Resources. Can you create the additional needed reports to organize collected log data quickly?
- How do you set alerts on anything in the logs to satisfy the monitoring requirements?
- How do you handle the ephemeral logging from containers or elastic workloads?
- Top three capacity concerns:
  - Events Per Second (EPS)
  - Storage
  - Licensing
- How do you size the environment?
- How does your investigation tool perform under 90, 180, and 360+ days of data (load factor)?
- How does the tool make it easy to look at log data on a daily basis?
- How can the tools help you prove that you are by maintaining an assessment trail of log review activities? Assessors will ask for a log that shows that you review other logs and not for the original logs from information systems. Yes, log analyst activities need to be logged as well—if this is news to you then welcome to the world of compliance!
- How do you enable fast, targeted searches across all in-scope systems components for specific data when asked? Remember, PCI is not about dumping logs on tape or disk, but about using them for cardholder data security.
- How do you readily prove, based on logs, that security (such as antivirus and intrusion prevention), change management (such as user account management), and access control policies mandated by the PCI requirements are in use and up-to-date?

These tools generally create few useful reports and alerts when deployed. On a more detailed level, here are some sample PCI-related reports and alerts for log review and monitoring.

Alerts used for real-time monitoring of in-scope servers are as follows:

- New account created,
- New privileges added to a user account,
- Firewall rules change,
- Multiple failed logins,
- Critical system restarted,
- Antivirus protection failed to load,
- Malware detected,
- Privilege escalation,
- Log collection failed from an in-scope system,
- Additions to administrative groups, and
- Group policy changes (if in an Active Directory environment).

NOTE

Alerts are only useful if there is a process and personnel in place to intake, analyze, and respond to alerts on a timely basis. In other words, if nobody is looking for e-mail alerts and is prepared to respond, they are next to useless.

Some of the recommended reports used for daily review of stored data are as follows:

- Traffic other than that allowed by PCI,
- Software update activities,
- User account changes on servers (e.g., additions, deletions, and modifications),

- Login activity on in-scope servers,
- User group membership changes,
- Password changes on in-scope servers and network devices,
- All administrator/root activities on in-scope servers, and
- Log review activities on a log management solution.

OTHER MONITORING TOOLS

Remember that the scope of security monitoring in PCI DSS is not limited to logs because system logs alone do not cover all the monitoring needs. Additional monitoring requirements are covered by the following technologies (as well as process requirements that accompany them):

- **Intrusion detection or intrusion prevention:** mandated by PCI Requirement 11.5.1 "Intrusion-detection and/or intrusion-prevention techniques are used to detect and/or prevent intrusions into the network—as follows—all traffic is monitored at the perimeter of the CDE, all traffic is monitored at critical points in the CDE, personnel are alerted to suspected compromises, and all intrusion-detection and prevention engines, baselines, and signatures are kept up to date."
- **File integrity monitoring:** mandated by PCI Requirement 11.5.2 "A change-detection mechanism (for example, file integrity monitoring tools) is deployed—as follows—to alert personnel to unauthorized modification (including changes, additions, and deletions) of critical files and to perform critical file comparisons at least once weekly."
- **Unauthorized changes on payment pages:** mandated by the new PCI Requirement 11.6.1 "A change- and tamper-detection mechanism is deployed—as follows—to alert personnel to unauthorized modification (including indicators of compromise, changes, additions, and deletions) to the HTTP headers and the contents of payment pages as received by the consumer browser, the mechanism is configured to evaluate the received HTTP header and payment page, the mechanism functions are performed as follows, and at least once every seven days or periodically (at the frequency defined in the entity's targeted risk analysis, which is performed according to all elements specified in Requirement 12.3.1)." This is broadly worded, but Branden worked with a bank that did this by polling the website every five minutes and checking to make sure we saw what we expected. There are services that will provide this as well, but just make sure you are coordinating with change control and have a good handle on the software included in your e-commerce site.

We will cover the critical issues related to these technologies in the section below.

INTRUSION DETECTION AND PREVENTION

NIDS and IPSs are becoming a standard information security safeguard. Together with firewalls and vulnerability scanners, intrusion detection is one of the pillars of modern computer security. When referring to IDSs and IPSs today, security professional typically refers to NIDS and network IPS. As we covered in Chapter 5, Building and Maintaining a Secure Network, the former sniffs the network, looking for traces of attacks, whereas the latter sits "inline" and passes (or blocks) network traffic.

NIDS monitors the entire subnet for network attacks against machines connected to it, using a database of attack signatures or a set of algorithms to detect anomalies in network traffic. See Figure 10.5 for a typical NIDS deployment scenario.

On the other hand, network IPS sits at a network choke point and protects such a network of systems from inbound attacks or outbound exfiltration. To simplify the difference, IDS alerts whereas IPS blocks. See Figure 10.6 for a typical network IPS deployment.

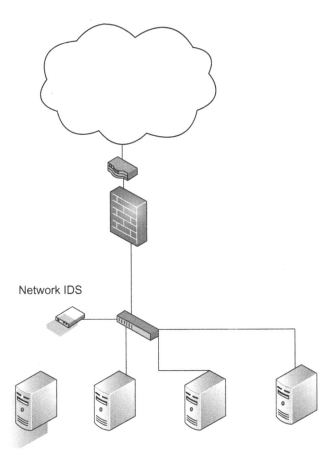

FIGURE 10.5   Network IDS placement.

NOTE

When looking at network intrusions, there is a delineation between attackers entering a network and attackers moving within it. Without a lot of micro-segmentation with firewalls in place, NIDS/NIPS only protects traffic entering or leaving a particular choke point on the network, or "North-South" traffic. For inter-network movement, or "East-West" traffic, including insider threats or attackers trying to move laterally across your network, you need to have HIDS/HIPS reviewing network traffic and connections, in addition to your NIDS/NIPS.

The core technology of picking "badness" from the network traffic with a subsequent alert (IDS) or blocking (IPS) is essentially similar. Even when intrusion prevention functionality is integrated with other functions to be deployed as so-called Unified Threat Management (UTM), the idea remains the same: network traffic passes through the device with malicious traffic stopped, suspicious traffic logged, and benign passed through.

Also important is the fact that most of today's IDS and IPS rely upon the knowledge of attacks and thus require ongoing updates of signatures, rules, attack traces to look for, and so forth. This is exactly why PCI DSS mandates that IDS and IPS are not only deployed but also frequently updated and managed in accordance with the manufacturer's recommendations.

In the context of PCI, IDS and IPS technologies are mentioned in the context of monitoring. Even though IDS can only alert and log attacks while IPS adds blocking functionality, both can and must

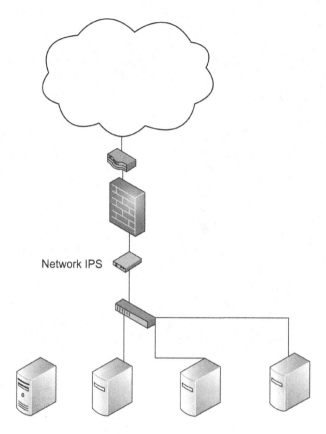

FIGURE 10.6   Network IPS placement.

be used to notify the security personnel about malicious and suspicious activities on the cardholder data networks. Below we present a few useful tips for deploying IDS and IPS for PCI DSS compliance and card data security. IPS is not required but can be used in the place of an IDS.

Despite the domination of commercial vendors, the free open-source IDS/IPS Snort may be the most popular IDS/IPS by the number of deployments worldwide. Given its price (free) and reliable rule updates, it makes a logical first choice for smaller organizations. It also shouldn't be taken off the shortlist even for larger organizations seeking to implement intrusion detection or prevention.

Although a detailed review of IDS and IPS technologies and practices goes well beyond the scope of this book, we would like to present a few key practices for making your PCI-driven deployment successful.

First, four key facts about IDS and IPS, which are also highlighted in the PCI standard:

1. IDS or IPS technology must be deployed as per PCI DSS. If another device includes IDS or IPS functionality (such as UTM mentioned above), it will likely qualify as well.
2. IDS and IPS need to "see" the network traffic in cardholder; for IDS, it needs to be able to sniff it and for IPS, to pass it through. An IDS box sitting in the closet is not PCI compliance (and definitely not security!).
3. IDS and IPS must be actively monitored by actual people, devoted (full-time, part-time, or outsources) to doing just that. PCI DSS states that systems must be set to "alert personnel to suspected compromises."
4. IDS and IPS rely on updates from the vendor; such updates must be deployed, or the devices will lose most of their value. PCI does highlight it by stating to "Keep all intrusion detection and prevention engines up-to-date."

The above four facts define how IDS and IPS are used for the cardholder requirement. Despite the above knowledge, IDS technologies are not the easiest to deploy, especially in light of the third bullet above. PCI DSS-driven IDS deployments suffer from a few of the common mistakes covered below.

First, using an IDS or an IPS to protect the cardholder environment and to satisfy PCI DSS requirement is impossible without giving it the ability to see all the network traffic. In other words, deploying an NIDS without sufficient network environment planning is a big mistake that reduces, if not destroys, the value of these tools. Network IPS, for example, should be deployed on the network choke point such as right inside the firewall leading to cardholder network, on the appropriate internal network segment, in the De-Militarized Zone (DMZ), or all of the above. For the wired networks, there are several IDS deployment scenarios that use special switch capabilities such as port mirroring or spanning. When one or more IDS devices are deployed, it is your responsibility to confirm that they can cover the entire in-scope network.

Port mirroring and spanning should be avoided whenever possible. Switching vendors' documentation will tell you that they do not scale for this type of monitoring, and you may not see all data when the network is busy. Don't forget virtual networks, as software-defined networking will have the capacity to do virtual span ports as well.

Network taps are the preferred method of deployment for IDS. Even if you decide to put IPS in-line, you should consider using taps to get the appliances in line. Even though all commercial IPS systems can be configured to fail open or "turn into a wire," if you do not use taps you may have to schedule a network outage whenever you have to swap out an appliance for maintenance or upgrades. In some environments, this can lead to failure to meet SLAs.

Second, even if an IDS is deployed appropriately, but nobody is looking at the alerts it generates, the deployment will end in failure and will not lead to PCI compliance. It's well known that IDS is a "detection" technology, and it never promised to be a "set it and forget it" means of thwarting attacks. Although in some cases, the organization might get away with dropping the firewall in place and configuring the policy, such a deployment scenario never works for intrusion detection. If IDS alerts are reviewed only after a successful compromise, the system turns into an overpriced incident response helper tool, clearly not what the technology designers had in mind. Even with IPS, a lot of suspicious indicators are not reliable enough to be blocked automatically, thus monitoring is just as critical as with IDS.

Despite the requirements to monitor security logs and alerts, many organizations deploy IDS and develop a no-response policy. As a result, their network IPS is deployed, it "sees" all the traffic, and there is somebody reviewing the alert stream. But what is the response for each potential alert? Panic, maybe? Does the person viewing the alerts know the best course of action needed for each event? What alerts are typically "false positives" (alerts triggered on benign activity) and "false alarms" (alerts triggered on attacks that cannot harm the target systems) in the protected environment? Unless these questions are answered, it is likely that no intelligent action is being taken based on IDS alerts—which begs the question, why did you spend all that money in the first place if you aren't going to respond to alerts? Some of the recent breaches of card data were directly attributed to ignored alerts from various security detection technologies.

The fourth and final mistake is simply not accepting the inherent limitations of network intrusion protection technology. Although anomaly-based IDSs might detect an unknown attack, most signature-based IDS will miss a new exploit if there is no rule written for it. IDS and IPS must frequently receive vendor signature updates, as mandated by the PCI DSS. Even if updates are applied on a schedule, exploits that are unknown to the IDS vendor will probably not be caught by the signature-based system. Attackers may also try to blind or evade the NIDS by using many tools available for download. There is a constant battle between the technology developers and those who want to escape detection. IPS/IDS are becoming more sophisticated and able to see through the old evasion methods, but new approaches are constantly being used by attackers like trusted server to trusted server or island hopping. Those deploying the NIDS technology should be aware of its limitations and practice "defense-in-depth" by deploying multiple and diverse security solutions. Sometimes a simple Denial of Service traffic flood can render an IDS or IPS inoperable.

INTEGRITY MONITORING

The idea of monitoring key system files for changes has a long history in distributed systems. As early system administrators engaged in an unequal battle with hackers who compromised almost every server connected to the Internet, the idea of a quick and easy way for verifying that system files was not modified and thus not subverted by hackers was worth deploying.

Indeed, just run a quick scan of a filesystem, compute cryptographic checksums, save them in a safe place, and then have a *known good* record of the system files. In case of problems, run another checksum computation and compare the results; if differences are found, then something or someone has subverted the files. Rapid system updates may make this process will require automation here as you will likely be patching multiple times per month.

That is exactly the idea of integrity checking and monitoring. The tools such as the pioneering *tripwire* (now developed by its corporate parent, Tripwire, Inc) have matured significantly and offer near real-time checks, an ability to revert to the previous version of the changed files, as well as a detailed analysis of observed changes across a wide range of platforms for servers, desktops, and even network devices.

NOTE

Question: What is the difference between host intrusion detection and integrity monitoring?

Answer: Many different types of applications are labeled as host-based intrusion detection. In general, the distinction is that with IDS, the end goal is the detection of malicious activity in a host environment, whereas an integrity monitoring system aims to provide visibility into all kinds of change. Detecting malicious change or activity is a big part of an integrity monitoring system but that is not the entire motivation behind its deployment.

As we mentioned, PCI DSS mandates the use of such tools via Requirement 11.5.2. Namely, "A change- and tamper-detection mechanism is deployed—as follows—to alert personnel to unauthorized modification (including indicators of compromise, changes, additions, and deletions) to the HTTP headers and the contents of payment pages as received by the consumer browser, the mechanism is configured to evaluate the received HTTP header and payment page, the mechanism functions are performed as follows, and at least once every seven days or periodically."

This means that the tools must be deployed on in-scope systems, key files need to be monitored, and comparisons are to be run at least weekly. Indeed, knowing that the server has been compromised by attackers a week after the incident is a lot better than what some recent credit-card losses indicate. For example, TJX card theft was discovered *years* after the actual intrusion took place, causing the company some massive embarrassment.

Some of the challenges with such tools include creating a list of key files to checksum. Typically, relying on the integrity checking tool vendor default (or even "PCI DSS focused") policy is a good idea. Here is an example list of such files for a typical Linux server:

- Configuration files in the/etc directory.
- All system executables (/bin,/usr/bin,/usr/sbin, and other possible binary directories), ESPECIALLY those setuid to root.
- Key payment application executable, configuration, and data files (including your Javascript payment scripts to help you be ready for Requirement 11.6.1)
- Log files/var/log (these require a special append-only mode in your integrity monitoring).

Also, just as with IDS and IPS, a response policy in case of breach of integrity is essential.

COMMON MISTAKES AND PITFALLS

By now you should be convinced that it is impossible to comply with PCI requirements without log data management processes and technologies in place. Complete log data is needed to prove that security, change management, access control, and other required processes and policies are in use, up-to-date, and are being adhered to. In addition, when managed well, log data can protect companies when compliance-related legal issues arise (e.g., when processes and procedures are in question or when an e-discovery process is initiated as part of an ongoing investigation). Not only does log data enable compliance but also allows companies to prove that they are implementing and continuously monitoring the processes outlined by the requirements.

- Logging in the PCI DSS is not confined to Requirement 10. As we discussed above, all the requirements imply having a solid log management policy, program, and tools.
- Logging in PCI is not only about log collection retention; Requirement 10.6 directly states that you need to review, not just accumulate logs.
- Log review in PCI does not mean that you have to read the logs yourself; using automated log management tools is not only allowed but suggested.
- A careful review of what is in scope must be performed. Otherwise, one creates a potentially huge issue for the organization in terms of having what is thought of as a solid PCI program, but then suffering a data breach and getting fined due to missing a wireless POS system or some other commonly overlooked but clearly in-scope systems. (Well, at least it becomes clear after your organization is fined.)
- Performing proper analysis on log data is critical. Whether manually or using automated rules, you must understand what the logs represent and whether the data is good. What happens if the baseline is set on a system that is already compromised and current traffic looks correct? And if using preconfigured rules, be sure to understand what is actually being used to make the decisions on alerting.
- Your logging tools purchased and deployed for PCI compliance are almost certainly useful for other things ranging from other compliance mandates (see the above example of PCI and SOX) as well as operational, security, investigative, incident response, and other uses.

CASE STUDY

Next, we present two of the case studies that illustrate what is covered in this chapter.

THE CASE OF THE RISKY RISK-BASED APPROACH

This case study covers deployment of a log management solution to satisfy PCI requirements at a large retail chain in the Midwest. Bert's Bazaar, an off-price retailer servicing the Midwest and southern US states, decided to deploy a commercial log management solution when their PCI assessor strongly suggested that they need to look into it. Given that Bert has a unique combination of a large set of in-scope systems (some running esoteric operating systems and custom applications) and an extreme shortage of skilled IT personnel, they chose to buy a commercial solution without seriously considering an in-house development. So, they progressed from not doing anything with their logs directly to running an advanced log management system.

The project took a few months following a phased approach. Bert's IT staff decided to implement it from the outside based on their risk assessment. They started from their DMZ firewalls and then progressed with feeding the following logs into a log management system, while simultaneously defining alerts and running reports from vendor's PCI compliance package.

Their project proceeded as follows:

1. All Internet DMZ firewalls,
2. Select internal firewalls that control access to payment processing systems,

3. DMZ front-end processing servers—operating system only,
4. Other payment processing servers—operating system only,
5. Databases that are involved in payment processing, and
6. Actual payment processing applications from all involved servers.

A few things need to be said about the above approach. One common piece of technology conspicuously missing from the list is network intrusion detection. The reason is that the organization chose not to implement it due to resource shortage (even though modern NIDS have improved, they still require people to provide care and feeding). The sequence is based on both their risk assessment and the complexity of log collection. The former led them to focus on the outside threat first, whereas the latter delayed some of the log collection efforts: it is much easier to forward Cisco ASA firewall logs to an analysis server, but a database logging configuration, collection, and analysis present a significant challenge (due to multiple factors from affecting performance to grabbing logs from a database itself in a secure and reliable manner to deciding exactly what you want to capture).

The project is a successful implementation of PCI logging requirements by using a commercial logging solution. The organization did pass their PCI assessment and was commended on their comprehensive approach to logging. In addition, the security team built a case that their PCI logging implementation actually addresses a few other compliance mandates (such as US SOX Act) because PCI DSS goes into higher-level details while covering essentially the same areas of IT governance. At the same time, a log management tool also bolstered its operational capabilities and overall IT efficiency.

THE CASE OF TWEAKING TO COMPLY

This case study is based on a major e-commerce implementation of an off-the-shelf log management technology in combination with in-house developed tools to address a unique need alongside PCI compliance. Upon encountering PCI compliance requirements, Wade's Webbies developed its own set of scripts to go through a Web server and payment application's server logs to identify hacking and fraud attempts. Such scripts were very useful but proved to be onerous to operate, update, maintain, and troubleshoot. Additionally, a few key IT staffers who helped develop the solution left to join a consulting company.

Thus, IT management decided to pick a commercial log management application, which will have to work together or integrate with their previous scripts (that still delivered unique value to the organization); they would use a vendor's collection and analysis log management infrastructure but retain an ability to look for fraud using their own methods.

Their log management project proceeded as follows:

1. Web server logs from DMZ Web servers,
2. Operating system logs from the same Web servers,
3. Custom payment processing application logs, and
4. Network logs from the DMZ (firewall, router).

The project approach was driven by the preexisting log analysis solution. Although the vendor solution was being deployed, they were adapting their scripts to run based on the log management vendor's API. Such API provided access to pre-analyzed as well as raw log data and allowed the organization to retain a large part of the effort spent on developing the scripts. At the same time, such API capability allows the users of the tools to take advantage of the vendor's advanced log management technology as well as regular updates and customer support.

Overall, this project was a successful illustration of a combined approach of using a homegrown and commercial solution and thus achieving combined benefits.

SUMMARY

In conclusion, we would like to stress a few points that were covered as well as leave readers with a few thoughts about how PCI logging fits into the bigger picture of IT governance and risk management. Despite the fact that this book is about PCI DSS, we do not recommend that you embark on a log management project or on a security monitoring project solely for PCI DSS. Taking control of your logs is useful for a huge number of IT and information security goals; thus doing logs "just for compliance" is akin to using an expensive and powerful tool as a hammer. Overall, a common scenario observed by the Branden and James is "buy for compliance (*such as PCI*), use for security" or, even "use for all the needed purposes." We recommend that the organizations that are subject to PCI DSS use the motivating power of PCI DSS to acquire the needed tools and then proceed to use them for solving all the problems in the whole IT security realm.

11 Cloud and Virtualization

Information in this chapter:

- Cloud basics
- Payment Card Industry Data Security Standard (PCI DSS) Cloud Examples
- So, Can I Use Cloud Resources in PCI DSS Environments?
- Containers and Kubernetes
- Maintaining and Assessing PCI DSS in the Cloud
- Tools and Best Practices
- Summary

You don't have to scour the deep pages of news websites to see how cloud outages are affecting major services. As I write this, another blip in a particular favorite cloud vendor took down several popular sites for more than an hour. We all are relying on the cloud in one form or another, and compliance with Payment Card Industry Data Security Standard (PCI DSS) in the cloud continues to baffle practitioners, assessors, auditors, and regulators alike. Organizations deploy cloud computing models for many tasks—from making their e-commerce offerings better to testing applications and storing data. PCI DSS and payment security issues intersect broadly with cloud computing.

CLOUD BASICS

Business is moving faster than ever and competitors appear from almost every angle. Technology is a major driver in your competition's ability to gain the advantage in your industry. Many corporate leaders leap to deploy technology in a way to gain an advantage, but government and industry regulations prevent the adoption of certain kinds of technology including—in some specific implementations or cases—the cloud. Slow-moving regulation can cause companies to scrap ideas altogether. In the business world, those that stand still will lose out on growth and profits.

While PCI DSS will be celebrating its 18th birthday in the year this book is published, new technologies are slow to make their way into the core requirements themselves. While frustrating, this is actually a benefit for the company being assessed as it creates flexibility in ways that rigid requirements by named technology do not. In PCI DSS 4.0, we *finally* see at least the acknowledgment of the existence of cloud, and some of the cloud-related challenges we've faced in the PCI space for the last 10 years (such as cloud-based Hardware Security Module [HSMs]). Merchants that want to leverage the power of the cloud are sometimes stuck between a slow-moving standard and an inexperienced Qualified Security Assessor (QSA)—who may not even know how to spell "IaaS" (Infrastructure as a Service)—to help them evaluate a solution for compliance. As much as it pains IT workers, compliance initiatives have the power to squash good ideas.

Do you do the right thing and abide by the letter of slow-moving compliance initiatives, or do you deploy technologies that can meet the control requirements while propelling your business forward? Many instinctively want to choose the latter, but how can we accomplish this and still pass the assessments we undergo? The improvements in technology since the first edition of this book animate the security and compliance community due to the rapid advancement and competitive nature of managing revenue and costs. The benefits are immense—and growing bigger as the power of the cloud and mobile technologies transform industries. Can we find a place for bleeding edge technologies in environments governed by compliance?

DOI: 10.1201/9781003100300-11

What Is the Cloud?

During one of our writing sessions, we're sitting in a coffee shop in our hometown early in 2022. Just observing the environment around us yields multiple examples of cloud technology enabling this business to move. You can place orders online using your phone and a website, the point of sale (POS) has a Software as a Service (SaaS) component, and you can pay with multiple methods, including contactless. It seems kind of silly to ask what the cloud is today, but we agreed it would be worth a nice level-set for this chapter.

While cloud computing is mentioned in many forums and media outlets, few people think about what the words actually mean—and what makes computing "cloudy." NIST's Definition of Cloud Computing in SP 800-145 says, "Cloud computing is a model for enabling convenient, on-demand network access to a shared pool of configurable computing resources that can be rapidly provisioned and released with minimal management effort or service provider interaction."

Further, they define these essential cloud characteristics such as on-demand self-service, broad network access, resource pooling, and rapid elasticity.

Cloud computing is also divided into three types:

- SaaS where you use a provider's applications over a network,
- PaaS where an organization deploys customer-created applications to a cloud, and
- IaaS where an organization rents processing, storage, network capacity, and other fundamental computing resources.

People in our industry will use the terms public, private, and hybrid cloud to describe how they will deploy any combination of two or more clouds' models.

Cloud computing usually happens at a massive scale (think Amazon AWS, Microsoft Azure, or Google Cloud) and makes heavy use of virtualization and low-cost software. As we have matured our deployment of compute technology to enable our businesses, we essentially continue to abstract up the way we interact with it. In today's world, you can deploy simple functions (anonymous or Lambda functions) to achieve a singular goal without having to worry about engineering the operating system (OS), buying the hardware, or dealing with the network. This gave birth to the widespread adoption of microservices where developers can build small segments of code to perform singular functions. Essentially, we don't really care about things like OSs or even server software. We choose higher-order methods for building technology to create flexibility and resilience at the expense of speed and customization (when you consider the speed of running compiled C over a Python lambda function).

Example: IaaS Amazon Cloud includes such components as Elastic Compute Cloud where you can run your own or Amazon's OS instances, Simple Storage Service for storage, and many other services.

Amazon includes this entry in their AWS PCI DSS FAQ:

"Question: What does this mean to me as a PCI DSS merchant or service provider?

Answer: As a customer who uses AWS services to store, process, or transmit cardholder data, you can rely on AWS technology infrastructure as you manage your own PCI DSS compliance certification.

AWS does not directly store, transmit, or process any customer cardholder data (CHD). However, you may create your own cardholder data environment (CDE) that can store, transmit, or process cardholder data using AWS services."

Cloud Badness

Many organizations have compiled lists of various risks, threats, and dangers of cloud computing. Every organization leveraging some form of cloud will face one or many of the items below. In our experience, allowing the usage of cloud technologies to grow uncontrolled without a strategy to architect and manage the footprint will grow the "we don't know what we don't know" problem. For security and technology professionals, this equals risk.

Here is one list of cloud threats by the Cloud Security Alliance (CSA) published in 2020:

- Abuse and Nefarious Use of Cloud Computing,
- Limited Cloud Usage Visibility,
- Metastructure and Applistructure Failures,
- Weak Control Plane,
- Insecure Interfaces & Application Programming Interface (APIs),
- Insider Threat,
- Account Hijacking,
- Insufficient Identity, Credential, Access, and Key Management,
- Data Breaches, and
- Lack of Cloud Security Architecture and Strategy.

These issues illustrate that cloud computing will include some of the risks of traditional IT environments as well as many new risks that do not exist in legacy IT.

CLOUD CHANGES EVERYTHING! BUT DOES IT?

As technology changes, we need to adjust how we act in the presence of these advancements, to avoid increasing our risk dramatically without the associated benefits. Yet, as humans, we force new problems into the frameworks of old solutions to try and make sense of them. When we look to solve problems, we ask ourselves where we have solved similar problems before. Information security and compliance is a notorious example of applying old methods to secure new things as security teams are constantly keeping up with the bad guys, and compliance tries to keep up with defense techniques designed by information security. By the way, cloud computing has already offered advantages to the attacking side, such as cracking passwords and storing stolen data.

Current generation protection mechanisms (firewalls and TLS anyone?) are generally poorly suited for protecting next-generation technology. As new technology provides expanded features, those features must be considered for what they do, but not in the context of how things have been done before. Using a port-level blocker to protect interactions at the application layer between the components of a SaaS application would not be as effective as something that is content, context, and identity-aware.

Consider how we have changed our shopping habits over the last 20 years. At the emergence of the commercialized Internet, consumers had two primary methods to buy products and services—either in person or via mail or telephone order. As businesses figured out how to generate revenue from this new channel, they had to do it in a way that didn't completely cannibalize their current business. As consumers, we've moved from casually shopping online to full online experiences, to omni-channel retail shopping, and now to mobile shopping as well.

Customers walking into a storefront today (for the few that still do) rarely carry lots of cash with them and instead will pay with some form of electronic payment. More of the customers are combining their physical and digital shopping experiences by using price check apps. One specific e-tailing app has a way to scan barcodes while in a store, and potentially have the same item delivered to you in a few hours at a better price. Merchants will need the optimal allocation of IT assets to meet customers on their terms—all while keeping the data secure and their IT environment PCI DSS compliant. New concerns not addressed by PCI DSS, such as ransomware, have hit some merchants hard as well.

Retailers are constantly experimenting with new ways to take products to market. They use data analytics as a way to maximize sales and dynamically reconfigure bundles for customers in the store as well as on the web. Cloud computing plays a major role in that by making advanced analytic algorithms available to wider populations of merchants. The goal for merchants is to change their business to capture the new reality of shopping to benefit their customers—and to do it fast. Given that online retailers have already invested heavily in technology as their primary pathway to market, extending to the cloud is a natural way to provide additional services to customers in an omni-channel retailing model.

CLOUD CHALLENGES AND YOU

One of the biggest changes in how we manage IT is the way that we procure technology. Instead of physically labeled rows of cabinets that show each machine, function, name, and IP address, data centers are virtual and the hardware type is almost irrelevant. As long as it supports the virtual fabric of the data center, it's good to run!

Both business and IT need flexible systems. This allows managers to better plan for their overall IT spend and maximize the utilization of assets deployed in normal operations. If deployments are approached with this type of flexibility in mind, jobs can be scheduled and scaled up and down as demand dictates. Every business has a peak season, and it's financially irresponsible to build fixed infrastructure solely while planning for your peaks. A better way is to plan for averages outside of your peaks, and then spin up cloud resources to handle high demand; a practice sometimes called "cloud bursting" since the capacity bursts up by using the public cloud resources. Online retailers shouldn't plan for sustained demand in the range of the traffic they get on Cyber Monday, they will save lots of money by contracting those peaks to a cloud provider.

One of the bigger challenges companies must address when considering a move to a cloud model is how they will work with the cloud to secure the operations. This is commonly known as the Shared Responsibility Model, whereby the cloud provider protects the infrastructure and you protect the things you are doing in your cloud instance. This critical analysis sits at the center of the "PCI and the cloud" debate.

Depending on your industry, there are ways around this. As an example with Cyber Monday, shopping around does not always equal purchasing. Instead of building a massive private cloud to manage everything, some companies leverage public cloud resources for browsing the catalog and then seamlessly transfer the process to private cloud resources for purchasing.

Technologists need to manage the finance teams in their firms. Irrespective of reporting structure, the Chief Financial Officer (CFO) and the Board have the final say in the budget allocated to IT and cybersecurity. So in order to get what we need, we have to think like a CFO and cater to his desires for running the business. Over the last five years, we have seen a tremendous shift from large capital outlays (CapEx) to operational charges (OpEx) for IT expenditures. The reason for this is that OpEx can more closely tie the spending on IT with the revenue associated with operations (think back to your Managerial Cost Accounting classes). With a more accurately predicted margin on the product, CFOs can smooth out the lumpy CapEx charges in the financial statements. Instead of large capital expenditures that end up going obsolete rather quickly, Chief Information Officers (CIOs) can help CFOs run a tighter balance sheet with less depreciation charges by moving these charges to OpEx through the use of elastic compute resources such as cloud.

The PCI Council offers some thoughts on cloud challenges as well in their PCI SSC Cloud Guidelines document, last updated in 2018 (available on the PCI Council website). Specifically, they mention:

"The distributed architectures of cloud environments add layers of technology and complexity that challenge traditional assessment methods. As a result, it may be particularly challenging to validate PCI DSS compliance in a distributed, dynamic infrastructure such as a public or multitenant environment."

The most recent guidance document contains specifics on how to deal with a number of common implementations that you may face. Keep in mind, guidance documents are not assessment documents. If your QSA comes into your assessment with that document printed out and starts assessing, they've made a wrong turn. This is one of the biggest challenges with PCI DSS and cloud, the standards are not as specific, which leads to interpretation problems. Your best bet is to ensure your QSA has significant experience with cloud technologies and assessing them before you sign the paperwork to bring them on board.

Leading researchers suggest that non-IT resources want CIOs to be more like a company executive and not just the top IT guy.[1] This means that the solutions brought to other executives areas should have the business in mind. Clearly, the ability to scale up and down to allow IT to move with the business is valued. Virtual and cloud infrastructure scales horizontally, not vertically. Meaning, instead of focusing on one massive process to run everything, the infrastructure scales out to a massively parallel group of smaller instances that do only their share of the work. While this is great for operations, it's not so great for audit.

Virtual assets in the cloud or Kubernetes clusters can be ephemeral, or only lasting for a short period of time, before they are recycled by the infrastructure as an idle resource. When it comes to security, this is a major problem. Just because an asset is no longer needed to perform work doesn't mean that its activity and logs can be discarded and forgotten. Just sit across from an auditor and tell them you can't produce the logs for your infrastructure because the instances no longer exist. Then tell them that you can't even produce the records of which instances were created, when they existed, and the jobs they performed because many of them only lasted for hours or minutes. You might witness a tantrum that would put a four-year old to shame!

Auditors and assessors need records of work performed and persistent logs from those jobs. PCI DSS specifically requires the maintenance of an inventory of in-scope systems (Requirement 12.5.1) as well as any bespoke software or scripts that are used to support the payment pages (Requirements 6.3.2 and 6.4.3). As a cloud user, you must know which resources are in scope at any given time, and keep the logs for those resources as well. Your assessor may not ask for it during your annual checkup, but you must maintain it for ongoing compliance. Years ago when these systems were physically racked, stacked, and labeled, this was pretty easy to do. Now when you can't even physically put your finger on the system running the job, you need tools to help you accomplish this task. In order to keep your auditors happy, you need to demonstrate command of your IT infrastructure. With cloud, there must be some level of automation in order to be able to keep up with the virtual assets that process cardholder data (or are otherwise in scope). This could easily extend to instances that were at one point in scope, but have now become dormant or just don't exist anymore.

Along with the challenges of inventorying ephemeral cloud assets, logging is another big one that can be troublesome in the cloud. As an experiment, look to see what logs your cloud provider shares with you. Are those logs sufficient to meet all of Requirement 10? Depending on your cloud provider, these logs may not be available to you in a way that will support your compliance initiatives. Any cloud-based infrastructure supporting production applications must generate running logs to satisfy both the security and compliance individuals responsible for the data contained within.

PCI CLOUD EXAMPLES

Early implementations of cloud infrastructure were analogous to the types of stories you might find in wild west flicks starring John Wayne. It was all about the technology. Let's demonstrate its abilities and practicality but not in a way that allows us to do things in a safe and secure way. Some of the earliest implementations were found in development and test environments to simplify technology deployments. Then we started to see non-critical services ending up in virtual or cloud infrastructures due to the sheer speed of deployment and resource maximization challenges. Now we see more and more critical jobs taking advantage of the cloud paradigm, and it's time for the long arm of the digital law to step in and de-risk the environment.

We've all heard a skeptic cluck their tongue when someone describes their desire to put something in the cloud. They proclaim "Without eyes on the hardware, you lose control of the device," and "if I can't see it, how can I secure it?" Physical control of a piece of hardware does not a secure platform make. In fact, it could even make the platform less secure.

Software-defined networking is an automation tool that professionals can leverage to defend their infrastructure (sometimes grouped in with Software-defined Wide Area Network [SD-WAN] when you start to look at a wide-area network over multiple transports). Temporary or ephemeral computing resources are hard for an attacker to control and leverage. A constantly changing network means that attackers must re-learn your setup with every iteration. When applying game theory to information security, we learn that the more moves the defender makes against an attacker, the harder it is for the attacker to make progress. Therefore, he gives up and moves elsewhere[2]. Dynamically reconfiguring physical assets is impossible, but building this resistance into a cloud-based infrastructure is not only possible but scriptable. Simply, any electronic asset that relies on physical security is more vulnerable to compromise than an electronic asset that doesn't need physical security to keep it safe.

The moral of this story is that it's safe to take the plunge. There has never been a better time to figure out how to leverage cloud for your critical workloads subject to compliance initiatives. As the saying goes, we know that we have arrived in a world of safe public cloud computing when NASDAQ offers products that leverage one.

SO, CAN I USE CLOUD RESOURCES IN PCI DSS ENVIRONMENTS?

This is a burning question that Chief Information Security Officers (CISOs), Chief Technology Officers (CTOs), CIOs, CFOs, and QSAs continue to wrestle with as the technology becomes more prolific. When we look for guidance from the PCI Council, they are surprisingly quiet. In fact, while there are over 50 instances of the word "cloud" in PCI DSS 4.0, only ONE (Requirement 11.4.7) contains a specific callout for something cloud-related. This requirement states that if you are a service provider demonstrating compliance to your customer, you must support external penetration testing (per Requirements 11.4.3 and 11.4.4). The rest of the instances are found in applicability notes or the guidance column.

One key thing to look for to help you is the term Third-Party Service Providers, or TPSPs, as any number of "as a Service" cloud deployments will likely affect the requirements for compliance for these entities.

At the very least, Requirement 12.8 "Risk to information assets associated with third-party service provider (TPSP) relationships is managed," Requirement A.1: "Additional PCI DSS Requirements for Multi-Tenant Service Providers," and their associated sub-requirements apply to cloud computing.

We now have some supplementary guidance that has matured from the initial release, and generally, it re-iterates that you as the assessed entity must perform all due diligence to ensure that the provider is able to meet all the requirements you need them to meet. Just like other parts of PCI DSS, you cannot simply pass the buck of responsibility in a contract. You as the merchant (or assessed entity) are *wholly responsible for the actions of your service provider.* You must include a few extra steps in your procurement and audit process ensuring the technology is safely supporting your business.

Compliance is notoriously behind the advancement of technology, so how can you leverage new technology in a way that doesn't question your compliance? The answer lies inside the standard itself, but it's not as cut and dry as we would like.

PCI DSS 4.0 improved upon best practices for implementing PCI DSS as Business as Usual (BAU) contained in Section 5 of PCI DSS in the front matter. While controversial when it comes to assessments (because BAU is not something that is in the *actual* requirements, with the exception of Appendix 3 for Designated Entities), managers should understand the implications of following the guidance provided here. There are not any specific requirements around assessing against the guidance, so therefore it is simply guidance. The Council's intent is to find ways to motivate companies to incorporate PCI DSS into their daily activities by calling it out specifically in the standard.

If you are expected to comply with PCI DSS and have not incorporated PCI DSS into your BAU process, you're not going to have a good time (you French fried when you should have pizza'd).

A company's security posture relies on a vigilant approach to defense that starts at the top, permeates through the organization, and ultimately to the front line. Rather than focus on PCI compliance, companies should implement security process into their BAU activities. Companies need tools to help them accomplish this daunting task, especially in the world of cloud. By focusing on security with your IT resources, PCI Compliance will come naturally.

Each business activity has IT support resources that support its operations. In order to keep up with the speed of innovation in your industry, you are most likely looking to tools and process to help your company get features to market quickly. DevOps, agile development, and rapid iteration have to balance capacity planning, defense, and audit controls. Attempting to tackle this with a manual process is virtually impossible. Security in the cloud is different, and you should be looking to do some of the following at a minimum:

- Build security controls into the workloads (or the data) themselves, irrespective of the platform it is running on. Having security follow the workload around is like putting on a life jacket when boating. Hopefully, you don't need it, but if there is a threat you are better protected.
- Add automation into logging and event monitoring, bringing the details into a central location for review.
- Add automation into your deployment pipeline so you can demonstrate compliance with any inventory requirements listed in this chapter as well as improve auditability, reliability, and deployability with infrastructure and policies described as code wherever possible.
- Consider which processes you drop into cloud resources carefully, and ensure that the underlying platform's security matches the risk associated with moving work onto that platform.

CONTAINERS AND KUBERNETES

Containers created both a nuanced complexity for IT service deployment as well as an ability to greatly simplify how software and services are deployed and managed. Allowing software to live in a specific sandbox creates the ability to make the workload ephemeral on your terms as well as infinitely mobile. Modern IT deployments will contain some level of containerization, which means that if you are managing a CDE, you probably have containers in there somewhere. Even software packages that you may install locally leverage containers for parts of their deployment. The installation may deploy private swarms or use preconfigured Kubernetes clusters for functionality and resilience, and they may not be properly configured to comply with PCI DSS or operate securely.

Containers by themselves are useful, but they become much more practical when you have an orchestration fabric that builds, deploys, moves, and tears down these workloads as required. Kubernetes (or K8s) and Docker Swarm can manage containers at the service level, but both require additional skills to make them production resilient.

You will find that containers typically are built following two different methods. The first would essentially look like a smaller virtual machine (VM). It contains an operating system and multiple software components (think application, database engine, logging, etc.) that would deliver a particular whole application or service. Think of this as a more flexible way to deploy a VM where the underlying fabric doesn't matter as much.

The other way you will find them built is to be more along the lines of one container one software one function. In the above example, instead of one container you would likely find a handful where each piece is in its own container that builds an application stack. You might even look at things like handling logging being deployed as a *sidecar* to the main container. This can create separation between the function of the container and the supporting elements that allow you to manage it.

Both examples require software inventorying and management of the software supply chain to ensure you are running non-vulnerable software in the containers supporting your CDE.

Networking with containers adds another layer of complexity that challenges your ability to comply with PCI DSS. Specifically in Kubernetes, you have a main node and cluster nodes. Kubernetes will run on top of VMs that have their own layer of networking in place, and then it will expand its own overlay network for the pods themselves. This enables the private network on Node 1 Pod 1 to interact with Node 2 Pod 1 containing the same apps. External traffic headed for the application is handled by an ingress controller, which is an app that is deployed in a pod on one or more nodes that acts like a traffic cop. By default, K8s and the Google Kubernetes Engine (GKE) overlay networks are *not encrypted* and generally allow for fully open pod-to-pod communication. So if your application accepts any credentials or sensitive data, that protection stops once you hit the ingress controller and is passed into the pods in the clear. That said, if you deploy the GKE according to Google's instructions, the overlay network is encrypted with IPSec tunnels. For more details on how encryption in transit works in the Google Cloud, see this resource: https://bit.ly/PCI-GCD

NOTE

We reference Google Cloud Platform, but any cloud platform that allows for a Kubernetes installation will require careful configuration by an expert to ensure you are using it securely. There are a number of threats you will face that differ from other types of technology deployments. OWASP is working on their Docker Top 10, currently in draft at the time of this writing, which will give you a clue on some things you need to consider. If wasps scare you, be sure to scroll past the title page fast! You can find the project here: https://bit.ly/PCI-OWASP-Docker

---

In addition, be sure you pay attention to the management layer that handles systems in your cluster or any PaaS or Cloud experience you are using. You need to ensure all admin access has multi-factor authentication (MFA) and you are tracking all actions by an administrator as well as the rest of PCI DSS. For example, if the PaaS service is provisioning at the VM layer and you have administrative access to those machines via SSH, how can you track an action by the admin back to the actual person if the VM does not tie back into a single identity management solution? In the case of GKE, you will, by default, have access to the nodes that will run your containers.

Be sure you have skilled professionals managing your container fabric so that default configurations or outdated software components do not put your ongoing PCI DSS compliance posture at risk. Read the Attestation of Compliance (AoC) for any of your cloud service providers to ensure they are compliant in the areas you need them to be. Just having an AoC isn't good enough, you have to read past the headline.

More Cloud for Better Security and Compliance?

If you meet with any of the payment brands, perhaps during their office hours at the annual community meetings, they will tell you that PCI DSS was never designed to put companies out of business from the costs of security controls. Its purpose is to reduce the risks associated with processing payment card data. IT innovation is pushing the limits on how we operate the digital side of our business, and PCI DSS requires that your security controls work in harmony with IT innovation. New IT infrastructure requires new security controls.

Whether you are in retail, manufacturing, transportation, or hospitality, your business will enjoy prosperous peaks and weather-challenging valleys. The size of your business is irrelevant—planning for peaks can be challenging in the world of IT operations. The cloud isn't the scary place that it used to be, and as an important stakeholder in your business (employees are key stakeholders) it's your responsibility to figure out how to maximize asset utilization in your operations. Be a hero to your CFO and show the business a way to operate your IT environment efficiently.

Take advantage of the flexibility of cloud and the ability to more closely tie the expenses of running your business with the revenue generated through operations (move to OpEx). Be the IT magician that can scale operations such that no matter the traffic load, your infrastructure responds with a snap. Do this with all of your auditing requirements met while keeping the data safe beyond just a compliance requirement. Leverage the cloud as a security tool to build a more resilient infrastructure that keeps attackers from gaining ground by constantly changing the game. And finally, free up cash to invest in other parts of your business, not in massive IT capital expenditures for assets that become obsolete quickly.

MAINTAINING AND ASSESSING PCI DSS IN THE CLOUD

You must test your cloud infrastructure much like you would your physical infrastructure, but the nature of software-defined security allows for much more real-time testing. PCI DSS has a number of controls that you must test periodically, but why wait for a compliance requirement to tell you to test something? That's like turning your firewall on for the day of the quarter that you test it, and then turning it off for the rest of the quarter assuming your network will be just fine. Attackers don't conform to a schedule, neither should you.

In order to maintain a healthy peace of mind toward PCI DSS, consider leveraging solutions with continuous monitoring and alerting to tell you when things are drifting out of compliance. Just like you build automation into other parts of your new IT, automate your compliance checking such that the systems do the work for you. After all, if new VM images are deployed automatically, how can compliance still be manual?

NOTE

Don't rely on a periodic check, make sure that your system has everything it needs to continuously monitor your environment for security and compliance violations.

When it comes to your assessment either by QSA or ISA, you may need to spend some time training the assessor on how your firm meets the controls with your cloud security tools. Just like security professionals struggle to keep up with the changes in technology, QSAs and ISAs are often presented with nuances in environments that don't fit into a conventional infrastructure. Remember, cloud evolves rapidly, therefore you should expect that QSAs do not have all the knowledge required to assess a complex cloud environment. Spend time walking your QSA through the process by which you designed your controls for the cloud. Ensure you tie back requirements to specific controls or features, and allow the QSA to test their effectiveness.

Enter the Matrix

The central point of any PCI compliance and the cloud exercise is the shared control matrix.

PCI SSC Cloud Guidelines (2018) contains such a high-level example of it, presented here as Figure 11.1.

The goal is to ensure that all parties involved have clearly identified which responsibilities are owned by the provider and which are owned by the customer of the service. Start by looking at their AoC and make sure your understanding of their responsibilities matches your understanding. This is where your legal team can help. Contracts can be a pain, but it's better to have the fight up front when you have leverage.

	Customer
	Provider
	Shared

Responsibility	Service Models		
	IaaS	PaaS	SaaS
Security Governance, Risk and Compliance (GRC)	Customer	Customer	Customer
Data Security	Customer	Customer	Customer
Application Security	Customer	Customer	Shared
Platform Security	Customer	Shared	Provider
Infrastructure Security	Shared	Provider	Provider
Physical Security	Provider	Provider	Provider

FIGURE 11.1   PCI SSC cloud guidelines.

TOOLS AND BEST PRACTICES

We would be remiss in not directing you to the Document Library section of the PCI Council's website where there are two Guideline documents that are worth a read. Keep in mind, one is from 2011 and the other is from 2018, so while the foundations may still apply, rest assured the technology is much more advanced in its security and compliance functionality and configurability. The two documents are:

- PCI DSS Cloud Computing Guidelines, 2018 and
- PCI DSS Virtualization Guidelines, 2011.

Kubernetes and the Cloud can be a downright daunting task to take on. We recommend working with experts to ensure you are designing your infrastructure with both security and functionality in mind. The elastic nature of these technologies can wreak havoc on your compliance program, so much so that many vendors now have PCI DSS compliance validation checks for your cloud.

The NSA and CISA maintain a document library full of guidance documentation and the latest revision of their Kubernetes Hardening Guide (version 1.1, updated March 2022) is worth a download and read if you are going to be supporting PCI DSS workloads in Kubernetes.

Here are a few general guidelines that they go into great detail, summarized here for you:

- Periodically scan your containers, pods, Kubernetes infrastructure, and deployment pipelines for vulnerabilities, missing patches, and misconfigurations.
- Remember to run everything with the least privileges possible (many installations run as root by default).
- Leverage network security controls to limit the blast radius of a security incident.
- Use strong, fine-grained authentication and authorization policies to limit user and administrator access.
- Ensure you have a solid, defensible log strategy that captures enough information to reconstruct ephemeral events.

This list is a high-level summary of items that you can start diving into, and you would do yourself a favor to keep that Guidance website bookmarked for quick reference into their work.

Perhaps the best reminder is your old tools, processes, and patterns may not work the same way in the cloud as they do on traditional infrastructure, specifically when you consider how these technologies talk to each other in different layers of the OSI Model. Make sure you have an expert with you and do your due diligence!

SUMMARY

The best and easiest way to become compliant in the cloud is to avoid exposure of payment data (encrypted or not) to cloud environments. It is useful to read the sentence a few times! Just like deleting payment data wherever possible is the easiest way to become compliant in traditional IT environments, avoiding toxic data in the cloud is the easiest way to achieve PCI compliance in any public cloud computing model. In essence, "shrink the scope" works in the cloud as well.

Also, it is better to have the payment processor handle more of the PCI burden and the merchant or cloud provider handle less. The exception to this rule would be cloud-based payment processors such as Shopify and Square. Your provider may perform these tasks on a merchant's behalf, but merchants are responsible and need to validate compliance—the cloud computing guidance is adamant about this.

Finally, a matrix of shared responsibility must be created by any merchant that considers utilizing public cloud providers. Make a matrix of shared responsibility and keep it with you! Remember: the merchant is on the hook, even if the cloud provider says they are doing a function that a merchant relies upon for compliance. The organization must involve legal departments in SLA and other discussions about regulated data in the cloud.

NOTES

1. Weill, P., & Woerner, S. L. (2013). The Future of the CIO in a Digital Economy. MIS Quarterly Executive, 12(2), 65–75.
2. van Dijk, M., Juels, A., Oprea, A., & Rivest, R. L. (2013). FlipIt: The Game of "Stealthy Takeover." Journal of Cryptology, 26(4), 655–713.

12 Mobile

Information in this chapter:

- Where Is Mobility Addressed in Payment Card Industry Data Security Standard (PCI DSS 4.0)?
- What Guidance Is Available?
- Deploying the Technology Safely
- Case Study
- Summary

Mobile technology continues to grow in significance as consumers and companies alike integrate tablets, phones, and other mobile devices into their daily work. The concept of Bring Your Own Device (BYOD) is fueled by Consumer-Driven IT movements everywhere, which in turn created a completely new push to a tablet-driven workforce with the Microsoft Surface, Samsung Galaxy, and Apple iPad Pro Tablets. In this case, individuals have leveraged mobile technology to create efficiencies in their personal lives, which then translates into ideas to become more efficient professionally.

And it created such harmony that companies started buying tablets with SIM cards instead of laptops and distributing those to their workforce who are increasingly not tied to a physical desk.

While BYOD-specific security and compliance topics are outside the scope of this chapter, we will be covering some of the key elements of mobility and how it integrates with Payment Card Industry Data Security Standard (PCI DSS 4.0).

WHERE IS MOBILITY ADDRESSED IN PCI DSS 4.0?

PCI DSS 4.0 has a few references to mobility as follows:

- In the front matter (page 14), tablets and mobile devices are listed as examples of end-user devices. If you see something in the standard referencing an end-user device, you should include mobile devices.
- Requirement 1.5.1, in the Guidance section, you must include mobile computing devices as in scope for this requirement. Take special note of the Good Practice example at the bottom of the Guidance section that discusses forbidding split-tunneling of VPNs on these devices and requiring them to auto-connect to a VPN on boot (which may be problematic depending on where you are enforcing your MFA requirement).
- Requirement 5's overview includes a mention of mobile computers as those subject to endpoint protection.
- Requirement 6.3.2 has a specific callout for a Mobile Device Management (MDM) system to be leveraged as an option for endpoint software inventory. It should also check for devices that have been jailbroken as those may allow for side-loading of apps or bypassing operating system level controls. Just be aware if you are reading this book and your company is larger than a few people, you most likely will need some kind of system to do this inventory in an automated fashion. If you don't have an MDM for your devices that interact with corporate assets, add that to your budget today.
- Requirement 9.5.1 excludes mobile devices that would be used for card capture in a Commercial-Off-The-Shelf fashion from scope.
- Requirement 12.2.1 mandates the inclusion of mobile phones and tablets to your acceptable use policy documents for end-user technology.

If you are considering adding a mobile strategy with card acceptance or in a manner that would connect to the cardholder data environment, you will need to consider these as well as many others. Remember, just because the requirement doesn't *mention* mobile doesn't mean you can ignore it in a mobile environment. As an example, any security patches released for a mobile device must still be applied within the required periods established in Requirement 6. Considering the number of zero-days that have been pushed in mobile operating systems in the past few years, be sure you have a solid understanding and control of the operating systems in use. This becomes *especially* important for Business Continuity where you may have mobile devices sitting offline somewhere as a backup. Branden ran into this during the start of the pandemic when a group of laptops that had been sitting in a closet powered off were suddenly redistributed and back in use, and boy howdy they were missing some critical patches. Don't forget to consider things like application updates, firmware or drivers, and other potential security problems.

Consider mobility, in the context of PCI DSS, as a method to do your normal work as opposed to something different and unique. If you approach it this way, it will fall into PCI DSS pretty clearly and the nuances of the mobile platforms become somewhat irrelevant. Your goal is not to reinvent PCI DSS compliant mobile solutions, but to apply the same precautions to mobile that you would anything else. The new Guidance, Applicability Notes, as well as the Customized Approach Objective text should all clearly guide you in the treatment of your mobile devices.

NOTE

Choose your mobile platform wisely! Not all platforms are alike, and even the ones that people advertise as secure can be used for nefarious purposes. If you are considering accepting payments through a mobile device, be sure to choose a solution that is tested or leverages something purpose-built for the capture process. Avoid hand keying in transactions as that can be risky and more expensive to service long term. Also, be sure that whatever device you use is *still getting updates to the operating system.* That old iPhone 5 in the drawer should **not** be used for mobile payment acceptance.

WHAT GUIDANCE IS AVAILABLE?

Since our last edition, the Council updated the Mobile Payment Acceptance Security Guideline documents to version 2.0. You can see the list of them by going to the PCI Council's website, clicking Resources, clicking Documents Library, and then filtering by Guidance Documents and Mobile. The PCI SSF document can be found by filtering by Software Security. As of the time of this writing, the following guidelines are available:

- PCI Secure Software Standard, v1.1 (2021),
- Accepting Mobile Payments with a Smartphone or Tablet (2014),
- Mobile Payment Acceptance Security Guidelines for Merchants, v2.0 (2017), and
- Mobile Payment Acceptance Security Guidelines for Developers, v2.0 (2017).

You may be looking at those dates and questioning why they are so far in the past. Surely mobile applications have matured in the last decade? The answer is yes, but the Council believes these documents cover the foundation for what is needed in today's environment. We expect the Council to continue to release updated guidance in this area.

The current documents touch almost all of the key areas where questions have popped up with various levels of detail. For example, the Accepting Mobile Payments with a Smartphone or Tablet document is only two pages but describes the basic concept of what they consider acceptable. Unfortunately, none of this has really made it explicitly into the Standard, so you may run into some difficulty depending on the third party you work with. Just remember, use the guidelines provided by the Council to help you build a safe solution, ensure the solution complies with the baseline PCI DSS standard, and use other security websites to bolster the security of the solution.

DEPLOYING THE TECHNOLOGY SAFELY

Mobility can be used safely and securely in the field, just like we discussed how cloud can be used safely and securely in Chapter 11, Cloud and Virtualization. The biggest challenge with any type of technology deployment is finding qualified people who fully understand the security and business implications of said technology. Remember back in the late 1990s when everyone wanted a website and we all had that one guy we knew who could do it? Maybe he was a brother-in-law, uncle, nephew, or just some guy at the gym, but we all knew someone who was a web wizard. Of course, reality was somewhat different. Nobody is a web designer after purchasing Adobe Dreamweaver for the first time or setting up their first WordPress site.

There are a few guidelines that you will find all over the web about using mobile applications in the workplace, so let's review a few.

Remember that mobile devices are just smaller computers. They can suffer from the same ills that your laptop can. If someone puts malicious software on the mobile device, it is compromised. Jailbroken or rooted devices remove specific controls set by the device manufacturer that are designed to keep untrusted software off of the device, so never jailbreak one you are using for payments. That also goes for side-loading apps from unofficial app stores. You also might consider only allowing them to use Wi-Fi (although in some use cases this is entirely impractical), and further locking them down with firewall rules, proxies, and policies that are centrally deployed. You will need to do something specific on the device anyway per Requirement 1.5.1, so consider defining and deploying a security policy for the devices. In addition, don't forget that mobile devices are just another IP device on your network. An attacker can use a compromised mobile device as a launching point to attack your network.

Along those lines, the data stored on the device must be protected. Most modern tablets and smartphones are encrypted by default and have protections to brick or lock the device if you fail to authenticate too many times—provided they are enabled and configured properly. An MDM comes in particularly handy here because if the device is lost or stolen, you can instruct it to wipe itself at its next check-in. Savvy readers are already starting to think about Faraday bags or other blocking techniques, which can obviously thwart this control. Based on the mobile nature of these types of devices, they can and do *grow legs* (meaning they often go missing). Being able to track these devices is an important addition to your security posture, but be sure you have set acceptable use policies for these and understand any limitations you may have under the law.

Here's another scary reality that we see often. Please, please, please do not store payment card information for your best customers anywhere on the device. Branden has seen situations where a merchant puts unencrypted payment card data with expiration and verification codes into a contact record, which syncs with iCloud, which syncs with a desktop or laptop, which syncs with Google, and so on. You get the picture.

Some MDM solutions segment the device to make secure areas, whereas others focus on the need to control the entire device. MDM solutions are still evolving, even at the time of publication. While the basic controls will be in place, more advanced controls may not be very mature yet. A quick internet search will give you details on bypassing MDM solutions, although most of them require specific scenarios in play before they will work.

When you choose to deploy these devices, consider getting a dedicated device for any part of your business that is handling payments—including your Point of Sale (POS) system. It's never a good idea to use your mobile POS as an attack platform to throw birds at pigs (or throw pigs at birds these days), to get your clan ready for a clash, or crush some candy. Keeping your digital work and pleasure separate will keep your customers and business secure!

Regardless, mobile technology deployed in the right way is something your business will be using today and in the future. Don't shy away from implementations that use mobility as they can be extremely useful, flexible, and cost-effective. All it takes is your creativity to make the technology safely work for you.

CASE STUDY

The case study below shows how a mobile implementation can go well.

THE CASE OF THE SUMMER FESTIVAL

Jennifer's Java is a café that specializes in free-trade coffee from small farms and growers throughout Africa and South America. She brews and serves coffee, sells pastries from a local baker, and offers her roasts in one-pound sacks for sale. She set up her shop off Main Street in her town and enjoyed frequent visitors. Because she is near the historic district of the town, the streets are frequently closed for festivals throughout the year. Unfortunately, during those festivals, her shop is somewhat blocked from the view of the street and people typically do not stop in.

To take advantage of the influx of people brought to the area, Jennifer decides to set up shop inside the next festival, Summer Fest, where she can sell iced coffee drinks to customers walking along the street. She buys a small table, rents a space, and prepares to serve customers, but she needs to process payments remotely for people who wish to pay for her wares with a credit card. She has heard of ways to process cards through her phone, but is skeptical of the security of the devices given the recent breaches.

She places a call to her credit card processing sales rep, Zack. He informs her that he has two options for her to process payments at the festival. The first is a "sled" that she can plug her phone into. All she needs to do is download an app, drop her merchant credentials into the app, and plug her phone into the sled to process payments. The second option is a payment terminal that looks exactly like the one in her store, but it has a cellular radio in it and a rechargeable battery. She opts for the second, and Zack delivers it to her two days before the festival.

During the festival, Jennifer had one of her single biggest days yet. The terminal worked great, and she operated it just like the one in her store. She could even tap into a loyalty program where people can enter their cell phones to get a text receipt and promotions.

As her business grew, she was looking to take the information from the loyalty program and tie it into a larger database of customers. Zack suggested that she purchase a tablet-based POS system that would sit on the counter to track orders electronically. The benefits of the system are significant in that she can remove a paper process in favor of an electronic one, and quickly understand her best products, bundles, features, and customers. She takes cards through an add-on supplied by the bank that plugs into the USB-C port. Because she leveraged a consultant on the Qualified Integrator and Reseller list to set it up, she is confident the system is safe. She pays the same firm a small fee every month to manage the devices and ensure the software is kept up to date.

SUMMARY

Mobility is a big technology driver in our personal and professional lives, and the ability to transact business over them is expanding. The Council provides documents that can be helpful to merchants and application developers alike—some of which are written with the small business owner in mind. Don't shy away from these technologies. Deploy them safely.

13 PCI for the Small Business

Information in this chapter:

- The Risks of Credit Card Acceptance
- New Business Considerations
- Your Point of Sale (POS) Is Like My POS!
- A Basic Scheme for SMB Hardening
- Case Study
- Summary

One of the central issues we face with respect to Payment Card Industry Data Security Standard (PCI DSS) is the sheer number of merchants that process transactions. The merchants that fall into the top reporting levels (Levels 1–3 for most payment brands) process a significant percentage of transactions both by themselves and when combined with others as a group, but they account for a tiny percentage of total merchants (less than 1/100 of a percent). That means if you are reading this book there is a significant chance you are a Level 4 merchant or another small business, and your head is exploding with the depth of PCI DSS. We've worked with companies big and small—some as small as a few employees. We feel your pain!

And it's not just us either. The outcry for help is loud enough to inspire Special Interest Groups and even entire markets whose participants build products for them. If you are a small business, do yourself a favor and seriously consider a Point-to-Point Encryption (P2PE), End-to-End Encryption (E2EE such as TransArmor from Fiserv), or some other outsourced solution using EMV terminals with encryption and tokenization to make this easier.

This chapter will explore several ways that you can manage PCI DSS as a small business, and hopefully never end up in a situation where you are facing fines and fees from a breach. Outsourcing will be one strategy to minimize your PCI DSS risk. The second is based on how you accept money. You don't have to accept payment cards, and we bet you will recall a business that was cash-only with an ATM in the corner. If you are outside the US, this is normalized to the point of being common. Both James & Branden have used an ATM at a pub outside the US.

THE RISKS OF CREDIT CARD ACCEPTANCE

Small companies tend to think that things won't happen to them because they are small enough to avoid being a target. In some respects, they aren't wrong. It's a numbers game, and criminals want the biggest payoff they can get for the lowest amount of effort and risk. Why would someone target a small business for minimal gains when they can go after a big box retailer and steal tons of information? Therefore, as a small business owner, I don't need to concern myself with information security. I need to focus on making my widgets and preventing fraud or physical threats.

Branden & James enjoy working with small business owners. Their passion is infectious! When speaking with a franchisee of a major brand, he told us that cashless payment transactions are simply a convenience for his customers. If he has an extra $15,000 at the end of a year to invest in his business, he'd rather invest in something that brings in revenue versus something that keeps his business safe from hackers. To him, that hack is a "Black Swan" event. He no doubt knows someone who has dealt with it, but probably dismisses that experience as something that won't or can't happen to him.

Perhaps a small experiment that we can all perform is to find your nearest single-location bar or restaurant. If you can find the owner, ask about their biggest worry for their business. It will not be a credit card hack, and we'd be surprised if that even made it into their top 10 concerns.

DOI: 10.1201/9781003100300-13

NOTE

We just did this at the business we are sitting at doing final edits and polish on the manuscript. We asked Anna what her top concerns were.

She said, in this order:

1. Price fluctuations,
2. COVID-19 (yes, still a concern in 2022), and
3. Staffing.

When we asked her about a data breach she said "It's not even on the list."

Anna uses an outsourced provider for her payment processing, so she is protected. When I asked if she even knew what PCI was, she looked at me funny. That's all I needed to know about the excellent choices she made with respect to electronic payments and her business.

Small businesses tend to view payment card acceptance as a necessary evil to reach their customers. There are many benefits to accepting payment cards such as less cash on hand, daily electronic wire transfers to your bank account, and an opportunity to track buying patterns of your frequent customers. Many small businesses actually prefer payment card transactions to other instruments like checks due to the risks associated with non-sufficient fund charges, the delays in converting the paper to cash, and indeed the basic handling of cash. But there are specific drawbacks as well that typically only manifest themselves when you have a problem. Small businesses don't focus on information security, so they won't know they've been breached until their acquirer makes the "Houston, we've had a problem" phone call.

If you end up on the wrong end of a payment card breach as a small business, you have a significant probability of losing your business. Imagine a small business that nets the owner $200,000 per year being hit with fines and fees totaling $100,000! It's like having your building 50% burned to the ground without fire insurance. Here's typically what happens:

1. A small business is informed by a payment brand (via their acquirer/processor) that their location has been identified as a common purchase point for a large number of known-compromised cards.
2. They must perform a forensic investigation ($30–70K).
3. The business will incur legal and consulting fees to help them navigate the process ($40–100K).
4. Fines come down from various payment brands depending on the size/scope of the breach and how good your lawyers are ($100K+).

All this because you entered into an agreement to accept payment cards, and the systems you own and operate were not built securely. And possibly because "That's always how we've done it."

This is why outsourcing becomes an increasingly compelling argument when weighing the cost of operating these systems with the risks of a payment card breach. For the most part, your customers don't see any real effects when their cards are stolen outside of the annoyance of replacing auto-bill entries. Some will just have new cards show up in the mail while others will notice bad transactions that are immediately reversed, and new cards then are mailed. Your loyal customers won't stop patronizing your business, and unless you are in the business of securing payment card data, you probably won't see a major hit in your brand value. There are plenty of examples that prove this point freely available to you with some clever searching.

So why don't more businesses outsource? Because the fees are generally higher! Think about it this way: if you are required to secure cardholder data, you can either spend the money to do it yourself by complying fully with PCI DSS, or you can incrementally pay an extra few basis points on every transaction to someone else to handle it for you. We've yet to meet a small business owner who was all in on payment card acceptance. Imagine the burden you could remove for a measly 50–150 basis points per transaction! As a small business owner or operator, you must make security and compliance a core part of your competency if you choose to operate in a manner that puts you in the cross-hairs of regulation.

As you are considering outsourcing and the Self-Assessment Questionnaire (SAQ) that each degree of outsourcing mandates, be sure that if you are lucky enough to be eligible for SAQ A you review the items on page iii, specifically: *"The merchant has reviewed the PCI DSS Attestation of Compliance form(s) for its TPSP(s) and confirmed that TPSP(s) are PCI DSS compliant for the services being used by the merchant."* You should do this for all relationships with service providers, but only SAQ A specifically calls this out.

NOTE

Are you seeing a trend here? While you will never hear anyone from the PCI Council say this, there absolutely are alternatives to accepting payment cards; if you are not investigating them, you are doing a disservice to yourself and your stakeholders. See Chapter 19, Emerging Technology and Alternative Payment Schemes, for more information. You don't have to know anything about PCI DSS, but if you dissect the contracts your company signed when you got your merchant account, you would know that you have to comply with certain security standards. You obviously can choose to ignore these standards but expect a low success rate if you point the finger at someone else after a breach. Finger pointing and litigation are standard fare, but both are expensive and unnecessary.

Small business owners need to know the level of risk they carry to understand how future actions alter that risk profile. For example, an over-leveraged company probably wouldn't choose to take on more debt to expand (liquidity risk), and a company relying on credit cards for customer revenue should know how security and compliance rules affect their business (compliance risk).

Of course, it's getting harder for business owners to learn about their risks, thanks to complex software packages being offered as a service. Business owners are attracted by the glitz and glamor of a fancy piece of software, yet they don't really understand how to use it or understand the liabilities associated with the information stored—that is, until a breach happens. *Cue the dramatic squirrel!*

NEW BUSINESS CONSIDERATIONS

Let's say you picked up this book because you heard about PCI DSS and you are looking to start your own business in the next few months. You know that you will be accepting payment cards, but you are unsure how to handle your compliance obligation. Here's a quick guide and some things to consider when setting up your process for accepting payments.

Your first reaction will be to get out your calculator and play with the bottom line, *how much does this cost me per transaction?* Understand that it is almost impossible to fully calculate down to the penny what it will cost you. Some offerings hide fees and other elements of interchange to where it is challenging to compare apples to apples—especially when you realize that not every card accepted has the same fees associated with it. That said, the cost is still a critical consideration for any small business owner, and you should understand what goes into that cost before you sign up for the service. We have helped companies set up their payment ecosystems over the last 20 years, and while the offerings and technology have changed, we all still gravitate toward the cost of the solution. Not all solutions are alike, so don't assume that you are making an apples-to-apples comparison when lining them all up in your spreadsheet. Here are five things you should consider while weighing your options:

1. Accepting credit cards costs money but provides convenience and physical security (less cash on hand). If you choose not to accept cards, you should understand the costs of dealing with cash, bad checks, and counterfeiting. You must also consider things like your average ticket size when making this decision. If you sell TVs, a cash-only acceptance will not be high-ticket-sale friendly. But if you are a restaurant, newsstand, or any place where the average ticket size is under $50, you may be OK. Don't forget, every year creates the opportunity for new electronic acceptance methods. It's not unreasonable to think by 2030 you would be able to operate without card acceptance thanks to the varied electronic payment methods available to you.

2. Look closely at the details in your card acceptance contracts and understand the differences beyond just the finances. The following six things typically make up the majority of the cost you might see (this list is not exhaustive, but makes up a significant portion of the cost you would pay):

    a. Will one ISO offer a complete outsourced solution, and take all the burden of PCI DSS compliance off your hands? (WIN!)
    b. Will they handle chargebacks for you?
    c. Will they cover fraud if someone uses a stolen card in your shop?
    d. What cards are accepted?
    e. How fast do you get your cash?
    f. How and when do they take their fees?

3. Choose not to accept cards but provide an on-site ATM or accept PIN-Debit with an outsourced provider (to push compliance back to them for member branded cards that can be used as PIN-Debit).

4. Go exclusive with one provider to potentially get a better deal but ensure you have covered PCI somehow (either yourself or outsourced back to the provider). These are harder to come by nowadays, and probably not viable. In the days of yore, examples of exclusive card agreements would be Costco (American Express), and Sam's Club (Discover Card).

5. Offset some of the costs of card processing by offering discounts to cash-paying customers. You may not be able to require people to pay for the privilege of using a credit card, but you can reward customers for paying with cash. You don't even have to give them discounts, it could be additional points in a loyalty program, a free gift with purchase or some other way to encourage folks to pay with cash or use debit.

These are all business decisions that are based on the assumption that you have to deal with cardholder data at some point, and you are better served by making it someone else's problem and treating it like a standard overhead cost. Focus on retailing, not processing payments, and you may just find yourself never having to deal with PCI DSS!

YOUR POS IS LIKE MY POS!

Point of Sale (POS) software tends to be the biggest focus on payments for small businesses. They understand that tracking the customer's sale and the card details plus all the magic that happens afterward starts at the POS. When you first start looking around you may feel like there are too many choices available. The reality is there are not lots of options out there, and the market is largely dominated by a few major players. The e-commerce world isn't too dissimilar in some respects, but the main danger with this side is that there are many free software packages available to process cards. Free isn't necessarily bad, but most small business owners need commercial support to get things running well. Free means you don't have to pay to license the software, but you still have to pay to operate it. The chances are that if you choose one of the major commercial players, you aren't the first to do so, and you can bet that there are other small businesses nearby that have the exact same system deployed in their stores.

You might be thinking, "Great! That means all the kinks are worked out and I will probably have a great experience with my software." In many respects, you are absolutely correct. But there is a hidden snake in the grass that many of us ignore. It's the collateral damage of a POS system being compromised because there is a fundamental flaw in the system—not the way it is deployed.

Criminals aim to maximize their payoff while minimizing their effort and risk of being caught. It's very game theory-esque. A criminal is less likely to target a single store and more likely to target some kind of common infrastructure shared by hundreds or thousands of stores. If he can find a way to break a POS terminal and can scale that hack from one store to thousands, he will do that. He might even be able to fly under the radar for a bit as the payment brands try to understand where the real issue is. It will start to look like a bunch of unrelated incidents until they see that they are all running the same software and then it becomes a major issue. We can also bet that those small merchants won't be fully compliant with PCI DSS, so even though the breach itself may not have been mitigated by a compliant solution, the fact that they are operating in a non-compliant fashion opens them up for fines and fees. That small business just became collateral damage in a larger, organized attack. It's unfair. You don't want to get caught in that web.

This chapter *is* designed to scare you a bit—but for good reason. Payment card data left unsecured is a cancer waiting to go malignant. You don't need to carry the risk of a breach on your shoulders, you need to make it someone else's problem. There are plenty of companies out there to choose from, and outsourcing can even make your position stronger from a negotiation perspective if costs from your current provider start to get out of whack.

A BASIC SCHEME FOR SMB HARDENING

So you have been sufficiently terrified of payment card processing and have already started looking to outsource. But since this isn't something you can do overnight, what can you do *now* to help mitigate much of your risk of an electronic intrusion at your store? One element is effective firewall controls that are probably built into the router you have at your location. If you are doing your best to block inbound traffic, have you considered what you are allowing out? Can someone access their Gmail account from a POS terminal or the back-of-house machine that collates daily sales data? What about a gambling website? What about accessing Dropbox or Secure Shell (SSH/SCP) for file transfers?

The majority of the guidance you probably have run into on network security controls focus on how to limit traffic from un-trusted networks into trusted networks. Outbound traffic tends to be much trickier for several reasons like:

- You have to do an analysis of your business-critical applications and the traffic they generate to function,
- You need to have policies in place governing access, and
- You should probably have some controls to prevent employees from going around your policies and rules.

The first one is sometimes the hardest one to accomplish—even as a small business. Traffic analysis is easy if you have the right tools, but small businesses rarely do. You may need to resort to using your firewall to tell you exactly what is typical traffic for your business.

For the record, you should not be allowing Gmail (or really any web-mail) access from a POS terminal, gambling websites, and definitely not SSH or FTP. We're not saying there aren't legitimate business reasons to do any of these things—well, wait. Yes, we are. Don't do these things from an in-scope PCI DSS device.

TIP

For a detailed post on how to do this for your business, visit this blog post by Branden: https://brando.ws/PCI-egress In it, you will learn how to handle firewalls in your small to medium sized business.

You will also probably want to start limiting traffic to certain websites. One easy (and cheap) way to do this is to set up a DNS Blackhole for certain websites. There are plenty of resources available online to show you how to do this, but suffice it to say, you can hide massive portions of the internet by routing lookups to domains to the loopback address of 127.0.0.1. Services like OpenDNS can be purchased to automate this for as little as $20/user/year. Imagine blocking Facebook, TikTok, and Instagram with a few entries in your DNS server! It's possible and will force your employees to use their personal devices to access non-business-related sites. Log this access though, as more and more applications are leveraging things like Facebook as core to normal operations.

CASE STUDY

You may not fully be able to convert to a cash business, but there are always strategies for reducing your risks. As a small business owner, you have much more to lose than an employee of a big business, so be sure you get good advice, read your contracts, and understand your risks fully before playing in the payment card space.

THE CASE OF THE OUTSOURCING DECISION

Michelle's Magnum Market is a new upscale wine shop that caters to selective wine consumers and wine stewards. Michelle has been a connoisseur of fine wines for many years and started a small wine club to source and taste fine wines from all over the globe. After much urging from her growing membership, she finally decided to open an official business location. She found a great location that requires minimal finishing costs for her store and is studying how to handle payment acceptance. She knows that cash only is not an option as her average ticket size will be well over $100, and she wants to provide a concierge-level service to her frequent customers to ensure they are serviced with minimal barriers.

She receives bids from several Independent Sales Organizations (ISOs) but is having a hard time selecting one as all of their features are vastly different. There are too many varied options among the suiters. She makes a table with her top two options to compare the merits of insourcing our outsourcing. She is computer savvy but does not wish to spend a bunch of time messing with her POS system if she doesn't have to. She ends up with something that looks like this in Table 13.1.

In order for her to choose to outsource her transactions, she must be willing to pay an extra $10,000 to completely remove the risk of a payment card-related breach from having a major effect on her new business. That's a pretty steep charge but works out to be around $830/month, well under the salary she would need to pay to hire someone to deal with all of her IT and security concerns, and less than what it would cost to hire a contractor to maintain the systems. In addition, the

---

TABLE 13.1

Basic Outsourcing Cost Analysis

Option	Xact Fee	Pct Fee (%)	Ave Ticket Size	Total Sales ($)	Total Cost
Michelle	$0.25	3	$125	$1,000,000	$32,000
Outsource	$0.25	4	$125	$1,000,000	$42,000

outsourced provider will allow her to make profiles for her top customers and include the payment card information there so she can charge her regulars without even asking for their payment cards. She also has the ability to set up a monthly wine club that automatically bills her customers for the wine they will receive as a part of their membership. Because she chooses to outsource, she is now able to do this without the fear of a PCI breach ending her business.

SUMMARY

Small businesses learning to deal with PCI DSS feel like they have an insurmountable hill to climb—so much so that many of them choose to ignore the problem and just pray that they will not be the target of a criminal attack. Companies have options when it comes to accepting customer payments, and they may opt to alter their business to accommodate these lower risk changes. For the most part, they absolutely cost more, but there are some interesting advantages that open up when you consider outsourcing this headache to a provider who bases their business around the flow and security of payment cards.

If you find yourself in this situation—be it a new company accepting payment cards or an existing company learning about PCI DSS—consider your options carefully. You have seen an outsourcing theme repeated heavily in this chapter and throughout this book. You should build some financial models to understand the impact of your decisions and be sure you fully understand your current risk and liability if you continue to operate your business as is.

If you take anything from this chapter, small businesses should remember the three Ds of Safe Payment Processing:

- Delegate (Outsource, you may pay a few extra basis points, but you don't have to worry about PCI DSS if you do it right),
- Destroy (After use), and
- Don't Store (Period).

14 PCI DSS for the Service Provider

Information in this chapter:

- Why Do Service Providers Have More Requirements?
- Variation on a Theme, or What Service Providers Should Care About?
- Service-Provider-Specific Requirements
- Case Study
- Summary

When we sat down in early 2020 to decide where to take this book next, one of the requests that came up from the past was a section dedicated to Service Providers. If your firm is a service provider and you have been reading this all along wondering when we would tackle the special things you need to be concerned about, this is the chapter for you. All of the advice we've been giving thus far for scope reduction, making compliance easy, and generally minimizing the effects Payment Card Industry Data Security Standard (PCI DSS) has on your firm are difficult to apply to service providers—at least to some degree. Using segmentation, data deletion, tokenization, and other technologies can help reduce the money you spend on PCI DSS, but chances are you have some kind of a requirement to handle this information on behalf of your end customer.

THE DEFINITION OF A SERVICE PROVIDER

From PCI DSS 4.0 on page 354, this is the definition they give to a service provider:

> Business entity that is not a payment brand, directly involved in the processing, storage, or transmission of cardholder data on behalf of another entity. This includes payment gateways, payment service providers (PSPs), and independent sales organizations (ISOs). This also includes **companies that provide services that control or could impact the security of cardholder data**. Examples include managed service providers that provide managed firewalls, IDS, and other services as well as hosting providers and other entities.

There are some additional nuances around telecommunication providers (can be exempt) as well as Multi-Tenant Service Providers (*a type of Third-Party Service Provider [TPSP] that offers various shared services to merchants and other service providers, where customers share system resources (such as physical or virtual servers), infrastructure, applications (including Software as a Service [SaaS] and/or databases))* and TPSP (*any third party acting as a service provider on behalf of an entity).* Just be sure you have reviewed all of these definitions to understand both the responsibility that your firm may have, as well as any service providers that *you* rely on that must have their compliance status tracked.

Ultimately, the easiest way to look at this definition when evaluating an entity to determine if they are a service provider or not is to ask this question: *Can this entity affect the security of account data in any way?*

If the answer is yes, they are likely a service provider.

WHY DO SERVICE PROVIDERS HAVE MORE REQUIREMENTS?

So by now you may be asking why the Council picks on service providers more than merchants. The concept of focusing on service providers, and in fact the genesis of the Visa CISP standard, was born because the networks didn't have visibility into all of the different companies that used their account data. Perhaps the largest differentiator between a service provider and a merchant is (with the exception of an acquirer or issuer processor that is directly connected to the payment networks) that there is no direct relationship with the payment brand itself.

Consider an example where a marketing firm decides to offer payment processing services to a specific type of merchant—perhaps a dry cleaner. Merchants open a processing account and then let the service provider manage it for them. The firm can make money by charging basis points on the processing fees back to the end merchant and provide added services like data mining and insights on how that dry cleaner can grow their business. In this case, the networks, who are the enforcement arm of the PCI DSS ecosystem, likely have no idea that this marketing firm is even involved in touching their data. The only contractual relationship that exists is between the merchant and the service provider directly, so unless the merchant is complying with PCI DSS and keeping that inventory of service providers who can affect the security of cardholder data under monitoring, there is a risk for a breach. The worst part is the merchant still owns the processing agreement, so if there is a breach it is the dry cleaner's liability, not the service provider.

In that same scenario, a breach would likely affect many dry cleaners, not just one. Simply being an aggregation point boosts the risks associated with operating a service provider; therefore, they need a few more controls to ensure they are protecting themselves as well as their clients both as a group and individually.

VARIATION ON A THEME, OR WHAT SERVICE PROVIDERS SHOULD CARE ABOUT?

We know merchants and service providers are different, but we also know that a merchant *can also be* a service provider. We also learned that sometimes the classification is tricky as in the case of the ATM operator in Chapter 3, Why PCI is here?, in which you really need to define all the elements of the transaction and challenge your assumptions.

Service providers need to care about their own PCI DSS status and be sure they are openly communicating this to their affected clients. Some services, like Amazon Web Services, post the details for you to download so you can inventory and share them with your QSA. Others will only give you a verbal, which is absolutely a risk for anyone working with them. They need to be able to clearly identify separations between their customers' data and ensure they are protecting their own infrastructure while providing secure services to their customers. Keep in mind, a theme throughout this book is you will not need to stop at PCI DSS when securing your business, *especially* if you are a service provider. The types of changes in 4.0 demonstrate how far the standards body lags behind what is actually happening from an attack perspective. Leveraging something like the NIST Common Security Framework or any other number of security guides will give you a fighting chance against the bad guys.

SERVICE-PROVIDER-SPECIFIC REQUIREMENTS

Let's go through the list of requirements by major category. To view these in context, be sure to refer back to the chapter in the book where we talk about the parent requirement for more details about what a merchant might have to do. There are 25 requirements (nearly double from PCI DSS 3.2.1) we will review here that come from Requirements 3, 8, 10, 11, 12, and Appendix A.

PROTECT ACCOUNT DATA

Requirement 3 has two specific subsections that apply to Service Providers. The first is Requirement 3.6.1.1, which mandates a documented description of all of the cryptographic architecture deployed to service your customers. You must include information about the algorithms, protocols, and keys, as well as key strengths and rotation schedules. You need separate keys with descriptions of the key usage for each key in your different environments (namely production and test, but use separate keys for *all* environments. Shared keys are bad, mmkay.), and an inventory of all of your hardware security modules, key management systems, or indeed any tool that is part of the cryptographic ecosystem. More documentation is probably better, so create the documentation with the assumption that the audience is the toughest of auditors you might welcome in the door.

Requirement 3.7.9 expands upon the key management requirement above to add controls for keys shared with customers. You need to have documentation on secure transmission and storage of keys, how they should be updated, and ensure the documentation you maintain is provided to your customers regularly.

IMPLEMENT STRONG ACCESS CONTROL MEASURES

Requirement 8 has three requirements for service providers. The first, Requirement 8.2.3, mandates that service providers use unique authentication factors for remote access to each customer's environment. On the simple side, leveraging a password manager could work here for unique passwords (as one of the factors presented in your multi-factor strategy) to each environment.

Requirements 8.3.10 and 8.3.10.1 were briefly discussed in Chapter 6, Strong Access Controls, where you must provide guidance as to the circumstances and frequency to which your customers must change their passwords if that is the only factor used in accessing their account data. Passwords must be changed at least every 90 days or you must have some kind of detection to know when an account has been compromised and subsequently force the customer to change their password. In 2022 and beyond, we would be surprised if service providers are *not* offering some kind of multi-factor option. The easiest way to get a guaranteed checkbox on this requirement is to add a second factor of authentication for your customers.

REGULARLY MONITOR AND TEST NETWORKS

There are three requirements in this section, and one of them will become a requirement for all entities complying with PCI DSS 4.0. Requirement 10.7.1 (which will be superseded by 10.7.2 and expanded beyond service providers to all assessed with 10.7.3 as of March 31, 2025) mandates the management and monitoring of critical security control systems to include network security controls (NSCs), IDS/IPS, FIM, anti-malware solutions, physical access controls, logical access controls, audit logging mechanisms, and segmentation controls. You will need documentation that shows you are doing this plus evidence to show when things occur.

Requirement 11.4.6 is the service provider stepped up version of 11.4.5, which just changes the testing requirement to at least once every six months and after any changes to segmentation controls or methods.

Rounding out this grouping of service provider requirements is Requirement 11.5.1.1, which is a best practice until March 31, 2025 where service providers must detect, alert on or prevent, and address covert command and control traffic as well as any communication traffic generally associated with malware. Modern IDS systems include indicators of compromise filters you can add to your detection suite, so make sure those are enabled, routinely updated, and alerts are going to personnel who can respond to them.

MAINTAIN AN INFORMATION SECURITY POLICY

Requirement 12 contains the seven specific requirements that must be addressed for service providers. Starting with Requirement 12.4.1, you must formally document accountability for maintaining PCI DSS compliance with a program charter. Your QSA will inspect this to ensure it's not just sitting on a shelf and is actively managed and communicated to the larger executive team as required.

Requirement 12.4.2 mandates quarterly reviews to confirm that your security personnel are doing their daily work in accordance with all security policies and operational procedures. This includes daily log reviews, configuration reviews for NSCs, applying configuration standards to new systems, responding to security alerts, change-management processes. Even the best-run teams will be able to demonstrate a response to at least one of these events every three months. Be sure it is documented and you review the results (Requirement 12.4.2.1), there is a remediation process documented for anything found needing adjustments, and that there is an official review and sign-off by the person assigned responsibility for PCI DSS.

PCI DSS 4.0 has a formalized process for reviewing and documenting scope every year (and upon significant changes to the in-scope environment), unless you are a service provider and Requirement 12.5.2.1 mandates this happen once every six months. Ensure you are documenting this properly for your QSA to examine. In addition, Requirement 12.5.3 includes significant changes to organizational structure to trigger a review of the PCI DSS scope and applicability of controls. The result of this review should be communicated to executive management.

Requirement 12.9.1 mandates that TPSP acknowledge in writing (i.e., in your master agreement or in the services agreement tied to the in-scope review for a merchant) that they are responsible for the security of any account data of which they can affect its security. It's the same old store, transmit, and process line but add in anything they have access to that could affect the security of account data. In addition, Requirement 12.9.2 mandates service providers support their customers' requests for any information that is required to support their own PCI assessment, specifically for Requirements 12.8.4 and 12.8.5.

Additional PCI DSS Requirements for Multi-Tenant Service Providers

The PCI Council updated Appendix A in PCI DSS 4.0 to more broadly address what they define as multi-tenant service providers. With the exception of one specific requirement embedded inside the standard itself, these exist in Appendix A1. Let's start with Requirement 11.4.7, which is grouped with the penetration testing requirements and mandates that multi-tenant service providers support external penetration testing requirements for their customers. Keep in mind, this is a best practice until March 31, 2025, but that doesn't mean you should ignore it until then. You are going to need a solid plan on how to allow penetration testing to occur that doesn't put your other clients' service at risk. If you are running single-tenant services, this is pretty easy as it should (theoretically) only affect the customer who is doing the testing. We suggest tracking any additional compute costs required to support the test and allocate those back to your end customer. This will ensure they are efficient in their testing.

For true multi-tenant environments, we suggest setting up a playground of sorts that is running the exact same code and infrastructure as your production offering (and you will need to prove this) and allow your customers to test that. This way you are sure to avoid one customer's over-zealous penetration testing firm from taking down your entire service. Again, we suggest tracking compute usage and charge those back to your customers.

On to Appendix A, Requirement A1.1.1 mandates logical separation in your multi-tenant environment. This means that you can only get access to each customer's environment after presenting a unique authentication factor as described in Requirement 8.2.3 and that customers are limited to their environment without specific authorization. This expands in Requirements A1.1.2 and A1.1.3 to ensure that a customer can only access their environment and not other customer environments at the provider and only access the resources specifically allocated to them. This is the separation we usually look for when we see multi-tenant environments. Each tenant or customer environment should be logically separated from all other environments, including the service provider's environment. Requirement A1.1.4 mandates that you test these logical separation controls at least once every six months in your penetration test for Requirement 11.4.6.

Requirement A1.2.1 adds logging requirements to your management environment such that you are consistent with Requirement 10 where logs are enabled for common third-party applications, active by default, and available for review only by the owning customer with locations that are clearly communicated.

In the case of a suspected or confirmed security incident, Requirement A1.2.2 mandates processes or mechanisms be in place to support and respond to any required forensic investigations to determine the impact and remediation plans for that incident. In addition. Requirement A1.2.3 mandates service providers maintain a process whereby customers can securely report security incidents and vulnerabilities to the provider, and those are then addressed and resolved according to Requirement 6.3.1.

OUTDATED SSL/TLS FOR CARD-PRESENT TERMINALS

Appendix A2 contains two requirements aimed at service providers that are leveraging outdated TLS and SSL for communication with hardware terminals for card-present transactions. The requirements are pretty straightforward (Requirements A2.1.2 and A2.1.3) and require remediation plans as well as a modern service offering. While we are aware there are still older terminals out there, this requirement should be less of an issue (if not almost completely irrelevant) as of this writing.

CASE STUDY

Philly's Phizzy Palate is a small craft beer garden that specializes in unique beers that challenge what connoisseurs know and love about beer. After becoming a certified cicerone, Philly found a small group of brewers that pushed the envelope of their respective sudsy styles and began ordering both the unique and a mainstream version of their beer to then pour for customers depending on their level of adventurism. He partnered with a payment and inventory service provider called Sudz to provide for the management of their front- and back-of-house systems that allowed for a digital menu with a percentage remaining in the keg as well as facilitating all the electronic payments. Philly even decided to experiment with payment methods and included the ability to pay with cryptocurrency.

The business was a wild success with patrons enjoying their drinks in the beer garden as well as taking beer to go in the form of cans and growlers. Before he knew it, Philly had people asking to franchise the concept in other cities nearby. Kori, a manager of the original location, gathered a group of investors and approached Philly to open a franchised location approximately 30 miles to the east on an area lake in a new business part that included apartments, houses, restaurants, and other retail and office space. After working out a few details, the franchise agreement was drafted and Kori was off to open her new location.

Philly knew that part of his long-term goals and success would come from working smarter, not harder, so he approached Sudz to ensure they could support a multi-tenant processing environment that would all roll up under his master merchant ID (MID), such that he could provide the Sudz software and analysis to Kori while charging a monthly maintenance fee as well as 50 basis points per transaction to manage her business for her. Kori received a weekly wire transfer to her account for any net profits after payroll was completed for her employees (all managed by Sudz). Philly had access into Kori's business details with a separate authentication credential, but Kori could only see her franchise details. This was done to ensure future franchises could replicate the model and each one can be its own separate tenant.

When it came time to do his PCI DSS validation, his acquirer let him know that he should fill out his Level 4 merchant self-assessment questionnaire, as well as require Sudz to send a service provider Attestation of Compliance (AOC) to him. What surprised Philly was when Kori asked for him to send along *his own* service provider AOC as well as Kori had no say in the systems being provided and was beholden to the franchise agreement.

Philly then asked Sudz to have their QSA perform the required assessment for his limited service provider role to Kori and charge him for this. Philly knew this made the most sense as the QSA for Sudz was well versed in how the software and relationships worked and could apply the controls build and managed by Sudz for his own attestation. He realized that by structuring his franchise agreement in the way he did, he had some additional PCI DSS requirements he had to meet as a result of being a merchant and service provider, earning extra money for a franchised store. His experience with Kori solidified the franchise model, so when he was approached by Alyssa to open a Philly's Peculiar Palate at the viewing area for a major airport, he had all of his documentation ready to go!

SUMMARY

Service providers are special, and they have earned the responsibility of demonstrating additional security controls to protect the account data they manage. If you are a merchant reading this chapter, keep these requirements handy so you can include them in your PCI DSS third-party management program. The security of account data and compliance with PCI DSS is a shared responsibility. Be sure you have clearly delineated which entity will own which pieces to maintain a complete PCI Compliance Program.

15 Managing a PCI DSS Project to Achieve Compliance

Information in this chapter:

- Justifying a Business Case for Compliance
- Bringing the Key Players to the Table
- Budgeting Time and Resources
- Educating Staff
- Project Quickstart Guide
- The PCI DSS Prioritized Approach
- The Visa TIP
- Summary

You have determined that your organization needs to comply with the Payment Card Industry Data Security Standard (PCI DSS) and, looking at the requirements, you are not sure where to start. Should you jump in and go through the 12 PCI DSS requirements and relevant Appendices linearly one at a time, documenting all of your requirements as in place? Or should you first figure out at what level you need to validate your compliance? How will you make sure that your fellow associates are on board with the changes you are proposing so that you can effectively and efficiently comply with PCI DSS? Is senior management behind you? How about the IT department that will actually be doing most of the work? How will you make the compliance effort come together? After putting the plan together, how will you ensure that your fellow associates have the training and information in front of them to help keep your company from falling out of compliance? Putting together a comprehensive plan will allow you to manage your compliance project efficiently and, in the end, achieve and maintain PCI DSS compliance as well as efficiently validate it.

This chapter will answer your questions about how to achieve compliance. You will learn how to justify putting in the effort and figure out if you need to comply at all. Once you know you must comply with PCI DSS, we will explore how you will bring all the players to the table to help build and enforce the compliance plan. You will read about tips on how to budget your time and resources so that you can achieve compliance quickly. Once you have your plan in place, you will need to get the message out to your staff and ensure they receive the right training to make sure your organization does not fall out of compliance. By the end of this chapter, you should have a clear plan on where to start with your own PCI DSS compliance efforts and the steps you will need to plan a program to meet compliance.

JUSTIFYING A BUSINESS CASE FOR COMPLIANCE

One of the first steps of any compliance plan is to justify putting in the effort. You must first figure out if you need to comply with the PCI DSS regulation and also figure out if you have overlap from other compliance plans already in place. Once you know compliance is a must, you need to figure out at what level you need to validate (although this should not impact the actions you take when securing cardholder data).

PCI DSS compliance validation applies differently depending on the volume of transactions you process and the medium by which you accept payments. Because compliance with the PCI DSS is mandatory, you could be hit with fines or higher processing fees today depending on your merchant level.[1] Another form of motivation should come from the fear of living through a breach. Fear, uncertainty, and doubt (FUD) have no place here, but let's not dismiss the motivational power of fear. If you have never had the opportunity to manage through a major breach, ask around in your industry. There are plenty of individuals that can help you frame your message properly such that you can make a positive impact and get the funding and support from the top that you need.

Figuring Out If You Need to Comply

Your first step with any compliance effort should be figuring out if you need to comply with a regulation. Regardless of the state of the economy, no company wants to waste time putting in measures that they are not required to have. Once you have figured out if you need to comply and what your validation requirements are, you will be in a good position to make your case to management.

NOTE

If you know you have card data in your environment, the next step is determining if you are a merchant or a service provider. Many merchants offer ancillary services to franchisees or even to other local companies to defray the costs of running their payment processing network. By doing this, many merchants end up being service providers and have slightly different reporting requirements for each payment brand. If you are accepting payments from any third party (like a franchisee) for processing, you are most likely a service provider. Consult with your acquiring bank or a Qualified Security Assessor (QSA) to clarify this before you go too far down your compliance project path!

Compliance Overlap

Once you determine that you have to comply, you need to look at the other compliance plans you have in place (if any). One sure way to fast-track your PCI DSS compliance program is to leverage investments made for other compliance or security initiatives. Compliance and information security initiatives often overlap (as shown in Figure 15.1) because most of the regulations are based on good

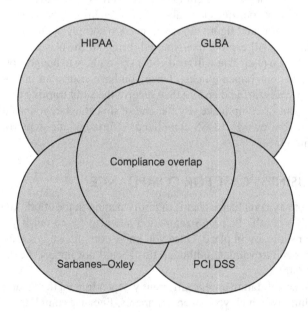

FIGURE 15.1   Compliance overlap Venn diagram.

business and security practices. So, pull out your Health Insurance Portability and Accountability Act (HIPAA) and Sarbanes–Oxley (SOX) compliance plans, and figure out which components you can reuse for your PCI DSS compliance plan. If compliance is nothing new to your organization, you may have invested in a control set that is unique to you, but maps to all of the major compliance initiatives. You can reuse those controls here as well. Who knows, you might find that you are already compliant but need to show that the measures you have in place are consistent with the PCI DSS regulations. For more information on how common compliance initiatives overlap, check your nearest search engine for a number of sources that show overlap. Check out the Unified Compliance Framework for a tool that can help you build out your controls.

The best place to start to figure out how to leverage your other compliance efforts is to set up a meeting with the team leaders from those projects. You need to get an idea of how the project performed and how it was accepted by management. The main point is to find out what the other teams have done in their compliance effort and see what elements you can bring over into your PCI DSS compliance plan. For example, HIPAA and PCI DSS both have rules regarding encrypting data. Can you use your encryption policy and procedure from HIPAA for PCI DSS compliance? That answer will come as you talk to your HIPAA compliance team leaders and review the policy and procedure to see if it already fits the PCI DSS encryption requirements found in Requirements 3.4–3.7. Your company policy for HIPAA compliance should mandate that you have encryption in place as you transmit protected health information across public networks like the Internet. Requirement 4 mandates the encryption of cardholder data as it moves across public networks. In this case, you do not need to recreate the wheel—you might just need to reclassify what type of data is required to be encrypted. Any efforts spent in leveraging your existing regulatory compliance will help to shorten the time it will take for you to become PCI DSS compliant.

NOTE

To help your organization determine how many new policies and procedures you will have to put in place to become PCI DSS compliant, consider completing Self-Assessment Questionnaire D (SAQ-D) in the early part of planning your compliance program. SAQ-D is a good tool to help demonstrate what compliance you already have and can show what you need to do to become compliant. SAQ-D can be downloaded from the PCI SSC website. SAQ-D is the most complete questionnaire, and may not be the exact one your organization follows. Review the guide available on the PCI SSC website to determine the appropriate one for your organization.

LEVEL OF VALIDATION

Now that you are on your way to planning your PCI DSS compliance project, you need to figure out at which level you need to validate. Unlike some regulations that present you with an all-or-nothing stance on how to validate your compliance, PCI DSS validation levels are based on how many credit-card transactions a merchant processes or a service provider processes/stores as well as on other related items you already read in Chapter 3, Why Is PCI Here? The more transactions you process, the more validation activities you may have to perform.

WARNING

Don't let yourself become complacent. If you are a Level 4 merchant across the board and are not required to do anything to validate your compliance with PCI DSS, remember this: by accepting even one card per year, you are still *required to comply with PCI DSS*. Many Level 4 merchants end up in big trouble when they realize they had to comply with PCI DSS regardless of their validation requirements.

For most organizations, validation consists of passing quarterly security network scans and completing an SAQ. If you process transactions in the millions, you need to have a QSA (or ISA if a merchant) validate your PCI DSS compliance through an on-site assessment. Remember, the five individual payment brands set their own enforcement requirements for PCI DSS, not the Council. It is possible (by volume, but level reciprocity could make the merchant a Level 1 across the board) to be a Level 1 American Express merchant, a Level 2 MasterCard merchant, and a Level 3 Visa Merchant all at the same time! To help you determine your merchant or service provider level, you can review the information in Chapter 3, Why Is PCI Here? Keep in mind, payment brands frequently alter their programs, so before you go too far into this process, visit the links in Chapter 3 to get the most recent levels from each of the card brands. Or better yet, call your acquirer(s) and ask them to help you determine your level.

WHAT IS THE COST FOR NON-COMPLIANCE?

The long-term costs (assuming the worst) associated with a breach far outweigh the costs of being compliant. Can your organization afford the fines and penalties, bad media press, and damage to its reputation? Breaches cost more during recessions as cash reserves are eliminated from companies facing dwindling or flat growth. Don't forget that the financial posture of your firm does more than just keep inventory and paychecks flowing, it also determines how much it costs your firm to borrow money (cost of capital), which affects every finance-driven business case your firm will undertake.

Your risk managers will tell you that the three things you can do with a risk is to resolve the issue, transfer the risk, or ignore the risk. The way PCI DSS states its 12 requirements—the only way to truly deal with the elements—is to resolve the issue or transfer the risk. Transferring the risk might mean that you outsource or bring in a managed service to deal with that requirement. Therefore, when you transfer the risk, you are still dealing with it indirectly. Ignoring the risk in PCI DSS is not an option. Even one non-compliant item in a Report on Compliance (ROC) or SAQ means you do not comply with PCI DSS. If you are compromised and found to be not compliant with PCI during the investigation, the fines are steep.

NOTE

Breach fines are calculated in different ways depending on the situation. Visa's Global Compromised Account Recovery program describes how Visa fines compromised merchants. They calculate fines based on the number and type of records lost. Your acquirer may be able to give you more information if you are interested in how the formula is calculated. MasterCard has a similar program, and your acquirer will have those details as well.

Penalties for Non-Compliance

Did you know that every quarter (if you are a Levels 1–3 Visa or MasterCard merchant) your acquiring bank is telling Visa and MasterCard if you have validated compliance? Both card brands are now actively fining merchants for non-compliance, but the amounts vary widely depending on your level. Keep in mind these numbers can change any time, and even if you are not compliant, you may not be getting fined today. Where these numbers may make sense is for new business initiatives or in a merger and acquisition scenario.

Let's take a minute to review the current fines that merchants of Levels 1–3 can expect to receive. Visa Fines:

- Level 1 merchants:
  a. $25K each month for non-compliance ($300K/year).
  b. Tiered interchange penalties, meaning that every transaction will cost you slightly more to process, potentially costing companies millions.

- Level 2 merchants:
  a. $5K each month for non-compliance ($60K/year).

MasterCard Fines:

- Level 1 and 2 merchants:
  a. Quarterly escalating fines of $25K, $50K, $100K, and $200K ($375K/year).
  b. Resets to $25K on the quarter following the $200K fine.
- Level 3 merchants:
  a. Quarterly escalating fines of $10K, $20K, $40K, and $80K ($150K/year).
  b. Resets to $10K on the quarter following the $80K fine.

While you may never find either of these programs detailed on the card brand's respective websites, your acquiring bank will have all the information relevant to your situation. Reach out to your acquirer first, then use the figures here (or the ones provided by your acquirer) to assist in your cost analysis. This information was obtained through previous online publications and through customer relationships and is subject to change at any time. The fines are global, but you may see differing enforcement of the fines as well as differing monetary amounts. These amounts are based in US Dollars and could be converted to your home currency for a baseline. Be careful when taking these figures to management. Validate these numbers through your acquirer based on the countries you process in to ensure you don't derail your compliance initiative before it starts. Remember, active fines come from both Visa and MasterCard in an opportunistic fashion, but any payment brand can fine you at any time.

If you suffer a breach and your organization is found to be out of compliance with PCI DSS, the penalties can be severe. Theoretically, the organization could be forbidden to store, process, or transmit credit-card information. A more likely result would be stiff penalties from the card brands used to recoup the costs associated with fraud and becoming a Level 1 merchant for one reporting period, thus dramatically increasing your compliance costs. Each case is handled individually on its merits. With the advent of new privacy laws in different states, you might be required to notify your customers of a breach and provide them with credit reporting services. Once notifications go out, you will lose control of the message. Looking at what it takes to comply, it should be easy to see how and why you need to put together your PCI DSS compliance plan.

BRINGING THE KEY PLAYERS TO THE TABLE

Once you have justified your compliance effort, it is vital that you bring all the players to the table to ensure that you are successful in becoming compliant. You need the correct corporate sponsorship otherwise senior management could reject any plan you put together. You need to look at your organization from the top down and identify each of the key people who are necessary to put the plan together, forming your compliance team. You need to identify the key members of your team to tackle components of the compliance plan and keep the project moving.

Compliance plans can be won or lost based on the participants you bring in to help you with the project. It is vital to bring the correct people to the table. Be selective of your team, as they will make putting together the compliance plan either a success or a failure. Remember what non-compliance can bring—failure is not an option.

WARNING

Be sure to get a good understanding of the current workload of the members you would like to invite to be a part of your compliance team. Many times, people are enthusiastic to be a part of a new project, but realistically they do not have the time to work on it. At the end, team members miss meetings or deadlines, which may impact deadlines associated with your compliance project.

If you are having trouble visualizing your team's work, consider getting a copy of *Personal Kanban: Mapping Work | Navigating Life* by Jim Benson and Tonianne DeMaria Barry (CreateSpace, ISBN-13: 978-1453802267) and using a *kanban* board to organize this project.

OBTAINING CORPORATE SPONSORSHIP

Management sponsorship is a critical success factor for any compliance effort. If senior management does not support the process, support from the staff will also be lacking. Why should they comply if your manager does not? As the leader of your compliance effort, you need to first work with your senior managers to make them aware of the issues and let them understand the justification of why they need to comply with PCI DSS. Make them understand the cost of non-compliance, and they will back you up as soon as they realize that the company could be in jeopardy for not complying. Start at the top, because the earlier you gain support from the CEO, the faster you will get support from her directs and other senior management.

Derek Milroy, our fantastic technical editor from the fourth edition, contributed this very important tidbit. Without the business bought in and involved in the efforts, you will just end up with a bunch of IT controls that are waiting to be broken. It's not just about controls, it's about a culture change in many cases. What good does a password policy do if the culture allows users to write it down on a sticky note and attach it to the bottom of their keyboard?

NOTE

Try to schedule a lunch meeting outside the office with the company CEO or other senior manager, where you would have her full attention, devoid of any distractions. Help her to understand the cost of non-compliance. Don't treat it like a stick to beat the CEO over the head with—they have plenty of that happening every day. Promoting FUD will get you nowhere fast, and the impression you make during these initial meetings will set the tone for the success of your program. Instead, learn about the business, the strategy, the plans, and figure out how to enable the CEO to get there without the burden of PCI Compliance. Executives manage risk every day—some better than others. Don't get banned from the adult dinner table because you cried wolf a bit too loudly.

When other employees in the company hear that a senior manager is sponsoring the team, the entire project will get more support which will help drive home the fact that the compliance effort is vital for the organization.

FORMING YOUR COMPLIANCE TEAM

Your compliance team is the focal point of your compliance project and is responsible for the success of the project plan. The best time to create your team is after you have received corporate sponsorship. Many times people who heard about the compliance project from a manager and want to participate will approach you. You need to get a good mix of people on the team to make the most impact. PCI DSS has requirements that can touch different departments in your company, so be sure to include at least one person from each of those functional areas. For example, PCI DSS requires you to build and maintain a secure network. If you don't include a team member from the networking group, you cannot be sure that a firewall is installed or maintained going forward. Don't forget to include the physical security and facilities teams as they help you meet various requirements (including much of Requirement 9) and the business folks when analyzing the various workflows that generate money from customers.

Roles and Responsibilities of Your Team

Your compliance team will help set the pace and scope of your compliance project. The selection of participants will make the project a success, but it is important to make it clear from the beginning what each team member is responsible for by assigning them roles and responsibilities. You will need your team to assist in the following ways:

- Work with managers and other team members to set the scope of the compliance project—mapping credit card data flows is critical and you must include both physical and logical flows,
- Select leaders for each of the areas where you need compliance,
- Analyze information needed for the compliance plan,
- Work with senior management to ensure that the end result is compliance, and
- Ensure you properly size and define the cardholder data environment.

Getting Results Fast

The best way to ensure a successful project and gain the respect from all levels of your organization is to get results fast (or at least score a few quick wins). As you are planning your compliance plan, you need to identify some low-level compliance issues that are relatively easy to fix and have your team tackle those first. People want to see results, and the faster you can show them results, the more confidence they will have in the project. If it takes you months to get the first item addressed, people might wonder if the organization will ever be compliant and become complacent about the effort as a whole, derailing all your efforts up to this point. Getting results early keeps the momentum and support moving in a positive direction for your entire project.

Notes From the Front Line

To give you a good example of how important it is to select the right team members, here is a real-world story of the first time Jessica was on a compliance team.

Jessica was approached by her manager, Ganesh, to be a subject matter expert for the company's PCI compliance project. Ganesh felt that Jessica's knowledge would be an asset to the team. The team leader sent out a meeting request and Jessica was excited to help make a difference in her organization. She showed up at the first meeting on time, ready to do what was necessary—even if it meant having to put in overtime to get the job done. That first meeting did not go so well. The team leader was 10 minutes late and only half of the team members showed up for the meeting.

During the meeting, Jessica began to realize that none of the other senior managers were briefed on the compliance project, and some even wondered whether they needed to comply with these new regulations. Even though there was no senior management support, the team leader knew the company needed to get into compliance or face trouble. When Jessica asked about the missing team members, the team leader thought that it was probably due to the lack of support from upper management.

After weeks of meetings, false starts, and many extra hours, the compliance team finally had senior management involved and then the wheels started to turn. The entire team showed up for a meeting for the first time, but they had to start over from the beginning. Jessica and the team leader soon realized that the meeting lacked the right people for the areas that need to become compliant.

After a few more weeks, the right people did get involved with the team, and miraculously senior management support was still there. The project took off like a wildfire. Jessica's team did a gap analysis and figured out what needed to be fixed and hit the ground running. After months of trying to put the team together, they were able to knock out the entire project in three weeks. Just like the expression about needing the right tool for the right job, you definitely need the right team for any compliance project you are attempting to pull off.

BUDGETING TIME AND RESOURCES

In order for your project to be a success, you need to ensure that it is managed correctly and that it does not take too long to complete. As important as it was for your team to get some results early on, you must continue to make sure that you set expectations, goals, and milestones. Figure out early on how you will manage the time and resources of your team and you will have a successful compliance project.

SETTING EXPECTATIONS

Setting expectations is a key factor when budgeting time and resources within your team. From the first stages of your compliance project, your team needs to know what to expect from you, other team members, and management. If this project is a priority, the team needs to know that all other tasks are secondary until the compliance plan is in place. You also need to be sure you set the right expectations with management, so they know what to expect with the compliance plan. Don't forget the ongoing costs associated with compliance as well. If you approach this as a project, your company will treat it that way. There are significant ongoing costs associated with complying with PCI DSS. Those can include things like hardware refreshes, software licenses or subscriptions, headcount associated with managing portions of your infrastructure, meetings, assessments and audits, and other expenses that you will find as you go along.

MANAGEMENT'S EXPECTATIONS

Knowing from the beginning what management expects out of this effort should be one of your first tasks. Before you bring the team together, you should talk to senior management to make sure you understand what they expect out of the project and the timeline in which the project must be completed. Be sure you understand the criticality of the compliance effort to the organization, as that will help you get a pulse on the project itself.

Once expectations (and the appropriate management sign-off) of the compliance project are in place, you need to document them and share them with all the members of your team. By having all team members of the compliance project working from the same set of expectations, you are one step closer to having a successful project. If management feels that the project needs to be done in four weeks, but the team actually needs eight weeks to complete the tasks, be sure to set the correct expectations.

ESTABLISHING GOALS AND MILESTONES

Once a timeline is in place, it is important to set goals for the team on when key items should be complete. You want to make it very clear when project items are due and when parts of the compliance plan need to be in place.

Start by listing the goals of the project and assign those goals to team members. Make it clear when goals need to be met, as some will have prerequisites that must be finished before you can move on to the next task. Having goals in place will keep the project moving in the right direction. Set up milestones for success and publish your plan to everyone involved to keep them up-to-date on the project's status.

A good way to keep your time and resources managed is by using project planning software such as Microsoft Project, which allows you to create Gantt charts that map resources to goals (see Figure 15.2). Gantt charts give you a way to easily report on your compliance project. If an item slips or is completed early, the chart will adjust and keep your project in line with the project timeline. There are so many free and paid solutions to help with project management that we would be remiss in listing all of them. Consult your favorite productivity group for examples.

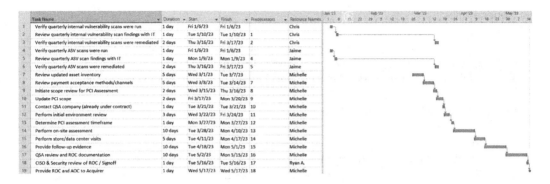

	Task Name	Duration	Start	Finish	Predecessors	Resource Names
1	Verify quarterly internal vulnerability scans were run	1 day	Fri 1/6/23	Fri 1/6/23		Chris
2	Review quarterly internal vulnerability scan findings with IT	1 day	Tue 1/10/23	Tue 1/10/23	1	Chris
3	Verify quarterly internal vulnerability scans were remediated	2 days	Thu 3/16/23	Fri 3/17/23	2	Chris
4	Verify quarterly ASV scans were run	1 day	Fri 1/6/23	Fri 1/6/23		Jaime
5	Review quarterly ASV scan findings with IT	1 day	Mon 1/9/23	Mon 1/9/23	4	Jaime
6	Verify quarterly ASV scans were remediated	2 days	Thu 3/16/23	Fri 3/17/23	5	Jaime
7	Review updated asset inventory	5 days	Wed 3/1/23	Tue 3/7/23		Michelle
8	Review payment acceptance methods/channels	5 days	Wed 3/8/23	Tue 3/14/23	7	Michelle
9	Initiate scope review for PCI Assessment	2 days	Wed 3/15/23	Thu 3/16/23	8	Michelle
10	Update PCI scope	2 days	Fri 3/17/23	Mon 3/20/23	9	Michelle
11	Contact QSA company (already under contract)	1 day	Tue 3/21/23	Tue 3/21/23	10	Michelle
12	Perform initial environment review	3 days	Wed 3/22/23	Fri 3/24/23	11	Michelle
13	Determine PCI assessment timeframe	1 day	Mon 3/27/23	Mon 3/27/23	12	Michelle
14	Perform on-site assessment	10 days	Tue 3/28/23	Mon 4/10/23	13	Michelle
15	Perform store/data center visits	5 days	Tue 4/11/23	Mon 4/17/23	14	Michelle
16	Provide follow-up evidence	10 days	Tue 4/18/23	Mon 5/1/23	15	Michelle
17	QSA review and ROC documentation	10 days	Tue 5/2/23	Mon 5/15/23	16	Michelle
18	CISO & Security review of ROC / Signoff	1 day	Tue 5/16/23	Tue 5/16/23	17	Ryan A.
19	Provide ROC and AOC to Acquirer	1 day	Wed 5/17/23	Wed 5/17/23	18	Michelle

FIGURE 15.2   Sample Gantt chart.

STATUS MEETINGS

The key to keeping your project on time is to have weekly (or daily if needed) team status meetings. The meetings should include your compliance team members, and each should report on what they have accomplished in the past week and what they will be working on in the next week. These meetings also give team members a chance to compare notes and bounce ideas off each other if they are stuck on a problem. Be sure to take notes or minutes and assign any new action items that come up. Any items that may impact the project timeline or resource requirements need to be placed into your project plan.

You should also have status update meetings with senior management on a regular basis. Depending on the length of your project, the meetings should be, at a minimum, once per month. During these meetings, you can go over your goals and milestones, and show how the project is progressing. It will also give the senior managers a chance to give their input on the project and reinforce the support you need from them.

Be prepared to hand out copies of your working project plan's Gantt chart. It will give a clear picture to your senior management team of where you are in the process and who is working on what issues. It is a good idea to send these charts to the managers beforehand to give them time to review the progress so that they can determine the guidance and support you will need.

If you are leading this team, you must strive for accountability. If deadlines go without recourse, expect the whole project to miss every future deadline you set. One trick Branden used was to send out daily status reports with every senior manager's name listed in a specific color to provide a visual reference to how their area's projects were going. Without fail, any manager who was resisting PCI DSS changed their attitude immediately after seeing their names turned red next to their peers.

TOOL

Here's a freebie for you all reading this far in the book. Branden stole and enhanced this status report from a colleague at his last job and found it to be incredibly useful. This report is sent out daily or weekly, depending on progress and timelines, and is designed to alert leadership on status and create space for asking for help. On the 'To' line of this report would be all the senior leaders in question as well as anyone specifically mentioned in the current report's iteration. In the 'CC' line could be more senior leadership and the managers of anyone on the 'To' line. Instead of a new email every time, we suggest replying to the last status report, updating the subject line, and pasting the new status on top (this way, people can scroll down to see the history). Be sure to remove any gaudy signatures at the end for brevity.

You will see a theme here; names, dates, and next steps; concrete, verifiable actions. You are communicating with senior leadership, so make sure this is consumable in a minute or two.

General rules:

- Every meeting on the topic should generate at least one line of text in the report.
- @ tag anyone who is mentioned in the report so that they see it.
- Highlight any upcoming deadlines (within 7 days) and @ the delivery person.

Report layout:

- Needs/Blockers:
  a. Hit them up front with anything you need or anything blocking you.
  b. Should include @ tagging people where possible and using red/yellow highlights to catch the eye.
- Watch Items:
  a. These things will turn into needs/blockers if not closely monitored.
  b. Note (@ tag) any people running critical path workstreams with any details or data and be sure to share target dates.
  c. Put risks that may pop up like resource contention.
- Completed from the previous update:
  a. Add anything in there that would be relevant.
  b. Great place to show the status of a larger ongoing workstream: 39 of 50 (+3 from last week) applications moved.
  c. Verifiable, visible, and concrete completed items. Setting up a meeting is not something you completed.
  d. Include people who completed as well as any dates.
- Next Steps:
  a. Here's where you talk about the next items for the workstream.
  b. If this is a big project that is near the end, just list all outstanding work.
  c. If you have many sub-projects that make up this project, group the next steps by sub-project.
  d. Put people who are doing the next step (@ tag) as well as dates.

People like seeing their name in green, and hate seeing it in red or yellow. This is extreme, but we guarantee you will see some results using this format.

EDUCATING STAFF

Training can make or break any compliance project. From the first meeting, ensure there is a training component to make all members aware of how the project will run and make sure they have all the necessary information to move forward with their part of the compliance project. Also, when your compliance program is in place, you need to make sure that part of that program includes training. Actions and plans to meet PCI DSS requirements must be maintained after they have been developed. The only way to do this is through a series of reminders and recurring training classes for your organization's employees. Having a training program in place from day one will go a long way in keeping your organization compliant after you have completed your compliance plan.

TRAINING YOUR COMPLIANCE TEAM

When your compliance team meets for the first time, your agenda should include an overview for all members. Items should include the following:

- An overview of the PCI DSS,
- An overview of the compliance effort for your organization,

- Why your organization is going through the process,
- A high-level review of the project plan to share goals and milestones, and
- A review of any elements the team might be submitting (i.e., how a policy should be written or how often to deliver status reports in some set format).

You could even use this book's Table of Contents as a guide for your training, making sure that you pull out the relevant portions for the teams you are working with.

Training your compliance team will help them understand how the plan came together and how to execute it to make your organization compliant. It will also get all members on the same page about what PCI DSS is and why your organization is going through the effort. You want to remove all myths around the project and level the playing field for your team members, so they can be successful in making your organization compliant.

TRAINING THE COMPANY ON COMPLIANCE

Compliance is boring. There, we said it. Getting people engaged on compliance initiatives isn't going to be easy, but the only way you will be able to maintain your compliance and minimize the effect PCI DSS has on your organization is to bake its requirements into your culture.

After your project is complete and you deem your organization to be compliant, you need to make sure the rest of the company knows that you need to maintain a level of compliance. You do not want to have a violation in the first week because an employee did not know about the need for compliance.

You need to put together a corporate compliance training program for all new employees and for existing employees to complete annually, which acts as a refresher course and also gives you a chance to present any information that has changed over the past year (Requirement 12.6 among others). Consider training anyone who comes into contact with a payment card. If this number seems daunting, try masking or truncating cardholder data for the majority of your users to reduce the number that need focused training. Your IT staff may also need training to ensure system administrators behave in a compliant fashion. Things like building hardening into the procurement process, logging checks and acknowledgments, and regular endpoint detection and response agent validations may not be part of your IT staff's DNA. If the new security processes are truly built-in (not bolted-on) then personnel from many IT teams will need to be refreshed on PCI-related processes for in-scope systems.

SETTING UP THE CORPORATE COMPLIANCE TRAINING PROGRAM

Be sure to set up your corporate compliance training program as an element of your compliance plan. Get the human resources department involved early on in the process to make sure that all employees of your organization receive the training. Many times you can leverage existing programs, like your current new employee orientation, to train existing employees.

NOTE

Keep your compliance training program upbeat and fun. Although security might be boring to most of your employees, it is fundamental to the success of your compliance efforts. One idea would be to have prizes at your training classes and offer them to people who get answers right during a question-and-answer session. People will be more likely to want to attend the training class if they can win a dinner, movies, or a gift card to any number of retail stores.

If you are reading this and laughing at how corny this sounds or thinking "this will never work in my company," you might be surprised. We have always found it interesting from a human behavior perspective when you find one or two motivators for influential team members. Others tend to fall in line!

The compliance training program is more than just creating a one-time training class for your employees. The following elements should be incorporated for a successful program:

- Create a new hire training class that all new employees are required to attend. It can be as simple as handing out this book to your new hires and making sure they understand the content by asking questions about PCI, or as complicated as bringing in a trainer to develop a program for you. The initial training will need to be comprehensive, potentially derived from this book's Table of Contents. Work with your human resources department to see if this training class can be injected into an existing orientation program or be sure you are a part of the process, so your training team is notified about new hires.
- Create an internal website that outlines key elements from the compliance training so employees have a good source to review information.
- Create a series of reminders to help keep the compliance effort on the minds of the employees. Good ideas for this are awareness posters, articles in your company's newsletter, and even "Compliance Days" where you can make a fun event around being PCI DSS compliant.
- Create a recurring annual training program for employees to make sure they are reminded about what they need to do to comply. Recurring training should update your employees on new developments (e.g., in 2009, we saw MasterCard change both validation requirements which were reversed and reinstated later, and add fines), changes in PCI DSS, or covering specific areas that your company struggles with. The recurring training program can work either as a live training class or as a Web-based training class that they can take when time permits. Either way the training is presented, it should be required to keep your organization in compliance.

With the right training programs in place, you can be sure that from the first meeting of your compliance team to the annual recurring training for your associates, your compliance efforts will have a lasting effect on your organization.

NOTE

One of the greatest tools in any compliance awareness program is the use of posters. With the use of posters, you can get the message out quickly. The posters you put out should have simple messages that grab people's attention. For PCI DSS compliance, simple phrases such as, "Display Your Employee Badge" or "Keep all Cardholder Data Under Lock and Key" will get the message to your employees quickly. Compliance posters are also a great way to get that first big result. You can create and put these posters up in the first part of your compliance planning efforts to give a kick-start to the project. When senior managers are walking around the office, they will see the posters and know that you are taking the compliance project seriously.

PROJECT QUICKSTART GUIDE

Putting a compliance plan together for PCI DSS can seem like an overwhelming task. You are probably asking yourself where to start. Who should be involved? When do you look at the PCI DSS SAQ? This section will get you pointed in the right direction and give you the first step toward getting your organization compliant with PCI DSS.

THE STEPS

We know how to plan a project to meet compliance, but when it comes to PCI DSS, what are the specifics you should be looking at to become compliant quickly and efficiently? For an overview of the steps, see Figure 15.3.

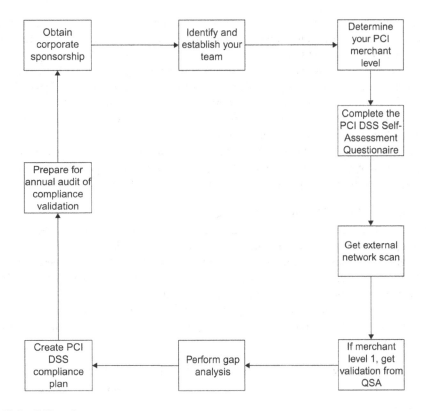

FIGURE 15.3 PCI project process.

Step 1: Obtain Corporate Sponsorship

Once you have corporate sponsorship, you will have the backing for all the steps of your compliance project plan. Be sure to meet with these members of your organization first to get the sign-off and acceptance that your company needs to be PCI DSS compliant. Remember, you need to make sure you get support from the highest level possible in your organization. Getting the backing from senior managers will help to ensure that the rest of the employees will be willing to work with you on getting compliant with PCI DSS.

Step 2: Identify and Establish Your Team

This is a critical step because it could make or break your compliance project. You need to be sure to select your team members from the appropriate areas of your company. Include the business leaders that have to worry about PCI DSS compliance and also the techies in the trenches who are setting up your networks. Having a good mix of key players will help your project succeed.

You should choose leaders for each of the 12 requirements of PCI DSS. If you break PCI DSS up into each requirement, you will be in a better position to complete your effort in a timely and concise manner. While this seems arbitrary, you will find that the latest revision of PCI DSS makes this a bit easier. You could also consider building a RACI chart that outlines everyone's responsibilities for all requirements by department. Remember, there can only be one accountable group per task! You should also set up a training class during your first team meeting to review what PCI DSS is, why your company has to comply, and the initial plan of what needs to be done to get into compliance.

Step 3: Determine Your PCI Level and Scope

You need to know what your PCI merchant or service provider level is, which will tell you how you need to validate compliance with PCI DSS. Talk with your team members who are from the business side and figure out how many transactions you perform. Or, if you are a merchant, call your acquirer(s). Then, refer to the card brand's websites to help you figure out your organization's level.

Knowing your level will set the stage for what exactly you need to do to comply as each level has different requirements for validating compliance. It is important that you determine this early on in the process because as you get closer to Level 1 (or Level 2 for MasterCard merchants), your compliance effort will take longer and involve more resources. If you are not at Level 1 from the start, you want to periodically review how many transactions you are processing—especially if you are close to the top of the range. If you jump to another level, you may also jump out of compliance.

As of PCI DSS 4.0, Requirement 12.5.2 mandates that you document and confirm scope at least once every 12 months (semi-annually for service providers). Be sure you follow all of those steps because everything after this step depends on the information confirmed in your scope exercise.

Step 4: Complete a PCI DSS SAQ or Hire a QSA

You need to complete the SAQ most appropriate for your business (many will use SAQ-D) in one of your first compliance meetings because the results of the questionnaire will give you clear guidance on how compliant your organization already is or is not with PCI DSS. The questionnaire can be found at the PCI SSC website. If you answer "No" to any of the questions, you are not in compliance. The questions on the questionnaire map directly to the requirements of the PCI DSS. When your organization has the questionnaire complete, it will indicate not only if you are compliant with PCI DSS, but what you need to do to become compliant. Even if you must validate as a Level 1, this exercise can provide a quick baseline for you.

Step 5: Set Up Quarterly External Network Scans From an Approved Scanning Vendor

Compliance with PCI DSS requires a quarterly network scan from an Approved Scanning Vendor (ASV), but Level 4 Visa, MasterCard, and Discover merchants may not have to submit their scans to their acquirer. All externally exposed Internet Protocol (IP) addresses must be scanned for vulnerabilities by an ASV, which means performing your own external scans will not make you compliant. The PCI SSC maintains a list of ASVs on their website. For more information, see Chapter 9, Vulnerability Management.

At the end of the network scan, the ASV is required to provide you with a report that will show you if your Internet-facing network is PCI DSS compliant. If your scanning partner discovers a vulnerability of a high enough severity, they will typically point you in the right direction toward a remedy.

One quick tip on your scans: do them as frequently as your infrastructure will support but remember that patching isn't always an overnight thing.

WARNING

You must select your ASV from the list that is maintained by the PCI SSC. If you do not use an approved vendor, any results you have, no matter how good they appear to you or your organization, can invalidate your PCI compliance efforts. Remember that you must have clean, quarterly external scans, except for your initial PCI DSS compliance where all you need is a recent, passing scan and documented policies and procedures requiring quarterly scans. Submitting scans with vulnerabilities that must be fixed for compliance proves you are not compliant with PCI DSS.

Step 6: Get Validated by a QSA (or an ISA)

This step is only required if you are at a merchant level that requires this (currently, Levels 1 and 2 in some cases) or your acquiring bank mandates it. You can also send some of your own employees to Internal Security Assessor (ISA) training, and perform some activities without the use of a QSA.

You want to engage the ISA or QSA to help you with Step 7 below. PCI Assessments are an annual process, where all components that are a part of how your company stores, processes, and transmits cardholder data are assessed. You can find a list of QSAs at the PCI Council's website. Keep in mind, Level 1 merchants are *not required* to use a QSA, and in fact can self-assess after having an employee complete the Internal Security Assessor program. Many companies opt to go the QSA route but remember that hiring a QSA does not transfer your liability to that QSA if you have a breach. You are still ultimately responsible for your ongoing compliance.

Step 7: Perform a Gap Analysis

After your team has gone through the SAQ, the network scan results, and potentially the reports from your QSA including a ROC, you now must prepare a document that lists out the gaps in your compliance. Your gap analysis document will set the stage for the creation of your compliance plan. To assist with your gap analysis, you should put together a worksheet that lists each requirement and indicates whether you are compliant or not. You can also use the worksheet to initially assign the requirement to a compliance team member.

Part of your plan should include building out some very basic documentation such as a data flow map for all of your card data to a list of in-scope systems. For those of you that must validate as a Level 1, you will already be required to do this. For those of you who are filling out an SAQ, this is required both for compliance and to drive your compliance process.

Step 8: Create PCI DSS Compliance Plan

Following the steps above, you now have the steps needed to create your PCI compliance plan. As discussed throughout this chapter, you should take all these elements and bring them into your compliance plan. Your plan should include the gaps that are standing in the way of your PCI DSS compliance efforts and what your organization plans to do to stay compliant year after year. Once all the gaps are closed, your compliance plan will be the live document that ensures you stay compliant with PCI DSS. If you need guidance on which gaps to tackle first, consider looking at the Prioritized Approach for PCI DSS and the accompanying tool in the Document Library section of the PCI Council's Website.

Step 9: Prepare for Annual Assessment of Compliance Validation

To maintain compliance, you should start over at Step 1 and begin the process again every year. The good news is that most of what you need to do is already complete, and you are mainly validating that you are still PCI DSS compliant.

THE PCI DSS PRIORITIZED APPROACH

For those companies that feel lost among the mountain of remediation that needs to be done, the PCI Council may have some help for you. The Council publishes the Prioritized Approach for PCI DSS and continues to maintain and update that document as they publish changes to PCI DSS. While the approach provides guidance to those individuals responsible for steering a PCI compliance project to completion, it needs to be customized for each organization to most efficiently meet your needs. There are two documents available for download—a written document outlining the approach and a spreadsheet to help manage your process.

NOTE

How can you use the PCI Prioritized Approach to make PCI DSS easy for you?

- Use the document to plan your PCI project from current state to compliant and secure state.

- Use the spreadsheet for ongoing planning of the next steps and identifying weak areas/next area to handle.
- Use the spreadsheet to track the status and create a report of compliance status for senior managers.

The PDF document describes the approach and gives some background on why the approach was created, it describes objectives, and it outlines the six milestones in their plan. The other document is a spreadsheet that contains the entire PCI DSS with a milestone number next to each requirement. Most companies that use this tool will add more columns to it to bring in their assessment data and will change the milestones to be in line with their particular project milestones. If you have no milestones defined, use these as a reference. Remember, you will probably need to adjust the milestones to fit more appropriately into your company's current compliance plan.

THE VISA TIP

While the Technology Innovation Program (TIP) is only from one of the payment brands, we felt it necessary to cover it here in this chapter as it is potentially a nice shortcut to obtaining compliance. One of the loudest complaints we hear from folks who feel that PCI DSS is forced upon them goes something like this: "If the payment system would just be secure, we wouldn't need this thing!" While that is technically correct, payment security is absolutely a shared responsibility. A secure payment system is a start, but so are secure enterprises.

As of this writing, the Visa TIP still allows companies to bypass specific annual reporting requirements by meeting a certain minimum set of standards. Unlike the Compliance Acceleration Program (CAP) that used fines and interchange penalties to motivate merchants to comply with PCI DSS, there is no true financial incentive to participate in the TIP today outside of lower compliance validation fees.

In order to qualify for the benefits of the program, merchants must meet the following baseline:

- Validate PCI DSS compliance within the previous 12 months or have submitted to Visa (via their acquirer) a defined remediation plan for achieving compliance, based on a gap analysis.
- Confirm that sensitive authentication data (i.e., full contents of magnetic stripe, CVV2 and/ or PIN data) is not stored, as defined in the PCI DSS.
- The merchant must not be involved in a breach of cardholder data. A breached merchant may qualify for TIP if they have subsequently validated PCI DSS compliance.
- 75% of your transactions must *originate* through any combination of enabled and operational chip-reading terminals (US merchants must have dual-interface terminals to support contactless), a PCI-validates Point-to-Point-Encryption (P2PE) solution, or an industry-standard tokenization solution that meets EMVCo's tokenization specification. An enabled device under this program means that your payment terminal must accept and process an EMV or contactless card (not just be capable of doing this). Note that the transaction itself does not need to be EMV or contactless, but the terminal must be capable of processing both of those payment types. Merchants that have upgraded their terminals with a slot for EMV and a contactless reader but cannot accept either in exchange for goods and services do not meet this requirement.

The TIP does not address card-not-present transactions but that transaction volume is included in the numbers used to determine the 75% qualifying level. If this is an issue, consider any number of strategies that could remove those transactions from the counts such as outsourcing card-not-present processing or creating a separate merchant relationship for your online store.

Merchants that choose to take advantage of the TIP may in fact be able to talk their acquirers or processors out of validating compliance entirely. This obviously would depend on the relationship you have with your providers as well as the way you process payments, but most acquirers are only required to report compliance back to the payment brand—not send along the ROC or SAQ. Therefore, participating in the TIP could ultimately remove your annual PCI Assessment requirement if you convince your acquirer to report your compliance in lieu of a ROC if you participate in the TIP.

The three main outcomes that Visa is shooting for as a result of these programs are:

- Bring the backend processing technology up to more secure levels as is seen in other parts of the world as dynamic authentication will reduce the amount of card present and counterfeiting fraud.
- Ensure cardholders that travel internationally can use the Visa card in countries where EMV is prevalent. Some cardholders have had trouble recently because their US-based issuers have not provided them with EMV-capable cards.
- Push merchants to accept dynamic data methods for payment by excusing them from liability in the case of a domestic or cross-border counterfeiting fraud.

SUMMARY

Planning a project to meet compliance can be so overwhelming that you wind up having false starts or not begin the project at all. Your compliance efforts do not have to end this way. By putting together a good compliance project plan, you will have what it takes to make your organization PCI DSS compliant.

From the start of your project, you need to take a close look at why you need to become PCI DSS compliant. Simply figuring out if you need to comply can save you weeks of time and effort that could be devoted to other compliance initiatives. Once you determine that you must comply, spend time understanding your current level, type of company (merchant or service provider), and what exactly you have to do to validate your compliance. Once you know your level, either you will have a QSA perform an assessment against your company or you will fill out one of the nine SAQs relevant to your business model. The Council's website has information on all nine SAQs, and what must be submitted for compliance validation purposes. You also need to figure out what is the cost to your organization for non-compliance. Can your organization afford the risk? With new legislation and fines constantly coming to market, nearly all situations will yield a firm "No."

Once you determine that you need to be PCI compliant and cannot afford the risk of non-compliance, you need to bring all the players to the table. You first want to obtain senior manager (C-Level) sponsorship to get the backing you need to complete the project. The corporate sponsorship process will also help you form your compliance team. Your compliance project starts by getting your team together and working through the planning process.

You must guide your team in the right direction and help them budget their time and resources effectively. First, you need to set expectations with your team and management about what the compliance effort entails. At this point, you can set up goals and milestones to help keep the project on a timeline and define when the project should be completed. It is important to have status meetings with your team and management during the process to keep everyone informed and moving forward.

As you start your compliance planning project, make sure that your team members get the correct training by providing an overview of what PCI DSS is and why your organization is going through this compliance effort. You should also train all the employees in your company, so they know what it takes to be compliant and to stay compliant. Setting up a corporate compliance training program will have a lasting effect on your organization—not only in keeping PCI compliant but also keeping your workforce thinking about security at all times.

Then, we outlined the nine steps you should take to become PCI DSS compliant. If you go through each of these steps, you will complete the first round of your compliance effort. Knowing that you are PCI compliant will help allay the fears of non-compliance by management. If you find yourself still needing a place to start, you can try out the new PCI SSC Prioritized Approach to compliance. Remember, the information provided may not directly apply to your organization, so you must customize it to make it effective.

At the end of your compliance effort, congratulate the team and encourage them to continue to keep your organization PCI DSS compliant.

NOTE

1. We feel obligated to inject some reality into this comment. We are only aware of a handful of instances where processing was terminated, and most of these were on the service provider side. The best advice we can give is to talk to your acquirer. In 2016, one acquirer we worked with shared that their Level 1 merchant compliance level was around 70%, but none of the non-compliant were getting fined (you are more likely to get hit with higher fees). As long as you are transparent with your acquirer on plans and progress, you should be able to get the time you need to complete a robust and sustainable compliance program.

16 Don't Fear the Assessor

Information in this chapter:

- Remember, Assessors Are *Generally* There to Help
- Dealing With Assessors' Mistakes
- Planning for Remediation
- Planning for Re-Assessing
- Summary

The title of this chapter might shock you a little bit. Why, you ask? Have you noticed that the words "audit" and "auditor" in reference to Payment Card Industry Data Security Standard (PCI DSS) are generally missing from this book? That's because the correct terms are "assessment" and "assessor" when referring to PCI DSS. While your Qualified Security Assessor (QSA) may be a CPA, it is not a requirement and most QSAs are not; instead many come from the IT security domain and some may be IT auditors. The procedures an assessor uses to validate your compliance with PCI DSS are called the Security Assessment Procedures (not the Auditing Procedures). We're, intentionally making this distinction as audit tends to be rigid and checkbox-y, while assessments have more nuance. Your assessor has flexibility, which ironically can both introduce and remove friction from your compliance process.

We are not suggesting that auditors are bad or that they cannot handle something like PCI DSS—they are just trained differently. Your internal audit group should be involved in the PCI DSS program from a self-assessment perspective, but remember, PCI DSS is assessed, and you work with assessors.

Whether it's your first on-site assessment or your first vulnerability scan, expect to find compliance gaps. While you may get lucky on your first go around, you should still have a plan in place to deal with this if it happens. It is a solid bet that you will have at least one finding from your PCI Assessment at least once in your career (if not literally every time). This may happen because you interpreted a requirement differently from an assessor, or it may be that you simply missed something that an experienced assessor would catch. When things go wrong, it's easy to blame the assessor. Having the right attitude can make all the difference.

Generally, assessors should not allow you an easy pass. And then the term "easy pass" is quite relative. If they do not properly report real gaps in your PCI DSS compliance they can lose their QSA status—or go into the dreaded PCI Council remediation process where they are closely monitored by the Council. In addition, history will repeat itself if you have a breach and become a statistic of how ignoring PCI and only paying it lip service will lead to bad outcomes.

REMEMBER, ASSESSORS ARE *GENERALLY* THERE TO HELP

When we sat down to start writing this chapter, we altered the title of this section to include *generally*. PCI DSS assessment work is a people business, and we would argue that *generally* people are well-intentioned humans that want to help others improve their security and compliance posture. We've all met someone who took things a bit too seriously or dug their heels in based on a fundamental misunderstanding of a situation.

In cases like this, it's up to you, the person on the other side of the assessment table, to take ownership of the situation and change the outcome. Normally it's a conversation to make sure that there are not any misunderstandings on either side of the table. In extreme cases, you may have to change your QSA or Qualified Security Assessor Company (QSAC). If your assessor is extremely familiar with UNIX servers but knows nothing about mainframes or cloud, he may struggle with assessing those environments. Providing vetting and oversight for the assessors that review your environment will help get you to the outcome you need.

NOTE

Douglas Squirrel and Jeffrey Fredrick published a book titled *Agile Conversations: Transform Your Conversations, Transform Your Culture* (IT Revolution Press, ISBN-13: 978-1-942788-97-3). We've found that the techniques in this book are foundational to conflict resolution in scenarios like the above. Finding common ground rooted in facts and building from there will get you to an acceptable outcome. We highly recommend this text.

When dealing with on-site assessors or approved scanning vendors (ASVs), most people fit into one of three groups.

1. Some people are intimidated by assessors. They see assessors as people with a lot of power, and they hope they will say and do the right things, avoiding the pain of a compliance gap.
2. Some look at assessors as their enemy. They believe they must wrestle with the assessor and win in the end (this is where the "auditor vs. auditee" mindset rears its ugly head).
3. Some people treat the assessor like a consultant ("a mandatory consultant" as the case may be) they've brought in to help bring their company into compliance. They respect the assessor's opinions and keep the assessor in the loop as they work out solutions.

While it might surprise you, the last group will get the most out of their assessor and will have the best overall experience—and likely the most secure cardholder data environment as well. This partnership should yield compliance with the least amount of friction, and will usually gain upper management support quickly for the funding required to resolve issues identified during the assessment.

As hard as it might be to believe, assessors are *generally* there to help you. After all, you are the one paying for their services. It's important to know how to work well with assessors so that your assessment will go smoothly and efficiently, and ensure that you get your money's worth. A good assessor will go over your company's systems, practices, and policies with a fine-toothed comb, and tell you what you can do to improve your security. Hopefully, your primary goal in becoming PCI compliant is to have your company become more secure and decrease the likelihood of payment card data theft or loss. When you realize that assessors provide you with a valuable service and that you're both on the same team working towards a common goal, you will have the most productive attitude. Remember that assessors have moral and professional obligations to follow the guidelines and procedures they've been given for the assessment despite the fact that you are paying for their services. It is not appropriate to ask them to compromise those obligations. The assessor's integrity is probably more important to them than the invoice they send you.

Assessors are trained by the Council and likely have performed many assessments (especially if they are the lead assessor or running an engagement alone), and they can give you great advice on what you can do to bring yourself into compliance by leveraging past experiences. As snowflakey as you may think your environment or business is, we would be surprised if an experienced QSA had not seen something similar enough to your environment to provide guidance on which adjustments to make to get you to compliance.

When you choose your assessor, interview them! This assessment is an important security project you will complete this year. Starting with the wrong assessor will make your pain so much worse. This is where having a person with an Internal Security Assessor (ISA) certification or a former QSA who knows how assessors are trained and how they operate on staff and with you during the assessment helps a lot.

Insist on setting up an interview with someone from your prospective QSA company. Understand their methodology. How will they ensure you exit the assessment process confident in the result? Nobody wants to receive a compliant rating only to discover that you have a compromise (sadly, there are examples of this that are well-covered in the media, even *days* after a compliant result).

Good assessors will bring a team of at least two QSAs to every engagement to make sure you get the most accurate result, balancing their expertise and specialties for your specific environment. Good assessors will come on-site and will not just interact with you via e-mail (Note that in a post-COVID-19 world, we understand that this shifted for a short period of time). Have you ever tried to explain to someone how to build a Lego Millennium Falcon from loose parts over the phone or, worse, e-mail? That would be one of the most frustrating experiences of your life. Don't expect your assessor to get a good view of your infrastructure over the phone. Finally, you get what you pay for! You don't always need to choose the most expensive bid, but if you get bids of $20K and $200K from the exact same scope, something is not right. Don't get stuck in an apples to oranges comparison. You will end up with sour grapes every time. In many cases, the cheapest assessor will end up being the least competent who may not even look (or look—but then overlook) at whole parts of the network and control environments.

Blaming your QSA after a breach is difficult if not impossible. It's been tried in the courts in the US and for the most part doesn't provide the monetary relief you may desire.[1] Depending on statutory and case law where you operate, you may have better or worse luck. Remedies generally are not relevant as you the merchant or service provider are responsible for your own compliance. It is in your best interest to have a solid assessment that helps you find and address hidden compliance gaps.

When you have the right attitude you will find ways to use your assessor to improve the security of your company. Seasoned assessors have a wealth of knowledge—even outside of payment security—and can be leveraged when bridging gaps in compliance. They have seen many technologies, policies, and practices others have put into place to mitigate risks, and should be able to give you choices to help you meet requirements that work best for your situation. For example, if cost is your main concern, an assessor may know of a low-cost or open-source tool that you can use to comply with certain requirements (the QSA may be efficient, "cost-effective" and "cost-smart," or they could be "cheap" and cut corners everywhere).

On the other hand if time is more important, the assessor may know of a solution that is quick to set up that will bring you into compliance. As you work on your remediation, it's important to keep your assessor in the loop. This way he can give opinions on what you've chosen to do and can give further advice. It will also likely make your next assessment much easier for both parties involved.

Don't forget this old business adage. Pick any two of the following when asking someone to provide you with a good or service: good, fast, or cheap! For QSA services, picking "cheap" with either of the remaining two may lead to spectacular (and costly) trouble later.

BALANCING REMEDIATION NEEDS

Do your homework when looking at ways to bridge compliance gaps. Depending on the problem you're trying to solve, there may be open-source tools, managed solutions, off-the-shelf software, or hardware appliances to consider. When looking at products and services that can help bring you into compliance, there are usually four main factors that you should consider:

- **Effectiveness:** Will the solution you're looking at really solve the problem and allow you to pass your next assessment? If it won't, it should be ignored.
- **Cost:** Normally cost is a factor in any decision made by a business. Sometimes decisions are based solely on initial cost, but costs of maintenance should also be considered. While one product or service is cheaper up-front, it may end up costing your organization much more in the long run.

- **Time to Install:** You probably want to get into compliance quickly. If you're not in compliance you may be facing fines, but the bigger issue is the exposure from missing security controls that a hacker dreams of.
- **Time to Maintain:** The time used to maintain a product will oftentimes be the most expensive part of adding it to your organization. Total Cost of Ownership calculations are critical to the remediation process (i.e., purchasing a log management solution instead of outsourcing the management to a managed service provider).

Depending on your exact situation, some of these may be more important than others, but they should all be considered when choosing a solution.

How FAIL == WIN

In some cases, failing an assessment ends up being a huge win for your company's security and compliance posture, and not even for just payment security. In many organizations, the security staff (or security-minded IT staff) would like to put certain security measures in place, but have been blocked by upper management because of cost or other priorities. Remember, upper management's job is to help the company make money, not spend money. Even after you have done a careful cost-benefit analysis and have determined that the benefits outweigh the costs, upper management may still say "no." A failed assessment may be the perfect time to help them to say "yes." If the assessor is requiring that you add something to comply with PCI DSS, you can use that as leverage with upper management to get it put into place. Build your business case and be sure to include the cost of non-compliance. Let them know that the assessor says you will not be compliant without that measure.

DEALING WITH ASSESSORS' MISTAKES

Assessors are human. Humans make mistakes. Yes, assessors make mistakes. While this does not happen often, there is a right way to deal with it when it does. The first thing to do is to talk to the assessor and have him explain how he came to his conclusion. Many times someone misunderstood a requirement or control or perhaps believed a compensating control mitigated a problem when the assessor doesn't agree. Having a good open dialog about what you believe is a mistake will often solve the problem quickly.

Many assessors find their roots in security (some find it in auditing, which can on occasion make this more difficult). Sometimes an assessor will "make up" a requirement because it just makes good sense, but when you ask the assessor to show you where in the PCI DSS that requirement exists, they will realize their mistake. Notice how that last sentence was phrased. Ask them to "show you where the requirement is in PCI DSS," don't scream at them to "PROVE IT!"

Before you go to the step in the next paragraph, consider why you think the assessor made a mistake. Is it because you personally have an attachment to a particular system or control? Was the assessor rude? Have you tried to fix the issue the assessor identified with no success? Or was he trying to sell you something that his company happens to offer? Assessors make mistakes, but don't assume that because an assessor feels a certain way that he is alone on an island where no other assessor would dare set foot. Before pushing back on the assessor, ask **yourself** this: "If I were breached tomorrow, could this be a cause?" If it is, don't waste time bullying the assessor. Take some time to research and look up the issue; don't argue because you happen to dislike his advice or don't want to deploy a particular technology or change a certain bad habit of your organization. Use that energy to fix the issue and close the issue that an attacker may use to break into your system.

On the other hand, if you know that this does not increase your risk and do not seem to be expressly spelled out in PCI DSS, consider continuing your conversation and pushing to find common ground.

NOTE

You may feel like you have compensating controls in place to solve a problem but the assessor doesn't agree. If the assessor does not agree with the control and you are a merchant, try working with your acquirer (sorry service providers, you do not have this option). If your acquirer chooses to accept the risk, they can absolutely do so. Most acquirers will side with an assessor, so be sure you present a good case if you choose to challenge the assessor. Most of the time it's easier to follow the requirement exactly than to try to get a mitigating control to fix the problem. See Chapter 17, The Art of the Compensating Control, to learn more about good and not-so-good compensating controls.

In some cases, you may need to push back on your assessor. Pushing back is when you challenge an assessor's results because you feel the outcome does not represent the situation. When you push back, be polite. Simply explain to the assessor your point of view and why you believe there was a mistake. If the assessor disagrees, ask him to explain his reasoning. If the assessor has explained why you didn't pass and you don't agree with his reasoning, you may need to talk to the PCI Practice Lead about the situation. Explain your situation and why you think a mistake was made. Most of the time, the lead will talk to the assessor to get his side of the story before coming to any conclusions. If the lead agrees with the assessor, you will need to fix the problem to be validated as compliant (or in extreme situations, change your QSAC).

Please avoid playing the "I WANT TO SPEAK TO YOUR MANAGER" card. Assessors are people too.

This really falls back to your skills in conflict resolution. First, strive to find some common ground and facts both sides can agree upon. Build from that foundation to find where there are opportunities to evolve. Whatever you do, don't end up in a viral TikTok.

Sometimes an ASV scanning tool will report a false positive—something uncommon but entirely possible at the time of publishing—especially if bespoke or other non-mainstream systems are scanned. This is when an assessment shows you have a vulnerability, such as a missing patch, that really is not vulnerable. This seems to happen more with remote scans since they have less access to the system itself. Any good assessor or ASV knows how to keep false positives to a minimum. When you do get a false positive, your ASV should work through it with you as they are required to operate a process for dealing with scan mistakes and other false positives. They may want to get more details from you so they can verify it as a false positive, and then fix the system so the error does not come back in the future.

If you are getting the false positive, chances are someone else is too.

WARNING

Don't forget, you get what you pay for! Most ASV scanning engines today are based on either Qualys or Nessus, but not all ASVs will produce the same results. Interview your ASV and ensure they are involved in the process, not just setting you up in a database for scans. You may need help interpreting the results or addressing false positives, and those features may cost more.

Some ASVs only run automated tools with very little human checking. This generally works well most of the time, but sometimes the scans can be complicated, and a false positive may end up in a report. If you get a report listing a serious vulnerability, first act as if it's true and see if there's something you can do to remedy the problem quickly. Do not start arguing before you have the data—after all, just because you told somebody to "go and patch the vulnerability" does not necessarily mean the scanner is wrong.

Depending on the situation, it may be a good idea to do some tests on your own. You already have a scanning solution on-site for the internal scans mandated by Requirement 11.3.1, so point it at the target in the external scan report (a solid second opinion if the tools are not the same). Depending on the type of vulnerability, you may be able to do some manual testing. For example, if your report says that a patch is missing, you may want to manually check the system to validate the finding. This can be particularly tricky if you are running systems that backport security patches to known-stable versions instead of sitting on the bleeding edge. Debian and RedHat systems are notorious for requiring an extra step to see if the version reported is *actually* vulnerable. If you are unable to find the vulnerability after your testing, it may be time to challenge your scanning vendor's findings and report it as a false positive. They should do additional tests to determine why the false positive happened, and fix the problem or remove this finding from your final PCI scan report.

PLANNING FOR REMEDIATION

A good rule of thumb when doing remediation is that it should be as transparent as possible so that it has a minimal impact on the business. Sometimes it is impossible to avoid affecting the business or a user. For example, implementing a much stricter password policy or disabling group accounts may have an effect on how people perform their jobs. For the most part, patches and system updates should be transparent to users.[2] The more transparent your remediation, the fewer problems you're likely to have while implementing it. As you plan your remediation process, always keep transparency in mind.

The first thing to do in planning for remediation is reviewing your gap analysis with your assessor. Your gap analysis describes the difference from where you are now to where you need to go to be compliant. Ask your assessor which risks he considers high priority. This is where good QSAs shine—being your consultant to help you get to a compliant state. You are paying him, so ask for his advice! Unlike auditors, a QSA may well share his experience with remediating and analyzing similar problems for other clients or in his past life as a security professional. This of course can all fall apart if you are using the Customized Approach, so just be aware of the details of your specific assessment.

NOTE

PCI DSS 4.0 creates a new requirement around any assessments performed under the Customized Approach. These must be done like traditional audits where the firm designing and implementing the control cannot be the firm assessing the control. From Appendix D: "if a QSA is involved in designing or implementing a customized control, that QSA does not also derive testing procedures for, assess, or assist with the assessment of that customized control."

For example, if the assessor feels that you have urgent risks that could easily be exploited at any time, you would want to work to remedy those first. In this case, the assessor should let you know as soon as he finds the problem and not wait until the rest of the assessment is done. This would then become your top priority, and you should follow your company's incident response plan.

Now that you have your results and understand what needs to be done to comply with PCI DSS, it's time to prioritize your risk. With the help of your assessor, work to determine which problems present the highest risk. If there are not any high-risk issues, the conversation should turn to the items that you can address that will get you some quick compliance wins and give you the biggest bang for your compliance buck. There are many tools that can be used to help you classify risks. Here are some that you might find useful:

- Common Vulnerability and Exposures (CVE): This is the industry standard, and much referred to, listing of vulnerabilities in products. Many products use CVE numbers to reference vulnerabilities.
- National Vulnerability Database (NVD): Supported by the Department of Homeland Security and has a great database of many types of vulnerabilities with scored vulnerability severities using the Common Vulnerability Scoring System (CVSS) method.
- Open-Source Vulnerability Database (OSV): This community-run database of vulnerabilities will give you a lot of great information on a vulnerability, including references, ways to test your system, and how to mitigate the problem.

Fun Ways to Use CVSS

The CVSS is a standard for scoring vulnerabilities that has become more widely used. Approved scanning must use CVSS scores for any vulnerabilities that have a CVSS score. PCI DSS 4.0 retains the use of CVSS for vulnerability severity (see Requirement 11). Most vulnerability databases will list CVSS scores, which are great in helping you determine the impact of a vulnerability. There are some vulnerabilities that may not have a CVSS score, but NIST provides a tool to help you estimate them on their website.

For example, let's say that your report shows that you don't have your credit card area physically secured. Since this is not a specific vulnerability with a specific system, there won't be a CVSS score for it, but you can use CVSS to help you determine the priority.

In this example, we'll use a physical security issue to show you how this works. While this system is mainly for computer security issues, it works pretty well for physical vulnerabilities as well.

The outdated example below is a bit contrived, but still illustrative of how you can leverage CVSS in unique ways. That said, there are some financial institutions that require things to be sent by fax…

Jeff is the afternoon manager for Teri's Tapas To Go, a small tapas bar near midtown Manhattan. When Teri built out the location, she found certain constraints as to where electric and telecommunications wiring could be placed. Thus, she has a fax machine near the bathroom to receive faxes containing orders with cardholder data on them. Because the fax machine is not visible by Jeff (or any employee) unless he is in front of the counter, he cannot closely monitor it. There are often times when Teri's staff is busy with customers and are not watching the fax machine. If they are too busy, they may not hear the fax machine and therefore delay checking for new orders. Anyone passing by the bathroom could easily grab a fax.

On the calculator page, Teri would start with the Base Scoring Metrics. This gives the CVSS calculator a base score to work from for the vulnerability.

Related exploit range is where an attacker would have to be able to exploit this vulnerability. If an attacker can compromise the system over the Internet or some other remote means, then it would be remote. In our case, with the credit card area not being physically secured properly, it would be **Local**.

Attack complexity is how difficult the attack is to pull off once an attacker has found the vulnerable target. If the attack requires other factors to be in place for it to work, it may make it complex. In our case, we'll say that this is **Low** complexity. Once an attacker knows where the credit card data is, it's easy for them to get to it.

The level of authentication needed is if an attacker must be authenticated to pull off an attack. This means that there is some test to verify who the user is that must be bypassed to attack the system. An example would be something like a fake badge to get access to the fax machine. In this case, an attacker would not because the fax machine is in a public area, so the level will be **None**, and there is no User Interaction required to create the vulnerability, so that will also be **None**. The scope will be listed as **Unchanged**.

Confidentiality impact describes how the exploit will affect the confidentiality of data in question. In our case, if they can access cardholder data by walking into a protected area and wheeling a file cabinet with all cardholder data in it out the door, it would be complete. Normally a heavy filing cabinet is pretty safe, but since Teri has faxes coming in with cardholder data and there is little to no protection of that data once it hits the fax machine. In this case, the confidentiality impact could be Partial (as in you are not getting ALL of the cardholder data), or Complete (as in you did get the complete card number). For illustration purposes, we'll choose **Low**.

Integrity impact describes how the attack will impact the integrity of data. In our case, it's not likely that integrity will be compromised, so we'll use **None**.

Availability impact describes the measure of how the availability of systems and data is affected. Since the attacker can walk off with a fax, the data is no longer available, so we'll mark that as **Low**.

The Impact value weighting allows you to give more weight to confidentiality, integrity, or availability. In our case, the biggest problem will be confidentiality, because the attacker just walked off with cardholder data, so we will choose Weight confidentiality. Scores are calculated dynamically, and we get a base score of 5.1.

Next we will do the temporal score metrics.

Availability of an exploit lets you determine if an exploit is actually available or not. In our case, we'll say that a **Functional Exploit Exists** since the attack would work much of the time, but there may be times when one of Teri's employees would catch somebody.

The type of fix available allows us to specify if there is currently any way to remediate the problem. We'll say that Teri has asked employees to keep an eye on the fax machine, which is a **Temporary** fix until she finds a better home for the fax machine.

Level of verification that the vulnerability exists allows us to specify how sure we are the vulnerability is actually present in the system. In our case, we know that the vulnerability exists so we'll choose **Confirmed**.

Finally, the environmental score metrics section allows you to add some customizations if required.

The Impact Subscore Modifiers allow you to model the impact the attack could have on your systems. In our case, one credit card number stolen on a fax won't bankrupt Teri, so we'll say it has **Low** Confidentiality Requirement. The scope should be set as **Unchanged**.

Now that we're done, our new overall score is 4.2.

There are many ways to prioritize risks associated with compliance gaps—more than we could review in the scope of this book. Don't spend a huge amount of time and effort prioritizing various compliance gaps, since in the end they all need to be fixed for PCI Compliance. But it's good to have a general idea in order to start where the fire burns the hottest.

PLANNING FOR RE-ASSESSING

As you are working through your gap assessment, include your assessor! Not only can she give advice on how to mitigate some risks and bring yourself into compliance, she can also help you set realistic completion dates. As you run into roadblocks, she can help you adjust the dates and remediation plan, and be there to support you through the process.

After this is done and everything is in place, plan to reassess yourself. We provide some self-assessment tips in Chapter 18, You're Compliant, Now What?

Validate that the identified gaps are closed before calling your assessor back out to save time and money. Provided you included your assessor during the remediation process, your re-assessment should be quick and painless. Then you will finally be able to have your PCI DSS compliance party!

SUMMARY

Don't feel bad if your first assessment does not end in a compliant report. Instead, use it to your advantage to better your company's security posture. Work with your assessors instead of against them. Remember you and your assessor are on the same team and the process of assessing should feel like a partnership. By following your assessor's recommendations, your assessment should be less painful and go by quickly. You should involve your assessor as you work to bridge your compliance gaps. The more you involve your assessor, the easier your reassessment will be.

NOTES

1. There does not appear to be copious case law related to QSA services, but the one that is present is Nat'l Union Fire Ins. Co. versus Trustwave Holdings, Inc., where the Superior Court of Delaware decided in 2016 to dismiss (in part) claims against Trustwave related to services provided as a QSA.
2. OK, yeah, we get it. Patches can sometimes have unexpected downstream consequences that require a rollback. Branden had personal experience with certain patches that could not be applied for weeks or months because of their nature (*cough* STRUTS *cough*). As your IT organization matures its capabilities, it will be more transparent. We believe in you!

17 The Art of Compensating Control

Information in this chapter:

- What Is a Compensating Control?
- Where Are Compensating Controls in Payment Card Industry Data Security Standard (PCI DSS)?
- What a Compensating Control Is Not
- Funny Controls You Didn't Design
- How to Create a Good Compensating Control
- Case Studies
- Summary

If Payment Card Industry Data Security Standard (PCI DSS) compliance by the book isn't controversial enough, we go full tilt when we consider what used to be edge cases but is now the norm in virtually every assessment, the Compensating Control. The slow movement of PCI DSS in general fueled the need for more guidance on intent of requirement, so much that early drafts of PCI DSS 4.0 removed compensating controls completely in favor of the Customized Approach (see Chapter 3, Why is PCI Here?).

Thankfully, the compensating control option is present in PCI DSS 4.0. The intent of the compensating control is to allow you to substitute an additional control in place of one that you cannot implement due to a technical or business constraint. They often look like a mythical compliance accelerator used to push PCI compliance initiatives through completion at a minimal cost to your company with the added bonus of consisting of little or no effort.

NOTE

We would be remiss if we didn't address the elephant in the PCI DSS 4.0 room: are Compensating Controls going away? Neither one of us are in the rooms with the framers of the Standard as they talk updates, revisions, roadmaps, or future plans. But here is what we know.

In the September 2020 draft of PCI DSS 4.0 (and perhaps in earlier drafts), Compensating Controls were completely removed from the standard. In fact, there was a whole section focused on the transition from Compensating Controls to the Customized Approach. Our gut tells us there was such an outrage that the Council was forced to put back the old language while simultaneously introducing this new method called the Customized Approach. During PCI DSS 4.0 introductory sessions held by the council, they reinforced the differences in usage between the Compensating Controls and Customized Approach.

What does that mean for your assessment? Compensating Controls will still be a valid option for at least the next few years, but if you have a stubborn process or system that cannot comply with PCI DSS as written, *it's now urgent* for you to work on de-scoping that particular system, changing it such that it can comply with the defined approach, or beginning to treat that with the Customized Approach so you are ready in the future if the next version of PCI DSS does not allow for Compensating Controls.

We discussed both the Defined and Customized Approach methods in Chapter 3, Why is PCI Here? This chapter only focuses on the compensating control aspect of the Defined Approach. The customized approach guidance peppered into the requirements can still be used as guidance to the intent of the requirement and should be considered when building your compensating controls.

Compensating controls are challenging. They often require using a risk-based approach that can vary greatly from one Qualified Security Assessor (QSA) or Internal Security Assessor (ISA) to another (note that QSA and ISA can be used interchangeably for the remainder of this chapter). The Council doesn't prescribe any specific risk-based model or thresholds, so it often defaults to a QSA and acquiring bank to approve and stand behind the control. This is one major area where the Customized Approach differs as it is heavily reliant on firms with mature risk management processes.

Be aware, there is no guarantee that a compensating control accepted today will also work one year from now, and the evolution of the standard itself could render a previous control invalid.

The goal of this chapter is to illuminate the reader on the nuances of compensating controls. After reading this chapter, you should know how to create a compensating control, what situations may or may not be appropriate for compensating controls, and what land mines you must avoid as you lean on these controls to achieve compliance with the PCI DSS.

WHAT IS A COMPENSATING CONTROL?

In the early years of the PCI DSS, the term compensating control was used to describe everything from a legitimate work-around for a business challenge to a shortcut to compliance. If you are considering a compensating control, you must perform a risk analysis on the scenario for which the control would be implemented and have a legitimate and documented technological or documented business constraint before you even go to the next step. The best tip we can give you is to remember the word *legitimate* and the phrase *perform a risk analysis* before proceeding to the next step. Anna being on vacation is not a legitimate constraint, and a 10-minute discussion of the gap and potential control is not a risk analysis. Your QSA should ask for the documentation from your thorough examination of the issue during a compliance review, and having it ready to go will make sure that you are efficiently using their (and your) time. If they do not, you can bet that your assessment isn't thorough, accurate, or really worth the paper the attestation came on.

If you think that compensating controls are easy, please read the note below.

NOTE

The compensating control paradigm has five specific points that must be met. For a compensating control to be valid, it must:

1. Meet the intent and rigor of the original PCI DSS requirement,
2. Provide a similar level of defense as the original PCI DSS requirement,
3. Be "above and beyond" other PCI DSS requirements (not simply in compliance with other PCI DSS requirements),
4. Be commensurate with the additional risk imposed by not adhering to the PCI DSS requirement, and
5. Address the requirement currently as well as in the future (you can't use compensating controls as a risk exception for forgetting to perform a periodic control).

Appendix B in the PCI DSS Requirements and Security Assessment Procedures document contains this information as well as some additional notes for those of you tasked with creating said controls. Appendix C contains a worksheet to be used when creating your compensating controls. Unfortunately, the filled-out example of this was deleted in PCI DSS 4.0, but your QSA should be well versed in filling one out.

An example of a valid control might be using a Write Once Read Many (WORM) file system, or some other sort of file system that becomes immutable after write, to store all of your logs. In this case, Requirement 10.3.4 would technically be met in other ways and you could potentially avoid building a separate alerting substructure if you can prove that the file system in question can be written to exactly once, and after that point anything stored there is read only. WORM file systems are not required for PCI DSS compliance, but if you decide that is your best option, you could use that as a compensating control for Requirement 10.3.4.

As stated earlier in this section, before immediately running down the compensating control route do your due diligence and made sure that you legitimately meet all of the requirements for a compensating control. Fifteen years ago companies relied on compensating controls because many key platforms did not have readily available solutions to certain PCI DSS requirements. Today's security environment is completely different. As a rule of thumb, if the operating system can meet the patching requirements in 6.3.3 it will probably have everything you need available to comply with PCI DSS.

WHERE ARE COMPENSATING CONTROLS IN PCI DSS?

Compensating controls are not specifically defined inside PCI but are instead defined by you or your QSA.

The changes found in PCI DSS 4.0 related to the customized approach may give an assessor or internal resource the best possible armor and guidance to date on the intent of requirements. The latest version of PCI DSS also includes a number of flexibility options that never existed in previous versions (see how Requirement 8 and password handling differ in 4.0 versus 3.2.1). Unfortunately, the completed compensating control worksheet from PCI DSS 3.2.1 that included a common, shared root password compensating control (in spite of our above example) is no longer in PCI DSS 4.0, mainly because the controls around shared accounts have been better defined to match the reality of systems in production today (see updated language in Requirement 8.2.2).

WARNING

Pay close attention to sub-bullets A, B, and C under list item 4 on pages 330 and 331. In our experience, this is where most companies go wrong and end up scrambling around assessment time to re-architect systems to support PCI DSS compliance.

As long as you have met the requirements in Appendix B for a compensating control, you should be able to build that control into your environment and satisfy PCI DSS under the Defined Approach. Compensating controls are ultimately accepted by acquirers or the card brands themselves in rare situations (start with your acquirer), so even after putting all of this information together you could face the rejection of your control and a significant amount of expense re-architecting your process to fit the original control. This is where an experienced QSA can really help ensure that your control passes the *sniff test*. If it smells like a valid control, it probably will pass. If you need examples of controls that did and did NOT pass the sniff test, look later in this chapter under the section titled "Funny Controls You Didn't Design" and in the case studies.

WHAT A COMPENSATING CONTROL IS NOT

Compensating controls are neither a shortcut to compliance nor a way to bypass or reassign risk. In reality, most compensating controls are actually harder to do and cost more money in the long run than actually fixing or addressing the original issue or vulnerability. Cost wise they are cheaper than assessing under the customized approach, so if you are looking at options to pass your assessment a compensating control may be what you need.

Imagine walking into a meeting with a customer who has an open, flat network, with no encryption anywhere to be found (including on their wireless network, which is not segmented either). Keep in mind, network segmentation is not required by PCI, but it does make compliance easier and is in fact listed as a potential added element for a compensating control in the PCI DSS 4.0 front matter. Usually in this situation, assessors may find a legacy system that cannot be patched or upgraded, but now becomes in scope simply because there is no segmentation in the network. This usually triggers the conversation about compensating controls. Now imagine someone in Internal Audit telling you not to worry about this massive problem with PCI DSS compliance because they would just "go get some compensating controls." Finally, imagine they tell you this in the same voice and tone as if they were going down to the local drug store to pick up a case of compensating controls on aisle five.

In their original incarnation, compensating controls were never meant to be a permanent solution for a compliance gap. Encryption requirements on large systems were made unreasonable early in the 2000s (or you could argue that these same encryption requirements forced innovation and progress on large systems). Not only was there limited availability of commercial off-the-shelf software, but also it was prohibitively expensive to implement. For Requirement 3.5 (Render PAN, at minimum, unreadable anywhere it is stored), card brands (largely Visa at the time) were quick to point out that compensating controls could be implemented for this requirement, one of those being strong access controls on large systems.

In the old days, assessors would typically do a cursory walk-through of the mainframe's controls and continue to recommend an encryption solution at some point for those systems. At one point, compensating controls were deemed to have a lifespan; meaning that the lack of encryption on a mainframe would only be accepted temporarily. After that, companies would need to put encryption strategies in place.

While concrete compensating control life spans never materialized, there are no guarantees that a compensating control that is valid for one assessment will be valid for the next. Compensating controls can be used for nearly every single requirement in the DSS—the most notable exception being permissible storage of sensitive authentication data after authorization (Requirement 3.3). There are many requirements that commonly show up on compensating control worksheets—Requirement 3.5 (primary account number [PAN] is secured wherever it is stored) being one of them.

Even with no defined life span, compensating controls are not an eternal free pass and shouldn't be viewed or sold to executive management that way. Part of the annual assessment process is to review all compensating controls to ensure that they meet the four requirements as currently defined by the PCI Security Standards Council. Remember that the requirements can change between versions of the standard, the original business or technological constraint must still exist, and the control continues to be effective in the current security threat landscape. If certain types of attacks are on the rise and a certain compensating control is not effective in resisting those attacks, it may not be considered acceptable during your next assessment.

To further cloud the situation, it is up to the QSA performing the assessment to decide to accept the control initially, but the acquiring bank (for merchants) has the final say. Substantial documentation and an open channel of communication to your acquirer are essential to ensure money is not wasted putting together controls that ultimately do not pass muster. If you are a service provider, you won't have that same authoritarian beyond your QSA. The reason for this is service providers typically do not have a relationship with a payment brand, they work for merchants directly. This is why selecting a great QSA that *understands the underlying technology he is assessing* is critically important.

Don't get discouraged, though! Compensating controls are still a viable path to compliance even considering the above caveats and descriptions of why you may not want to use them.

We would not be true security professionals if we didn't have a fun story or two to tell based on experiences of coaching companies or individuals through PCI Assessments. No names will be used, and the details will be altered to protect those who were most likely being forced to try the old "Push Back on the Assessor" routine. We hope you enjoy reading them as much as we enjoyed listening to them.

FUNNY CONTROLS YOU DIDN'T DESIGN

Some of the most cherished stories and experiences come from customers and vendors that had the right intentions, but never seemed to follow the basic doctrines listed above on how good compensating controls are made. By the way, if you read this and think, "Hey!! They are talking about ME!" We're not.

Pinky swear.

Before Branden was heavily involved in PCI, he did some IT auditing for a bank that was owned by his employer. He knew the drill of responding to audit findings. They usually start with a meeting, bringing all the key stakeholders together to mull over a comprehensive spreadsheet detailing all of the deficiencies. Findings are separated out in the "To Fix" pile, and the "To Push Back" pile, each individual item being assigned to an expert to either fix the issue or push back on the auditors. "We don't need that control because of a control over here," or "This gap does not apply to our environment," are the common phrases uttered in these meetings. Eventually, a happy (potentially unhappy) medium is established, and the audit or assessment is closed out.

The same process is often applied to PCI DSS and the compensating control dance that commences.

Before we poke fun at the following examples, please understand that we are only illustrating a point. At no time were these suggestions made by people who didn't understand both the requirement and the capabilities of the technology in question. These people were professionals; based on their credentials and experience, they should have known better.

Encryption has always been a hotly debated topic. Our favorite failed compensating control for Requirement 3.5 comes from a vendor that called Branden late one afternoon. He brought in their product team and tried to convince Branden that a Redundant Array of Independent Disks (RAID) using RAID-5 was essentially an equivalent to encryption. Their argument stated you could not take any one drive and reconstruct useful data that could be considered compromise worthy; thus, their RAID cards should be considered valid to sell to companies as an encryption checkbox for PCI Compliance.

To their point, if one drive (probably damaged) falls off a truck during transport, the technology does prevent someone from reconstructing all of the data from that system. If the system was large enough, chances are that the data on the drive may not be much use to a bad actor. But that's not really the goal of the requirement, is it? Physical theft prevention is covered in other areas of the standard. The point of the requirement is to render the data unreadable anywhere that it is stored. RAID may render parts of the data unreadable (or un-reconstructable) on one physical drive, but it does not render it unreadable in any other circumstance. A simple compromise of one area of the system could lead to the access and theft of massive amounts of unencrypted data.

Speaking of encryption, disk-only encryption inside data centers is not very useful either, unless additional user credentials are tied to the decryption process. Another favorite was a vendor that offered PCI compliance through an encryption appliance that was completely transparent to the operating system. So basically, the vendor was only protecting the data as it sat on a disk, in a secured facility, with gates, cameras, and Buck, the not-so-friendly security guard that looks like his previous job was bouncer of a night club—but now equipped with a Taser®. If cardholder data sat on disk drives installed in the unlocked part of a post office, then any reasonable technologist would see the value of encrypted data while physically on disk. But since we have physically hardened data centers, the solution doesn't really do anything other than line a salesperson's pocket.

Contrast this concept with whole disk encryption for a laptop. Laptops are frequently lost or stolen, and whole disk encryption (depending on configuration, of course) would absolutely serve the needs of keeping data secure when its physical container is not.

But even after all these fun stories about encryption, the real problem comes when managing keys. Once companies figure out that encryption technologies are available for their platforms, they realize that key generation and management is a whole different problem that may require additional hardware and software to fully enable as well as lots of process.

One vendor, who apparently thought a severe case of weekend-itis had firmly set in, made a case for using the COBOL Random Number Generator (RNG) to spit out 16 digits (technically 128 bits of data) for use as an encryption key. People can come up with some really creative ideas when the fear of failing an assessment looms.

The vendor did actually have some good intentions. Yes, they were focusing on randomizers and at the end it technically produces a 128-bit key. However, anyone with a basic knowledge of encryption will quickly find the problem with that approach. The problem isn't that COBOL's RNG is less than random, but instead you have eliminated a giant section of possible key space! A 128-bit key generated in the manner described above is the equivalent of (approximately) 53 bits of encryption, thus making it computationally feasible to brute force that key. With enough resource and horizontal compute capacity, it could be feasibly broken in a few days to a few months. Knowing the keyspace contains only digits makes it even easier as there are only 29 billion possible combinations. It was a good thought to try to solve a problem but ultimately would not pass.

HOW TO CREATE A GOOD COMPENSATING CONTROL

We've spent quite a bit of time setting up this section. We talked about what compensating controls are, what they are not, and some of the best-misguided attempts to create them. Before we discuss these good examples, please remember they should be used for illustrative purposes only. We have over-simplified the scenarios for brevity, and things are rarely this simple in the corporate world. Ultimately, compensating controls must be approved first by a QSA, or barring that, your acquiring bank. In our assessor days, we dreaded someone bringing an article about PCI to an interview during an assessment to bully his way through to compliance, so please don't do that with this chapter. Now let's walk through a couple of examples of how to create a good compensating control.

Let's start with a common compensating control that QSAs will define and implement at a customer. A Level 1, brick and mortar retailer with 2,500 stores has some systems in their stores that do not process cardholder data. These systems are a high risk to this customer's cardholder environment because they may access both the Internet through a local firewall and the corporate intranet and webmail system, and users log-in to that machine with the default administrator account. Store managers and retail operations claim that the systems are required for day-to-day business because each store is empowered to customize their operations to better fit the local market. Managers believe this drives innovation and helps them maintain a competitive edge over their peers.

If the retailer chooses not to segment the network, all of the systems in the store are now in scope, and they must meet all of the applicable requirements of the PCI DSS. Doing this will add significant expense to the IT infrastructure, and will probably force a call center to be staffed up to manage the volume of calls that will come in for things like password resets.

What do you do? Do you crush the retailer's aspirations to innovate by telling them they must deploy active directory to these machines, lock them down Department of Defense tight, and staff a call center? That is one option. But, if you made that recommendation, then you missed something important—understanding the business and limiting the impact that your compliance recommendations make. Instead, consider this compensating control.

Any number of network components could be used to create some segmentation in this environment. Let's say that we have a virtual local area network (VLAN) aware switch at the location that can have access lists (ACLs) tied to it. Why not create a new VLAN for just the point of sale (POS) network? Then create some ACLs around it to make it look like it is segmented behind a firewall. Now the threat of the in-store PC is effectively mitigated provided that the ACLs are appropriately secure.

NOTE

"Wait a second," you might say. "ACLs? Those are not stateful and cannot be used for compliance with PCI according to Requirement 1.4.2!" They most certainly can be used for compliance as we discussed in Chapter 5, "Building and Maintaining a Secure Network." Requirement 1.4.2 refers specifically to untrusted networks which can be troubling, but if you are able to leverage an ACL that can prevent unauthorized traffic from reaching a trusted asset, you may have the beginnings of a compensating control. Using ACLs internally may be perfectly acceptable. Where you can (technology permitting), use reflexive access lists (RACLs) that will basically look and feel like a stateful inspection firewall. You may need to review the memory and overall capacity of your switches when going through this analysis, but keep in mind that most switches developed for business in the last three years have this capability and more.

"But my store networks are different in every store," you say. "I can't just slap something in there like that and expect it to work globally!" If this is the case, is your store support group is overloaded with break-fix calls? Maybe this could be an opportunity to shore this up and make each store based on a consistent footprint. Keep in mind where your scope lies with any sort of jump server and the networks those servers connect to.

Barring that, how about this twist?

Let's say that you are running a Windows variant as the operating system powering your POS. You are already required to put some kind of anti-virus and malware removal tools on there. Most of those come with software-based firewalls that could be administered remotely, or used in combination with a client-side VPN to completely bypass any trust levels established on the local network. Deploying firewall capabilities to the POS itself could be viewed as appropriate segmentation depending on the policy attached to that firewall. It is neither a transparent solution, nor is it very pretty, but it works.

The first solution above is really less of a compensating control and more of a way to reduce the scope of PCI. The best thing you can do for your company is reduce the scope of PCI (or any compliance initiative) to the bare minimum required, and then manage that subset of your infrastructure for security and compliance. The second example above truly is a compensating control. It meets the original intent and rigor of the original PCI requirements and provides a similar level of defense as the original requirements (reduce the vulnerability to payment systems), goes above and beyond the base requirements of PCI (firewalls are not required on devices that do not leave the premises), and it is most definitely commensurate with the additional risk imposed by not meeting the original requirement.

Take a closer look at those two suggestions. The first may be "free" to your company depending on what is already in place! You will need to adjust business process and prepare your IT community to deal with the change, but you may not need to spend any hard dollars rolling this solution out (unless your equipment cannot do this in the first place). The second suggestion, which is actually the compensating control, probably requires capital outlay for software licensing and training or consulting to build out the environment. Upon rollout, things will break that will result in potential losses to the business.

WARNING

Without fail, companies that push major changes into large environments often face some kind of hardware or software error during the final rollout. Keep in mind, large environments always vary just a little bit among locations. Be sure to have a solid contingency and rollback plan. If you subscribe to a DevOps way of work, a focus on smaller changes will de-risk any Big Bang changes.

Are you starting to get the hang of this thing? How about another example?

A Service Provider has a large mid-tier UNIX installation, like Solaris or AIX, that runs critical areas of the payment process, including long-term data storage. For various reasons, encrypting the data is not an option on these machines. How do we make this service provider compliant with PCI Requirement 3.5?

This is a real-world example that comes up frequently. Encryption implementations have come a long way. The words "my platform does not have a solution for encryption" are no longer valid for platforms that can comply with PCI. When presenting the following control to customers, it is shocking how fast they find a way to encrypt their data.

While systems like this could be bolstered by moving from discretionary access control (DAC) to mandatory access control (MAC) to act more like a Mainframe, the requirements specifically talk about storage. These days, most storage is somewhere on the network in a Storage Area Network (SAN) and may not be physically connected to the host machine. MAC might help you in some aspects of PCI DSS, but it may no longer be strong enough in non-Mainframe environments to meet requirement 3.5.

A better option that wouldn't affect system performance significantly might be looking at external tokenization engines to protect the data while it sits on disk. Several companies have products that would allow you to extend the life of those legacy systems (remember, they still must be maintained and be able to get security patches) through tokenization. This would help you outright meet Requirement 3.5 and serve as a compensating control for Requirement 3.6 as it would not necessarily apply.

Even if you were able to convince a QSA that switching to MAC is a fabulous compensating control for 3.5, things are never that easy. Some security professionals inside companies love the idea of converting to MAC as it allows them to have more granular control over their systems and data. Practical ones know that converting an existing system requires so much effort that the costs typically outweigh the benefits. In fact *conversion* is probably more like a *replacement* for a change this large. This is a perfect example of how a compensating control might look good on paper (it's only three words when you use the acronym! "Convert to MAC!"), but in reality would be much easier to just meet the implied requirement to encrypt that data (or build a new system from scratch that begins with MAC).

One more example, and then it's time for you to get creative!

A medium-sized retailer with less than 500 stores is struggling with Requirement 10.2.1.1 to "capture all individual user access to cardholder data." All of their data is stored in a large DB2 database that runs on a mainframe. They run massive batch processes at regular intervals, and their space constraints prevent logging every single access to a row. Do you tell them to go back to their board for new budget dollars to buy lots and lots of drive space to store logs?

Before we proceed, consider the intent of the requirement. Reliable logs are valuable in investigating a breach quickly. Without them, it may take forensic examiners days, or even weeks, to determine the source of a breach. Once the source has been identified and analyzed, forensic companies must attempt to determine how many card numbers may have been exposed. If there are no logs, the assumption is that everything could be exposed, meaning that fines will add up pretty quickly.

The idea is not necessarily to make a log record that includes every single card number that is accessed but to be able to identify which cards are accessed through the data contained in the logs.

If we were to log the actual query performed against the database during a batch process, with knowledge of the date and time that the query was run and exactly what that query will do, we should then be able to determine, with reasonable certainty, which cards were accessed. It's common for batch processes to run on a daily basis, usually using the data from the previous day to produce its output. If we must determine what could have been exposed from January 1 to January 8, we could look at the data that would have been accessed by that batch process during those days.

Logging the query, and all the other elements required by 10.2.2 about that action, would generate a reasonably accurate list of records that would use a fraction of the drive space required by creating an entry that has every single record exposed (as well as bringing that log into expanded PCI DSS scope where you have card numbers that must be protected! How circular!).

CASE STUDIES

Now that we have explored examples of what some humorous (yet invalid) compensating controls look like and what acceptable ones might be, let's walk through a couple of case studies to help us further illustrate the process.

The Case of the Newborn Concierge

Nora's Newborn Nursery is a small chain of daycare centers specializing on infant and newborn care, with minimal medical staff on-site to assist with minor issues that can come up while providing ongoing and routine child care. Her customers tend to be affluent and busy professionals that can sometimes have strange schedules and benefit from a service designed to target professionals with young children.

Nora founded her business on the principle that her customers should never have to worry about the transaction process. Once a customer signed up for the service, they would leave a credit card on file to be pre-billed for services to be rendered during the following week or month. Her customers simply drop off the newborn, briefly discuss any problems or issues that are going on, and get on with their day. Nora invested in some basic IT systems and a mobile app that allows her customers to get reports on their children while care is happening, as well as schedule additional services like routine checkups, wellness care, and seasonal immunizations. For those customers who choose not to use the app, her systems can alert or update her customers via text message or e-mail.

Most of her customers pay monthly or weekly, so her transaction volume is projected to make her a Level 2 merchant in the next 12 months. As a Level 4 merchant, she heard about PCI DSS through a presentation at the local Chamber of Commerce, but has not implemented anything at this point to comply with the standard.

Because she has a small IT staff, building sophisticated networks simply isn't an option.

She calls a consultant and sets up some time to meet. During the first conversation, the consultant describes how a centralized database and processing system could be valuable for her to invest in so that each location doesn't have to worry about on-site storage. In addition, she is looking at Heathcare Information Portability and Accountability Act (HIPAA) Security and Privacy rule compliance issues with the healthcare data she inevitably stores during the course of her business.

Nora, with advice from her consultant, decides that the best course of action is to invest in a hardened, centralized computing infrastructure that houses both the applications and data that her locations will use. She will continue to store information about her active customers in an encrypted format, and ensure that hardened environment meets both HIPAA and PCI DSS compliance. For her employees, they will connect to that environment through a virtual desktop infrastructure like AWS Workspaces, Citrix, or VMWare Horizon. This allows her the freedom to implement any number of IT solutions in her locations, such as removing PCs in exchange for iPads or other tablet computers, or even allowing her employees to bring their own devices into the workplace. The connection between the centralized location must be encrypted, and there must be adequate controls in the software to prevent the theft of sensitive information through screen scraping or even lost credentials.

Nora now complies with PCI DSS by building this compensating control for all the machines and network devices in her diverse environment that may not be able to directly comply with PCI DSS without a massive investment, and she knows that her IT future is both flexible and secure.

THE CASE OF THE CONCIERGE TRAVEL AGENCY

Sally's Sojourns is a medium-sized travel agency that focuses on personal getaway travel. Because they never process payments on their own, they are a classic concierge-like service provider that holds payment card information for their customers and passes it along to the various merchants that make up the vacation experience. Because Sally prides herself on arranging travel excursions to remote parts of the globe, several of her vendors are outside the United States and can only accept credit card information through e-mail, she must find a way to add some security to her business processes to meet Requirement 4.2.2. She knows that she cannot invest in all of these vendors to provide computing services for them, but must find a way to continue to do business with many of these merchants as they provide a personal touch that has earned Sally a fantastic reputation in the industry.

Sally decides to invest in some Data Loss Prevention (DLP) technology coupled with an in-line e-mail quarantine program that will look for and encrypt any e-mail found to contain cardholder data. The remote users will get an e-mail with the sensitive data redacted, and a link that directs them to a TLS-enabled e-mail web application where they can view and process the end customer's payment card. In addition, any inbound e-mail found to contain cardholder data will be immediately quarantined into the same system, and the original securely erased from the original system that processed the e-mail.

Now she is able to meet Requirement 4.2.2, and has narrowed the scope of PCI DSS as her e-mail infrastructure may be removed from the scope of PCI DSS.

SUMMARY

Good compensating controls are the result of a marriage between art and science. The best ones embody the definition of elegance: something that is pleasingly ingenious and simple. We've discussed what compensating controls are, what they are not, some funny examples of how to go wrong, three solid scenarios from which we created good controls, and two case studies that illustrate the discovery process.

Compensating controls are not the golden parachute of compliance initiatives and will probably be gone in the next revision of the standard. While they are here, effective ones require work to ensure they will pass the scrutiny of both a QSA and an acquiring bank (or card brand). Rarely do they reflect a lower total cost and compliance effort to the organization than simply meeting the original requirement. PCI DSS is based on many good (not best) standards of practice for security and should be viewed as a baseline by which to operate not a high-water mark to which you aspire. Compensating controls may help you lower the bar of compliance in the short term, but remember, only you can prevent a security breach.

18 You're Compliant, Now What?

Information in this chapter:

- Security Is a Process, Not an Event
- Plan for Periodic Review and Training
- Payment Card Industry (PCI) Requirements With Periodic Maintenance
- PCI Self-Assessment
- Case Study
- Summary

Congratulations, you made it! Your Report on Compliance (RoC) or Self-Assessment Questionnaire (SAQ) is done and you are ready to complete your Attestation of Compliance (AoC), your vulnerability scans came back clean, and your compliance status is validated. You are DONE! Depending on where you were when you started, you may have worked long and hard to get here. So now you can kick back, relax, and enjoy your flight until you land at your next annual assessment, right? It would be great if it were that easy, but unfortunately it's not. Security (and PCI compliance in particular) requires constant vigilance, both for new controls deployment and for event monitoring. In this chapter, we will discuss how you can best spend your time to ensure you maintain compliance into the future. We will discuss why you should think about security as a process instead of an event. We will then make suggestions on periodic review and training that should be happening in your organization. Lastly, we will outline some suggestions for performing a self-assessment on your own network.

SECURITY IS A PROCESS, NOT AN EVENT

Security is not something that can be achieved and then forgotten about. Contrary to some security vendors' claims and management hopes, you cannot install a magical device on your network that will make you eternally secure. Security is a process of constantly assessing your risks and then working to mitigate them to a reasonable level. These risks are ever-changing, so processes and technology to address them should be ever-changing as well. To put this concept another way, the concept of security is akin to a journey, not a particular destination.

Along those same lines, all compliance efforts are a process—including Payment Card Industry Data Security Standards (PCI DSS) compliance, which is intended to place a focus on the security of cardholder data.

One thing to keep in mind is that you are never 100% secure. Even if you've done everything to secure your systems, an attacker can still find ways in (sometimes through low-tech ways like social engineering). It's difficult to prove that you are secure, while it's relatively easy to prove that you are insecure. To prove that you are secure, you must prove that you have addressed every possible threat (remember, these are constantly changing). To prove insecurity, you only have to find one attack vector that allows you past the rest of the security controls in place. Thanks to what feels like a never-ending stream of zero-day attacks, that vector could be something you had not even considered. It could be an exploit known to only one attacker in the world. If that attacker decides to target your company, then despite all you have done it could successfully compromise your network.

One key thing to remember is the more complex a system is, the harder it is to secure. It is very difficult to have a system that's completely risk-free while actually doing something useful, like serve a webpage or allow a user to send e-mails. In general, today's systems are very complex, and therefore hard to secure.

NOTE

Complexity is a smokescreen for competitive advantage. Systems that truly create durable competitive advantage are elegant, not complex. Every technology and security professional must dedicate time to removing complexity in favor of things pleasingly ingenious and simple. At Branden's last job, he was faced with complex systems that routinely failed. That's when his right-hand man (and our technical reviewer for this book), Yousef Hamade, passed along an amazing article that we want to pass along to you. Richard Cook's, "How Complex Systems Fail" summarizes 18 specific vulnerabilities in complex systems.

Yousef gifted this knowledge to us, and now we're gifting it to you. It's definitely worth the read to find examples of systems you manage that meet these criteria and then find ways to de-complicate them in a pleasingly ingenious and elegant way.

Risks, technologies, and your organization are changing constantly. Attackers find novel ways to break systems every day. Geopolitical movement opens and closes threats against your organization. Hacktivism is a present threat to your ongoing security posture. New technologies and software are implemented in your network on a regular basis. New people come to your company and current employees forget things from time to time. People need to be trained regularly.

It's impossible to be PCI compliant without approaching compliance and security as a process. All of the requirements require some sort of maintenance. Logs need to be reviewed, systems and policies need to be updated, and security assessments need to be performed. These are all part of the security process that keeps your company as safe as possible from attack.

NOTE

All of the requirements mandate some sort of maintenance. Please remember that while your compliance is validated by a QSA or ISA, it is maintained by you and you alone. Validation is a moment when you feel like you accomplished something—and you did! Security is an ongoing state of vigilance, with compliance as a by-product.

PLAN FOR PERIODIC REVIEW AND TRAINING

It's important to plan now for future review and training. Working with technology in an organization can get very hectic, and if you put off planning then you are far less likely to do it. It's important to review your security policies and practices often to verify they're actually in place. Many PCI DSS requirements mention monthly, quarterly, annual, or otherwise periodic processes that you define and perform targeted risk assessments against.

Section 7 of the front matter gives us definitions for the various forms of periodicity in the standard. Although perhaps the worst definition is *promptly* given that it relies on a reasonableness standard. If you have questions on any of the periods mentioned in the standard, reference Section 7 for their respective definitions.

NOTE

Here are some examples from PCI DSS requirements and testing procedures that mention ongoing process:

Requirement 1.2.7: "Configurations of NSCs are reviewed at least once every six months to confirm they are relevant and effective."

Requirement 3.2.1: "[...] A process for verifying, at least once every three months, that stored account data exceeding the defined retention period has been securely deleted or rendered unrecoverable."

Requirement 11.2.1: "Authorized and unauthorized wireless access points are managed as follows: [...] Testing, detection, and identification occurs at least once every three months."

Requirement 11.3.1: "11.3.1 Internal vulnerability scans are performed as follows: At least once every three months."

More examples are covered in the next section of this chapter called "PCI Requirements with Periodic Maintenance."

Many times companies write great policies but they never enforce them, and so they are never actually followed. Train and test your employees often so they are aware of your security policies and re-emphasize their importance so that employees are more likely to follow them. Recall the new Requirement 12.6.3.1 that mandates training specific to phishing and social engineering. One way to meet this could be routine phishing simulations that help employees distrust links and attachments in emails. You need to get creative on these, and you will have people yelling at you. But ultimately, as long as the info provided in the lure is all public, it's real enough for an attacker.

As an example, in Branden's last job, he received a ton of complaints over a phishing lure that advertised a holiday party with a link to RSVP. The only things specific to the company were the location (the address of which was public on our website) and the name. The rest was generic enough to really apply to any company. Drinks, food, one guest/spouse allowed, meet us in the common area but RSVP now so we can ensure you will be fed. Definitely was a step up from pAyRoLl HaS fOuNd An eRrOr iN yOuR pAyChEx.

NOTE

Perform training sessions that are brief and frequent. For example, Branden's last company experimented with two-minute animated/live action videos that illustrated a security problem in a comedic way and then had two multiple choice questions at the end. The response was massively positive. Coworkers talked and laughed about the videos, and they actually cheered when we told them they wouldn't have to sit through an hour-long course on cybersecurity at the end of the year. Here are some ideas of things you may want to review with employees at your organization:

Passwords: What makes a good password? Remind people never to share their password with anyone for any reason. Warn employees of common mistakes such as writing passwords on a post-it note and sticking on the computer monitor. You also may be working to eliminate passwords or stop constant rotation. If this is the case, use it as an opportunity to educate users on your company's position related to passwords.

Social Engineering: Be suspicious of *everyone*. Make policies for visitors clear to ensure that a malicious visitor won't leave with information they shouldn't have. Also, you should review policies for verifying an employee's identity when they make requests (such as password resets) over the phone or in some other non-face-to-face situation.

Physical Access: Verify that everyone knows what a visitor's badge looks like and knows what the company policies are with regards to where visitors are allowed to go and where they are not allowed to go.

Correctly Storing and Destroying Sensitive Material: Help employees keep up-to-date with company policies that require sensitive data to be destroyed. For example, it's important that employees are trained on destroying paper and electronic media that contains confidential data when it's no longer needed.

Your Information Technology (IT) staff also needs to be regularly trained on security. For example:

- **Secure Coding Practices:** Software engineers don't necessarily need to be security experts; however, it's important that they understand secure coding practices. Anyone working on a Web application should be aware of cross-site scripting (XSS) and Structured Query Language (SQL) injection bugs which are shockingly prevalent given their age and ease of remedy. Programmers should also be aware of unsafe functions that may be available in their language, and their safer alternative functions (for example, printf() vs sprint()). Requirement 6.2.2 mandates this.
- **Systems Training:** Systems administrators should be kept up-to-date with security practices that are related to the systems they administer. They should know how to securely install and configure these systems. Many of the Requirement 2 items mandate that.

Finally, security professionals at your company must be trained regularly. Depending on the size of your company, this may be a few or several employees. These people are responsible for securing your systems every day. They must receive periodic training to help them be aware of new technologies and new attacks.

Regularly review the PCI requirements and compare what is asked with what you have at that moment. Focus on the requirements that cause your company trouble. Set aside a day per month for your review. A good rule of thumb is to review all manually validated PCI requirements at least quarterly and ensure your automated ones are alerting you to problems as soon as discovered. Reviewing these requirements on this schedule should keep you in great shape for your quarterly scan and annual assessment as well as keep you up-to-date with any changes in the PCI requirements, plus the documentation you generate can be part of the work your QSA reviews during your next assessment. Your self-assessment process can be as detailed as walking through the testing procedures of the PCI DSS or reviewing SAQ D.

PCI REQUIREMENTS WITH PERIODIC MAINTENANCE

PCI DSS has many requirements that mandate ongoing actions with varying outcomes. Some requirements have documentation outputs that are reviewed during your annual assessment, and other requirements actions are in fact the compliance activity. Finally, some requirements don't have an actual maintenance requirement, but there is documentation that must be updated before an assessment, so we'll cover those as well.

WARNING

If you remember one thing from reading this entire book, let it be *you are never "done" with security*. Also, while validating your firm's PCI compliance is your QSA's task, maintaining compliance and data security is yours and yours alone.

Before we continue on with this section, you are going to quickly realize that periodic requirements fall into two specific categories: those that are explicit and those that are nuanced. Some will be monthly or annually, and others will just be periodically and promptly.

BUILD AND MAINTAIN A SECURE NETWORK AND SYSTEMS

No major updates here in PCI DSS 4.0. Requirement 1.2.7 requires a review of all Network Security Controls (NSCs) such as firewall/router rules and configurations every six months. That means that when your annual assessment is due, you should have documentation from at least two of these reviews; that is what your QSA will be asking for. The reviews should be detailed enough to show that an engineer checked every item and validated that it was still needed.

Your assessor will also review documentation for two other requirements in this domain, and while they may not have to be updated through a formal process, many companies have failed parts of their PCI Assessment because they forgot to do something simple like update a configuration standard that referenced outdated, or known vulnerable software. Be sure that during your normal review for Requirement 1.2.7, you review and update your firewall and router configuration standards. Do the ruleset review first and note anything that is not in the standard, then go update the standard so that it matches what is in the ruleset. While it may seem overly picky, an assessor would be right if he noted outdated configuration standards for Requirement 1.2.1.

In addition, go back through all of your in-scope system types and ensure that their configuration is up-to-date for Requirements 2.2 and 2.3. Companies fall short of this requirement when they reference out-of-date software packages or versions that have security vulnerabilities in them. For example, if your configuration standards for a new mail server still say to start with a stock Solaris 5.7 build with Sendmail 8.9, an outdated and vulnerable version of Sendmail, you would not be able to pass that requirement.

PROTECT ACCOUNT DATA

Requirement 3 has two key items to address, and one that may just need to have a fresh set of eyes. Requirement 3.2.1 mandates that you create retention requirements for account data and have a quarterly (technically once every three months) requirement to purge old data by way of manual review or automated disposal process. Even if your process is 100% automated, take the time each quarter to make sure that the processes are in fact functioning correctly. During your assessment, expect your assessor to ask you to produce your oldest set of retained data. They will then check to make sure that it does not exceed the retention requirements set forth in the aforementioned review.

WARNING

Our guidance from Chapter 7, Protecting Cardholder Data, still stands: It is usually easier to avoid storing data than to protect stored data. This is not a traditional way to think about data security, but it is one way of thinking about it, which is extremely useful for painless PCI DSS compliance.

Consider expanding that quarterly process to include a review of the actual requirements to retain data. The business, regulatory, and legal environments can easily change more than annually (maybe not all at the same time, but one of the three will happen at least more than annually), so use that time to be sure that you do not need to alter your data retention requirements. If you do, republish the information and perform a new review to make sure you are in compliance with your own policy.

NOTE

Time and time again, companies write policies in good faith and then completely ignore them in practice. As an example, Matt works for a large regional grocery chain that is a Level 2 merchant. His company's corporate policy is actually more restrictive than PCI to require all critical and high-risk security patches to be deployed within 10 days and all cardholder data to be encrypted internally over the wire. When Matt's assessor was performing the assessment, she noticed that one process for the florist shop inside his stores did not encrypt the cardholder data over the wire. When Matt confronted the department responsible for the florist shop's systems, the response he got back was "Well, it's not a PCI requirement so we just did the minimum," thus completely ignoring the corporate policy. Usually, you don't find that just one policy is violated—there tend to be many. This would be a clue for his assessor to dig deeper to ensure that policies requiring the minimum PCI requirement are actually being followed. Moral of the story? If you have a corporate policy that exceeds the base requirements of PCI, FOLLOW IT. There is a reason why that policy is in place!

Requirement 3.7.4 states that keys should be rotated once they have "reached the end of their cryptoperiod (e.g., after a defined period of time has passed and/or after a certain amount of ciphertext has been produced by a given key), as defined by the associated application vendor or key owner, and based on industry best practices and guidelines." This formerly was a pre-defined period to be an annual key rotation requirement for all keys used for the encryption of in-scope data. Expect some challenges with your assessor here as they will ask for your analysis to justify the period you chose. They may still want to see annual or semi-annual changes, and you may need to educate them on what an acceptable cryptoperiod is for your particular implementation. Your assessor will first look at your key management processes and make sure the requirement to rotate is documented, and then will check your implementation to see if you actually did rotate the key per the document. This becomes challenging on new installations with longer cryptoperiods (say a new installation with a three-year rotation requirement), so again, expect an education session. While you are reviewing your documentation for this, take a look at the overall key management processes and procedures and ensure they are up-to-date for Requirement 3.7. Common gotcha's here include forgetting to update the key management processes when you change encryption technologies. That's a big, red flag for an assessor, and it is pretty easy to spot.

Maintain a Vulnerability Management Program

Vulnerability management is a task that is easily seen as ongoing. New vulnerabilities, viruses, and malware are found every day, and companies need to take the appropriate precautions to ensure that they are protected. Requirement 5.3.2 uses that indefinite term periodic. To comply with this requirement, you must perform periodic scans of your in-scope machines.

TOOLS

We cover the vulnerability scanning tools that help with external and internal network scanning in Chapter 9, Vulnerability Management and Testing.

With the ever-changing landscape of attacks and malware, you probably should not be using what we traditionally think of anti-virus tools. You should now be using Endpoint Detection and Response (EDR) tools to better protect endpoints against malware and other malicious behaviors. In addition, Requirement 11.3.1.3 mandates that you run authenticated scans against internal systems after any significant change, but at a minimum Requirement 11.3.1 has a quarterly internal scan requirement. You should probably be scanning systems more frequently (or including detailed vulnerability checks during Continuous Integration and Continuous Delivery [CI/CD] build processes). I would suggest weekly if your systems can handle this. More of the quality vulnerability vendors offer unlimited scanning, or you can use freeware tools such as Nessus as well for internal scans and "unofficial" external scans (those not performed by an ASV).

To determine how often you should scan your systems, perform a risk analysis of these systems and include elements such as the criticality of the systems, amount of processing power, business hours and uptime requirements, bandwidth, and the frequency by which you update your antivirus definitions. Such risk analysis is in fact prescribed in Requirement 12.3.1 and must be performed annually. It's a slippery slope with many variables, but more frequent scanning followed by the ongoing remediation is clearly better. If you do your homework, you can take your assessor on a journey through your logic, with documentation to back it up.

Critical and high-risk security patches must be installed within one month of their release. This particular requirement will quickly ruffle the feathers of system administrators, particularly those of mainframes and large databases. These systems have high availability requirements and typically are not brought down frequently to install patches. When looking at Requirement 6.3, be sure that the patches you are considering installing are actually security related. Only those patches must be installed according to this schedule. Alternatively, if you have a way to mitigate the vulnerability without installing the patch, do that. Given the nature of some virtual systems, it may be possible to patch without taking the actual service down, so don't get lazy. You should take a risk-based approach on your patches and prioritize critical systems first. Then you can patch the remaining systems within three months (quarterly) or longer instead of one.

NOTE

A good example of an (old) action that could be used to mitigate a security vulnerability instead of deploying a patch is the Microsoft Graphics Rendering Engine vulnerability from early 2006 (MS06-001). In their notes, unregistering the dynamic-link library (DLL) mitigates the vulnerability until the patch is deployed. This type of mitigation is acceptable for PCI DSS compliance.

Finally, be sure that you scan your public-facing web applications at least annually, or after any changes for Requirement 6.4.1. Your assessor will review your policy and procedure documents, as well as review the output from processes like the above to make sure it is occurring as prescribed. If you do not want to go through this process, Requirement 6.4.1 allows you to use a Web Application Firewall (WAF) in lieu of the above process. Most companies end up choosing a hybrid of the two. They may have a WAF protecting their applications and APIs and also perform an automated web application security scanning as needed. Keep in mind that both scanning and WAF monitoring are ongoing tasks; scanning is periodic while WAF management is continuous. Also, keep in mind that scanning is not terribly useful unless vulnerabilities found by the scanner are actually fixed!

IMPLEMENT STRONG ACCESS CONTROL MEASURES

Strong access controls are key to preventing unauthorized access to your data. As of PCI DSS 4.0, Requirement 7 finally mandates a review of all access granted to cardholder data be performed at least every six months. We recommend more frequently than that (quarterly has a nice ring to it). This will help to keep only those with a business or job-related requirement to access in-scope data part of the access groups that grant this type of privilege. Now that QSAs are getting a shot to review this process, it might be time to do a little more than the rubber stamps. In Branden's last position, he would have his team review their entitlements and specifically write justifications on why they need them. It's amazing how quickly people don't need access to certain systems anymore when you ask them to do a write-up about it.

For those that do have a requirement to access in-scope data, be sure that users inactive for more than 90 days are disabled or removed (Requirement 8.2.6). To save time, build an automated process to do this, and assess the process quarterly. Be sure to document everything you find! While you are doing this, think back to the last time you changed your password. Did that one change work for all systems you access? Were there systems outside of your corporate identity and access management system that had to be changed manually? Did that system force you to do it at least quarterly? If not, follow up on that now. Don't wait for your annual assessment to learn that your systems are not requiring quarterly password changes (Requirement 8.3.9).

NOTE

In one of those (frankly kind of rare) excellent moments with PCI DSS, it's password guidance is actually in line with current security thinking and guidance from NIST. Requirement 8.3.9, if implemented correctly, effectively allows you to remove the forced password rotation requirement for password known not to be compromised. What's a good way to determine if an account is compromised? Successful username and password authentication but a failed Multi-Factor Authentication (MFA). Yes, that means that your entire workforce should have an MFA requirement. The former RSA employee in Branden is rolling his eyes and saying, "Duh, you guys."

Do you use off-site storage for tape backups or hard copy media? If so, be sure you visit it at least annually and review its security. Some of these facilities have annual assessments performed and can provide the documentation to you upon request. If they do this, be sure you have a chance to review the methodology used by the assessment company, and it includes common security controls in the scope of the review. SOC 2 reports are often provided for this type of due diligence. You may want to do this in conjunction with your annual media inventory process for Requirement 9.4.1.2.

REGULARLY MONITOR AND TEST NETWORKS

It's time for one of our more frequent periodic review elements—daily log review for Requirement 10.4.1 and a periodic review for 10.4.2. Chances are you don't have a team of people driving themselves insane by reading every log generated by every in-scope device. PCI DSS 4.0 actually discusses how to do automated log review (10.4.1.1). You most likely have some tools to collect, aggregate, normalize, and correlate these logs. As part of that process, the log management tool should be intelligent enough to find items that are not part of normal operations and create alerts for your staff for follow-up. Have your internal assessment group periodically assess this process to make sure it is working as designed. It is more important to review the ongoing process for log review, making sure it is current and active than to review every single log manually.

Next comes Requirement 11. Several sub-requirements under Requirement 11 have some kind of periodic action associated with them. Starting with Requirement 11.2.1, testing, detection, and identification of authorized and unauthorized wireless access points are performed quarterly (or every three months). As we discussed in Chapter 8, Using Wireless Networking, doing a quarterly walk-through may not be the best idea from a resource and threat mitigation perspective. If you only have one location the logistics might work, but from a security protection perspective, you are not doing everything you should. If you have chosen to deploy Wireless Intrusion Detection/Prevention technology instead, perform a quarterly assessment of the systems to ensure they are properly alerting and deploying defense and containment measures that you configured.

Requirement 11.3 requires that both internal and external scans are performed at least quarterly, with clean scans being the desired outcome for both of those operations. Save each of those clean quarterly scans in a special place because your assessor will need them as part of the on-site assessment review. Here is another requirement that can benefit from network segmentation as a scope reduction exercise. Companies are required to scan all in-scope internal systems and all external IP Addresses. PCI DSS scoping instructions state that systems connected to networks that process cardholder data are in scope for PCI DSS, even if they do not process or store cardholder data themselves. Thus, putting firewalls between these systems will reduce the amount of work you need to do for your internal scans. Externally, you can reduce the scope of your scans by air-gapping networks (meaning that the networks that process cardholder data externally are physically disconnected from ones that do not) or other strong segmentation techniques. Every situation is slightly different, so it is best to check with your QSA or ISA on which method works best for you.

Although those quarterly scans should address most of your vulnerabilities, you must also perform a deeper inspection of both internal and externally facing systems and applications at least annually with a Penetration Test (Requirement 11.4). Two common mistakes companies make are forgetting to validate that segmentation is working as designed (Requirement 11.4.5 and A.1.1.4 for Multi-tenant service providers) and neglecting to perform the penetration test from an internal perspective as well as an external perspective. If you claim large areas of your network are out of scope due to a firewall or other type of segmentation, be sure you have a penetration tester prove that segmentation is effective. The penetration test is one of the most critical periodic requirements used by PCI DSS. The quality of your assessment will directly impact the likelihood of being caught up in a breach due to an external (or internal) attack. Your penetration test should be based on an industry-accepted penetration testing approach (such as NIST SP 800-115) and will include at least the following elements:

- Network attacks,
- Application attacks,
- Social engineering,
- Modem penetration testing (if applicable), and
- Wireless penetration testing (if applicable).

Once your test is performed, be sure to address any findings and have them rechecked to make sure your fixes worked.

Finally, Requirements 11.5.2 and 11.6.1 have periodic options to consider. Both require critical file comparisons to be performed at least weekly, meaning that all in-scope technologies (including the Point of Sale [POS] and browser-based payment pages) should have some kind of change-detection mechanism such as file integrity monitoring run on its files (11.5.2) or on the response from the server (11.6.1). Whether you go with a commercial solution, or script something using a hashing utility like *sha512sum*, be sure that you run those comparisons at least weekly and for the second part of the review, follow up with any exceptions that come out of the process. The only reason an exception would be generated by the file integrity process is if you deployed a system update or patch and can track the exception back to a change control ticket, or if something bad was happening (maliciously or not) to the system. Both should be followed up on and closed appropriately.

MAINTAIN AN INFORMATION SECURITY POLICY

If you have not had enough with documentation, here are some more periodic requirements specifically for your information security policy and framework. Requirement 12.3.1 mandates an annual risk assessment be performed on any PCI DSS requirement that provides for flexibility in its periodicity, and potentially as a part of that you can conduct your policy review as well as review other risk-related items in Requirement 12.3. Your organization probably already performs some kind of annual risk assessment as a part of normal operations. You may be able to tag along with that, but be sure to include an assessment of risks relevant to PCI DSS. If you ignore all in-scope systems and don't include the risks associated with storing cardholder data, the risk assessment is not much help to your PCI efforts. Including your policies in the risk assessment might be a nice way to kill two birds with one stone. Be sure to update your policies to address findings in the risk assessment! Your assessor will look for this!

One of the more abstract requirements built into the top of every major requirement is an overall operational review to ensure that everything in the major requirement is documented in policy and operational procedures. Your assessor will want to see your definition of these items and will want to see evidence that you are following the process. This is a re-packaged and more broadly applicable version of the requirements tagged at the end of all the major requirements in PCI DSS 3.2.1. If you were passing those, this should be an easy one to cover as well.

Requirement 12.5.2 mandates a deep PCI DSS scope documentation process and review that is confirmed either annually or after significant changes to the in-scope environments. This was normally done as part of your PCI Assessment preparation, but now it's an official requirement. If you are a service provider, this is a semi-annual requirement.

Security awareness training is something that is often overlooked, but critical to maintaining a secure company (Requirement 12.6). You must demonstrate this ongoing educational process is reviewed annually and updated as needed based on new threats and vulnerabilities, and that every person (contractors or any other individual coming into contact with the CDE must receive this training) receives this training upon hire and annually thereafter until they are no longer with the firm. Multiple methods of communication are required for the training to be valid, and you must track a formal acknowledgment by the individual that they have read and understood the information security policies and procedures. Limiting this type of training to only once per year will meet PCI DSS, but it is a bit too relaxed to be considered a security best practice. Find fun ways to engage your employees on information security. Do demonstrations or exercises often. Consider posting things in break rooms or common areas where employees congregate. Add something to their pay stub. Or even involve them in a demonstration like "Find the Bad Guy" where you have an employee walking around with a fake badge, or maybe no badge at all. Offer prizes like Starbucks or iTunes gift cards. You will be amazed at how well this will improve the weakest link in your security chain: people. Don't forget to include social engineering and phishing (and related) attack awareness (Requirement 12.6.3.1) and awareness about the acceptable use of end-user technologies defined in Requirement 12.2.1 (Requirement 12.6.3.2).

For those companies that leverage Third Party Service Providers (TPSPs), Requirement 12.8.4 mandates the review of the compliance status of those providers periodically, which means you will need to do a risk assessment and document the period by which you will review these TPSPs, and provide the documentation to show you are doing it, the results of the reviews, and how those results are addressed and closed (if applicable).

None of us want to invoke an incident response policy, but like your last will and testament, it needs to be defined and planned in case something bad happens. Requirement 12.10.2 mandates annual testing of the incident response policy. Instead of hiring someone to steal something from your company, consider doing a table-top exercise whereby you simulate a relevant and creative incident, and walk through all the steps in your plan. This will help your employees understand their roles and will ferret out problems or gaps in the process. Just make sure your simulation covers all seven bullets in Requirement 12.10.1 in the test. In addition to doing this, you must train your staff with security breach responsibilities so they have the specific skills needed to respond (Requirement 12.10.4). This may include sending key employees to forensics training, or Continuing Professional Education classes around breaches and their aftermath. You must have 24×7 coverage to respond to suspected or confirmed security incidents (Requirement 12.10.3), which may require you to augment staff with a managed service provider.

When thinking about how you want to manage your 24×7 coverage, you must consider what all must be included. Requirement 12.10.5 states that your incident response plan must include monitoring and responding to alerts from these systems (and anything else that provides security telemetry): intrusion-detection and intrusion-prevention systems, NSCs, change-detection mechanisms for critical files, detection of unauthorized wireless access points, and the change-and tamper-detection mechanisms for payment pages. As you run your plan as part of incident response or a table-top exercise, Requirement 12.10.6 states that you must modify and evolve the plan based on what you learn, the changing threat landscape, and new industry developments.

Finally, new incident response Requirement 12.10.7 now formally defines a type of incident for PCI DSS to include a response procedure for when stored account data is found anywhere it is not expected. It should include instructions regarding account data retrieval, secure deletion, and/ or migration into the cardholder data environment. You also need to document whether sensitive authentication data is included with this account data. To close out the process, you must perform a retrospective to understand where the data came from and what mechanism put it in this unexpected place. Finally, execute any remediation that you need based on newly discovered data leaks or process gaps.

PCI SELF-ASSESSMENT

In addition to the elements called out earlier, take the time to review all of the requirements at least once before your assessor shows up. You should be going into an assessment by a QSA or ISA knowing that you will pass. Don't rely on the assessor to find all of your gaps. Instead, show your assessor that you have been compliant all year long. You'll be amazed at how much faster your assessment goes, and how much more confident your management will be when asked about your current PCI DSS posture.

One tip that seems to work very well these days is hiring a consulting firm to do a pre-assessment and work with you and the QSA during the assessment. Does it double or more your PCI Assessment fees? Absolutely. But ensuring a pass the first time through will save you money in the long run.

The PCI Security Standards Council provides some great documents to help you with your self-assessment. For example, SAQ D (for either merchants or service providers) can help you to determine your company's current compliance level in a Yes or No format. You should periodically review these documents and use them in your own assessment processes, and look for ways to improve your company's security posture.

CASE STUDY

You have read plenty of case studies in this book where someone made a mistake that lead to a breach. It's not that there are no GOOD programs in this world; it's just that we (should) learn from others' mistakes. Those lessons will hopefully prevent us from walking off the proverbial cliff. However, in this chapter, we're turning the tables and presenting a case study where a company got it right. Not only right, but knocked it out of the park!

THE CASE OF THE COMPLIANT COMPANY

Peggy's Panang Palace, a national Thai food chain, enjoyed quick success with its authentic food. Peggy's vision was to create two sides to the business and started with a high-quality dining experience in freestanding restaurants. Once she had her recipes down, she figured out how to prepare something very close to the same quality and taste in a mass-produced way, and opened hundreds of stores in shopping malls across the country. Her success spread like a wildfire, and before she knew it, she was managing a billion-dollar enterprise with more than 3,000 locations.

She began accepting credit cards in her mall locations five years ago and quickly ascended through the levels to become a Level 1 merchant. Before she became a Level 1 merchant, she attended many conferences and seminars geared toward restaurateurs and heard alarming stories about how people lost their restaurants because a hacker breached their POS systems and stole credit card data. Peggy was determined not to let that happen to her.

Peggy began investing in security soon after hearing these stories and had a full enterprise security assessment performed to see how she stood up against the NIST CyberSecurity Framework (CSF). She further invested in a program to address the gaps discovered during the assessment, and within two years had a mature cybersecurity program, complete with compliance management. She hired a small staff of individuals to handle her information security and compliance needs, and after completing several internal assessments against PCI DSS, she set out to find a QSA.

Her QSA came on board during the next quarter and was duly impressed at how organized her processes and systems were. Through segmentation, End-To-End Encryption, tokenization, and other scope reduction techniques, Peggy had reduced the scope to the point of interaction (or the payment terminal), and a few routers and switches in between. Overall, it was less than 1% of her total infrastructure. She also was sure to complete internal pre-assessments before the QSA arrived, and had all the documentation built and ready to go.

Peggy approached compliance as a cost of doing business and was sure that she invested in security to cover her compliance needs. Her company went into each assessment KNOWING the outcome would be positive, and never had an issue passing her compliance assessment, and building security best practices to cover security threats where PCI DSS did not.

SUMMARY

Security is fleeting. You've got it one minute and it's gone the next, but there are some steps that can be taken to keep yourself as secure as possible. Working with management and employees, you can keep your company in a good position to combat many attacks now and in the future. Things you can do to maintain your security include keeping your policy up-to-date, periodically assessing your security, and periodic training.

It doesn't matter how many times we say, "security first!" If some organizations don't get security with all of its complexities and ignore it for years, "compliance first" becomes a real choice for them. At least they can understand it. And then later, "compliance first" becomes "compliance ONLY," checklists replace risk awareness, and flowcharts replace critical thinking about their threats and vulnerabilities. And then hackers get them!

Reading this chapter should make it clear that maintaining ongoing PCI DSS compliance and data security is your job, not ASVs, not QSAs, not your bank's. It is yours and yours alone! Plan now to train and review the employees and IT staff regularly to keep them reminded of and up-to-date on company policies.

PCI DSS guidance is regularly updated as new attacks surface. Be sure to review the PCI requirements regularly to keep yourself up-to-date. Regularly assess your systems to ensure they are still PCI compliant and secure. Similarly, regularly review your policies to verify they are up-to-date and are working at your company.

19 Emerging Technology and Alternative Payment Schemes

Information in this chapter:

- Emerging Payment Schemes
- Bitcoin, Ethereum, and Crypto
- Predictions
- Taxonomy and Tidbits
- Case Study
- Summary

After getting this far in the book, you may be thinking that Payment Card Industry Data Security Standard (PCI DSS) compliance is both insurmountable and unsustainable. We disagree on both counts, but we're writing this from our side of the page, not yours. We also know how difficult it can be to go through this process and maintain your status over time. We have seen many companies where PCI DSS just wasn't a good fit. Be it culturally, technically, or simply the sheer willpower to get it done, PCI DSS may be one of those things that you choose to avoid.

Branden has spent the last decade or more of his career convincing people to *avoid* PCI DSS at all costs. If you are not selling compliant and scope-reducing services to merchants and service providers, you should be taking a serious look at what you are doing to reduce the effect that PCI DSS has on your customers.

Even if you have reduced your scope as far as possible, don't despair! There are some interesting emerging technologies and alternative payment methods that could be useful to you as well as things you need to be aware of in case someone tries to place a square peg of ZigBee through the triangle hole of PCI DSS. Keep in mind, as a society we have been trained to reach for the plastic payment option. Before you change your payment acceptance strategy, you need to consider things like average ticket size, how often you directly interact with the customer, and your customer experience lifecycle (time between card entry and money movement). Each of those things will affect your customer's behavior while at your business. For example, everyone can move to a cash-only business, but if you are selling furniture and televisions where the average ticket price is over $100, putting an Automated Teller Machine (ATM) out front will probably not get you the customers you need at the rate you need them to survive.

EMERGING PAYMENT SCHEMES

This section used to be titled New Payment Schemes. After reviewing what is in here, it's not as new and shiny as it once was. Even though what you read here isn't brand new, some of these technologies are not ubiquitous. If you are not using any of these technologies, consider reading the overviews below and talking to an expert to determine if your business would benefit from any of them.

Getting customers to part with precious Dollars, Pounds, Yen, and Euros isn't new, but some of the ways we do it are. Over the last 15 years, we've seen tremendous advancement in technology and interoperability between handheld devices and fixed ones. From scams to legitimate business needs, there are new problems, solutions, and opportunities to attack this issue.

EMV

In the last edition of the book, EMV was something new, strange, and largely understood in the United States. By now, merchants have figured out how to make the dip action almost as fast as the swipe, and it seems like a significant number of cards now have a contactless option (perhaps accelerated by COVID-19). And then we have ApplePay, SamsungPay, WalmartPay, StarbucksPay, and AmazonPay.

We also predicted that magstripe would decline dramatically, but in our observations, we still see cards swiped at a number of merchants. More than half of the merchants we shop at offer EMV terminals for tapping or dipping these days, and it's rare to see a non-chipped member-branded card.

EMV is commonly implemented as Chip & Personal Identification Number (PIN) outside the US, but here in the States the closest tagline we can use is Chip & Choice—not very elegant. The reason for this is that any intermediary between the cardholder and the issuer can choose to lower the security of the transaction down to what will likely be Chip & Sign. So for you EMV cardholders in the US who travel internationally, you will present your chip like every other citizen in that country, but instead of using a PIN a receipt will print out for you to sign. The holder of the terminal may look confused until they hear you speak. About the closest thing we have to Chip & PIN is a transaction that rides the Debit rails.

Let's be clear—EMV is not hack-proof. In fact, there is some great research out there that shows hacks for both online and offline transactions. That said, it is a huge step forward in transaction security from a counterfeiting perspective. For more information, check out Dr. Ross Anderson's page (https://bit.ly/PCI-DRA) for a good number of papers on this topic.

Ultimately, you need to make the right choice for your business. Some businesses are somewhat chargeback proof. When Branden worked at a large payment processor, a client who ran a large chain of hair salons asked if they needed to replace all their terminals. The payments manager said they had not had a chargeback in years (who does a chargeback on their hair stylist anyway?). Branden advised them to just watch this statistic. If fraud and chargebacks were not a big deal for the salon, wait until you need to replace the terminal to move to EMV.

MOBILE

Let's continue with mobile. While we discussed the technology and its applications in Chapter 12, Mobile, there is still much to discuss from an emerging payments' perspective. Smartphones are ubiquitous. Businesses realize that these devices are everywhere and are always on the lookout for ways to monetize them.

One of the simplest mobile payment options doesn't even require a smartphone. SIM-based payments are commonly used in the US to attract charitable donations after natural disasters, but they can also be used to pay for taxis, parking, and even items in vending machines. They typically require the user to send a text to a five- or six-digit number with some code associated with it, and the charge will show up on their mobile phone bill at the end of the month. As a business, you may choose to accept SIM-based payments in this realm.

SIM-based payments use the same SIM chip that authenticates your phone to your carrier to figure out who purchased something and bill them accordingly. It works on eSIMs as well, so newer phone owners won't really notice anything different. It's a neat solution for on-the-go, small payments; or for something that is self-service in a manner where the storefront is automated or electronic. You must have the ability to receive the confirmation of these payments in your store, which will require you to both have a contract to accept them and a reliable Internet connection. Just like an online payment card transaction, if your Internet connection goes down you won't be able to receive the payment information unless you invest in sophisticated over-the-air technology (which still must have two-way connectivity to function).

If your business ONLY accepted SIM-based payments, you wouldn't need to worry about PCI DSS unless you were somehow getting payment data back from the provider (unlikely this is the case). It's an interesting alternative, and depending on the ticket size and how someone's phone plan is set up, it might work. For individuals with company phones, however, this type of payment scheme may not work or may cause problems for the individual at the end of the month.

NOTE

You must understand that regardless of your situation, any time money is exchanging hands there is a possibility for fraud to occur. There is no silver-bullet solution, and part of doing business is taking on risk. There are several variables to consider when deciding how to accept payments for your business. Those are:

- **Ticket size:** How big is your average transaction size? Certain thresholds may be conducive to one method over another, and you may notice more fraud from certain types of schemes depending on the ticket size. Payment cards are good for higher ticket sizes, cash for low, and others fall somewhere in between.
- **Transaction volume:** How many transactions are you running per day?
- **Customer volume:** How many customers do you see per day (each with a potential to pay in their own special way)?
- **Average sale time:** How long does it take for someone to go through the line? For high-volume, rapid transactions your options may be limited solely based on speed.

With any change in payment acceptance you can expect you will see a change in fraudulent activity. Just like someone can spoof a magstripe card by capturing and reprinting the data, SIM cards can be spoofed, ported, or swapped in the same way. You may end up accepting a fraudulent payment, allow someone to exit your store, and end up having the equivalent of a chargeback hit you without much recourse. Fifteen years ago this type of spoofing was difficult to do and typically required equipment purchases into the six-figure range. Now with some parts you can get from eBay and knowledge, you can do this for under $2,000. If you are able to compromise someone who has access to mobile network operator infrastructure (for example, at that fun mobile phone kiosk in the mall that sells bedazzled cases), it might only cost you a 100 bucks. If your storefront is unattended, this may not be an issue if the ticket size is small. It's no different than any other kind of fraud. But if you are using SIM-based payments in places where your average ticket size exceeds $10, you may find yourself learning quite a bit about fraud (the painful way).

NEAR-FIELD COMMUNICATION (A.K.A., TAP & GO)

NFC technology has been used in the payment space for years as an alternate, dynamic payment mechanism. Payment brands released products like Blink (Visa) and PayPass (MasterCard) where Radio-Frequency IDentification (RFID) chips were embedded in traditional plastic cards as an alternative to swiping. You simply wave your payment card over the reader and walk out with your goods. No signing, no PINs, nothing static to capture and replay. In fact, this is one of the two technologies you can use to qualify for Visa's Technology Improvement Program (TIP) which can effectively eliminate the requirement to validate compliance annually (See Branden's blog [https://www.brandenwilliams.com] for thoughts on ending PCI assessments). Some NFC payments might be SIM-based as well, thus going through a carrier instead of a payment scheme. Some geographies have different adoption rates than others, so you should understand your options when building your payment strategy for each area you are doing business.

NFC payments have a huge advantage to merchants as they are an element that allows you to qualify for Visa's TIP program along with accepting EMV transactions. For those of you reading this outside the US, you can also qualify for the TIP program if you already accept EMV or Chip & PIN. It might even work to your advantage, especially if you can deploy some level of point-to-point encryption in your network to encrypt the information that EMV considers routing but can in fact be used to push fraudulent transactions through in other parts of the world. Keep in mind that the Visa TIP only works for Visa, and you may have a couple more hoops to jump through for other payment schemes for the same benefit.

Many smart devices come with NFC capabilities to present your payment cards in the ApplePay or SamsungPay ecosystem. At the time of this writing, nearly every card we use has gotten itself set up for NFC payments through mobile devices. It requires a bit of work to get it done, and it does lend itself to fraud opportunities—for example if you have not set up your card for ApplePay and you fall for a scam where someone adds it to their phone. This doesn't change anything for you as a merchant as it will use your existing infrastructure to complete the payment.

NFC carries its own risks as well. In spite of information being dynamic, computing power increases at incredible rates. Cryptanalysis is not only possible but becomes feasible in some cases when bad guys put their efforts to try to reverse these algorithms. What does that mean for you? It means that while the risk of a spoofed card is reduced to almost zero with EMV, it is still possible and can still happen. The rate is so low that you can probably write it off as a cost of doing business, but you should understand your liability if you end up in that situation.

Finally, when looking at ApplePay, SamsungPay, and other implementations of the EMV Tokenization Standard, you must realize as a merchant that you could have many different representations of a payment card number. In a perfect world, each method of acceptance would use a number specific to the context of the payment. ApplePay and SamsungPay do this today where the number the merchant sees is not the same number on the plastic in your wallet. It's fully routable, but if you were to capture that number and try to put it in a magstripe, it won't work. If you are trying to do analytics or track customers based on the payment card number, you now have to worry more about a card getting canceled and re-issued. You must realize that James's Discover card may have four or more different numbers that could be used to run a transaction to the same instrument.

THE PAYMENT ACCOUNT REFERENCE

This brings us to the Payment Account Reference or the PAR.[1] Because of the problems above and the need to better combat money laundering and illicit transactions, the PAR was created to identify an account without divulging personal information about the account holder. In the above case, when the transaction is returned to the merchant, a PAR will be included (look at EMV Tag 9F24 or Fields 51 or 55 in ISO 8583 as an example) so that multiple references to the same person's account will always have the exact same PAR. This reference will survive card replacement, ApplePay, SamsungPay, and any other new schemes that come up. It's meant to help end users identify financial responsibility that a bank or payment card provider will vet as part of the account opening process.

The PAR is a 29 alpha-numeric character string whose first four characters are a BIN equivalent to identify the financial institution, and a unique 25 character value to identify the account owner. This represents the safest way to identify an account owner in your business analytics to learn more about buying behaviors and preferences.

SQUARE, PAYPAL, AND INTUIT

We would be remiss if we didn't mention a creative little scheme started by Square years ago! This solution allows you to both accept payments with phones and tablets, and create the equivalent of a digital wallet whereby users can put payment information into an app on their phone and use that app to pay for goods and services. It's not quite the same as the Starbucks app where you can register your Starbucks card and pay via a barcode on your phone as you still are passing your actual payment card information to the merchant for processing. Merchants like the technology as it can enhance their ability to provide top-notch service to their customers. Consumers like it because they can almost get to the point where they just need a smartphone to live their lives.

Paypal, Intuit, and several others have also entered into this realm, but really only on the merchant side to aid in processing via a mobile device such as a phone or tablet. They work by plugging a dongle into your device that will accept a swipe at a minimum and full tap and dip in a perfect world. This makes payment acceptance for small businesses a breeze when they are doing events outside of their physical storefront. Think about all the outdoor festivals you have been to and all those extra wireless terminals you see. As a merchant, I'm definitely looking to that device as a way to save money and time. No longer do I have to take the card to the back of the store for processing, I can swipe it right in front of the customer and get them out the door.

Keep in mind, using Square won't excuse you from your PCI DSS responsibilities. Generally with companies like this, you do not actually own the Merchant ID (MID) that the transactions are processed under, it belongs to the provider such as Square. This means that they are directing your PCI Compliance requirements, and they could in fact tell you that just by using the solution you are fine. Depending on how you have it set up, you may have greatly reduced responsibilities and risk, but that means the breach will likely come from somewhere else—like physical theft of paper records. Your biggest risk with Square may simply be losing track of the tiny dongle.

Square may have been one of the first on the scene, but they are not the only game in town. Paypal, Intuit, and many others have released competing solutions, not to mention the myriad of apps that can accomplish this as well. We'll also talk about Paypal's traditional digital wallet options in the next section as we transition to card not present.

Google Checkout, Paypal, and Stripe

Let's spend a few minutes talking about card-not-present transactions. Online retailers have to deal with PCI DSS just like brick-and-mortar ones do, but the security at online retailers tends to be much better because they live with electronic fraud every day. Brick-and-mortar stores tend to focus on theft and fraudulent payment devices more than they do an external attacker constantly pounding on their door to steal things.

Google, Paypal, and Amazon offer products to merchants that take the burden of payment processing away. These may be offered in multiple delivery methods, but the way to ensure you are exempt from PCI DSS is to ensure you are redirecting your users to the provider's payment portal during the payment portion of the checkout process. If you are accepting the card information and passing it to the processor on the user's behalf, you are still in the middle of the transaction and must comply with PCI DSS. Both allow you to set up a recurring payment for subscriptions as well, so businesses with those models can take advantage as well.

Essentially in these schemes you would get your user all the way to entering payment information and then pass them to the provider with key information related to the transaction. The user would then choose how to pay within those systems (there are multiple methods) and then be routed back to you after the payment has been completed. You will get funds sent your way as a daily deposit but without the payment card information attached.

Some disadvantages include losing track of the user while they check out. Some e-commerce merchants focus on their user experience so much that passing their customers to a third party during the most critical part of the transaction may be unacceptable. Third-party payment providers aren't new, so we would largely argue that using these services won't dramatically increase your cart abandonment rate. Another disadvantage may be the cost to process. Doing the processing directly may cost less per transaction, but in theory, those savings should be used to secure your network and deal with PCI DSS compliance. With some analysis, you may learn that it is cheaper in the long run to outsource your online payments to any number of companies like this. Some things to look out for include:

- How long does it take for cash to show up in your account?
- What is the chargeback (or equivalent) process like?
- Do you have any minimum transaction volumes to adhere to (dollars or numbers)?
- What is your liability if money is exchanged on a stolen account?

Stripe is a service built by developers, for developers, and attempts to address many of the issues with losing control through a great API and fantastic service. It's a great alternative to consider when looking at outsourcing card not present transactions. PCI DSS 4.0 maintained the requirements for companies filling out the SAQ (specifically SAQ A-EP) that may bring some elements previously considered out of scope to be now in scope, so find your nearest PCI DSS expert to assist you in your unique situation!

3-D SECURE

Branden teaches in a cybersecurity master's program, and back in the mid-2000s his university actually had a class dedicated to electronic payments that covered 3-D Secure extensively. Originally released in 2001 under the Verified by Visa brand, the protocol is designed to provide e-commerce merchants with an assurance that a payment accepted under this method will not result in a chargeback (i.e., fraud). Other payment brands quickly adopted the technology as SecureCode by MasterCard, ProtectBuy by Discover, J/Secure by JCB, and American Express SafeKey by American Express. 3-D Secure 2.0 is now current as of 2016 and fixes a number of problems with the original protocol.

Why are we discussing a technology released in 2001 under the Emerging Payment Schemes? For our readers in Europe, we can hear your eyes rolling. Your merchants have been using this technology since its inception. For those of you in the United States, you may not know what this is even though you probably have shopped at a merchant that used the protocol.

Essentially 3-D Secure inserts the issuing bank into the buying process directly as a way for them to provide additional validation on the transaction. If issuers approve the transaction through this process, they accept all the liability for fraud associated with it.

In a typical e-commerce transaction without 3-D Secure, the authorization process looks very similar to a card present transaction. The information is transmitted from the merchant to a processor/acquirer, through the network, back to the issuer, for approval or denial, and all the way back. But if the payment card was used fraudulently and the issuer approves the transaction, the merchant may still see a chargeback and have to deal with losses from that transaction. The criticism is that issuers are generally incentivized to approve all transactions that come through this channel because the burden of defending against a chargeback falls to the merchant. This obviously reduces trust in the payment system from the merchant side, so this is where 3-D Secure comes in.

If you have ever shopped on a website, entered your payment information, and then seen a strange interstitial page pop up during the *processing* screen with your bank's logo on it, you have gone through the 3-D Secure process. If your bank thinks the transaction might be fraudulent, they will often ask you to supply your bank login information on the next screen as assurance you are the authorized user of the card. Newer implementations may have the bank text the mobile phone on file with a code that is entered into an intermediate page to validate the transaction.

Merchants have a love–hate relationship with 3-D Secure. On one hand, they are guaranteed to get paid on every approved 3-D Secure transaction. On the other hand, 3-D Secure introduces friction into the buying process and they lose control of the experience for arguably the most critical part of an e-commerce transaction—what immediately happens after a buyer clicks "Purchase." Issuers can deny transactions even if merchants believe that there is a low risk of fraud. Merchants can still accept the transaction even if they do not get the approval through 3-D Secure, but they will now own the fraud risk. This may be desirable with repeat customers or repeat payments where the Issuing side doesn't have all of the details required to accept the risk of the transaction.

Merchants can pick and choose which transactions they want to send through 3-D Secure, so it can be a very useful anti-fraud tool for high-value transactions like jewelry, electronics, and appliances. We know we would feel much safer shipping out $2,000 washer and dryer set knowing that we are guaranteed to get paid.

BITCOIN, ETHEREUM, AND CRYPTO

We debated adding a section like this into the book when we began writing in 2020, but now in 2022, there is absolutely no way we could exclude it. From meme coins to ElonMania to Bitcoin Billionaires, this non-traditional, decentralized digital object of value is here to stay.

As a company, you may be thinking how you could accept crypto as a payment method. There are a few items to consider to make sure you understand how it will affect your business. Crypto falls outside the scope of PCI DSS, so anything you do here would offload your compliance risk.

Here are some things to think about as you consider expanding your payment acceptance to include cryptocurrencies:

1. You need to carefully consider the coin(s) you will accept, and understand that if they are not pegged to a fiat currency that the value will fluctuate dramatically enough for your prices to potentially change by the hour or minute. Some stablecoins are pegged to fiat currency and can be an easy way to dip your toes in those waters.
2. Transactions on the blockchain are FOR-EVAH. We imagine for legitimate businesses this is not really a problem. Just remember it will always be available as long as the blockchain for that coin is public. If you are leveraging the smart contract portion of the coin, this can be tremendously useful as a non-repudiated way to quantify the relationship between you and your customer.
3. You still have processing fees, and sometimes they can be more than card processing (especially with Debit transactions). Each coin has different fees for the network and you need to understand how they work.
4. Your wallet is only as secure as you make it. Turn to your nearest search engine and look for cryptocurrency fraud, theft, money laundering, or illicit purchases. The former is a reminder that nobody is guaranteeing the value or the amount of cryptocurrency in your wallet, and if someone manages to get control of your wallet, your coins will be gone forever. The latter is part of the stigma of an unregulated monetary exchange medium that could increase the reputation risk of your business.
5. Technology is difficult. Imagine explaining how to pay for a coffee using Bitcoin to your grandmother. Branden's grandmother loves her iPhone (93 years young!), but she distrusts it and would never understand why she can't pay for something by writing a check. We love GG so much!

Cryptocurrency may be something you want to accept for your business, and it definitely will exempt you from PCI DSS for those transactions. If nothing else, it may be worth experimenting with in small doses to get a feel for how it may work for you in the future.

PREDICTIONS

We wanted to take an opportunity to give you our thoughts on who the leaders might end up being when it comes to all this fancy technology. You are only allowed to read this portion of the book if you understand that we do not have a crystal ball, and we cannot tell the future. All we can do is stand back here, yell into the void, and let things happen naturally. That said, here are a few thoughts on where things are going.

The smart devices have revolutionized how we live our lives. It's more than annoying when our carriers refuse to work or the devices crash as they have become the centerpiece of our digital world. Businesses know this, and they are doing everything possible to integrate with our devices in a way that both makes doing business with the consumer easier and can use analytics and personal service to increase ticket size and loyalty.

Because of this, the concept of a physical payment card may have a shorter lifespan than we think. As avid travelers, both of us would love to consolidate what we bring with us by carrying fewer things in our pockets. Branden lives for the day when all he has to carry around is his smartphone such that he can (legally) drive his car, pay for dinner, present on a fun security topic, and run through security to hop on a plane home without problems. Any way you can tap into this device without re-inventing the wheel will probably work to your advantage. The key here is to not invest heavily in a technology that locks you in for the long haul. If some new crypto-wallet goes belly up or never has wide-scale adoption for your customers, you want the ability to change your back end to accommodate some other scheme that will.

Along those lines, magstripe cards are at the end of their life. If you are a small business owner and are looking for technology to differentiate and power your business, skipping EMV and going right to the smartphone might be your best bet. Smartphones are proving to be a disruptive technology in the payment space, and we feel that they will become central to payments like they have become central to our digital lives.

TAXONOMY AND TIDBITS

In this section, we will go over some basic definitions that are useful to those of you who feel a bit overwhelmed by what you are reading thus far in this chapter.

EMV

EMV, known as Europay, MasterCard, and Visa when you spell it out, is a global interoperability standard for payments meant to boost assurance in payment card transactions, specifically at the point of interaction (POI—the point where the information is read off of a customer's payment card). Some areas of the globe use Chip & PIN, but Chip & PIN is just one possible implementation of EMV. It's incorrect to use EMV and Chip & PIN interchangeably. The chip contains cryptographic algorithms to authenticate the card and can be presented by themselves or used with a cardholder signature or PIN. PINs are optional and may not be used for every implementation. The majority of EMV transactions are done online (as in authorized in real time back to the issuer), but offline transactions may happen in some geographies.

EMV is not ubiquitous, so you may see different implementations in different places depending on where you go. Most new terminals deployed today have the hardware to do NFC or contactless, EMV, and traditional swipe transactions, but the presence of hardware doesn't mean the presence of capability. If you are doing a technology refresh, go with the fully capable terminal and turn on the specific features as your processor is prepared to handle them. In Visa's case, you must be able to accept both a contactless and an EMV transaction at a payment terminal, *and process that transaction correctly* if a customer presents either of those at 75% or more of your total terminals to qualify for the TIP. There are other nuances with this program as well as other payment brands' programs, so check with your acquirer for details.

EUROPE VERSUS THE US VERSUS THE REST OF THE WORLD

Europe is a bit different than the US or the rest of the world when it comes to payments, including the EMV topic we discussed above. If you are a global business, you may be struggling with the differences between Visa and MasterCard in Europe and how those must be balanced with other global operations. In some cases, you might find some requirements relaxed while others are more stringent. Rest assured, you will need to fully investigate these differences and it's a bit beyond the scope of this book. It's not that we don't want to take the time to write about it; it's more like the situation changes so frequently that we fear that this would become rapidly outdated and not useful to the readers.

In addition to requirements, the penalties vary from place to place. You will find selective enforcement by some payment brands with inconsistencies between each brand on how they enforce and how big the penalties are. We discussed some of those penalties earlier, and those should be used as a benchmark. You could end up paying more or even less than what you read about. Your acquirer may even refund some of those penalties, further invalidating the numbers. Do yourself a favor and check with your acquirer for any up-to-date information on global enforcement.

ONE-TIME USE CARDS

Have you ever shopped at a firm that you didn't really trust to cancel your membership when asked? Or just looked at a particular site and knew that while the company was legitimate, the security of the website probably was not? Enter one-time-use cards!

Branden recently signed up for a site that required him to enter a credit card to get access to the 30-day free trial. Knowing that he wasn't sure what was behind the actual paywall, he didn't want to deal with an extensive cancellation process. Branden used Privacy.com to set up a temporary card that had a monthly charge limit on it and used it only for this site. Upon seeing the content, he realized it was not actually helpful and looked for the "Cancel" button.

It didn't exist. Literally. There was no actual way to cancel the subscription anywhere online, and there were no instructions for a number to call.

So Branden just closed the temporary card he created and, like the Bobs, let Milton's payroll just "work itself out."

These cards work like every other payment card but understand if you are trying to do any kind of analytics on using the card number as your key, you will find yourself with some confusing data when you try to identify trends or your most valuable customers.

Many issuers offer one-time-use cards natively, so you may not have to go down this road. There are even entire business models based on this. We are aware of a company that does medical billing and consolidation where they take over insurance reimbursement and have the office staff run a one-time, hand-keyed transaction into their terminal to get their funding with everything cross-referenced by a patient. Not a model that would work in a single-payer structure, but they are processing millions of dollars.

CUSTOMER EXPERIENCE

Our readers are largely charged with securing the infrastructure or complying with PCI DSS, but you will have another force that will dictate how you do business—the customer experience. This may dictate more about how you build and manage your payment systems than any other single force in your company. Many of our customers are experimenting with all of the emerging technologies above with varying impact and success. Collecting money from a customer is an important part of the experience, but mostly to the business. You can expect that your company will experiment more with this in the coming years in ways that will challenge your compliance status. Wireless terminals, kiosks, festivals, third parties, pay-by-cellphone, cryptocurrency, and integrated physical and virtual shopping experiences will impact everything you are doing with respect to payments.

Are you responsible for a call center? Consider using new software to direct callers to enter in their credit card number using the touch-tones on their phone. Doing so would take the majority of the Voice over Internet Protocol (VoIP) system out of scope, saving you money and time demonstrating compliance with PCI DSS.

Your challenge (you must accept it, or you will find yourself looking for work!) is to meet the business folks with solutions to their payment acceptance problems. Don't put the "NO" in inNOvation, put the YES in succYESs (OK, that was a stretch but the "y" is silent). Be creative. Learn how the business wants to operate. Learn what is important for them. Learn about the customer. Only then can you adequately put your brainpower to use to come up with solutions that solve both the business and security needs with the compliance requirement.

CASE STUDY

If you read the next case study and think, "Wow, these sound crazy far out in the future," they might be for you but someone is doing this today. Concept stores, like concept cars, are fully functional and in limited use, but help businesses push themselves to the fringe to figure out what works and what doesn't. In fact, some of this may be happening right under your nose!

THE CASE OF THE CASHLESS COVER CHARGE

Melissa's Mainstage is an intimate concert hall in SoHo, Manhattan. Melissa focuses on bringing local, regional, and some national acts through her venue but keeps the seating under 300 people. Her goal is to charge under $10 for cover for every act, sometimes as low as just a few dollars, and donate some portion of the fee to a local charity for the needy. She has had a few instances of cash missing from the daily take as well a few customers wanting alternative payment options to cash when coming through the door. She accepts major credit cards once inside, but the door is cash only. She decides to take advantage of SIM-based payments on a trial basis and allows customers to send an SMS with the event name to a five-digit code that will place a charge on their cell phone bill. Since the dollar amount is typically very low, she doesn't see any major customer challenges. The first week she put the plan into effect, she had an amazing 97% adoption rate effectively reducing her cash risk by the same amount. She could track each cover by phone number and validate any transaction by simply checking the cell phone of the customer at the door. For the 3% that chose cash, she could choose to motivate them by making a cash cover charge slightly higher than the SMS payment. Or, as long as the adoption rate remains high, she could just opt to accept cash as a non-preferred alternative.

To fully understand Melissa's decision, you must realize that this change does not in any way affect her PCI compliance posture. She still does her normal compliance work for her bar and merchandise sales, but she now has a cashless solution for the door as well. She knew that by piloting and ultimately implementing this solution she would not create a PCI headache in the process.

SUMMARY

The world moves pretty fast just like Ferris Bueller said. By the time you are reading this book, these technologies will be even further down the path to maturation and probably embedded in more than a few retailers around the world. Remember that you can pilot or even adopt different payment methods that may or may not have any impact on your existing PCI DSS compliance. If you use a Qualified Security Assessor (QSA) or Internal Security Assessor (ISA), you will probably be educating him in this process as well. When you prepare for your meeting, be sure to give yourself plenty of time to walk through the technology and implementation, and bring an expert along with you that can answer any specific questions that the assessor may have.

Go forth and experiment! We are consumers too, and we're pretty excited about the creative ideas you all will implement.

NOTE

1. You can learn more about this here: https://bit.ly/PCI-PAR.

20 PCI DSS Myths and Misconceptions

Information in this chapter:

- Myth #1 Payment Card Industry (PCI) Doesn't Apply to Me
- Myth #2 PCI Is Confusing and Ambiguous
- Myth #3 Payment Card Industry Data Security Standard (PCI DSS) Is Too Onerous
- Myth #4 Breaches Prove PCI DSS to Be Irrelevant
- Myth #5 PCI Is All We Need for Security
- Myth #6 PCI DSS Is Really Easy
- Myth #7 My Tool Is PCI Compliant, Thus I Am Compliant
- Myth #8 PCI Is Toothless
- Case Study
- Summary

The Payment Card Industry Data Security Standard (PCI DSS) transformed the way many organizations practice information security. While we've *heard* that something other than a breach can bring information security to the boardroom, PCI actually accomplishes this for many organizations—both large and small. You may be early on in your PCI DSS journey, but your firm is most likely not. In addition, there are likely other security and compliance standards that your firm must manage given the ever-evolving cybersecurity world. While it should be clear to our readers that following all of the PCI DSS guidance will not magically make your organization secure or prevent all incidents, the standard contains many of the common security requirements that are essential for protecting account data and can be useful for other types of sensitive data as well.

Throughout this book, you've learned about other types of standards you can use to build your information security program. The National Institute of Standards and Technology (NIST) Common Security Framework (CSF) is a freely available reference to build a foundational information security program that would only need to be tweaked for PCI DSS. When you are looking for bang for your buck, this is exactly one of those ways to "shortcut" compliance to PCI DSS 4.0.

As of today, "PCI DSS is intended for all entities that store, process, or transmit cardholder data (CHD) and/or sensitive authentication data (SAD) or could impact the security of the cardholder data environment." The aforementioned quote from Section 2 on page 4 of the PCI DSS document reminds us that the *applicability* of PCI DSS is in fact nearly universal even if the enforcement is not.

In this chapter, we look at common PCI DSS myths and misconceptions. We will also dispel those myths and provide a few more tips on approaching PCI DSS.

Let's get to the myths!

MYTH #1 PCI DOESN'T APPLY TO ME

Myth #1 is pretty simple, but, sadly, very common: "PCI DSS just doesn't apply to us, because we are small, or we are a University, or we don't do e-commerce, or we outsource *everything*, or we don't store cards, or we are not a permanent entity, and the list goes on." More recent versions include "we use tokenization, we use EMV, or we encrypt end-to-end." "We outsource everything

DOI: 10.1201/9781003100300-20

and thus have no PCI responsibilities" may be true in specific circumstances, but in most cases that is just that—a myth.

This myth can quickly placate key stakeholders in the firm, making employees oblivious to PCI DSS requirements and, almost always, to information risks and security requirements in general.

An older example might be health care providers attempting to comply with the Healthcare Information Portability and Accountability Act (HIPAA). An old publication from *SC Magazine* entitled "PCI-DSS: Not on health care provider's radar"[1] (notice the incorrectly hyphenated "PCI-DSS" in the title...) reports:

However, since Medicare reimbursement is not at risk with PCI-DSS compliancy, it has been virtually ignored. It doesn't help that major health care publications are openly misinterpreting the PCI-DSS standards for health care providers, with statements such as: "[Providers] do not have to worry about compliance with PCI standards... they aren't storing any card numbers."

While this is an article from 2009, don't be surprised if a new class of workers comes through your company and says PCI is *like, so 2009.*

A Perfect Example of Myth #1 at Work!

PCI DSS applies to those who accept, capture, store, transmit, process, or *any entity that could affect the security of payment account data.* Want to guess the percentage of health care providers that accept cards? In the US, that number is probably close to 100%. Outside of the US, things are different. The paper mentioned earlier confirms: "In 2009, virtually all health care providers take credit cards—and virtually none of them are PCI compliant." Today the situation is different but not because of a conscious effort from individual health care providers. Most likely, cards are processed through the software they use to run the practice or through a standalone terminal, which generally works in a compliant manner out of the box these days. In larger health care organizations, PCI DSS sometimes becomes a baseline framework that is used to justify HIPAA compliance. PCI is definitely not the priority, and the fragmented nature of health care billing, when compared to services provided, complicates compliance (think gift shops or cafeterias in hospitals that are often run by third parties).

NOTE

Question: If I only accept cards from June to August each year and I only use a dial-up terminal, I am "safe from PCI," right?

Answer: Wrong. Even though your scope of PCI DSS validation is very, very small, you are definitely subject to its rules because you accept payment cards. PCI DSS applies to those who accept, capture, store, transmit, or process credit and debit account data. If you do, it applies to you—end of story.

But, with only three months out of the year, your transaction volume is probably extremely low, and perhaps your portable terminal is quite secure. Your *validation* requirements may state that you don't have to do anything. The important part is to know exactly what your responsibilities are for payment security and perform those.

Interestingly enough, one of the data elements required to be protected under HIPAA is customer payment information, which often means "credit account data." This means that HIPAA technically preceded PCI DSS when it comes to cardholder data security. However, this doesn't stop health care providers from struggling with both regulations.

NOTE

Question: If I use external tokenization and cardholder information never enters my environment, am I OK?

Answer: Possibly! If your merchant agreement does not mention PCI DSS, none of your employees can see the data, and it is not handled anywhere on your systems, your PCI responsibility might be nonexistent. Be sure you understand what your responsibilities are and make sure they are clearly written in your contracts.

If cardholder data touches your systems—sometimes even if the data is encrypted—those systems (and probably more) are in scope for PCI DSS, which means your organization has a responsibility to comply with PCI DSS.

Admittedly, different things need to happen at your organization if you have absolutely no electronic processing or storage of digital cardholder data compared to having an Internet-connected payment application system. The scope of compliance validation will be much more limited in the former case and so your PCI project will be much, much simpler. For example, if a small merchant "does not store, process, or transmit any cardholder data on merchant premises but relies entirely on third-party service providers to handle these functions" he is only responsible for validating a portion of PCI DSS. Specifically, he would be responsible for the parts of seven requirements for a total of twenty-nine questions.

Let's explore this example in more detail. Payment card brands such as Visa and MasterCard label merchants that process fewer than 20,000 e-commerce transactions a year or fewer than 1 million card present transactions are categorized as Level 4. Level 4 merchants currently are recommended to validate their PCI compliance using a Self-Assessment Questionnaire.

In addition, as described in PCI DSS standards, if a merchant matches the criteria below, he is eligible to fill out SAQ A. The criteria are as follows:

- The merchant accepts only card-not-present (e-commerce or mail/telephone-order) transactions,
- All processing of account data is entirely outsourced to PCI DSS compliant third-party service provider (TPSP)/payment processor,
- The merchant does not electronically store, process, or transmit any account data on merchant systems or premises, but relies entirely on a TPSP(s) to handle all these functions,
- The merchant has reviewed the PCI DSS Attestation of Compliance form(s) for its TPSP(s) and confirmed that TPSP(s) are PCI DSS compliant for the services being used by the merchant, and
- Any account data the merchant might retain is on paper (for example, printed reports or receipts), and these documents are not received electronically.

Additionally, for e-commerce channels, all elements of the payment page(s)/form(s) delivered to the customer's browser originate only and directly from a PCI DSS compliant TPSP/payment processor.

Explained simply, the aforementioned criteria describe a situation where a merchant accepts credit cards as payment, but does not have any electronic storage, processing, or transmission of cardholder data. Think about it for a moment. PCI DSS doesn't apply if you do not store, process, or transmit any account data. PCI DSS would absolutely apply to you if you put a custom-built application into a cloud provider even though that would move it off-premises. It's more about who can affect the security of payment data. This example highlights the fact that card acceptance is sufficient to make the merchant fall under PCI even if they have outsourced nearly all the responsibility to a third party.

You may be thinking this is overwhelming. The important part is to understand exactly what your obligations are with your acquirer or processor. Make sure it is clearly spelled out in your contract so that you know what you have to do to protect yourself in case of an incident.

A subtle point brought to life by an increasing use of EMV technology needs to be clarified: payment card brands may relax some of the PCI DSS validation requirements if the merchant uses new (and presumably more secure) payment methods, however, merchants will still be required to maintain PCI compliance at all times.

MYTH #2 PCI IS CONFUSING AND AMBIGUOUS

Myth #2 is just as pervasive: PCI is confusing and ambiguous. At first, it might seem like it is true: after all, this whole book is written about it!

Let's be real for a moment. *PCI DSS is confusing and ambiguous.* People made careers out of navigating that ambiguity dating back to the original Visa CISP days in the early 2000s—and that includes both of us.

Sometimes you will find people who believe the problem of PCI DSS is so small it's worth ignoring (by the way, they may be right). For example, when confronted with the need to change their business processes to avoid storing account data (a simpler task as you now know) or with the need to secure existing account data (a harder task compared to not storing it), smaller organizations may activate Ostrich-Head-in-the-Sand-Mode and try to pretend the problem is unclear, unsolvable, or confusing instead of tackling it head-on.

Namely, those under its influence often proclaim things such as:

- "PCI just confuses us—we can't do it."
- "We don't know what to do, who to ask, what exactly to change."
- "We don't know whether we are compliant and hiring somebody to give us that answer is expensive."
- "PCI is confusing. Until you give us something better, we will not do anything different."

Sometimes it also devolves into the following:

- "Just give us a simple task list and we will do it. Promise!"

The reality is quite different. PCI DSS documents explain both what to do and then how to validate it. There can be a world of grey in what is intended to be a black-and-white determination of compliance. You just need to take the time to understand the "why" (the spirit of the standard and cardholder data security), the "what" (the list of PCI DSS requirements), and "how" (common approaches, guidance, and practices related to PCI).

PCI DSS 4.0 certainly added weight to the paper that an assessor or assessee must read through and carry around, and if that is what someone is alluding to when they say it's confusing, we concede that can be correct. The good news in 4.0 is there is quite a bit of clarification in that added weight. The ambiguity is demonstrably lower today than in 2015 when the last version of this book hit the shelves.

PCI can be easier to understand than other existing security and risk management frameworks and regulatory guidance in spite of its length and breadth. Looking at some of the advanced information risk management documents (such as ISO27005:2018 "Information technology – Security techniques—Information security risk management" or NIST 800-30 "Guide for Conducting Risk Assessments") with their hundreds of pages of sometimes esoteric guidance, PCI DSS is a refreshing reminder that standards can be fairly straightforward.

Most of the gray area talk you hear about PCI DSS typically comes from individuals that are trying to find creative ways not to do anything to their business or their technology is deployed in ways that they don't fully understand.

Let's compare what PCI says and what some other guidance documents say:

Requirement 5 of PCI DSS gives 12 whole pages of guidance on requirements, all stemming from the below high-level sections:

- *"5.1 Processes and mechanisms for protecting all systems and networks from malicious software are defined and understood.*
- *5.2 Malicious software (malware) is prevented or detected and addressed.*
- *5.3 Anti-malware mechanisms and processes are active, maintained, and monitored.*
- *5.4 Anti-phishing mechanisms protect users against phishing attacks."*

Go look at those pages and review all the details associated with malware that guide you on the types of systems, the types of software, and now a new requirement (Requirement 5.4) to help protect users against phishing attacks. That's a lot of content, but it's also prescriptive enough for any practitioner to absorb and understand what must be done to comply.

ISO27002[2] states: "Precautions are required to prevent and detect the introduction of malicious software, such as computer viruses, network worms, Trojan horses, and logic bombs."

Even though PCI DSS needs some focused attention from merchants and service providers, it is more specific versus confusing when compared to other industry security guidance. While the original PCI creators had BS7799/ISO17799 in mind, their standard ended up being simpler to objectively measure than its ISO-created inspiration but lost of few things that people consider important (e.g., all the security project management requirements).

There are definitely areas in the PCI security guidance that can be made more specific. For example, when PCI DSS was updated from version 3.2.1 to version 4.0, dozens (hundreds?) of clarifications and explanations brought up during the review phase made their way into the final version (see the PCI DSS Summary of Changes document available on the PCI Council website for details).

As PCI DSS continues to mature, the remaining ambiguity diminishes by adapting to the needs and requirements of merchants as threats evolve.

Finally, security cannot be reduced to a simple checklist even if you fill out an SAQ to validate your PCI DSS compliance. PCI DSS 4.0 specifically ties specific requirements to the risk assessment work you perform in Requirement 12.3. PCI guidance is as close to a checklist as we can get without increasing risk.

MYTH #3 PCI DSS IS TOO ONEROUS

The next myth is closely related to the last one. Sometimes, it becomes too expensive, too complicated, too burdensome, just too much for a small business, with too many technologies or even simply "unreasonable" and "too much security."

"PCI is too hard" becomes true if merchants are treating their account data in a particularly negligent way. Think massive transaction record files with unencrypted PANs on a website or payment terminals allowing remote access open with no password.

For example, we discussed flat networks in Chapter 4, Building and Maintaining a Secure Network. As a reminder, it means a network that is not segmented by firewalls (or other equivalent network choke points) into zones. Such network design means that if a single system handles account data, the whole network is in scope for PCI DSS. Yes, that means all servers, all desktops, all network devices, all mobile phones and tablets, all IP-based phones and cameras, all VoIP phones, the Roomba, and everything else connected to it becomes subject to all PCI DSS requirements. Flat networks exist at merchants of all sizes making PCI DSS compliance very hard as the scope grows from a single system or a handful of systems to hundreds or thousands of systems. Every system will need to be scanned for vulnerabilities, have its security configuration verified, have logging enabled and monitored, and all applicable controls from PCI DSS in place and functioning. In this case, "PCI is hard" is not a myth, but PCI DSS will not be the reason to blame: the operators of that kind of network will be.

WARNING

If you think PCI is too onerous, please stop and consider this: do you think that wearing a seat belt while driving is too onerous? How about brushing your teeth every day? How about actually operating your business?

New tasks often seem onerous. When you were three years old, it is very likely that brushing your teeth was seen as a huge task—and an annoying one as well since you were literally brushing teeth that would be falling out of your head in a few years.

So, if you happen to think PCI and data security are too onerous, start exploring and it will stop being onerous over time.

Similarly, if a simple change in a business process will lead to the removal of stored cardholder data, do it! PCI will indeed be "too hard" if you don't conduct a review of risky business practices with the intent to change and reduce risk. Delete everything you can, and then secure the rest.

People who complain about PCI DSS being too hard are often split into two camps:

- "Please, please make PCI easier by letting us skip the requirements," or "JUST SAY YES ON THE SAQ!" Those are laggards.
- "We know that our security program makes us PCI compliant; please make it easier for us to prove it!" Those are leaders.

As you can guess, the organizations that fit into the first camp and those that fit into the second camp are very different. While some in the first will miss the joke in *ScanlessPCI* (an old joke site set up by a band of security experts to poke fun at some of the organizations that ignore security), the second camp is often concerned with relating their risk-focused approach to PCI's mostly control-focused approach.

It is possible to make PCI easier even for those in the first camp, those people who just "want it to go away." Acquirers make doing the right thing easier for merchants (while making doing the wrong thing harder): things like not storing account data, outsourcing processing, or using tokenization. For example, some merchants store account data because they are under the mistaken impression that such data falls under the "Financial Rule of Thumb" of storing financial records for seven years. Such actions are making PCI DSS much more difficult or, in the case of storing CVV2 or other prohibited data, impossible. Even for chargebacks, which obviously don't go back seven years, storing the PAN and other sensitive data is just not needed today.

On the other hand, in the second camp, you sometimes hear things like "we have a good security program, and we manage our risk well! Why should we spend time on that PCI thing? We are probably in good shape already!" These organizations are likely doing a good job with security and want to quickly prove compliance. In this case, making PCI easier will include making it easier to assess, validate, and prove compliance and overall make the whole assessment experience a little less painful. Still, it will not be harder than building a net new risk management program.

All that said, why would you even want to tackle all of this for your entire organization? Nearly every business will benefit from some technology or process you can use to reduce the scope of PCI DSS dramatically. For example, end-to-end encryption technologies could reduce a brick & mortar merchant's scope to the terminal only.

You will make PCI harder for yourself by making the wrong decisions or by avoiding difficult conversations related to changing outdated business practices. For example, developing your own web application complete with credit card processing will increase your PCI scope likely beyond your ability to handle. Using a third-party checkout service will do just the opposite and make PCI and data security easier. Review the previous section on Myth #2 and remember that your PCI experience becomes so much easier when you avoid handling account data.

MYTH #4 BREACHES PROVE PCI DSS TO BE IRRELEVANT

Nearly two decades of living with PCI DSS compliance have rendered Myth #4 less relevant, but perhaps that is because we have breach fatigue and in every case the breached entity was found not to be compliant with PCI DSS. In order for PCI DSS to be truly successful, the industry needs to demonstrate both high compliance rates and low breach rates. Meaning, 100% compliance rates reduce breaches to zero. Branden's experience at acquiring institutions tells us neither of those are true. Compliance rates continue to be well below 100%—even for Level 1 merchants—and breaches continue.

There is a give-up mentality present at some organizations that then develop a negative, destructive mindset toward PCI DSS and do a bad job with compliance and data security. We believe organizations that go through the motions are more likely to suffer a breach. Organizations that validate PCI compliance and subsequently suffer a breach must understand where their processes broke down. If a similar organization related to you suffers a breach, learn as much as you can to give your firm a better chance.

We both are private pilots, and any time there is a crash in general aviation you can bet we both are scouring every data source available to us to understand what may have led to it. It can be quite unsettling listening to someone's final broadcast on the radio—a joyless necessity in the process of learning. We both want to be safe pilots, and that means we must learn from others' mistakes to avoid our own.

QSAs carry some of the blame as well. A prominent QSA firm found Heartland Payment Systems compliant in 2008 when they very clearly were not. Blatant security mistakes, severe configuration weaknesses, forbidden data storage, and even compromised systems were missed by the easy grader assessor who focused much more on writing quickly instead of accurately. Selecting a QSA helps to focus on the value you will receive and not simply on price or the method of billing. Try to squeeze every penny of valuable security advice during that face time (or Zoom time) in the assessment process. Have somebody from your organization certify as an Internal Security Assessor to make things go more smoothly. Some firms like to hire both a QSA and a second firm to consult during the entire process (Branden did this at his last firm).

Data breaches remind us that basic security mandated by PCI DSS is necessary but not sufficient. As you learn more about security, you usually come to realize that nothing guarantees breach-free operation. Let's pick a few examples from PCI DSS and check whether they are a good idea as well as whether they guarantee the absence of breaches. Table 20.1 shows excerpts from PCI DSS as well as their relation to data protection and data breach prevention.

Table 20.1 allows us to conclude that while most PCI DSS controls are necessary to prevent account data loss and theft, few of them can be considered sufficient on their own.

NOTE

Recent breaches remind us that PCI DSS is insufficient on its own. Only an ongoing and adaptable cyber risk program with quality strategy and execution gets you to a more secure end-state—even if it truly never ends.

Remember, you are never *done* with information security!

TABLE 20.1

PCI DSS Requirements for Data Security

Requirement Number	PCI DSS Requirement	Importance for Data Security	Guarantee Lack of Account Data Loss?
2.2.2	If the vendor default account(s) will be used, the default password is changed to a strong, unique password.	Default passwords are still a frequent avenue for attackers.	No.
2.2.4	Only necessary services, protocols, daemons, and functions are enabled, and all unnecessary functionality is removed or disabled.	Extra non-functional scripts are often abused to get access to systems.	No.
2.2.7	All non-console administrative access is encrypted using strong cryptography.	Leaking an admin password or session exposes the system to attackers.	No.
3.2.1	Account data storage is kept to a minimum through the implementation of data retention and disposal policies, procedures, and processes…	Theft of data is bad, mmkay.	Yes! No data means no data breach.
5.2.1	An anti-malware solution is deployed on all system components known to be affected by malware.	Viruses, ransomware, and other malware can lead to the theft of account data.	No, even with anti-malware tools malware can still spread to the systems.
7.2.1	An access control model defines appropriate access depending on the entity's business and access needs…	Entitlement bloat expands your attack surface.	No, as other means of breaking in can be used by attackers.
8.3.6	[Passwords must be] a minimum length of 12 characters (…) [and] contain both numeric and alphabetic characters.	Long, complex passwords are much harder to guess.	No, even complex passwords can be guessed or systems compromised without the passwords.

One of our colleagues likes to say that every breach proves PCI DSS is necessary. PCI DSS is a great start for security, but a really bad finish, as we discover in the next myth.

MYTH #5 PCI IS ALL WE NEED FOR SECURITY

Myth #5 is probably the scariest one of all: PCI is all we ever need for security. People in the grasp of this myth would proclaim things that would shock every security professional; for example:

- "We have handled PCI—we are secure now."
- "We worked hard and we passed an assessment. Now we are secure!"
- "Our QSA told us we are secure."
- Or even, in its more extreme form, "I filed my PCI compliance documents, now I am compliant and secure for a year."

Remember back in the late 1990s when executives proudly proclaimed, "I have a firewall, I'm secure" and then refused to pay attention to *overblown* security concerns. At the very least, a firewall might block some suspicious connections, which is more than can be said for your Report on Compliance that, on its own, does not provide any protection.

Another common manifestation is an organization that doesn't pay attention to data security suddenly stung by PCI DSS requirements. More often than not, management will direct IT do "that PCI security thing." It often leads organizations to focus on "pleasing the assessor" and then forgetting that a happy assessor does not mean that your organization is protected from information security risks.

Validating PCI DSS compliance does not mean that you are done with PCI DSS. Now you need to maintain compliance—something that needs to happen daily. It certainly does not mean that you are done with security nor does it mean that you are secure, just that you validated PCI compliance and hopefully made an honest step towards reducing your risk. Your QSA only validates your compliance at a point in time. Merchants and service providers are solely responsible for maintaining compliance between assessments.

Validating PCI compliance does NOT mean that:

- You are "done with PCI," and now can ignore it.
- You are "done with security," and your data requires no ongoing protection.
- You are "secure," or as even secure as you need to be.

PCI DSS mandates minimum acceptable security controls, not maximum or optimal. PCI validation attests that those specific minimum-security controls were in place at the time of assessment (or perhaps simply shown to a QSA without further examination).

PCI is basic security at best—a low bar to hop over that was never meant to be an end state. No document can guarantee ongoing compliance, just as excellent police work can never guarantee a crime-free environment. People don't expect police, prosecutors, and laws to *end* crime—so why do some people think that QSAs, security vendors, and PCI DSS documents will end cybercrime? This is a useful thought to keep in your head as you are finishing that PCI validation.

WARNING

If you hear somebody assert his firm was PCI compliant and then suffered a breach, please pause abandoning PCI DSS as a lost cause. It is hard to say for sure without understanding the details surrounding the incident. In every case we have seen in the field, the breached firm failed to do something to comply with PCI DSS. The standard itself, the PCI Council, or any other regulatory entity is not at fault for poor execution of standards designed to help merchants stay safe—even if there are things in the standard that we could argue are not as secure as they could be. In fact, even when they say, "we were compliant," they rarely mention *when* they think they were compliant.

Finally, PCI is about account data security—not the rest of your private or regulated information, your organization's intellectual property, or identity information such as Social Security Numbers (SSNs). It only covers confidentiality and not availability or integrity of cardholder data (though it very clearly covers the integrity of log data). These quick examples show that there is a lot more to data security than PCI DSS, and there are clear areas where PCI does not focus for a good reason.

Specifically, perfect PCI DSS compliance and validation will not:

- Secure your non-cardholder data, such as SSNs.
- Secure your trade secrets and other intellectual property.
- Secure your "out of scope" systems and networks.

- Make you automatically compliant with any other international, national, state, or industry regulation.

It might only minimally affect:

- The security of non-PCI data entangled with payment account data and systems.
- Your readiness to address other regulations.

Thus, you are certainly not done with security even if you maintain ongoing PCI compliance. Another of our colleagues likes to say that you likely need "PCI+" or even "PCI++" to deal with risks to your systems and data today.

MYTH #6 PCI DSS IS REALLY EASY

The next myth, #6, is the opposite of myth #4: PCI is easy: "we just have to say, 'Yes' on a questionnaire and get scanned." As you become more familiar with PCI DSS, you might start to feel that PCI is not that scary. It is about getting a scan from your ASV, then answering *yes* to a bunch of lengthy questions. Some merchants even think that the fees they pay related to PCI DSS compliance on their monthly statement means they are compliant, or the bank is providing protection.

For merchants and service providers that don't have to go through an on-site assessment with a QSA, PCI DSS compliance is indeed validated via external vulnerability scanning by an ASV and via filing an SAQ—often representing a subset of the full requirements. Simply answering yes to the questions might get you over the documentation finish line, but it definitely does not accurately represent the current state of your compliance program. Instead, it may be a more accurate representation of the treatment of End User License Agreements. Dr. Hugh Thompson said at an RSA conference ages ago, "What buttons do I have to push to throw birds at pigs?" Only select "yes" if you know it to be true.

WARNING

PCI DSS is not easy. It is not easy for a large company that needs to collect all the evidence for compliance validation from different systems and then maintain evidence between assessments. However, these activities, if not easy, are actually useful for security and overall manageability in that company.

PCI DSS can be pretty easy if all card processing is outsourced to a reliable and secure processing provider who does not allow you to touch the data. Some external tokenization solutions offer similar benefits for simplifying PCI compliance. We're not even sure why merchants still manage lots of their own PCI DSS scope. The entire ecosystem has built products and services to let merchants do what they do best—marketing and supply chain management. In that case, maybe PCI is really easy!

Here is an example: Requirement 1.2.3 mandates "An accurate network diagram(s) is maintained that shows all connections between the CDE and other networks, including any wireless networks." We show a few examples of such diagrams in Chapter 4, Building and Maintaining a Secure Network. Answering "Yes" to this question means you:

1. Have a diagram available,
2. Made sure that the diagram is indeed current, and all network connections are reflected on it,
3. Know the locations of cardholder data (itself a massive project at many organizations),

4. Verified that there are no other locations of cardholder data (previous PCI DSS updates placed additional emphasis on such discovery efforts),
5. Confirmed that it shows all connections to all locations of cardholder data,
6. Know which wireless networks are deployed and where, including those deployed by divisions and other business units (and possibly rogue as well), and
7. Mapped connections from networks and systems that can manage systems housing cardholder data.

Clearly, this takes more than reading a book (we suggest telling your friends and colleagues about *this* book) or clicking "Y" on a survey. This is what turns minutes into months and simple tasks into projects.

A slightly simplified reality is that a typical small merchant who processes cards online would at least need to do the following:

1. Get a network vulnerability scan of the external systems from an ASV, resolve the vulnerabilities found, and then rescan to verify,
2. Do the things that the SAQ questions refer to and maintain evidence that they were performed,
3. Answer the questions affirmatively (providing details that were needed) and retain the proof of that validation, and
4. Keep up with periodic maintenance and other requirements until you no longer wish to accept credit cards, i.e., maintain compliance.

In other words, achieve PCI DSS validation and then maintain PCI DSS compliance for as long as you plan to accept cards. You can only answer yes if you have grounds for saying yes on the questionnaire and can prove it, even with no assessors or acquiring banks looking over your shoulder.

NOTE

Question: My management told me to ignore everything, including security hardening of my servers and even response to an ongoing hacking incident and focus on pleasing the QSA. What should I do?

Answer: Aside from giving your LinkedIn profile a touch-up? What you need to do is try to tie all the key security things you know you need to do (we are assuming here that you actually know what those things are) and tie them to PCI DSS requirements. Under a PCI umbrella, management should be more accepting of what you actually need to do for security. The end result should help achieve both PCI DSS compliance and security. Some people might object to such tactics as "gray area" or "unethical," but there is nothing unethical in using a compliance framework—PCI DSS in this case—to improve security.

Specifically, even on the vulnerability scanning side, the perception that you can get a PCI scan and be done is misguided. PCI DSS requires you to run both internal and external network vulnerability scans at least quarterly (in reality, twice per quarter since you would need to fix the vulnerabilities and then rescan to confirm closure) as well as after every major network change. Internal scans can be run by in-house security staff, while the external scans must be performed by an ASV, and these are then used to satisfy your PCI Validation Requirements and may be submitted to your acquiring bank.

Furthermore, the specific requirements provide details on the process of such scans. Requirement 11.3.2.1 mandates remediation of all vulnerabilities with a CVSS score of 4.0 and higher for external scans and Requirement 11.3.1.3 mandates remediation of all high-risk and critical internal vulnerabilities as defined in PCI DSS Requirement 6.3.1. In essence, this is not a scan-and-be-done function, but a scan, fix, and maintain lifecycle.

NOTE

Don't be fooled into thinking that the PCI DSS scanning validation requirements only apply to systems that process or store account data. If you are subject to PCI DSS scanning requirements, all of your externally visible systems are subject to security scanning (by an ASV) as well as those systems involved in processing, storing, and transmitting the data and the ones directly connected to them. Many organizations have challenges scanning systems with cardholder data especially when those systems are virtual, located in other environments, or are not under the full control of the merchant. Companies can work with their QSA and ASV to reduce the scope if certain controls and segmentation are in place and enforced.

For more information on segmentation and how that could affect your scanning requirements, check this document available on the PCI Council's website: Guidance for PCI DSS Scoping and Segmentation.

MYTH #7 MY TOOL IS PCI COMPLIANT, THUS I AM COMPLIANT

Believing that your network, application, or tool is PCI compliant with the resulting conclusion that this achieves compliance for your organization is foolhardy. This myth manifests itself in statements such as "My payment application vendor said his tool is PCI compliant" or "they put together a network and it is PCI compliant." Be advised, no tool can make you compliant. We've seen merchants confuse a PCI Software Security Standard listed (formerly PA-DSS-certified) application with a PCI DSS compliant organization. PCI DSS 4.0 states that "Software that is PCI SSC validated and listed provides assurance that the software has been developed using secure practices and has met a defined set of software security requirements." That's it. No guarantees.

TOOLS

The official validated software lists on the Council's website contain all of the validated payment applications that can be used by merchants. Acquirers may refuse to onboard merchants that use applications missing from the list or if they are running specific versions of the applications which are not on the list.

While using this resource will get you a list of products, you still must deploy them as prescribed by both PCI DSS and the Implementation Guide from the vendor. Don't forget to ensure the software package is still being maintained and you get patches that may be required to maintain PCI DSS compliance.

In reality, there is no such thing as a PCI-compliant tool, application, configuration, or network, no matter what a vendor's marketing department says. PCI DSS compliance applies to organizations only. You can struggle toward, achieve, and validate PCI DSS compliance only as an organization. Using a compliant application is only a small piece of the entire puzzle.

Despite that, we have been asked multiple times by various industry colleagues about certain pieces of IT infrastructure being PCI compliant. Here is one recent example.

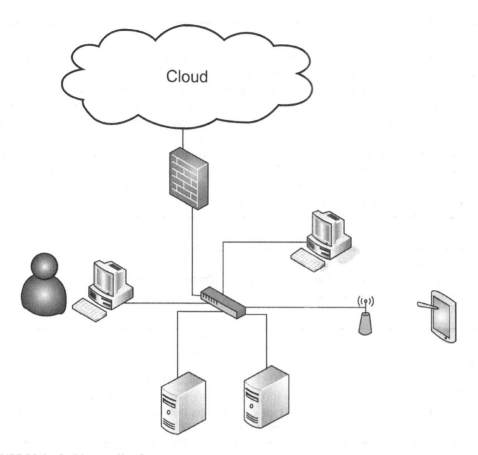

FIGURE 20.1   Is this compliant?

Figure 20.1 was shown to Branden with the question "Is this PCI compliant?" Even though some people will start debating this with crafty arguments for yes and no, the immediate response was "there is no way to tell." There are simply too many things that can make or break the PCI DSS compliant status of an organization. For example:

- What are the password policies on these servers? Are they compliant with many require-ments such as "8.2.6 Inactive user accounts are removed or disabled within 90 days of inactivity" or "8.3.9 Passwords/passphrases are changed at least once every 90 days"?
- Is logging performed? Does this logging meet Requirement 10? Namely, is logging suf-ficient to reconstruct the prescribed events?
- Are vulnerability scans performed "at least once every three months"? Are discovered vulnerabilities remediated?
- Is file-integrity monitoring software (or change detection software) deployed to alert per-sonnel to unauthorized modification (including changes, additions, and deletions) of criti-cal files and perform critical file comparisons at least weekly (see requirement 11.5.2)?
- Moreover, are the security policies "established, published, maintained, and dissemi-nated to all relevant personnel, as well as to relevant vendors and business partners" per Requirement 12.1.1? Or is a "formal security awareness program […] implemented to make all personnel aware of the entity's information security policy and procedures, and their role in protecting the cardholder data" prescribed by PCI DSS Requirement 12.6.1? What about the operational procedures for all the security tasks?

WARNING

Your security policy is pretty darn important for your PCI DSS compliance program (since it is mandated in Requirement 12 which we cover in Chapter 7, Protecting Cardholder Data) as well as for data security. However, here is the dirty truth about policy: it does *nothing* to secure your data unless it is actually followed and enforced by security technology and process. If someone tells you, "Well, we have some administrative controls that do this," that's a clue to dig and ask more questions.

Furthermore, we hypothesize that this is exactly why finalizing policies, procedures, and processes is listed in Phase 6 of "PCI DSS Prioritized Approach." Some security professionals say, "policy comes first," and they might be right. But policy needs to be actually implemented to have ANY impact on data security and risk.

The above lists only a few of the reasons for why the above-pictured environment might or might not be part of a PCI DSS compliant organization.

Thus, "no way to tell" is the only correct response. There is no way to judge the PCI compliance state of isolated servers pictured on a diagram.

NOTE

PCI DSS compliance applies to the entire organization. PCI DSS also does not have any partial compliance—there is only compliance with all applicable requirements or not compliant. In some cases, payment brands or acquiring banks may allow you to complete certain phases of the Prioritized Approach in the quest for compliance, but those are either associated with technology advancements and implementations or special one-off cases.

Answering the question posed above is only possible when considering all the conditions, criteria, and requirements, and the only way to achieve this is to follow your own path through the PCI DSS requirements. The PCI DSS Prioritized Approach lists the recommended, risk-based order for following the requirements that can be helpful on your journey. The document can be found on the PCI Council website. Table 20.2 shows an example from the document.

As we mentioned, PCI DSS combines technology, process, policy, awareness, and practices as well. For example, Requirement 12 covers your security policy, incident response practices, security awareness, and other nontechnical safeguards and controls. Don't focus on isolated pieces; rather, build the big picture, track a path, and move ahead towards PCI DSS compliance and improved data security.

MYTH #8 PCI IS TOOTHLESS

This myth embodies the view that data security measures are only deployed due to regulatory pressure, such as from PCI DSS, and not from a genuine need to reduce risk to information and transactions. This myth is often used to justify inaction by merchants who believe that even if they are breached and found non-compliant, their business will not suffer. Similarly, people read news stories and see companies after a breach return to profitability quickly without any internal context so they need not care about PCI and security. Finally, they claim that compliance costs more than non-compliance without doing any research into this subject, which then leads to faulty decision-making.

While it is in nobody's interest to remove merchants or service providers from the payment ecosystem, it has happened in the past and can happen in the future. The payment ecosystem works

TABLE 20.2

PCI Prioritized Approach Milestones

Milestones	Goals
1	**Remove sensitive authentication data and limit data retention.** This milestone targets a key area of risk for entities that have been compromised. Remember, if sensitive authentication data and other cardholder data are not stored, the effects of a compromise will be greatly reduced. If you don't need it, don't store it.
2	**Protect systems and networks and be prepared to respond to a system breach.** This milestone targets controls for points of access to most compromises and the processes for responding.
3	**Secure payment card applications.** This milestone targets controls for applications, application processes, and application servers. Weaknesses in these areas offer easy prey for compromising systems and obtaining access to cardholder data.
4	**Monitor and control access to your systems.** Controls for this milestone allow you to detect the who, what, when, and how concerning who is accessing your network and cardholder data environment.
5	**Protect stored cardholder data.** For those organizations that have analyzed their business processes and determined that they must store Primary Account Numbers, Milestone Five targets key protection mechanisms for that stored data.
6	**Finalize remaining compliance efforts and ensure all controls are in place.** The intent of Milestone Six is to complete PCI DSS requirements, and to finalize all remaining related policies, procedures, and processes needed to protect the cardholder data environment.

when transactions are flowing through it. Removing transactions means removing revenue. So even though the threat of paying to clean up a breach should be a big motivator for your firm, PCI does have teeth in the form of fines and extra overhead you may need to do if you don't maintain your compliance.

PCI DSS non-compliance and resulting loss of cardholder data packs a punch to include fines, lawsuits, mandatory breach disclosure costs, investigation costs, potential card processing rate increases, the cost of additional security measures, and potentially the cost of victim credit monitoring. Fines can be substantial, but they are not the only way money will leave your organization:

- **Breach disclosure costs:** Although it is not the direct consequence of PCI DSS non-compliance, these costs result from breaches caused by blatant disregard for both data security and PCI compliance.
- **Consulting fees:** Companies have to pay people like us to whip them into shape quickly. We're not cheap.
- **Legal fees:** In case of suffering a breach and then being found non-compliant, the chance of a negligence lawsuit increases. State or Federal data breach laws pave the way for Attorneys General to sue your firm.
- **Fines:** The card brands are not very vocal about fines unless it gets disclosed in a settlement. You can research assessed fines from prominent breaches of public firms.
- **Publicity:** While brand damage related to a breach is likely only temporary, it is definitely something negative that your public relations team will need to manage.

To top it off, a victim merchant can be labeled Level 1 or a Designated Entity requiring Special Validation (DESV) irrespective of their actual merchant level. These firms are now subjected to an annual QSA assessment at their expense. While every breach may not incur all of the costs above, it's reasonable to assume there are unexpected expenses that will arise post-breach.

NOTE

Let's be real for a second. How damaging is a breach, really?

If you are trying to understand how this might affect your firm, do not look at the "Cost Per Record" studies put out by the Ponemon Institute. It will get you laughed out of the room. Be sure to read all the fine print on the limitations of that research. After doing so, you will learn why it is really meant for entertainment purposes only as the source data is estimated, anecdotal, and not clustered by industry or merchant size.

A more accurate representation is thinking about a breach like a large-scale natural disaster (a hurricane might be appropriate). Will you go bankrupt from a breach if your business is healthy? Probably not. But what will happen is your balance sheet will look much different after dealing with a breach. Your assets will be lower, the makeup of those assets will be different, and you will have higher expenses. This affects your cost of capital, which means if your business planned on opening ten locations in the 12 months following that breach, your plans just changed.

If your firm has a data breach the health of your business will suffer. Research shows that it generally is a temporary loss. But if your competitors don't have the same type of loss, they can take advantage of your breach to accelerate their position in the market.[3] You can't predict the degree of your losses, but you will have losses. In the very worst case (especially if you are a small business), your business will simply be gone as has happened with some merchants over the years. Or, its name will become synonymous with data breach, like Target's did. If compliance costs look to be too much for you to handle, your only course of action should be to completely outsource your payment processing to someone else. Besides, in what right mind would a retailer want to be a payment processor?

Overall, it is much more useful to think of customer and cardholder data protection as your social responsibility and not as something you do because of the threat of a stick. Companies talk about corporate social responsibility (CSR),[4] but often forget that caring for the private data of their customers is a practical and simple form of CSR. What fits the definition of "embracing responsibility for the impact of their activities on the environment, consumers, employees, communities, stakeholders, and all other members of the public sphere," more than caring for those precious bits and bytes from the card itself?

CASE STUDY

Next, we present a case study that illustrates what is covered in this chapter.

THE CASE OF THE CARDLESS MERCHANT

Sometimes, merchants unknowingly accept PCI-related risk and can be left facing substantial fines.

Payton's "P-Funk All Stars" Party Palace is a recent startup attacking the ever-popular, all-inclusive children's birthday party celebration. Payton recently left her position at a retailer to start her company. Her previous experience included only a basic understanding of PCI and that compliance was important and mandatory. When Payton was looking for the ability to accept major credit and debit cards, she made sure to find an Independent Sales Organization (ISO) that offered management of her Point of Sale (POS) devices.

Upon receiving the contract from her ISO, she noticed that she would still be filing compliance documentation for her own Merchant ID (MID), but one of the ISO's divisions, Rocky's Rockin' Payments, would be leasing and managing her POS equipment. For an extra fee, they also agreed to perform settlement services and reconciliation reports. Payton was working on a budget and preferred a transactional-based fee for management instead of hiring someone part time to perform this function.

Six months into her venture, her business was booming. She received a peculiar call from someone in the fraud department of her ISO asking very odd questions about her setup. She learned that her business was identified as the possible source of a cardholder data breach. After explaining that she outsourced all of her maintenance and upkeep to Rocky's Rockin' Payments, she was informed the business unit was sold to another company and that the MID was still issued to her directly, therefore she was responsible for paying for fines and the forensic investigation.

Payton was crushed. How did she end up in this situation? She was now facing significant fines that could affect her ability to meet her creditors and payroll.

Payton made one critical error. While her knowledge of PCI was critical to how she set up her payment processing environment, she mistakenly thought that having a third party manage her systems would cover her in the case a breach occurred. In reality, Payton was responsible for keeping up with her compliance, and she failed to ensure that Requirements 12.8 and 12.9 were met with respect to her outsourcer.

Had Payton's transactions been processed under Rocky's Rockin' Payments MID, she may only be facing lost business due to consumer confidence versus facing fines and fees associated with the breach.

SUMMARY

Here are all the myths again:

- Myth #1 PCI Doesn't Apply to Me
- Myth #2 PCI Is Confusing and Ambiguous
- Myth #3 PCI DSS Is Too Onerous
- Myth #4 Breaches Prove PCI DSS to be Irrelevant
- Myth #5 PCI Is All We Need for Security
- Myth #6 PCI DSS Is Really Easy
- Myth #7 My Tool Is PCI Compliant, Thus, I Am Compliant
- Myth #8 PCI Is Toothless

Now that you know how to tell the difference between myth and reality, you are one step closer to running an effective PCI DSS program and becoming an organization that cares about its customers by protecting their data.

Remember that PCI is generally basic security. Hackers have long been exploiting a threat vector by the time a requirement becomes mandatory in PCI DSS. If you need evidence of this, look how long it took PCI DSS to include a phishing requirement, payment script monitoring, or even MFA from anywhere. By focusing on immediately useful parts of PCI DSS, you can start towards a full-scale risk management program, backed up by implemented and maintained controls. Then, after validating that you are compliant, don't stop! Continuous compliance and security is your end goal, not just passing an assessment. For example, remember that leveraging a compensating control should generally be a temporary situation, not excuses to never do the right thing.

Overall, it is much more useful to develop a security and risk mindset not a compliance and assessment mindset. Just as there is no true guaranteed job security today, there is no guaranteed security either. There is only one thing: doing the best you can do and aiming for above average so that attackers leave you alone for greener pastures.

NOTES

1. See the article here: https://bit.ly/PCI-HC.
2. ISO/IEC 27002:2013, available at https://bit.ly/PCI-27002.
3. See https://brando.ws/PCI-Attitudes.
4. Sometimes corporate social responsibility (CSR) is defined by stating that the business must accept all responsibility for the results of its activities on the nature, environment, customers, employees, and even public at large. Moreover, commercial organizations must actually work in the public interest by encouraging the community and choosing to discontinue practices that harm the public sphere or can be seen as unethical. CSR research is maturing but evidence suggests that businesses are more often pushed to focus on things other than profit, whether it is good or bad.

21 Final Thoughts

Information in this chapter:

- A Quick Summary
- On Time Travel
- Interact With Us!

A QUICK SUMMARY

You made it! What a journey we've been on together. We hope you enjoyed tagging along with us as much as we enjoyed bringing you with us. While this book represents thousands of hours of work curating, collecting, and presenting information for consumption, it also relies on the decades of experience that the entire team earned in the field dealing with Payment Card Industry Data Security Standard (PCI DSS). We're proud to bring this book to you.

PCI DSS 4.0 represents a major overhaul of PCI DSS, and while they changed nearly every page and requirement from the last version, we have a few closing thoughts for you.

TIMELINES

First off, deep breaths. The Council did the industry a solid with the extended timelines we all have to comply with the new requirements. Technically, you have the opportunity to complete one or even two more annual assessments on PCI DSS 3.2.1 before you are required to move to 4.0. The action you can take now is to compare your last assessment with the new version and see which new requirements will be tricky, as well as which requirements might become easier to comply with due to clarifications or the dropping of outdated controls. After this analysis, you may decide that your next assessment will be on PCI DSS 4.0, especially since the *new requirements are still considered a best practice until March 31, 2025*. If you have not done your assessment for this year, bring this text and PCI DSS 4.0 along with you and take notes so you can determine your best pathway forward.

COMPENSATING CONTROLS AND THE CUSTOMIZED APPROACH

The Customized Approach is a way to boil requirements down to control objectives and apply more traditional audit methods to determine the effectiveness of controls designed and deployed. But what does this mean for Compensating Controls? We think they are probably going away—sooner rather than later. We would not be surprised if PCI DSS 4.0 is the last official version of the standard that allows for Compensating Controls. If your assessment relies heavily on Compensating Controls, it's time to do a serious evaluation of what is next for you. As always, we recommend scope reduction first for speed, cost, and simplicity, then meeting the defined approach as written, then looking at a Customized Approach option.

If you arrive at the Customized Approach as the only viable option, reach out to your QSA to discuss a pathway forward.

WE PLAY CATCH-UP

Some of the new controls shouldn't be a problem for you because we're guessing you were already doing them. Things like educating your staff about social engineering and adding to your defensive posture in response to phishing. A solid SPF, DMARC, and DKIM strategy may be all you need, and if you have made it a focus to improve your email delivery in the last few years, chances are one or all of those are part of your strategy.

Authenticated scans have been around since vulnerability detection started, and we hope you have had this enabled to get the most accurate result for your vulnerability management program. Bugs like to hide behind authentication screens of both operating systems and applications. You should be performing authenticated scans in general to ensure you are finding all the things you need to fix.

THE CHALLENGING ONES

There are many new requirements to this version of PCI DSS that will add to the level of effort required to build, run, and assess your PCI DSS compliance program starting with the massive number of inventories you now need to maintain. If there is a person, process, software, hardware, or any other object that has the ability to affect the security of account data, it must end up in an inventory somewhere. Not only does this create failure points if you miss something, but this all needs to be kept up to date. Don't try to do this by hand. You will need software to help you meet this requirement and maintain your sanity.

The monitoring and management of web content and applications might be something you have already addressed, but the new requirements meant to combat JavaScript skimming will represent a significant effort for companies that rely on that channel for moving product and services. For service providers, looking for covert command and control traffic might be one of the more technically challenging aspects of PCI DSS 4.0.

Risk assessments are confusing and vary greatly between companies. This version of PCI DSS defines several new areas where risk assessments need to be performed. If your firm has an immature risk management program, don't fret. You are not alone. But it's time to up-level how you define, assess, and manage risk to ensure you are meeting the control objectives laid out in PCI DSS. There are free documents (NIST SP800-30), paid documents (ISO 31000), and an entire framework built upon quantitatively measuring, reporting, and managing risk (FAIR). Any of these options can help you build and mature your risk assessment program. Those take time to build, so this may be one of your first immediate actions after reading this book.

Finally, what may seem like some of the most challenging changes will be easily met through the maturation of your information security program. For example, if you have been doing a great job of alerting when anomalous behavior occurs, but a terrible job of responding, remediating, and documenting the steps you took to address that alert, now is your opportunity to continually improve what your teams do. The NIST Cybersecurity Framework focuses on five functions you must do well to give your program a chance at repelling attacks. In the olden days, we focused on three: protect/prevent, detect, and respond. Back at Branden's days at RSA, he discussed how firms were generally investing 90% in prevention, 10% in detection, and nothing in response instead of investing equally in all three. For NIST's five functions of Identify, Protect, Detect, Respond, and Recover, we also recommend equal investments (or at least equal capabilities) across the five. The dollars may not be balanced at 20% per function, but if your firm is great at identification and spends a lot on protection, but can't really detect or respond to things happening in real time, PCI DSS 4.0 can help get you there.

ON TIME TRAVEL

One thing that we love about writing is the sense of time travel. James and Branden started this project in 2020 while we were in quarantine and trying to pass the time. We learned quite a bit about the collaborative nature of writing a book these days, and couldn't have done it as rapidly and as well without our trusty toolkit that includes git, GitHub, Slack, and Markdown. The experience that we had with all of our tools working together nicely just felt right.

While we started working on this book in 2020, the heavy lifting was completed in the first half of 2022. James and Branden had spirited debates with other industry colleagues about new requirements, new requirement organization, and this weird Customized Approach thing that looks to gobble up Compensating Controls in the next version of PCI DSS. When this book is in your hands, you will see stories that go back years, as well as brand new stories we wrote in the first half of the year.

We hope that we achieved our goal, which is to be the kind of book that has a prominent place in your office. We hope its pages will become warn, bent, and crinkled. We want these pages to be marked up with highlighters, notes in the margins, and tape flags (a personal favorite of Branden's). We hope this book will be the reference you will use to gather inspiration for solving problems you face right now and into the future.

Mostly, we hope that you enjoyed reading this as much as we enjoyed writing it. As the world is returning to meatspace, we genuinely look forward to meeting you all at a conference or gathering soon!

INTERACT WITH US!

It wouldn't be the 2020s if we didn't have a dozen different ways to reach us. That's a bit overwhelming, so we'll streamline it for you. If you have comments on the book or just want to reach out, please engage with us!

We view this project as a living being for the next few years as we see companies tackle various implementations and new requirements we discussed in the book. The hub for information on the book will be our website, www.pcibook.com. We will have blog posts, a link to our GitHub Repository (github.com/captbrando/PCI-Compliance-5th-Edition) that has links to tips and tools and will support the public errata and issues for the book, and more ways to interact with us. There are already a few blog posts for you to check out! We're discussing truncation, thoughts on logging, and ways to build a solid MFA strategy that includes a risk-based component. Some links in the book may change, and as we discover them we will post them to the public book GitHub repository.

We have a Facebook community for the book if you would like to join the discussion there. You can find that at https://www.facebook.com/PCIComplianceBook.

The entire book team is of course on LinkedIn and some on Twitter, so if you want to reach the author team, you can find James at https://www.linkedin.com/in/jameskadamson/ or @JamesKAdamson, and Branden at http://www.linkedin.com/in/bwilliams or @BrandenWilliams. Andi Baritchi wrote our Foreword, and you can find him at https://www.linkedin.com/in/andibaritchi/ or @andibaritchi. Yousef Hamade is our technical editor (this book is so much better because he is here) and can be reached on LinkedIn at https://www.linkedin.com/in/yhamade/.

We look forward to future communications and can't wait to see you at an industry event soon!

Index by Requirement

Note: Locators in *italics* represent figures and **bold** indicate tables in the text.

A

Appendix A
Requirement A1.1.1, 222
Requirement A1.1.2, 222
Requirement A1.1.3, 222
Requirement A1.1.4, 222
Requirement A1.2.1, 222
Requirement A1.2.2, 223
Requirement A1.2.3, 223
Requirement A2.1.1, 111
Requirement A2.1.2, 223
Requirement A2.1.3, 223

R

Requirement 1
Requirement 1.1.1, 52
Requirement 1.1.2, 52
Requirement 1.2.1, 53, 261
Requirement 1.2.2, 53
Requirement 1.2.3, 53, 124, 294
Requirement 1.2.4, 46, 53, 54, 71–72
Requirement 1.2.5, 53
Requirement 1.2.6, 53
Requirement 1.2.7, 54, 264, 266, 267
Requirement 1.2.8, 54
Requirement 1.3.1, 55
Requirement 1.3.2, 55
Requirement 1.3.3, 55, 57, 124–125
Requirement 1.4.1, 55, 56
Requirement 1.4.2, 55, 56, 259
Requirement 1.4.3, 56
Requirement 1.4.4, 56
Requirement 1.4.5, 56
Requirement 1.5.1, 56, **153–154**, 207, 209
Requirement 2
Requirement 2.1.1, 59
Requirement 2.1.2, 59
Requirement 2.2.1, 59, 60, **153–154**
Requirement 2.2.2, 60, **153–154**, 292
Requirement 2.2.3, 43, 61
Requirement 2.2.4, 61–62, **153–154**, **292**
Requirement 2.2.5, 62
Requirement 2.2.6, 61–62
Requirement 2.2.7, 62, 76, **153–154**, **292**
Requirement 2.3.1, 124, 126, **153–154**
Requirement 2.3.2, 124, 126
Requirement 3
Requirement 3.2.1, 2, 18, 19, 22, 30, 37, 74, 100, 101,
142, 220, 255, 264, 267, 271, 289, **292**, 303
Requirement 3.3.1, 22, 101, *102*
Requirement 3.3.1.1, 102, 104
Requirement 3.3.1.2, 104
Requirement 3.3.1.3, 104

Requirement 3.3.2, *102*, 119n2
Requirement 3.3.3, 101, 102, 119n2
Requirement 3.4.1, 104
Requirement 3.4.2, 104
Requirement 3.5.1, 104, 106
Requirement 3.5.1.1, 104
Requirement 3.5.1.2, 106
Requirement 3.5.1.3, 106, 132
Requirement 3.6.1, 108
Requirement 3.6.1.1, 220–221
Requirement 3.6.1.2, 108
Requirement 3.6.1.3, 109
Requirement 3.6.1.4, 109
Requirement 3.7.1, 109
Requirement 3.7.2, 109
Requirement 3.7.3, 109
Requirement 3.7.4, 109, 268
Requirement 3.7.5, 109
Requirement 3.7.6, 109
Requirement 3.7.7, 109
Requirement 3.7.8, 109
Requirement 3.7.9, 221
Requirement 4
Requirement 4.1.1, 110
Requirement 4.1.2, 110
Requirement 4.2.1, 110, 124, 126
Requirement 4.2.1.1, 111
Requirement 4.2.1.2, 111, 124, 126, **153–154**
Requirement 4.2.2, 112, 262
Requirement 5
Requirement 5.2.1, 142, 143, 292
Requirement 5.2.2, 142
Requirement 5.2.3, 142
Requirement 5.2.3.1, 142
Requirement 5.3.1, 142, **154**
Requirement 5.3.2, 142, 268
Requirement 5.3.2.1, 142
Requirement 5.3.3, 142
Requirement 5.3.4, 142
Requirement 5.3.5, 142–143
Requirement 5.4.1, 143
Requirement 6
Requirement 6.2.1, 144–145
Requirement 6.2.2, 145, 266
Requirement 6.2.3, 145
Requirement 6.2.3.1, 145
Requirement 6.2.4, 145, 146
Requirement 6.3.1, 145, **153–154**, 223, 296
Requirement 6.3.2, 40, 150, 199, 207
Requirement 6.3.3, 145, **153–154**, 255
Requirement 6.4.1, 146, 147, **153–154**, 269
Requirement 6.4.2, 146, **153–154**
Requirement 6.4.3, 148, 199
Requirement 6.5.1, 53, 149
Requirement 6.5.2, 149

Alphabetical Index

Note: Locators in *italics* represent figures and **bold** indicate tables in the text.

Printed in the United States
by Baker & Taylor Publisher Services